Research and Practice in A

Series Editors
Christopher N. Candlin
Macquarie University
Church Point, Australia

Jonathan Crichton
Communication, Int Studies and Languages
University of South Australia
Magill, Australia

"Hanks makes an original, detailed, and compelling case for the fundamental distinctiveness and practical importance of Exploratory Practice (EP), a radical form of practitioner research bringing teachers and learners (and others) together as co-researchers seeking deeper understandings of what it means to be engaged in language teaching and learning."

—Dick Allwright, *Lancaster University, UK*

This flagship series was created and overseen by Professor Christopher N. Candlin, and continues his work by providing the essential cross-over between research in applied linguistics and its practical applications in the professions. Books in the series address the growing need for professionals concerned with language and communication issues to keep up to date with applied linguistic research relevant to their practice. Central to this agenda, the series offers students and practising professionals rapid and authoritative access to current scholarship and research on key topics in language education and professional communication more broadly, emphasising the integration and interdependence of research and practice in a useable way. The series provides books with a common structure, each book offering a clear, up-to-date and authoritative overview of key concepts, research issues and developments in the particular topic, identifying: research evidence for the main ideas and concepts competing issues and unsolved questions the range of practical applications available for professional and organisational practice that draw on such concepts and ideas a synopsis of important issues open for action and practice-based research by practitioners/students. These state-of-the-art overviews are supported by selected cases studies of the practical applications of research and 'how to' research guides and resources, all designed to extend and localise knowledge of the topic and its relevance for the reader. Throughout the books, readers are encouraged to take up issues of enquiry and research that relate to their own contexts of practice, guided by reflective and exploratory questions and examples that invite practical connections to their work. Written by leading scholars and practitioners, the books will be essential reading for MA or PhD student in Applied Linguistics, TESOL, Communication Studies and related fields and for professionals concerned with language and communication who are keen to extend their research experience.

More information about this series at
http://www.springer.com/series/14504

Judith Hanks

Exploratory Practice in Language Teaching

Puzzling About Principles and Practices

Judith Hanks
University of Leeds
Leeds, United Kingdom

Research and Practice in Applied Linguistics
ISBN 978-1-137-45343-3 (Hard cover)   ISBN 978-1-137-45344-0 (eBook)
ISBN 978-1-137-45711-0 (Soft cover)
DOI 10.1057/978-1-137-45344-0

Library of Congress Control Number: 2016950476

© The Editor(s) (if applicable) and The Author(s) 2017
The author(s) has/have asserted their right(s) to be identified as the author(s) of this work in accordance with the Copyright, Designs and Patents Act 1988.
This work is subject to copyright. All rights are solely and exclusively licensed by the Publisher, whether the whole or part of the material is concerned, specifically the rights of translation, reprinting, reuse of illustrations, recitation, broadcasting, reproduction on microfilms or in any other physical way, and transmission or information storage and retrieval, electronic adaptation, computer software, or by similar or dissimilar methodology now known or hereafter developed.
The use of general descriptive names, registered names, trademarks, service marks, etc. in this publication does not imply, even in the absence of a specific statement, that such names are exempt from the relevant protective laws and regulations and therefore free for general use.
The publisher, the authors and the editors are safe to assume that the advice and information in this book are believed to be true and accurate at the date of publication. Neither the publisher nor the authors or the editors give a warranty, express or implied, with respect to the material contained herein or for any errors or omissions that may have been made.

Cover image © Cvorovic Vesna / Alamy Stock Photo

Printed on acid-free paper

This Palgrave Macmillan imprint is published by Springer Nature
The registered company is Macmillan Publishers Ltd.
The registered company address is: The Campus, 4 Crinan Street, London, N1 9XW, United Kingdom

To my parents and my siblings (all of them!)

General Editors' Preface

Research and Practice in Applied Linguistics provides the essential crossover between research in applied linguistics and its practical applications in the professions. Written by leading scholars and practitioners, the series provides rapid and authoritative access to current scholarship and research on key topics in language education and professional communication more broadly. Books in the series are designed for students and researchers in Applied Linguistics, TESOL, Language Education, Communication Studies and related fields and for professionals concerned with language and communication.

Every book in this innovative series is designed to be user-friendly, with clear illustrations and accessible style. The quotations and definitions of key concepts that punctuate the main text are intended to ensure that many, often competing, voices are heard. Each book presents a concise historical and conceptual overview of its chosen field, identifying many lines of enquiry and findings, but also gaps and disagreements. Throughout the books, readers are encouraged to take up issues of enquiry and research that relate to their own contexts of practice, guided by reflective and exploratory questions and examples that invite practical connections to their work.

The focus throughout is on exploring the relationship between research and practice. How far can research provide answers to the questions and issues that arise in practice? How should we warrant the relevance of research to practice? Can research questions that arise and are examined in very specific circumstances be informed by, and inform, the global body of research and practice? What different kinds of information can be obtained from different research methodologies? How should we make a selection between the options available, and how far are different methods compatible with each other? How can the results of research be turned into practical action?

The books in this series identify key researchable areas in the field and provide workable examples of research projects, backed up by details of appropriate research tools and resources. Case studies and exemplars of research and practice are drawn on throughout the books. References to key institutions, individual research lists, journals and professional organizations provide starting points for gathering information and embarking on research. The books also include annotated lists of key works in the field for further study.

The overall objective of the series is to illustrate the message that in Applied Linguistics there can be no good professional practice that isn't based on good research, and there can be no good research that isn't informed by practice.

Christopher N. Candlin and Jonathan Crichton

Acknowledgements

My own fragile, partial, and developing understandings are represented in this book. If there is one thing I have learned, it is that developing understandings takes time – varying and unpredictable amounts of time. Sometimes we experience the joy of a sudden illumination, but more often it is a long, slow process of accumulation of ideas, thoughts, and experiences. An evolution in thinking. The joy comes not from the end result, satisfying though that may be. The real enjoyment is in engaging in that entirely human endeavour of working together to develop understandings that are relevant to our lives, thus making our lives more liveable.

I am immensely grateful to all those who have collaborated, not only with this book, but also in a myriad of incalculable, immeasurable ways, in researching, learning, and teaching, over days, months, and years. Such collaborations range from a conversation over a cup of tea, when inspiration hits, through talking at workshops and conferences and during projects, to everyday working together inside and outside classrooms. Any *mis*understandings, mistakes, or misinterpretations are of course my own; any understandings are the work of many minds, curious and enquiring.

Above all, my thanks go to my family, especially Helga Hanks, Peter Stratton, Patrick Hanks, Francis, Emily and Rosie Hanks, the Buckleys (Ruth, Paul, Emma, James, Jessica), and the Winters (Isaura, Voise,

Adrianna, Orland, Clara). In addition, my friends: Joan Allwright, Charlotte Armstrong, Bee Bond, Simon Borg, Caroline Campbell, Haynes Collins, Mandy Deacon, Ian and Louisa Graham, Peter Howarth, John Jones-Parry, Jane Kay, Kashmir Kaur, Carol Martin, Inés Kayon de Miller and all in the EP Rio Group, Becky Moore, Jess Poole, Morag Samson, James Simpson, Assia Slimani-Rolls, Akira Tajino, Martin Wedell, Zongjie Wu, the contributors to the case studies and vignettes, and *all* those friends and colleagues (learners and teachers, necessarily nameless here) who made this work possible. I also want to thank my editors: Chris Candlin, an extraordinary powerhouse of the intellect who is sadly missed, and Jonathan Crichton, whose rigorous, insightful, thought-provoking comments were invaluable in developing my own understandings of what it was I was trying to say. Finally, my deepest thanks go to Dick Allwright: an inspirational teacher, researcher, learner, thinker.

Contents

1	**General Introduction**	1
	Introduction	1
	What Is Exploratory Practice?	2
	Why this Book?	8
	Who Is this Book for?	9
	Who Am 'I'?	11
	Where Is Exploratory Practice in the World?	12
	What's the Impact of Exploratory Practice?	13
	Before Beginning	15
	And Finally…	17

Part I	**The Historical and Conceptual Background to Researching Practice**	21
2	**Introduction to Part One**	23
	Introducing Forms of Practitioner Research	23
	Why So Many Names for Practitioner Research?	24
	But Isn't Exploratory Practice Just a form of Teacher Research?	26

	But Isn't Exploratory Practice Just a Form of Action Research?	26
	Practitioner Research as a Family	28
	Mapping Part One	30
3	**From Research to Practitioner Research: Setting Exploratory Practice in Context**	**33**
	Introduction	33
	What Do We Mean by 'Research'?	33
	What Is 'Research'?	35
	Quantitative Research	37
	Qualitative Research	38
	Mixed Methods Research	39
	Summary	40
	What Do We Mean by 'Practitioner Research' in Education?	41
	What Are the Underlying Assumptions Guiding Practitioner Research?	47
	Who Are the Practitioners?	48
	What Is the Proper Subject Matter of the Research?	50
	So What Makes It Research Rather than Random Looking Around?	51
	Phronesis: Ethical, Practical Wisdom	52
	Problematising Practitioner Research (i): Power, Ownership, and Funding	53
	Summary	55
4	**Perspectives on the 'Family' of Practitioner Research**	**57**
	Introduction	57
	Why So Much Interest in Practitioner Research?	58
	Working for Improvement (i): Action Research	60
	Working for Improvement (ii): Reflective Practice	63
	So Why Don't Practitioners Engage in Research?	67
	Lack of Time and Resources	68
	Lack of Expertise	69

    Lack of Relevance of Research Agenda/Findings   72
    Lack of Respect   73
    Problematising Practitioner Research (ii): The Discourse of 'Improvement'   76
    Summary   78

5 The Evolution of the Exploratory Practice Framework   81
    Introduction   81
    Definitions   82
    The Background   83
    Where Did It All Begin?   84
    Puzzling and Understanding, Rather than Problem-Solving   86
    The Evolution of the Exploratory Practice Framework   88
        Stage One: Relevance, Collegiality, and Theory-from-Practice   88
        Stage Two: Developing Understandings   91
        Stage Three: The Importance of 'Quality of Life'   96
    Bringing the Story Up-to-Date   103
    Problematising Exploratory Practice: A Critical Look   105

6 Puzzles, Puzzling, and Puzzlement   107
    Introduction   107
    Why Does Exploratory Practice Promote 'Working for Understanding'?   108
    Why Does EP Promote Puzzlement? What Is It, and Why Is It Seen as Somehow Different?   112
    Where Do Puzzles Come From?   117
    So What Differentiates These Questions from the Kind of 'Problems' (or 'Puzzles') Found in Other Forms of Teacher Research?   119
    What Do Learners Puzzle About?   121
    What Do Teachers Puzzle About?   123
    Problematising Puzzling   125
        A Note of Caution   126

The Risks of Sharing Puzzled Thoughts	127
Summary	129

Part II Developing Understandings from Practice — 131

7 Introduction to Part Two — 133
Introduction	133
Resisting the Discourse of Improvement	135
Inviting Practitioners to Dare to Question	138
So How Might this Work in Practice?	140
Mapping Part Two	140

8 Integrating Research and Pedagogy — 143
Introduction	143
Puzzling Over Bringing Research and Pedagogy Together	144
Exploratory Practice as Researchable Pedagogy	147
So What Do You Actually *Do*?	149
Case Study 8.1: 'Why Are Some Students Not Interested in Learning English?': A Story of Developing Mutual Understandings	149
Case Study 8.2: 'Why Are My Learners Not Taking Responsibility for Their Learning?': A Story of Gaining Deeper Understandings	153
Case Study 8.3: 'Why Do the Students Seem Reluctant to Take Responsibility for Themselves?': A Story of Stepping Back for Understanding	156
Case Study 8.4: 'Why Do My Students Want Lectures While I Want Discussion?' – A Story of Collegiality	161
Summary	165

9 Collegial Working 167
Introduction 167
Is Exploratory Practice Transplantable to/in Other
    Contexts? 168
What Do Learners Think About It? 171
How Does All this Relate to the Exploratory Practice
    Principles? 177
    Case Study 9.1: 'Why Do I Ask My Students to
      Reflect on Their Learning?': A Story of Mutual
      Development. 177
    Case Study 9.2: 'Why Don't We Bring EP and Learner
      Autonomy Together?': A Story of Integration 181
    Case Study 9.3: 'Why Don't We Use EP in Our
      'Zemi' Classes?': A Story of Sustainability 184
Summary 188

10 Continuing Personal and Professional Development 191
Introduction 191
Learning as an Ongoing Process 192
Who Else Can Be Involved in Working for
    Understanding? 195
    Case Study 10.1: 'What's the Link Between EP and
      CPD?': A Story of Personal and Professional
      Development 196
    Case Study 10.2: 'Why Incorporate EP in Teacher
      Education Programmes?': A Story of Overcoming
      Burnout 200
    Case Study 10.3: 'Why Don't We Integrate Theory
      and Practice in Pedagogy?': A Story of Inclusivity
      and Relevance 205
    Case Study 10.4: 'Why Do Teachers and Learners
      Struggle in the Classroom?': A Story of Quality
      of Life 209
Summary 212

Part III Understandings for Practice — 215

11 Introduction to Part Three — 217
Introduction — 217
Issues of Culture, Identity, and Meta-puzzling — 218
The Relationship Between Principles and Practices — 218
   Understanding — 219
   Collegiality — 220
   Relevance and Sustainability — 222
   Quality of Life — 224
The Importance of Trust — 225
The Exploratory Practice Principles as a Network — 226
Mapping Part Three — 228

12 Puzzles, Puzzling, and Trust — 231
Introduction — 231
What Puzzles You? — 232
Practitioners Getting Started — 239
Refining Puzzled Questions — 242
A Caveat: How Versus Why — 243
Moments of Transition — 245
Puzzling About Puzzlement — 247
The Need for Trust — 255
Summary — 262

13 PEPAs, Culture, and Identity — 265
Introduction — 265
Identifying 'Potentially Exploitable Pedagogic
   Activities' (PEPAs) — 266
   Starting Off: 'Normal Pedagogic Activities' — 267
   From Activities to PEPAs — 269
Avoiding Recipes — 274

	Developing Understanding(s) of Classroom Cultures	
	and Identities	274
	Cultures of Pedagogy	276
	Cultures of Identity	282
	Summary	288
14	**Conclusions**	291
	Introduction	291
	From Research-as-Practice to Practice-as-Research	292
	Language, Culture, and Identity in Exploratory Practice	295
	Problematising Problem-Solving	297
	Looking Ahead: What Next for Exploratory Practice?	301
	Exploratory Practice as a Form of Research	301
	Case Study 14.1: 'What Happens When Exploratory Practice Moves Beyond the Classroom?': A Story of Explorations in Research	301
	Exploratory Practice as a Form of Scholarship	305
	Redefining Notions of Pedagogy, Scholarship, and Research	307
	Implications and Impact	310
	Suggestions for Future Research	311
	Conclusion	314

Part IV   Resources   317

15	**Exploratory Practice Voices**	319
	Interview with Dick Allwright	320
	Interview with Bebel A. Cunha	333
	Interview with Inés Kayon de Miller	335
	Interview with Assia Slimani-Rolls	339
	Interview with Akira Tajino	343

Interview with Judith Hanks 346
A Final Few Words from Dick Allwright 349

References 353

Index 373

List of Figures and Table

Fig. 2.1	The 'family tree' of practitioner research	30
Fig. 5.1	Three processes of practitioner development	95
Fig 6.1	Puzzling about practice	120
Fig. 7.1	Pulled in opposing directions	135
Fig. 7.2	Bringing explorations into/from practice itself	136
Fig. 11.1	The exploratory practice principles as an interconnected whole	227
Table 13.1	My normal classroom activities	268

1

General Introduction

Introduction

It has become axiomatic that research into classroom language learning and teaching should be participatory, egalitarian, and empowering. Just how these three aims might be achieved, however, has been the subject of much debate. Over the decades, practitioner research has been increasingly recognised as a force for developing understandings of educational processes and practices (see Cochran-Smith and Lytle 2009; Tudor 2001; Zeichner and Noffke 2001), and is now a well-established field, with a plethora of different approaches to educational investigations. These approaches fall roughly into the following areas: Action Research (Burns 2005, 2010, 2015; Nunan 1993; Wallace 1998), Reflective Practice (Edge 2011; Farrell 2007), and, most recently, Exploratory Practice (Allwright 2003; Allwright and Hanks 2009).

Exploratory Practice (EP) has come to the fore as an original form of practitioner research which integrates research and pedagogy. EP foregrounds the importance of 'why'; of puzzling, being puzzled, and puzzlement; and acknowledges that exploring such puzzles (as learners, teachers, teacher educators, and researchers) aids our understandings of issues relevant to our language learning and teaching (Allwright 2003; Allwright and Hanks 2009; Gieve and Miller 2006a). This book critically examines the powerful notions of understanding, and developing understandings, in linguistically and culturally diverse contexts (Holliday 2013; Kramsch 2009). In living and valuing our experiences, we gain understanding(s) of the range and depth of complexities of researching language learning/teaching life.

What Is Exploratory Practice?

Exploratory Practice is a form of practitioner research in which learners as well as teachers are encouraged to investigate their own learning/teaching practices, while concurrently practising the target language. It offers a way of avoiding 'burnout' by integrating teaching, learning, and research (Allwright 1993, 2003, Allwright and Hanks 2009). But what is it and where did it originate?

Concept Box 1.1 gives a thumbnail sketch of the story of EP, highlighting the crucial importance of practitioners and researchers in Rio de Janeiro, Brazil, on the development of EP ideas and practices.

> **Concept 1.1: The Story of Exploratory Practice**
>
> Exploratory Practice originated in the early 1990s in the work of Dick Allwright (Lancaster University) together with language teachers and teacher educators in Rio de Janeiro working at, to name but a few, the Cultura Inglesa, the British Council, and the Pontifical Catholic University (PUC-Rio). They began to seek ways of better understanding what was going on in their classrooms – using language points from the syllabus as a way of researching issues of language, pedagogy, and social relations inside and outside the classroom. In other words, they were integrating language learning and teaching with research itself.
>
> EP has since developed worldwide in many different ways – necessarily different, for one of the central tenets of EP is that there is no single ideal way of learning or teaching a language. What these ways have in common is that teachers and learners are taking ownership of their classroom language learning lives, and are thus best positioned to research, and report on, their own teaching and learning experiences.

At first glance, EP may seem quite similar to other forms of practitioner research, such as Action Research and/or Reflective Practice. There are indeed some points of congruence. For example, all place an emphasis on education as a social process, and aim to empower practitioners; they all include elements of reflection; and all claim the arena for research should be the classrooms, and the pedagogic practices, of practitioners. Yet there are also important aspects which establish EP as quite distinctive. In the philosophical underpinnings of the EP framework, and in the explicit attempt to unite research with pedagogy (Allwright 1993), EP seeks to go beyond other forms of practitioner research. It does so by prioritising understanding over solutions, and by emphasising the importance of *agency*, of learners as well as teachers, in the learning/teaching enterprise.

> **Quote 1.1: Allwright on Exploratory Practice**
>
> Exploratory Practice […] is a way of getting teaching and learning done so that the teachers and the learners simultaneously develop *their own understandings of what they are doing* as learners and teachers.
>
> (2006: 15)

Definitions, however, are difficult to pin down, as the field is fluid, with currents of thought influencing developments in all areas. I will examine these similarities and differences in more detail in Part One. For now, though, a brief definition, as given by Allwright in Quote Box 1.1, will suffice. Having been involved in EP for so many years, these seem like self-evident truths, but, despite definitions like the one above, I am frequently asked, 'What *is* EP?'. In answer, I have written this book. To begin, I turn to a colleague, Jess Poole, a teacher of English for Academic Purposes (EAP), and a learner herself, who has worked with/in EP in the UK since 2010. I asked Jess, 'How would you explain EP to someone who has never heard of it before?' Her reply is presented (published with her permission) in Vignette 1.1 below.

> **Vignette 1.1: Mutual Inquisitiveness**
>
> Hiya
>   I found it a bit hard to try and encapsulate what I think EP is without sounding very woolly!
>   But I think it is a way to be more human with your students. It removes some of the barriers and hierarchies and can be a great reminder that maybe the best learning is mutual inquisitiveness, an openness to discussing things that might not immediately make sense, puzzles …and a willingness to admit you don't (nor should) have all the answers, but that looking for them and reflecting on them is a valuable process in and of itself.
>   Hope you are having a great time! ☺
>   Jess
>   Jess Poole, June 2015

Exploratory Practice recommends that the enquiry we undertake is integrated into our normal pedagogic practices – our habits and our common world of learning and teaching – using typical learning and teaching techniques as tools to aid our understanding, while also enhancing the processes of learning and teaching. Concept 1.2 highlights this notion of integrating research and pedagogy, which will be examined in more depth throughout the book.

> **Concept 1.2: Integration of Research and Pedagogy**
>
> Too often in the history of our field, research has been seen as entirely separate from learning and teaching. Exploratory Practice aims to mend this rift by bringing research and pedagogy together. In other words, research, learning, and teaching are seen as different facets of the same thing, with normal teaching/learning activities being used to both help the learning and teaching along *and* to aid research. Since the ultimate aim of research is (or should be) a more profound understanding of a concept, issue, or behaviour, the notion put forward in EP of *integrating research and pedagogy* should not be seen as radical, yet it is frequently overlooked as a key concept for practitioner research.

EP downplays the goal of explicitly working for (social, political, classroom) change, arguing that attempting *change without under-*

standing is a lost cause; if change is to be worth implementing, we (the practitioners) need to have a collective understanding (Allwright 2005a), about what is happening, and why (if we agree that change is advisable) change should be effected. Prabhu calls this a 'sense of plausibility' (1987: 104), which is essential for any meaningful change to take place.

> **Quote 1.2: Prabhu on a Sense of Plausibility**
>
> A good system of education [...] is not one in which all or most teachers carry out the same recommended classroom procedures but rather a system in which (1) all, or most, teachers operate with a sense of plausibility about whatever procedures they choose to adopt, and (2) each teacher's sense of plausibility is as 'alive' or active, and hence as open to further development or change as it can be.
>
> (1987: 106)

But we must first question the drive for change. The current obsession in our society with increased 'efficiency' or 'effectiveness' fails to recognise that superficial/mechanical measures for improving efficiency or effectiveness do not necessarily lead to better teaching or learning. The system is predicated on a deficit model which, as Breen, in a searing critique, puts it, '[assumes] that whatever teachers [and learners] achieved before is no longer adequate' (2006: 206–7). The field is awash with attempts to measure performance, to identify and control 'competencies'. But these fail, for the simple reason that 'Nobody ever grew any taller by being measured'. Even the most practitioner-friendly forms of education and research tend to position learners as recipients, teachers as problem-setters and problem-solvers, and academic researchers as experts who help with, or more often guide, the problem-setting and solving.

Partly in reaction to these issues, EP rejects the more common approach of starting with 'problems' and trying to solve them. Instead, it advocates the notion of 'puzzling' about language learning and teaching.

> **Concept 1.3: Puzzling, Puzzlement, and Being Puzzled**
>
> Arguing that solving the problem may be successful, but will not necessarily yield an explanation of why the problem happened in the first place, EP aims instead to focus on *developing understanding(s)*. That is to say: 'puzzling' or 'puzzlement' or 'being puzzled' about an issue in the language learning lives of teachers and learners. This focus means moving away from 'how (to)', and embracing instead *'why'*, as the deeper rationale for research.

As we shall see in Chapter 5 and beyond, this allows practitioners (ie *all* those engaged in the language learning/teaching enterprise) to step back, to consider carefully, and to share our understandings about our practices, with the aim of comprehending what it is that we do and why it is that we do it. This focus on understanding has noble antecedents in the work of Heidegger (1962) and Dreyfus (1991). Dreyfus explains Heidegger's view of understanding as an integral part of what it is to be human: to try to understand understanding is to engage unconsciously or consciously in/with/through our humanity:

> What Martin Heidegger is after in *Being and Time* is nothing less than deepening our understanding of what it means for something (things, people, abstractions, language, etc.) to be. Heidegger wants to distinguish several different ways of being and then show how they are all related to human being and ultimately to temporality. (Dreyfus 1991: 1)

The focus on working for understanding in EP also connects with van Manen (1990), writing about phenomenology, when he argues that research is an ongoing process of questioning and beginning to know the world. This places an emphasis on curiosity as the driving force for research.

> **Quote 1.3: van Manen on Research**
>
> ... to do research is always to question the way we experience the world, to want to know the world in which we live as human beings. And since to *know* the world is profoundly to *be* in the world in a certain way, the act of researching – questioning – theorizing is the intentional act of attaching ourselves to the world, to become more fully part of it, or better, to *become* the world.
>
> (1990: 5)

In a compelling investigation of the notion of curiosity, Manguel (2015) ranges beyond education to encompass language, literature, philosophy, and science. He links our humanity to our imaginations – this soaring of the spirit is what it is to be human, he argues. For any intellectual endeavour, curiosity is a prerequisite; it leads, it is hoped, towards those small epiphanies, or illuminating insights, which together create a state of puzzled enquiry. If, as he suggests below, our 'Why?' is powerful enough, we can open the doors to sustainable, fascinating explorations of ideas and thinking which encourage us in our human (and therefore constantly partial, frequently flawed, endlessly ongoing) endeavour to understand and grow.

> **Quote 1.4: Manguel on the Importance of Asking 'Why?'**
>
> 'Why?' (in its many variations) is a question far more important in its asking than in the expectation of an answer. The very fact of uttering it opens numberless possibilities, can do away with preconceptions, summons up endless fruitful doubts. It may bring, in its wake, a few tentative answers, but if the question is powerful enough, none of these answers will prove all-sufficient. 'Why?', as children intuit, is a question that implicitly places our goal always just beyond the horizon.
>
> (2015: 4)

In EP, teachers *and* learners (and teacher educators, educational psychologists, family members, administrators, and so on) are encouraged to puzzle about their own learning and teaching practices (see Concept 1.4). In the field of healthcare, Iedema et al. (2013) describe a similar concept, that of productive, shared intelligence. They maintain that:

> …through taking the time to observe their work and talk about it, practitioners develop a shared ability to question the taken-as-given, and a shared sense of what are the main opportunities and challenges. (Iedema et al. 2013: 8)

Practitioners are then encouraged to work together in collaborative efforts to develop their understandings, to build what Iedema et al. call 'collaborative attention' (2013: 14) which provides a rich stream of potential understandings of practice. In doing so, practitioners, whether in healthcare or in education, frequently find reassurance that they are not alone in wondering about a particular issue, and discover that peers can be as helpful (if not more so) as those designated 'experts.' As we shall see in Part 2 of the book, this is of interest because it relates so closely to issues of motivation (or lack thereof) which permeate language education, and research in language education.

> **Concept 1.4: Learners and Teachers as Co-researchers: Relevance and Collegiality**
>
> EP strongly encourages collegial ways of working, and this implies sharing of questions that have been puzzling teachers, learners, and teacher educators, working together to deepen understandings of the issues, and disseminating findings to each other. Above all, encouraging practitioners to set the research agenda (by airing what is puzzling) and to discuss together means that the research that is carried out is directly relevant to the participants themselves. Since 'lack of relevance' is a reason frequently given by teachers in explanation for their lack of engagement in research activity, the emphasis given in EP to collegial ways of working, including learners and teachers as co-researchers, offers an upsurge of potential for practitioner research.

Why this Book?

This book aims to bring the story of Exploratory Practice up-to-date, to address critical questions that have arisen as it has become more established on the world stage, and to deepen and broaden the scope to include not only language learners, but also teachers, teacher educators, educational psychologists, and researchers who engage in EP. After all,

> Teachers [...] are also necessarily all lifelong learners. (Wedell and Malderez 2013: 166)

Since its inception in 1990, EP has grown quickly, with many more practitioners becoming involved, writing, but more importantly "doing-being" (The Rio EP Group, in Allwright and Hanks 2009) EP. In the 2000s, EP flourished, with a number of publications (eg Allwright 2001,

2003, 2005a, b; Gieve and Miller 2006a; Hanks 2013a, 2015a, b; Miller 2003, 2010, 2012; Slimani-Rolls 2003, 2005; Yoshida et al. 2009) disseminating research into, and ideas about, the framework. However, some publications are difficult to access, some have been misinterpreted by 'outsiders', and others need further explication.

In this book I intend to go beyond the 'introduction to Exploratory Practice' of Allwright and Hanks (2009), by bringing together key research, papers, texts, ideas, and arguments to examine the experiences of practitioners (teachers, teacher educators, psychologists, researchers, *and* learners) doing EP in a variety of contexts. I analyse this innovative combination of research methodology and pedagogy, moving from practice to theory to practice again. It is timely to trace the history of EP in depth, discuss the developments, and analyse the field with a more critical eye. However, while I bring *critical attention* to EP, and other, related, forms of practitioner research such as Action Research and Reflective Practice, my intention is not to *criticise* any of these movements. There is a fine distinction between the two, which is all too often forgotten.

EP teachers, teacher educators, and learners have rightly been focused on developing their understandings locally (Allwright 2003) and sharing their insights with each other. In *The Developing Language Learner* (Allwright and Hanks 2009) we deliberately foregrounded the importance of learners, challenging what was then a near-ubiquitous focus on teachers. Now it is time to draw back the camera, without losing depth, to consider the field of second language education as a whole. In doing so I aim to acknowledge the work of teachers, teacher educators, psychologists, administrators, researchers, and learners… in short, all those who are, and should be, involved in second language education.

Who Is this Book for?

The book is conceived as an accessible guide for *anyone* involved in research and pedagogy who may be interested in EP. This includes:

- teachers (novice or experienced)
- teacher educators
- learners
- educational psychologists
- researchers (whether they are teacher-researchers, learner-researchers, academic-researchers, or others).

In other words, all those who are interested in aspects of practitioner research, applied linguistics, and education, whether doctoral students or undergraduates, professors, lecturers or tutors, teachers or learners, all are seen as the audience for the book. For questions still arise. EP holds enough promise to have inspired teachers, teacher educators, and learners around the world. If someone is interested in trying it out, how might they go about integrating research into the pedagogy of second language education? What challenges do practitioners wanting to try EP for the first time face? What can we hope to learn from other people's experiences with EP? In addition, the academic world has begun to take notice of this younger sibling in the family of practitioner research, with newcomers asking, 'But what do you actually *do* in EP?' Researchers have begun to critically examine EP as a subject in its own right, as a lens through which to see the world, developing their, and our, understandings of this innovative new form of practitioner research. But what are those understandings, and how are they connected to the comet's tail of previous pioneering work in the field of second language education? And what are the challenging questions that are asked of EP itself?

The examples and discussions to be found in these pages offer springboards for practitioners to launch their own explorations of their language learning/teaching practices. The central idea, then, is to assist anyone seeking inspiration for research methods that will help the learning along, rather than taking attention away from the work of language learning and teaching.

Who Am 'I'?

As a practitioner and a researcher myself, I am both language teacher and learner and researcher, and thus my positioning throughout this book is as 'one-of-us' (including a variety of groups as 'us'). In order to provide some background to my stance, I should outline my history as a language teacher, learner, teacher educator, and researcher. Since the book also showcases the stories of others, in the form of narratives and vignettes, I present my own narrative (below) on an equal footing.

> **Vignette 1.2: A Teacher's Story**
>
> I began teaching English as a Foreign Language (EFL) in 1987. Like so many others, I took an entry-level qualification (then called the Certificate in Teaching English as a Foreign Language to Adults – CTEFLA) shortly after I had graduated from university. I didn't know what I wanted to do, and only intended to stay in the field for about six months. Over the years, I worked as an EFL teacher in London, Italy, Singapore, and with every job my knowledge grew. I became an examiner for the Cambridge suite of examinations (eg First Certificate; Proficiency in English) and, later, a Teacher Trainer for pre-service and in-service teacher education programmes. But I was conscious that the more I thought I knew, the less I really knew: my *understanding* needed attention.
>
> I first became aware of Exploratory Practice (EP) in 1997 when I was studying for an MA in Applied Linguistics for English Language Teaching. I was attracted to the underlying principles of EP, which resonated with my own beliefs about language teaching and learning, and the ways in which research might be conducted. Above all, as a person on the verge of burnout myself, and ready to leave the profession, I was particularly attracted by the notion of *avoiding burnout* (Allwright 1993; Allwright and Bailey 1991) that EP proposed.
>
> Over the years I worked with Dick Allwright, Isabel (Bebel) Azevedo Cunha, Inés K. de Miller, Assia Slimani-Rolls, Morag Samson, Akira Tajino, and Zongjie Wu, to name but a few, to develop the conceptual framework underpinning EP. In 2009, following five years of research and writing, Dick Allwright and I published *The Developing Language Learner: An introduction to Exploratory Practice* (Allwright and Hanks 2009). We coined the phrase 'key developing practitioners' (referring to learners) as a way of stressing that it is learners as well as teachers who are central to the learning, teaching, and research enterprise; we put forward five propositions

> about learners, and discussed seven principles for 'fully inclusive practitioner research.'
>
> My work continued as I researched issues raised by implementing EP in my own context English for Academic Purposes (EAP) with my colleagues for the first time. I wondered: What challenges would we have to face? What would the relationship be between the EP principles (which might seem a bit 'woolly' to some) and our own practices as we tried EP out? My colleagues and I had never done EP in EAP before – what would happen to the idealistic principles as they met the harsh realities of an EAP pre-sessional course? This book draws on the empirical research I conducted as part of that doctoral work.
>
> I have since moved to take up an academic post in a university, yet still consider myself a practitioner: a practitioner of teaching, a practitioner of research, and a practitioner of learning.

Throughout this book there is interplay between my understandings of EP as a vibrant form of practitioner research and my interest in providing a critical analysis of EP. I acknowledge here my own predispositions towards EP, which provide me with extensive knowledge of the history and development of the framework, yet I also acknowledge my desire to critically examine the ideas, concepts, and practices of EP. In providing this explanation of who I am and where I come from (metaphorically speaking), I intend an open and vigilant stance, so that such a highly reflexive undertaking may be achieved.

Where Is Exploratory Practice in the World?

As we shall see, EP has become established as a viable form of practitioner research in a range of different contexts, whether at primary school or secondary school, at college or university level, in teacher education, or as a form of continuing professional development (CPD). In the UK, practitioners are now researching their own EAP contexts (see, for example, Hanks 2013a, b, 2015a, b), and teachers and managers are using EP as a form of CPD (eg Slimani-Rolls and Kiely 2014). Fascinating developments have been taking place in Brazil (Miller and Barreto 2015; Miller et al. 2015), China (Wu 2004; Zhang 2004; Zheng 2012), Japan (Smith 2009; Stewart et al. 2014; Tajino 2009), Taiwan (Chu 2007),

Turkey (Bartu 2003; Özdeniz 1996; Dikilitaş 2015a, b), the United Arab Emirates (Gunn 2010), and the USA (Crane 2015; Tarone 2006; Tarone and Swierzbin 2009), to name but a few.

At the cutting edge is the EP Group in Rio de Janeiro, Brazil. Teachers and learners there have continued to demonstrate their innovative ideas, for example by running their own 'learner and teacher conferences'. This annual Exploratory Practice Event has been going since the late 1990s, and since 2003 learners as young as eleven present alongside novice teachers, experienced teachers, researchers, and academics. For a description of this event, with photographs and commentary from the participants themselves, see the Rio EP Group contribution (Chapter 14 in Allwright and Hanks 2009), and the EP Facebook page. All these issues are worth investigating; as EP matures, it is taking its place in the world, a world which, on the surface at least, seems ready for discussion of the living framework of practice-theory-practice on which EP is based. The following chapters seek to address these questions in a variety of ways, with a range of voices from different cultures and contexts.

What's the Impact of Exploratory Practice?

When EP began (in the 1990s), our work took place in a pre-'impact' world. Since then, much has happened. The potential *impact* of research needs also to be explored and discussed. How does the kind of fully inclusive practitioner research that we in EP have been advocating impact upon the field and its practitioners, and, importantly, empower the practitioners to explicitly state their contributions to the field?

This is central to the EP framework. The blurring of ancient boundaries between research and practice and the development of our (practitioner) understandings generates public engagement with research, where the definition of 'public' includes learners of all ages and all walks of life, as well as teachers and teacher educators, psychologists, administrators, and family members. Arguably, then, the language and conceptual work of EP has begun to seep into the discourse of research; we see the adoption of the words 'understanding', 'puzzle', and 'quality of life' (though the deeper implications of these concepts are frequently missed) in the discourse, and the field has begun to wake up to the potential of collaboration and sustainability. For example, the Research Council UK's 'Pathways to Impact' document defines 'impact' as twofold, both academic:

> … [the] contribution that excellent research makes to academic advances, across and within disciplines, including significant advances in understanding (http://www.rcuk.ac.uk/innovation/impacts/ accessed 27 November, 2015)

and economic/societal, which:

> … embrace all the extremely diverse ways in which research-related knowledge and skills benefit individuals, organisations and nations by:
> - […] enhancing quality of life, health and creative output (ibid.)

Interestingly, the notions of quality of life, collaborative working and explicit links between research and practice, all of which are central to this definition of impact, have for many years been integral to the EP framework. Although it is too much to claim that the writers of definitions of 'impact' were influenced by EP principles, these ideas are clearly in the air, and must have come from somewhere. The hitherto hidden contributions of Exploratory Practitioners to the overall discourse of research in our field are (over-) due some acknowledgement. Our responses to the impact(s) of research and our impact(s) upon research are crucial not only to the field, but to society at large, as we educate within and outwith the language classroom. Leaving aside the sinister *misuses* of the concept of 'impact' so eloquently elaborated by Collini (2012), there are elements here that are entirely apt. Research, by this definition, must be relevant to the 'users'. Who else could the 'users' be but language learners and teachers, and anyone connected with second language education?

Before Beginning

> In suggesting we need to collaborate with those who are the 'subjects' in our study, we advocate an axiology, an *ethics*, of relationships and collaboration. (Iedema et al. 2013: 73)

It is worth noting some of the ethical dilemmas involved in reporting on practitioner research. It has become commonplace to use pseudonyms in place of the names of participants, thus masking their identity. However, this seems to run counter to the egalitarian belief systems of most forms of practitioner research, and EP in particular. Codes, pseudonyms, and other ways of ensuring anonymity paradoxically disempower the practitioners, distancing them again from the very research that they might be interested in conducting. Hiding participants behind false names is in danger of being an unethical stance, which pushes learners and teachers back towards the bottom rungs of the hierarchy. EP actively argues against such subjection/objectification:

> [The principles of EP] reflect our ethical concern to respect the fact that practices are essentially social, and the epistemological notion that understandings are collective as well as individual. (Allwright 2005a: 360)

There are no 'objects' or 'subjects' – we are all potent actors in our classrooms and our research, and we all have useful things to say.

Consequently, in this volume I have given proper acknowledgement to the authors who have (voluntarily) provided ideas, interviews, stories, and experiences for this book. They deserve the same respect from the field as that given to a professor or researcher. I have therefore invited contributors to use their real names wherever possible. Participants were free to withdraw at any time, and informed consent was established, not only at the beginning, but at regular intervals. Nonetheless, there were some cases where it was necessary to use pseudonyms (eg where contributors had given permission for their words or stories to be used, but preferred not to use their names), and I have respected this also. Where first names only are used, these are monikers agreed with the participants. I would like to thank the participants for their contributions throughout, and for allowing me to reproduce their work here. Interested readers can see the photographs and comments that practitioners *themselves* have shared:

> Exploratory Practice Facebook Group:
> https://www.facebook.com/prática-exploratória-exploratory-practice-190518727649222/
> Teacher Research Facebook Group:
> https://www.facebook.com/Teacher-Research-for-Professional-Development-2013-408365679200768/
> IATEFL Research SIG website:
> http://resig.weebly.com/

Plan of the Book

Part One: historical and conceptual background.
Part One critically examines notions of research, practitioner research, and the debates surrounding them. What happened before EP, and where does EP come from, conceptually and theoretically? What are the key concepts and research issues in practitioner research in education more generally (eg issues of empowerment, ethics, collaboration, and collegiality)?

Part Two: practical applications 'Understanding from practice'.
Part Two considers how research has been applied, and examines what interesting research possibilities are raised by the practice of language teachers and teacher educators. How do practitioner-researchers investigate their puzzles? What benefits do they see, and what obstacles do they need to overcome? Are the challenges and opportunities they face similar, or are they very different? What can other practitioners learn from their experiences? How does EP 'work' for people in different linguistic and cultural contexts?

Part Three: researching in/through/by EP 'Understanding for practice'.
Part Three offers a guide to do-able research activities that readers can engage with as part of their regular practice as teachers, learners, teacher educators, etc. It also raises questions about the important research issues in the field that readers can undertake in a practice-based way. Issues of beliefs, ownership, and trust in practitioner research in (language) education are analysed. Part Three concludes by looking ahead, and, following EP practices, raises a number of puzzling questions, or *meta-puzzles* which offer opportunities for future research.

Part Four: Resources
Part Four provides interviews with key figures in the EP field. Their commentaries provide valuable insights into the thinking behind developments in the EP framework.

This volume offers a close examination of developments in EP, focusing on its potential for uniting research and pedagogy in mutually beneficial and meaningful ways, for and by practitioners. In the coming chapters, I examine the growth of the EP principles, over the past twenty-five years, into a flexible, robust framework for practitioner research. I begin with research, and examine its relationship to practice, examining currents of thought between 'then' and 'now', and consider how practitioner research, and more specifically EP, has evolved. In the complex world of language learning and teaching, EP highlights the intercultural nature of classrooms and the fluidity of notions of (learner/teacher/researcher) identity in such contexts. By encouraging an attitude of curiosity (Hanks 2015b), and enabling the agency potential (Gieve and Miller 2006b) of practitioners, EP affords sustainable opportunities for developing our understandings of language learning and teaching (Allwright 2005a).

In this book, I focus first on the importance of understanding *from* practice, and on the notion of research-as-practice: reconfiguring teachers, teacher educators, educational psychologists, and researchers as people-who-learn, as well as positioning learners as potential researchers and teachers, all of whom have insightful, relevant things to say about the processes of learning/teaching a language. This leads to the notion of understanding *for* practice: examples of people engaging in EP in a variety of ways, relevant to them, in their complex linguistic and cultural contexts. But this calls attention to the need for Trust (Candlin and Crichton 2013a, b) in the field. Practitioners working together for understanding and mutual development need to trust and be trusted to engage in seriously playful, rigorous, practice-as-research.

And Finally…

Any writer must decide upon an order and a structure for a book. In keeping with the reflexive, exploratory and reflective nature of the work, there are strong currents of reiteration in the book, with each iteration developing understandings of research, theory, and practice as the story continues to unfold. However, the reader also has some say in the matter.

You have a choice as to where to start, where to pick up, and where to leave off. I have said that here, for the first time, is a full, in-depth review of the historical and conceptual background to EP, examination of the philosophical underpinnings of the EP framework, and discussion of the practical applications of EP, showing examples of EP in different contexts. But different readers have different concerns, and I would encourage a more eclectic approach to reading, to suit individual interests and analyses.

For those who are more interested in the historical/conceptual background, Part One is a logical place to start. Others, who may be more interested in the practical applications of/for EP, may prefer to jump straight to Part Two, where they will find examples of EP in different contexts from around the world. For those who are keen to begin incorporating EP into their own practice, Part Three is the place to begin. Finally, Part Four provides a compendium of useful resources in the shape of interviews with key people in EP.

I hope you will read on with a curious mind and a readiness for playful approaches to the perplexing, fascinating, imaginative world of language education.

Further Reading

Allwright, D. & Hanks, J. (2009) *The Developing Language Learner: An introduction to Exploratory Practice*. Basingstoke: Palgrave Macmillan. This book introduces the ideas of EP, focusing on the experiences and issues of language learners and their teachers. Of interest to anyone keen to find out about the principled framework of 'fully inclusive practitioner research' and the 'five propositions about learners'. A central text for anyone interested in EP, in learners, or in language learning and teaching.

Dreyfus, H.L. (1991) *Being-in-the-World: A commentary on Heidegger's Being and Time, Division 1*. Cambridge, MA: The MIT Press. For anyone who is interested in the philosophical underpinnings of a range of phenomenological and epistemological approaches to research, practice, and thinking, this scholarly work makes Heidegger's thinking, about profound understanding, about being-in-the-world, and about clarity, accessible. Commentary on *Dasein* and understanding is particularly relevant, but for those with the time and inclination, the whole book is worth dedicated attention.

Iedema, R., Mesman, J. & Carroll, K. (2013) *Visualising Health Care Practice Improvement: Innovation from within.* London: Radcliffe Publishing Ltd. Although working in a different field (healthcare), the ideas and arguments presented in this book are closely related to those of EP. In trying to make visible the invisible, assumed practices, and in respecting and acknowledging the pre-existing wisdoms of practitioners, Iedema et al. explicate the notion of research-as-practice, a first step towards what I propose here: (exploratory) practice-as-research.

van Manen, M. (1990) *Researching Lived Experience: Human science for an action sensitive pedagogy.* New York: The State University of New York. Phenomenology and Qualitative Research Methodology are forensically and poetically analysed in this helpful book. In suggesting that researchers and educators need to focus on the 'lived experiences' of practitioners, van Manen provides an alternative vision of what it is to be scientific, of the importance of human experience in developing our understandings of pedagogy.

Part I

The Historical and Conceptual Background to Researching Practice

2

Introduction to Part One

Introducing Forms of Practitioner Research

Despite the blossoming of research *for* and *by* practitioners over the years, we still understand little about the challenges that must be overcome, or the benefits that may be gained in this field of activity. As Zeichner and Noffke (2001), in their seminal article on practitioner research, maintain, there is a need for greater understanding of the implications of, and for, practitioners wishing to engage in research into their own educational practices in language learning and teaching.

> **Quote 2.1: Zeichner and Noffke on the Needs of Our Field**
> We need close investigation of the conditions that facilitate and obstruct the ability of educators to conduct research on their own practice.
> (2001: 324)

In this, the second decade of the twenty-first century, the need to consider both challenges and obstacles to practitioner research is becoming ever more urgent. How might practitioners, already overloaded with work, manage to incorporate research into their practice, and why should they bother? In Part One I examine some of the ways in which this question has been addressed: first from the broader perspective of research in social science, second from views of practitioner research in education, and in English language teaching more specifically, and finally via perspectives of Exploratory Practice (EP).

Practice is naturally where EP has tended to remain; it deliberately focuses on the lived experiences (van Manen 1990) of teachers and learners rather than promoting publications. But as a consequence there are relatively few articles and books easily available to readers contemplating EP, and there is little published work that examines the stages of evolution of the EP framework. Here, then, I bring such work together to review the development of the principles and framework against a backdrop of developments in practitioner research more generally.

Why So Many Names for Practitioner Research?

Before examining EP, however, it is worth taking a moment to distinguish between the many forms of practitioner research. Cochran-Smith and Lytle (2009) provide a helpful overview of the plethora of different approaches available to practitioners interested in investigating their own classrooms. Under the umbrella term of 'practitioner inquiry', they consider Action Research (AR), Teacher Research, Self Study, Scholarship of Teaching, and 'Using Practice as a Site for Research.' They rightly point out that:

> …it is not our intention to blur important ideological, epistemological, and historical differences (Cochran-Smith and Lytle 2009: 39)

They aim instead:

> …to illuminate important differences at the same time that we clarify commonalities. (ibid.)

Their multidimensional vision, which encompasses similarity as well as difference, is a useful introduction to some of the key issues involved here.

First, a brief word about names and naming is required. The field seems to be endlessly proliferating in different names for different kinds of research in language education. I have named some major forms above, but there are many more. So why do we need to give them different names?

> **Concept 2.1: Frequently Asked Questions About Practitioner Research**
> Why insist on the umbrella term 'Practitioner Research'?
> Isn't Exploratory Practice just a form of Teacher Research?
> Isn't Exploratory Practice just a form of Action Research?
> Isn't Action Research just a form of Reflective Practice?
> Or should that be the other way around: Is Reflective Practice just a form of Action Research?
> And why don't we just call all of it Teacher Research and have done?

This question is addressed by Wu (2004), when he argues that: "*Naming* is the language that brings understanding into interpretation and manifestation." (Wu 2004: 309)

It is the process of using language to name things (objects, concepts, thinking) that leads us towards understanding. Using practitioners' daily lives, and mundane experiences, much of which remain un-named (because automatic, assumed, commonplace) as the locus of research opens up the potential for deep understanding. The research takes place in the taken-for-granted background, the 'being-in-the-world' (Dreyfus 1991) of *Dasein* (Heidegger 1962), against (and with) which the reader/teacher/learner makes sense of experience. It behoves us, then, to be precise in using terms and terminology.

But Isn't Exploratory Practice Just a Form of Teacher Research?

Exploratory Practice, like Action Research and Reflective Practice (RP), is one form of practitioner research. In other words, it is research done by practitioners – and 'practitioners' in EP are taken to mean '*practitioners of learning, or teaching, or teacher training, or…*' As we shall see in the ensuing chapters, EP explicitly includes learners, administrators, educational psychologists, and teachers and teacher educators – all those ghosts in the room (Muir 2015) that populate our classroom language learning lives. Hence, 'Teacher Research' is too limiting a term, because here the researchers are not only teachers, but also learners, administrators, managers, curriculum designers, educational psychologists, and so on. So, the answer to this question must be 'no': Exploratory Practice is more than Teacher Research, because although it includes teachers, it also encompasses learners, teacher educators, psychologists, etc.

But Isn't Exploratory Practice Just a Form of Action Research?

This question is often asked by those new to the concept of EP. Interestingly, there are those who 'get' the differences immediately, and those who struggle. EP has its own identity, its own way of being and behaving, and its own clear purpose, a purpose quite distinct from that of AR (or other forms of practitioner research). In Part One, I trace the links as well as the distinctive qualities of AR, EP, and RP, and investigate the philosophical underpinnings that characterise EP in particular.

As a very brief *aide memoire*, however, it is worth considering the following points when trying to identify what form of practitioner research is being talked about:

- *Are learners included as co-researchers?*
  Thus far, the AR literature has not attempted to include learners (though there is always time for that to change) as co-researchers. So if

learners are being positioned as equally responsible for, and able to conduct investigations into practice, and if teachers (and teacher educators, educational psychologists, researchers, etc.) are being positioned as people-who-learn-too, we're talking about EP.
- *Does the search for profound understanding come before attempting problem-solving?*
Since EP explicitly prioritises working for understanding over problem-solving, it is clearly differentiated, both in intent and in execution, from AR. It may be an unkind reading of AR, but it is clear from the literature that a large majority of AR projects begin by identifying problems, and engage in attempts to improve the situation. That is not to criticise (somebody needs to attempt to improve the situation now and then), but merely to state the difference. So, as a quick 'rule of thumb', if the practitioner-researchers are *puzzling*, if they are asking 'why' (rather than 'how to' or 'what'), and trying to access a profound understanding of the situation, by working collegially, and by using their normal pedagogic practices as investigative tools, we're talking about EP.
- *Does the search for understanding aim to integrate research and practice?*
An essential criterion for EP is the use of 'what we normally do' in the classroom as a way (or ways) of investigating whatever it is that puzzles us. This, like the positioning of learners as potential teachers, and teachers as potential learners, is something that is unique to EP: the use of everyday classroom activities as a way of engaging in research and scholarship, without adding to the already-heavy burdens of teaching/learning. In Parts Two and Three we will see examples of what this looks like in (exploratory) practice.

In sum, if the answer to these three questions is 'yes', we are talking about EP. Over the years, these criteria have been honed into a set of principles, which provide the philosophical underpinning for the EP framework. As noted earlier, a definition of EP includes the notions of collegiality (learners as well as teachers, and potentially also administrators, assistants, parents, and researchers – in other words, those who are peripheral, but connected, to the classroom), sustainability, and puzzlement. Crucially, it aims to unite pedagogy and research, by using language learning activities as a way of conducting investigations.

Nevertheless, there is a problem with this rather reductive way of presenting things. For, just as AR influences, and is influenced by, issues thrown up in, say, RP, so too has EP impacted on the discourse. It is a sign of a healthy field that these vigorous and various forms of practitioner research are able to listen to one another, and respectfully acknowledge differences, while also celebrating shared values.

Practitioner Research as a Family

So the names we give to things are significant. In Concept 2.2 (prompted by an IATEFL ReSIG online discussion in 2015 - see Wyatt Burns & Hanks, 2016), I probe the attempts to subsume EP. Trying to wrap everything up under one name may seem tidy, but in fact such a move fails to recognise the philosophical differences underpinning these different forms of practitioner research (for a detailed analysis, with definitions, of AR, Teacher Research, and Classroom Research, see Bailey 2001). Those who try to conflate one or more of these, by, for example, stating that EP is merely a form of AR, or that all can be put under the umbrella term of 'Teacher Research', might think they are merely being pragmatic, but this loses sight of the distinct identity of each form, and in the end leads to a lack of precision.

Concept 2.2: On Names and Naming

One thing that is puzzling me is the issue about names and naming. Why do some people say, 'EP is just another form of Action Research'?

As I explore this puzzled thought, the following metaphor takes shape: I have a brother. In many ways he's very like me: we both have dark eyes, dark curly hair (going grey); when we were very young we were even taken

> for twins sometimes. As adults we share many values, a sense of humour, and our political outlook is similar. But if you were to call my brother 'Judith', he'd think you were a bit odd.
>
> That seems to be important: this brief list of names (Action Research, Classroom Research, Exploratory Practice, Reflective Practice, Teacher Research, and so on) are not arbitrary labels. The names tell us something important about what happens, about the approach, about the deeper philosophical underpinnings and defining characteristics as well as the surface-level activities of each. If one is promoted as a superordinate, that places it 'above' the others, as if this one is the patriarch, while the others are merely offshoots.
>
> But in considering more equal relationships between EP, RP, and AR and others, that glimmers for me: – I think they can happily stand next to each other in the rambunctious 'family' of practitioner research.
>
> After all, there's plenty of room... isn't there?

These are family members – carrying similar DNA, but decidedly individuals with distinct identities. EP shares much with both AR and RP, but each has its own history, its own life, its own future. A certain amount of jostling is to be expected, as a brother or sister, or a half-sister or step-brother, claims attention and space that she or he thinks is due. But in the end, the important point is to respect one another, acknowledging admiration and influence as well as differences of opinion.

As we shall see in the following chapters, these attempts to reduce complexity fail to acknowledge the distinct philosophical and conceptual differences characterising each movement. Instead, a diagram in the shape of a family tree (see Fig. 2.1) may help to clarify the situation. In this representation, 'practitioner research' is an all-inclusive trunk from which the various forms spring. Each (life-)form has its own distinct identity, with a set of values, principles, theories, and activities, some of which may be shared with another form (or 'sibling', to extend the metaphor). But this sharing does not mean that one can simply absorb another. It is equally as nonsensical to assert that EP is merely a subset of AR, or that AR is a subset of RP, or, indeed, that AR and RP are subsets of EP (Fig. 2.1).

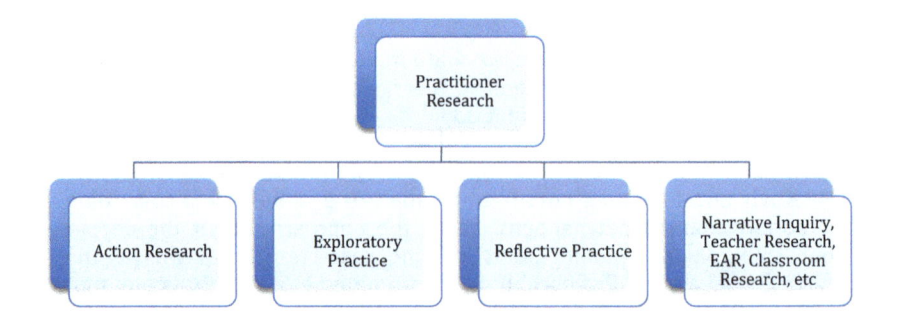

Fig. 2.1 The 'family tree' of practitioner research

This is a more satisfying (and less colonial) way of looking at the field. It allows each approach to have its own identity, while also acknowledging the many positive relationships between them.

Mapping Part One

Part One maps out the historical and conceptual background to the field of practitioner research, with a view to setting EP in context. What are the origins of EP, and how have they influenced the principles that guide Exploratory Practitioners? I outline the arguments around key paradigms in practitioner research such as AR, or RP, and I show why we place EP as a younger sibling in this rambunctious 'family.'

I start by examining the roots of EP, considering definitions of research and practitioner research, examining the growth of different forms of practitioner research, and the evolution of the EP framework. Chapter 3 considers definitions of research, and practitioner research: What are some of the key questions about practitioner research in second language education generally? Chapter 4 examines some of the defining characteristics of practitioner research, focusing particularly on AR, characterised by the divergent pulls of 'action' (for change/improvement) and 'research' (to investigate and reflect on matters), and RP, characterised by the notions of *reflecting in* and *on* practice, also with the goal of improving matters. Chapter 5 traces the emergence of EP as a movement in its own right, and uncovers some of the deeper philosophical influences that characterise EP. Chapter 6 focuses on the importance of puzzlement as a 'way in' to practitioner understanding(s) in EP. This emphasis on revealing understanding is central, and needs considerable thought. The act of *being puzzled* enables us to reveal our developing understandings to ourselves, and thus it allows a greater depth. And, because understanding is always to be further developed, with multiple possibilities, we can begin to uncover a wealth of understandings (in the plural) which exist in the moment, and in our own worlds – our personal/personalised versions of *Dasein* (Heidegger 1962). Through puzzlement we can glimpse the hidden capacity that we all (teachers, learners, researchers) have, but which is all too often concealed by the rush to find solutions to problems. Puzzlement, then, is the 'dark matter' of our universe, and requires our attention.

Before going further with the notion of puzzlement, though, we need to address the twin issues of what is 'research', and what is 'practitioner research.'

3

From Research to Practitioner Research: Setting Exploratory Practice in Context

Introduction

In this chapter I first consider the notion of 'research' in education. What does it mean, and why does it matter? I then examine the proliferating field of practitioner research. This is a wide and varied field, however, so I progressively narrow the scope. Starting with the origins and influences of practitioner research, I consider the reasons for its recent growth. Despite its popularity, a critical look shows that there are a number of questions which remain unanswered. In later chapters, we see how Exploratory Practice (EP) seeks to address some of these questions.

What Do We Mean by 'Research'?

> All research is interpretive: it is guided by a set of beliefs and feelings about the world and how it should be understood and studied. […] Each interpretive paradigm makes particular demands on the researcher, including the questions he or she asks and the interpretations the researcher brings to them. (Denzin and Lincoln 2003: 33)

The notion of 'research' in education, and in social science more generally, is itself a site of conflicting definitions, as many have discussed (see Cohen et al. 2007; Denzin and Lincoln 2003; Richardson 2001). Many of the concepts and terms are contested territory, and excite strong feelings in different (and often opposing) camps. It is therefore worth stating from the outset what the terms 'research' and 'practitioner research' are taken to mean here. The following brief definitions are not presented as final iterations of what should be used; rather, they are expositions of the thinking underpinning EP more broadly, and this book in particular.

> **Concept 3.1: The Current 'Holy Trinity' of Research**
> Crucial aims for research are often characterised as a need for:
> - impact
> - rigour
> - originality
>
> But who wields the power to define what is conceived of as rigorous, original, impactful?

We might be in favour of originality, rigour, and impact as abstract concepts, yet it is clear that these are not neutral terms. As Flyvbjerg (2001) puts it, the problem for social science is that it tries to objectivise background practices while stuck with the paradox that context-independence (as required by 'scientific rigour') is practically impossible in studying the social. In a more recent analysis of the question, science (and by extension, scientific research) is depicted as a highly complex state of affairs:

> ...science […] could no longer be understood as a neutral means to representing and capturing the 'real'. Instead, it came to be understood as a complex endeavour that links a diversity of efforts, interests and investments. It is an endeavour that operates with multivariate perspectives, partial benefits, contestable outcomes and ethical implications. (Iedema et al. 2013: 47)

In education, too, this is crucially important. But what is often left unsaid is that such directions, in second language education at least, should also be meeting the pedagogical needs of language learners, teachers, and teacher educators, *without leading to burnout*, as Allwright and Miller (2013) have pointed out.

> **Quote 3.1: Allwright and Miller on a Vision for the Future**
> We look towards a world in which technicist thinking is reversed – a world in which teachers and learners become so engaged in working for understanding that, even in the face of institutionalised pressures, they feel strong enough to put classroom life issues before technical improvement, and so be able to resist the debilitating threat of burnout.
> (2013: 111)

What Is 'Research'?

I use a relatively simple statement here, one which is situated in a social and political context, but draws on themes common to many in the field. Following a pragmatic perspective (see Gibbons and Sanderson 2002; Robson 2002), we can use the working definition given in Concept 3.2 below.

> **Concept 3.2: A Working Definition of Research**
> Research is purposeful, systematic, ethical, and critical investigation which takes place in a socially constructed world, with the aim of deepening human understanding.

Of course, such wording is necessarily partial and incomplete, as will become clear in later chapters. For now, though, I limit myself to this brief operational definition. But this then raises the question: What is *good* research? Yates (2004) provides one thoughtful response that is useful for our purposes here.

> **Concept 3.3: What Is 'Good Research'?**
>
> Yates (2004) argues that there are three themes which tend to recur in descriptions of 'good' research:
>
> - It is technically convincing (impressive in design, using innovative methods, and systematic throughout).
> - It provides a clear contribution to knowledge (ie something that was not known previously), perhaps completely or partially changing our way of looking at things.
> - It truly *matters*, whether to individuals in a particular context or to the world more generally.
>
> Do you agree with these three themes?
> Is there anything missing?

The points above indicate some of the reasons why many practitioners shy away from research. Arguably, if research has to fully meet all these criteria in order to be considered 'good' enough to be worth doing, it might be beyond even the best of us (unless we are Nobel Prize-winners). In fact, there is plenty of good, and worthwhile, research which aims at, but does not meet, all of these criteria. Perhaps we should call the former 'superb research', and allow for the silent majority to be acknowledged as 'good', in the Winnicottian (1971) sense of 'good enough'. Good enough to contribute to understandings in the field, good enough to build upon, good enough to inspire others.

The complexities of belief systems surrounding an individual researcher's approach influence choices of, for example, data collection/generation, tools and forms of analysis, and even the language used to write up the research. The belief systems of the researcher will affect not only how s/he views the world, or indeed what s/he is *able* or *willing* to see, but also *what* s/he decides to research and *how* to go about conducting that research. Because of the incomprehension caused when researchers committed to different paradigms clash, it is important to make explicit the assumptions underpinning the research.

> **Quote 3.2: Kuhn on Research Paradigms**
> ...the proponents of competing paradigms practice their trades in different worlds. [...] Both are looking at the world, and what they look at has not changed. But in some areas they see different things, and they see them in different relations one to the other.
> (1996: 150)

As Kuhn (1996) cogently argued, in any study the shape the research takes will depend on the perspectives of the researcher, whether s/he believes that that 'the truth is out there' just waiting to be discovered, or that knowledge is a co-construction of participants engaged in meaning-making. What is considered acceptable as 'research' depends very much on the viewpoint taken: whether positivist or post-positivist, or interpretive or phenomenological, whether qualitative or quantitative, or a mixture of the two, in approach.

Quantitative Research

Traditional ideas of what constitutes appropriate research methodology include the sense of a search for 'truth' and an attempt to define '… natural and universal laws regulating and determining individual and social behaviour' (Cohen et al. 2007: 7). In the field of education, this has often meant an alignment with what are thought to be scientific methods. Governed by a belief in the need for observers to discover precise and pre-existing truths, large-scale surveys or controlled experiments are used to try to prove or disprove the researcher's hypothesis. Key values are objectivity, validity, replicability, and generalisability, as Creswell (2003) has pointed out. Such work attempts to define, measure, and analyse causal relationships between variables, and it has frequently been criticised for failing to take the complexities of social interactions into account.

> **Quote 3.3: Creswell on Quantitative Research**
>
> A *quantitative* approach is one in which the investigator primarily uses postpositivist claims for developing knowledge (ie cause and effect thinking, reduction to specific variables and hypotheses and questions, use of measurement and observation, and the test of theories), employs strategies of inquiry such as experiments and surveys, and collects data on predetermined instruments that yield statistical data.
>
> (2003: 18)

Qualitative Research

However, a number of alternative perspectives have developed. These come under the umbrella of what may be broadly defined as qualitative approaches to research. Much qualitative work emphasises engaging in collaborative meaning-making which is rooted in the context of the real world. It seeks '…to say something sensible about a complex, relatively poorly controlled and generally "messy" situation' (Robson 2002: 4).

> **Quote 3.4: Denzin and Lincoln on Qualitative Research**
>
> Qualitative researchers stress the socially constructed nature of reality, the intimate relationship between the researcher and what is studied, and the situational constraints that shape inquiry.
>
> (2003: 13)

Despite this 'messy' appearance, certain common themes can be identified in qualitative approaches. For example, seeking to 'understand the subjective world of human experience' (Cohen et al. 2007: 21) and providing 'insights that will enrich our understanding' (Richards 2003: 9) are central, defining characteristics.

A range of strategies for enquiry can be used, including case studies (Duff 2008; Stake 1995, 2003; Yin 2003), ethnography (Hammersley and Atkinson 2009; van Maanen 1995), ethnomethodology (Garfinkel 1967), and grounded theory (Glaser and Strauss 1967; Strauss and Corbin 1990), though there is some debate amongst the grounded theorists themselves as to just how qualitative or quantitative they are (see

Charmaz 2003; Glaser 1992). A more recent development, narrative enquiry (Clandinin and Connelly 1995; Johnson and Golombek 2002; Lieblich et al. 1998), has developed, not least from Mishler's (1986) pioneering work introducing the notion of the interview as a tool for eliciting illuminating narratives from practitioners. EP sits firmly alongside these research methodologies in a long, respectable, tradition.

Mixed Methods Research

At the turn of the twenty-first century, debate about research had become polarised to such a degree that researchers operating within one paradigm found it difficult to speak to those from another. They even resorted to 'name calling instead of substantive arguments' (Flyvbjerg 2001: 2). This attitude of mutual incomprehension has been described as 'paradigm wars' (Gorard and Taylor 2004) or 'science wars' (Flyvbjerg 2001). Considering such hostility, Gorard (2001) identifies two 'villains' in these debates about approaches to research: those who only accept numerical data as relevant, and those who reject all numerical evidence in favour of more 'humanistic' data. However, in recent years, a more conciliatory tone has developed, with many now subscribing to a 'mixed methods' or 'combined methods' approach (Creswell 2003; Gibbons and Sanderson 2002; Gorard and Taylor 2004).

> **Quote 3.5: Gorard and Taylor on Mixed Methods Research (MMR)**
> The dichotomy between qualitative and quantitative [...] betrays a misunderstanding of the qualitative basis underlying all measurement, and of the importance of patterns in qualitative analysis.
> (2004: 167)

Choosing to use 'mixed methods' in research design, it is now argued (Creswell 2003; Hashemi and Babaii 2013), can offer the best of both worlds. Here, a diversity of methods are employed in order to meet the needs of the research question, the researcher(s) and participants, and the context or situation. The focus is on the methodological avenues open to a researcher, and the assumption is that s/he will make the most appropriate choices to aid comprehension and explanation of the situation under scrutiny. This implies using a range of techniques form both traditions, for example, large-scale surveys alongside in-depth interviews as tools to collect data. But as Riazi and Candlin (2014) point out, it is not as simple as just picking a few methods, instruments, or tools. We need also careful, thorough, consideration of the ontological, epistemological, and methodological implications of our choices.

> **Quote 3.6: Riazi and Candlin on Mixed Methods Research (MMR)**
> Whichever of the purposes one follows, carrying out MMR is no easy task for the researcher since it entails clarifying how the three characteristic and axiomatic aspects of research – ontology, epistemology and methodology- inform the conceptualisation and implementation of the research problem with an MMR framework. Ontologically, for example, the research problem needs to be conceptualised so as to represent the multi-layeredness or multi-dimensionality of the phenomenon. Epistemologically, the quantitative and qualitative data and analysis should provide evidence for understanding and interpreting its different layers or aspects.
> (2014: 161–2)

Despite this sensible route away from confrontation, then, it is clear that all too often, one side wins out, whether philosophically or practically (see Riazi and Candlin 2014, for a comprehensive analysis). The underlying belief systems of the researcher influence everything s/he does, from the choice of what to research and where, to how the research question is framed, what tools are used to investigate, and how the data are analysed, reported, and discussed. Even the language used to express the 'findings' or 'interpretations' reveals the position of the researcher (Clark and Ivanič 1997; Holliday 2002). Thus, as Bryman has argued (2007, 2009), the 'mixed methods' approach is problematic, trying to please two masters, and in the end perhaps pleasing none.

Summary

In the end, though, whatever research methods are chosen, there is a clear need for those involved in education (at any level, in any role) to understand more about what goes on in language learning and teaching. And one way to access such understanding is to involve *practitioners* in investigating their own language learning and teaching experience. In other words, to engage in practitioner research which investigates the lived experiences (van Manen 1990) of those involved in the educational enterprise.

What Do We Mean by 'Practitioner Research' in Education?

A working definition of practitioner research in education includes the notions of purposeful, systematic, and critical investigations outlined above. It delves into the practices of those working within their own schools and classrooms and seeks to explain, explore, and understand the world of classroom language learning and teaching. Arguably, in communicating the findings of their research, and exchanging information in a more public arena, practitioners stand to gain from practitioner research, most notably in developing their understandings of language learning, and enhancing their quality of life. A working definition (as outlined in Concept 3.4) is therefore used here.

> **Concept 3.4: A Working Definition of Practitioner Research**
>
> Practitioners (teachers, teacher educators, learners, etc.) conducting purposeful, systematic, ethical, and critical enquiries into their own practices, in their own contexts, with the aim of extending understanding(s) of educational processes and human behaviour.

A brief review of practitioner research shows that some writers, for example Robson (2002) and Richards (2003), have substituted the words 'enquiry' or 'inquiry' for 'research', perhaps as a way of making it more accessible to those outside the world of academe, to practitioners who are encouraged to engage in research. This question of accessibility is crucial for EP and other forms of practitioner research. If practitioners are to contribute to the body of knowledge about language teaching and learning, then surely they should also be included in the research process.

Practitioner research grew out of a number of social, political, and philosophical developments. These appear to follow one another chronologically, though there is a high degree of overlap. The great political movements which developed during the nineteenth and twentieth centuries (communism, feminism, socialism, civil rights, and other emancipatory movements) are reflected in developments in education. At the same time as minority groups in society were beginning to express their voices, teachers were developing a sense of the importance of their own experiences in education.

One key figure in all of this, from an educational perspective, was John Dewey, working in the USA in the early part of the twentieth century. In highlighting the notion of education as a social activity, Dewey (1938, 1963) argued for a more democratic process of learning and teaching and slowly educational researchers took up the call. In various ways they attempted to open up the realms of education and research in the 1950s and 1960s and beyond.

> **Quote 3.7: Dewey on Education as a Social Process**
> ... there is incumbent upon the educator the duty of instituting a much more intelligent, and consequently more difficult, kind of planning. He [sic] must survey the capacities and needs of the particular set of individuals with whom he is dealing and must at the same time arrange the conditions which provide the subject-matter or content for experiences that satisfy these needs and develop these capacities. The planning must be flexible enough to permit free play for individuality of experience and yet firm enough to give direction towards continuous development of power [...] education is essentially a social process.
> (1963: 58)

Dewey's ground-breaking work has, in various ways, influenced the forms of practitioner research under discussion here. For example, he argued powerfully that:

> The trouble with traditional education was not that educators took upon themselves the responsibility for providing an environment. The trouble was that they did not consider the other factor in creating the experience: namely, the powers and purposes of those taught. (Dewey 1963: 45)

And he identified the potential mismatch between experience(s) and education, which might lead to 'mis-education'. He therefore proposed an alternative:

> When education is based upon experience and educative experience is seen to be a social process, the situation changes radically. The teacher loses the position of external boss or dictator but takes on that of leader of group activities. (Dewey 1963: 59)

But Dewey stopped short of empowering the learners to be leaders of group research activities; his premise was based on an assumption that such decisions still rested with the teacher. Rooted in his time, he did not explore the potential to empower learners to enquire as equals with teachers and other educational professionals into their learning/teaching/researching practices. So for our purposes, although he was a landmark figure in pointing the way towards enabling teachers to take their place as researchers, his work could only prefigure the principles underpinning the EP framework.

As Dewey's ideas took hold, the emancipatory and highly politicised movements of the 1960s and 1970s both influenced and were influenced by educational researchers such as Stenhouse (1975) and Lortie (1975) who developed notions of empowering teachers to do research themselves, rather than relying on external researchers. Stenhouse, for example, argued strongly for the notion of teachers as researchers.

Quote 3.8: Stenhouse on a Call for Different Expectations

… the long-term improvement of education through the utilization of research and development hinges on the creation of different expectations in the system and the design of new styles of project in harmony with those expectations.

The different expectations will be generated only as schools come to see themselves as research and development institutions rather than clients of research and development agencies. […] Communication is less effective than community in the utilization of knowledge.

(1975: 222–223)

Unfortunately, however, Stenhouse's call for different expectations seems to have fallen on deaf ears, despite a generally positive consensus of opinions across the field. Schools continue to be seen as clients (or 'end-users') of research and development agencies. And, as he noted, the two barriers to teachers studying their own work themselves (which Stenhouse had advocated) are still psychological and social, with very little support given to teachers wanting to engage in researching their own practice, and almost none to the notion of pupils joining in such engagement.

Lortie is often cited in connection with the phrase 'apprenticeship of observation', but what is rarely mentioned is the fact that he also noted two major limitations on the notion of students serving as apprentices for a later career in teaching: first that the student sees the teacher from a specific, and often limited, vantage point, and second that 'student participation' in lessons is usually imaginary rather than real (Lortie 1975: 62). Nevertheless, Lortie remained optimistic that teachers could be empowered to research their own classrooms, though this was seen as a 'half-way house' between classrooms and universities.

> **Quote 3.9: Lortie on Forming a New Cadre of 'Teacher-Researchers'**
>
> I conceive of the role as both practical and visionary; teacher-researchers would work directly on teaching problems while searching for better solutions [...] They could form a liaison between classroom teachers and outside researchers in research institutes and universities. They could channel ideas for research and disseminate useful findings. [...] To expect teachers to contribute to the development of their occupational knowledge seems reasonable; to the extent that they do, their future standing and work circumstances will benefit.
>
> (1975: 242–244)

A radical moment in history saw Freire (1970, 1973) advocating the idea of learners taking control of their own learning in a highly politicised, critically aware way. Working to develop literacy in rural Brazil, he argued against the notion of an outsider coming in to 'tell' the peasants what and how to read. Instead, he raised the possibility of workers choosing for themselves, using the literacy teacher only as one of many resources available to them. Crucially, he suggested that education is not one-directional, but rather a constant flow, back and forth, in a dialogic relationship between people (whatever their role), drawing on, and feeding into, an ongoing, living conversation.

> **Quote 3.10: Freire on a New Way of Thinking About Education**
> The role of the educator is not to 'fill' the educatee with 'knowledge', technical or otherwise. It is rather to attempt to move towards a new way of thinking in both educator and educatee, through the dialogical relationships between both. The flow is in both directions.
> (1973: 125)

Freire also argued for a highly politically aware approach to literacy teaching and learning, encouraging a critical awareness as readers interpreted the (written and unwritten) signs and messages around them. So learners (and teachers?) were at last getting hold of some of the power to set their own agendas for learning and teaching, which can also be extended into researching. Freire and colleagues (see also Freire and Shorr 1987) were challenging traditionally accepted hierarchies of knowledge and knowledge transfer from authorities (eg professional academics/researchers, or institutions such as ministries and governments). Their ideas contributed to the fertile ground from which the EP principles grew.

In language teaching, Stevick (1976, 1980, 1990, 1996) worked alongside others in teacher education to promote the notion of 'humanism' (see also Moskowitz 1978) in language teaching and learning, seeing the learner (and the teacher) in a 'holistic' way. That is to say, Stevick advocated an attitude of recognition and respect for '… the whole, complex person, not only in each student, but in yourself and your colleagues as well' (1996: 254). This was based on an understanding of learners and teachers as *human beings* in the classroom, and as people who have important insights into the learning/teaching process.

> **Quote 3.11: Stevick on the Intricate, Delicate Process of Language Teaching/Learning**
>
> ... I fear outside experts from whatever field who seek or who even accept some sort of intellectual hegemony over mere language teaching practitioners. [...] I fear any teacher who emphasizes copying over creating. [...] I fear whoever [...] focuses more on teaching language than on teaching people.
>
> What, then, do I hope to find? First of all, I know that the kind of teaching I have called for makes heavy demands on the teacher – demands on time and skill, of course, but also on flexibility and commitment. So I hope that in the future we will all find a growing public appreciation not only for the value of our product, but also for the special intricacy and delicacy of the process that we are responsible for guiding.
>
> (1996: 249)

Stevick (1996) argued for a recognition of, and respect for, the contributions that learners and teachers offer for the field of language education. This, developed to its full capacity, leads to Johnson and Golombek's (2002) promotion of *teachers* as the people best placed to investigate classrooms, and Cochran-Smith and Lytle's (2009) notion of 'Inquiry as Stance'. However, there are a number of obstacles to overcome.

Often when people think of 'research' they make a number of assumptions: that it should be large-scale, objective, and replicable, and that its findings should be generalisable. Traditional ideas about research emphasise the need for product and improvement. But as has been pointed out (Allwright and Bailey 1991; Borg 2010, 2013; Burton 1998), there are major problems with this attitude when we consider the context of language education. The fluid, ever-changing dynamics of individuals and groups working in a class, and the infinite variety of variables inside and outside the classroom, as well as the ethical dilemmas involved, mean that research with experimental/control groups is deeply flawed, and large-scale questionnaire-based studies often remain at a superficial level. Classrooms are highly complex social situations, where traditional notions of research simply fail. I'll return to this point below, but first we need to critically examine these assumptions. In moving towards a clearer definition of practitioner research, a number of questions about the underlying assumptions need to be addressed (see Concept 3.5).

> **Concept 3.5: Questions for Practitioner Research**
> What are the underlying assumptions about what guides the research?
> Who are the practitioners?
> What is the subject matter of the research?
> What makes practitioner research 'research' rather than just random looking around?

These questions link directly to the development of the EP framework, as we shall see in Chapter 4. We will therefore consider each of them in turn.

What Are the Underlying Assumptions Guiding Practitioner Research?

In their extended discussion of practitioner research, Zeichner and Noffke (2001) suggest 'trustworthiness' as a more appropriate criterion than 'validity'. They posit that the world of the classroom, which is fluid, complex, and placed within a particular (and ever-changing) socio-political context, requires other benchmarks, such as trustworthiness, resonance, systematicity, and clarity, to be brought into play. Further, Burton (1998) argues that the complexity of human relations and learning, the unique and transitory nature of the teaching/learning experience, and ethical concerns surrounding such research point towards the need for a more interpretivist approach. Miles and Huberman (1994) list a set of binary pairings to be considered in different forms of qualitative or quantitative research traditions.

> **Concept 3.6: Cornerstones of Research**
>
> There are many ways of characterising the cornerstones of qualitative and quantitative research. The defining characteristics of quantitative research have remained fairly stable, while those of qualitative research seem more fluid and open to debate. For example, 'resonance' often replaces 'dependability', and 'trustworthiness' may be seen in place of 'credibility'. Despite the large number of terms for apparently nebulous concepts, there does seem to be a consensus. For example, Miles and Huberman (1994) suggested the following pairings, which have remained (despite differences in nomenclature) relatively constant:
>
> | Quantitative | Qualitative |
> | --- | --- |
> | (i) Objectivity | (i) Confirmability |
> | (ii) Replicability | (ii) Dependability |
> | (iii) Validity | (iii) Credibility (or 'trustworthiness') |
> | (iv) Reliability | (iv) Transferability (or 'resonance') |

Such approaches take up Geertz's notion of 'thick description' (Geertz 1973) and allow for the complexity of different participant perspectives in classrooms to be represented. In doing so, practitioner research goes some way to answer Denzin and Lincoln's (1998) call for representations of a multi-layered reality, involving the practitioners themselves.

Who Are the Practitioners?

In much of the literature to do with classroom research, the term 'practitioners' is glossed as 'teachers' (Altrichter et al. 1993; Freeman 1996) and a whole field of 'teacher research' (Lortie 1975; Stenhouse 1975) has grown up over the years, with Borg (2010, 2013) a recent contributor to the field. Positioning teachers as researchers has the advantage of allowing them to develop as professionals, who have a unique understanding of the world of the classroom and who can also make a substantial contribution to knowledge. Kiely (2006), for example, cites the benefits for teachers, students, and institutions that practitioner research offers, and the complementary nature of teacher/researcher identities that may develop.

The social and political changes that allowed teachers to move from being consumers to 'producers and mediators of educational knowledge' (Zeichner and Noffke 2001: 299) increased the potential for gaining insights into the world of teaching and learning. Others have encouraged teachers to examine their own principles and classroom practices:

> … both the dynamic nature of the individual's experiential pedagogy and any evolution in what may be the collective pedagogy of the wider professional community – *and* how these may be related to each other – are significant issues for both teacher education and research on language teaching. (Breen et al. 2001:498)

Certainly, then, teachers (as the practitioners of teaching) are central to this definition of practitioner research. But in EP we ask: Is that enough?

EP seeks to broaden the remit to include learners as 'key developing practitioners' (see Allwright and Hanks 2009). We can trace this move back to Freire's (1970, 1973) work as mentioned above, and also to moves in other fields such as psychotherapy (eg Casement 1985). Here 'patients' (ostensibly the clients or end-users of psychotherapy) are recognised as having a contribution to make not only to their own therapeutic development, but also to the development of the therapist. For example, Casement argues for opportunities for analysts to engage in creative learning from patients:

> Opportunities for learning from the patient are there in all caring professions. […] I hope […] that those in allied caring professions will be able to play with the ideas I explore here and to relate them to their own spheres of work. (Casement 1985: xii)

Just as the caring professions stand to gain from listening to patients (or 'clients'), so too can the world of education learn much by giving space to learners, and conceptualising them as co-researchers alongside teachers. In other words, teachers learn, learners (potentially) teach, as well as the other way around.

What Is the Proper Subject Matter of the Research?

Related to the two points above, there have been calls for an 'ecological perspective' in describing the complexity of classrooms and language teaching (Tudor 2001; van Lier 1996, 2009). Practitioners are positioned as having potential as theorisers and theory builders (Lave and Wenger 1991): they have access to insights and a deeper understanding of the complexity of language teaching than 'outside researchers'. For example, Tudor (2001) argues that classroom language teaching merits investigation, and that such investigations must include the perspectives of those most closely involved in learning and teaching. In other words, he calls for classrooms to be investigated from the *inside*, considering the complexities of different points of view, identities, and contexts. At the same time, Johnson and Golombek (2002) call for promoting research, *for* teachers and *by* teachers who are working and researching in their own classrooms, as a way of promoting theorising. And Richards suggests that practising teachers can 'draw strength from our shared understandings and experiences' (2003: 9).

Freeman's (1996) suggestion that teaching *itself* has the potential to be research points to the notion put forward by Allwright (1993) that teachers might use their own practice as a methodological tool for investigation. This later became a central plank of the EP principles, as we shall see in Chapter 5.

> **Quote 3.12: Freeman on Teacher Research**
> When pursued in a disciplined manner, teaching itself becomes a form of research. It is a matter of balancing and assembling different points of view, each of which knows – or can know – aspects of the story of teaching and learning.
> (1996: 112)

In sum, a growing consensus has developed regarding concepts such as multiple perspectives, and a multi-layered and complex reality as crucial. Whether the research is data-driven, with local implications, or whether it is aiming for grand theory, makes a difference to what is (or who are) studied, by whom, and using which methods. In other words, the proper subject of practitioner research is (amongst other things) enquiry into classroom learning and teaching and the local meaning-making in which practitioners are constantly engaged. We will return to these points in Chapter 4.

So What Makes It Research Rather than Random Looking Around?

This last point raises the issue of the *purpose* of practitioner research, and the *purposeful and systematic* nature of research. It is helpful here to note the point made by Allwright and Bailey: '… it is not enough to know that ideas do work; we need also to know why and how they work' (1991: 197). In other words, there is a need for purposefulness in research – not to find 'the answer' but rather to understand *why things are as they are*. A working definition of practitioner research, then, includes the notions of purposeful, systematic, and thoughtfully critical investigation.

In EP we promote the idea of 'enquiry as process'. More recently, Cochran-Smith and Lytle (2009) have proposed the notion of 'inquiry as stance' (2009: 3) in contrast to the more commonly accepted notion of 'inquiry as project' (ibid.). This has useful implications for anyone interested in researching their own contexts through EP, as we shall see in Part 2.

EP also argues for learners to be included as co-researchers (see Allwright 2003; Allwright and Hanks 2009) alongside teachers in the investigative enterprise. This links with Freire's (1973) pioneering work, which challenges the 'mechanisation' of education (in a system which encourages uncritical acceptance of 'production') by encouraging a dialogic and actively critical approach, involving learners and teachers as potent and potential researchers. And this in turn goes even further back, to the Aristotelian notion of *phronesis*.

Phronesis: Ethical, Practical Wisdom

Informing the above discussion is the concept of *phronesis*. This revisiting of Aristotle's notion was a formative moment in conceiving research in the social sciences more broadly, as Flyvbjerg (2001) has discussed. We will return to *phronesis* in Part Three, so a brief discussion of the meaning of the term is required.

> **Quote 3.13: Flyvbjerg on the Nebulous Concept of *Phronesis***
> Whereas *episteme* concerns theoretical *know why* and *techne* denotes technical *know how*, *phronesis* emphasizes practical knowledge and practical ethics.
> (2001: 56)

According to Flyvbjerg (2001), *phronesis* sits alongside the technicist, problem-solving approach of *techne*, and the contemplative reflection of *episteme*; it

> ...goes beyond both analytical, scientific knowledge (*episteme*) and technical knowledge or know-how (*techne*) and involves judgements and decisions made in the manner of a virtuoso social and political actor (2001: 2)

Flyvbjerg cites Aristotle as arguing that 'every well-functioning society was dependent on the effective functioning of all three intellectual virtues' (ibid.: 60). This is helpful for our purposes as it gives long-overdue value to the importance of context, and to the expertise of those actors in their context (for our purpose: learners and teachers and all those involved in second language education).

In the field of education, Carr (1987, 2004) has posited a return to the Aristotelian notion of *praxis*, and cited *phronesis* (or as he defines it, 'practical wisdom') as a way of promoting the 'integrity of educational practice and oppos[ing] all those cultural tendencies which now undermine and degrade it' (Carr 1987: 174). He argues that without *phronesis*, 'deliberation degenerates into an intellectual exercise, and "good practice" becomes indistinguishable from instrumental cleverness' (ibid.:

172). Sound judgement, in his view, must be combined with practical knowledge (relating to 'good' practice) and rooted in the particularities of social context. As we shall see, this relating of wisdom to ethics and practice is central to the ideas of EP.

Problematising Practitioner Research (i): Power, Ownership, and Funding

Alternative definitions of practitioner research in education typically offer opportunities for greater involvement from teachers, as Cochran-Smith and Lytle (2009) suggest.

> **Quote 3.14: Cochran-Smith and Lytle on a Thriving Movement**
> Considerable evidence shows that, during the last decade, despite all the forces working against it, the practitioner research movement has continued to thrive in parallel with other initiatives that aim to democratise the locus of knowledge and power
>
> (2009: 34)

In Chapter 4 we will investigate several forms of the practitioner research movement in more depth, relating them to EP. But first, a pause for reflection.

Although the discussions of research definitions (in Concept Boxes 3.2, 3.3 and 3.4) seem to offer clarity, a number of questions remain. What is meant by 'systematic'? Does it relate to a coherent system of theoretical constructs? Or is it more to do with '… a meticulously planned method for carrying out the research' (McDonough and McDonough 1997: 41)? When considering the variety of research projects and the range of contexts that teachers work in around the world, how can systematicity be ensured? What is the research agenda, and who sets it? How may purpose be defined, and who sets the criteria for this? Whose understandings will be extended, and why? What really counts as 'making public the research'? And who gets to decide this?

One of the many criticisms of practitioner research (summarised in Borg 2013, pp. 18–22) is that it is seen (by non-teachers?) as limited, naïve, and descriptive. Currently, 'scientific' notions of experiment and empirical observation block the possibility for professionals in education asking deeper questions about education itself (see Borg 2013). Research has been colonised by those who want to see it as a *particular form* of science – not the exciting, edgy, imaginative work of, say, particle physics, or the search for dark matter, but a more technicist, measurable, controllable, and limited way of thinking that has been (mis-)labelled 'scientific'. This betrays a fundamentally narrow view of what 'science' or 'scientific' is and can be.

This uneasiness is exacerbated when questions are asked about the 'territory' of research (Breen 2006). In summarising the criticisms of teacher research, Borg (2010) has noted a number of concerns raised by those who are at some level, and perhaps for different reasons, opposed to the notion of practitioners researching their own contexts. This raises another set of questions: Who sets the research agenda? Who does the research? Who benefits from the research? In other words, who *owns* the research?

When alternative definitions are used, some of these problems seem to be resolved, but thorny questions remain. These doubts are masterfully drawn out by Walker (1995, cited in Zeichner and Noffke 2001: 310) and may be summarised as follows:

- Who sets the research agenda?
- Who carries out the research? (and on/with whom?)
- Who reports on the research? (and to whom?)
- Who benefits from the research?

Who decides what is valued in research, and why, and who has the right to decide what is acceptable as research and what is not, has been much debated elsewhere (Breen 2006; Johnson and Golombek 2002; Zeichner and Noffke 2001). Such discussions have profound effects on practitioner beliefs about what research is done, how much can be done, and how it may be carried out. The attempt to resolve such 'cognitive dissonance' (Festinger 1957), whether by changing cognitive behaviour or by changing environmental cognitive elements, takes place in a site of struggle, for beliefs around research and pedagogy are ideologically loaded, rooted in conceptions of society, behaviour, and values. EP is no exception to this, as it sets up a 'problematic shift in power relations' (Breen 2006: 216), which may cause difficulties for the more traditionally minded. Issues of power, ownership, and funding permeate definitions of research. The problems faced by teachers contemplating practitioner research are exacerbated when a more 'traditional' definition of what constitutes 'research' is applied, whether this is done by the academic community or by the teachers themselves (see Cochran-Smith and Lytle 2009, for an extended discussion of this matter). We will return to this discussion in Chapter 4.

Summary

Despite such doubts, practitioner research is now a well-established form of inquiry in its own right. Because of the contributions of giants such as Dewey, Freire, Lortie, and Stenhouse, not to mention Bourdieu (1991) and Fairclough (1989), we know that issues of power and power relations are central to debates about research in education. Teachers and learners are slowly becoming more involved in language education research, not only as the subjects/objects of research projects, but also as researchers themselves. However, there are continuing attempts to stifle this potent mix, and the next chapter shows the story of teachers as researchers and their struggle to be recognised and acknowledged as knowledge-holders and theory-makers in the field.

Recommended Readings

Cochran-Smith, M. & Lytle, S.L (2009) *Inquiry as Stance*. New York: Teachers College Press. This contemporary text brings the historical discussion of practitioner research bang up-to-date, provides a helpful analysis of the complicated and complexifying field, and encourages readers to begin to see themselves as powerful agents in education processes.

Dewey, J. (1938/1963) *Experience and Education.* New York: The Macmillan Company. A giant in the field of education, Dewey's pioneering work challenged traditional and hierarchical notions of teaching and learning. He analysed assumed roles and relationships in the classrooms of his time and paved the way for a new way of conceiving teacher contributions to education and research.

Freire, P. (1973) *Education for Critical Consciousness.* New York: Seabury Press. Freire's work is crucial for an understanding of the radical nature of work including learners alongside teachers as the people most concerned in what happens in their language learning/teaching efforts.

Lortie, D.C. (1975) *Schoolteacher: A sociological* study. Chicago: University of Chicago Press. All too often, mention of Lortie remains rooted in the famous phrase 'apprenticeship of observation' but Lortie has far more to offer the field than that. His sympathetic reading of the potential for teacher-researchers, and perhaps even learners, is worth revisiting.

Stenhouse (1975) *An Introduction to Curriculum Research and Development.* London: Heinemann. Stenhouse goes beyond the research and development of the curriculum to introduce the idea of the teacher as researcher. This ground-breaking idea is as sensible as it revolutionary – a shock for the established order, perhaps, but a crucial development in our field.

4
Perspectives on the 'Family' of Practitioner Research

Introduction

This book focuses on Exploratory Practice (EP), but in order to understand EP, we need to consider earlier influential movements in educational research. What are the questions, answered, unanswered, and unanswerable, that are raised here? To begin with, I consider a range of approaches to practitioner research, focusing particularly on two closely related movements: Action Research (AR) and Reflective Practice (RP). Each of these is clearly differentiated, while also acknowledging the family relationships, and shared values, that tie these various family members together. In doing so, I critically consider the challenges that practitioner-researchers face, and raise further questions about practitioner research.

Two major questions are considered here. First, 'Why so much interest in practitioner research?' The chapter begins by elucidating the benefits of practitioner research in language education, and sketching the contributions of several related, but different forms. Second, 'Why don't practitioners engage in research?' The chapter ends by considering the hindrances that potential practitioner-researchers face, with a view to understanding how/why/whence the EP framework of principles (which will be discussed in Chapter 5) emerged.

Why So Much Interest in Practitioner Research?

As teachers became more articulate about research and teaching, and with the encouragement of major educationalists such as Dewey (1938, 1963, 1944), Lortie (1975), and Stenhouse (1975), they began to actively research their own contexts. This notion of practitioner research has grown in healthcare and psychology, as well as in education. And this stems, at least in part, from the realisation that:

> [Teacher research] has undeniable transformative potential to enrich and improve the work of teachers, the experience of learners, and the effectiveness and credibility of organizations. (Borg 2013: 230)

The advent of practitioner research broke the log-jam of teachers who were interested in their classrooms, in their teaching, and in learning, but who were unable to take enough time to train and act as fully qualified professional academic researchers. Over the past twenty years there has been a great surge of enthusiasm, with journals, websites, and conferences focusing on teachers engaged in researching their own contexts.

> **Quote 4.1: Johnson and Golombek on Teacher Involvement in Research**
> ... narrative inquiry enables teachers not only to make sense of their professional worlds but also to make significant and worthwhile change within themselves and in their teaching practices.
> (2002: 7)

As a result of the shift to these more practical approaches, and a more equitable view of teachers' experiences, a sense of optimism infused publications of the late 1990s and early 2000s. As shown at the end of Chapter 3, questions were being asked about *whose* knowledge would be privileged in the teacher research genre, and there was a sense of increased respect (at least in some quarters) for the importance of research done by practitioners in language education.

Ideological commitments to the benefits of practitioner research have led to impassioned declarations from those who encourage teachers to engage in fruitful explorations of their practices, in their classrooms—in other words, investigating their sense of *Dasein* (Heidegger 1962), of 'being-in-the-world' (Dreyfus 1991). As many have argued (eg Johnson and Golombek 2002; Tudor 2001; Zeichner and Noffke 2001), researching classroom practice is best done by those who are most closely involved in the world of the classroom itself; our understandings as classroom practitioners are most meaningful to us, the learners and teachers, teacher educators, etc. Arguably, this increases the potential for deeper understanding *because* it is situated in, and stems from, everyday life.

Quote 4.2: Tudor on Understanding Classrooms

... in order to understand precisely what takes place in our classrooms, we have to look at these classrooms as entities in their own right and explore the meaning they have for those who are involved in them in their own terms.

(2001: 9)

Tudor (2001) argues that if we are to understand what happens in classrooms, then we need to move away from the notion of the external researcher looking in, and, instead, position practitioners themselves as the key observers. This empowering view echoes the arguments of many others (Burns 2010; Cochran-Smith and Lytle 1999, 2009; Johnson and Golombek 2002), and it is central to the various forms of practitioner research that have grown up over the past two decades. For example, Zeichner and Noffke (2001) have positioned practitioner research as an inherently political act, adding an altruistic dimension. They present a compelling argument for practitioner research as a positive force in the world of education.

Quote 4.3: Zeichner and Noffke on the Potential of Practitioner Research

When practitioner researchers choose to make their inquiries available to others, their work becomes a potential source of knowledge (a) for other researchers and practitioners, (b) for the curriculum of teacher education and professional development programmes, and (c) for educational policymakers.

(2001: 315)

All this looks very promising. But as we shall see later in this chapter, practitioner research is problematic for the status quo. It asks questions that those higher up in the hierarchy would, perhaps, prefer to suppress. This desire to 'speak truth to power' is characteristic of the early stages of an important form of practitioner research called Action Research. As mentioned earlier, AR has a sister in Reflective Practice, and they are both prevalent in the fields of healthcare, psychology, and education.

Working for Improvement (i): Action Research

The movement which became known as Action Research, developed beyond the work of Dewey (1938) in education and Lewin (1946) in psychology in the second half of the twentieth century (see Zeichner and Noffke 2001, for a comprehensive account of these developments). Perhaps as a result of the political and social climate in the West at this time, the main focus for AR was the fight for social justice, as Carr and Kemmis (1986) pointed out.

> **Quote 4.4: Carr and Kemmis on Action Research and Social Justice**
> ... action research, by linking research to action, offers teachers and others a way of becoming aware of how those aspects of the social order which frustrate rational change may be overcome.
> (1986: 179–180)

Definitions of AR are varied, though, and have proliferated over the years (see, for example, Elliott 1991; Kemmis and McTaggart 1988). Eventually, the term became so ubiquitous that it now means many things to many people. McNiff and Whitehead (2002) suggest that in some ways there is 'no such "thing" as action research' (2002: 15). They also offer an extended discussion of critiques from within the AR movement, which I will not wear out with repetition here. Some of those working in the AR arena (eg Altrichter et al. 1993; McNiff et al. 2003; Kemmis and McTaggart 2003) have emphasised the political dimension. So, for example, McNiff & Whitehead characterise action researchers as

4 Perspectives on the 'Family' of Practitioner Research

sharing a set of beliefs about values and having a common aim of trying to change life into '… futures which are more in tune with their values' (2002: 17). This begs the question, though, of *whose* values take precedence. Moreover, what if there is no agreement about these values? And what if the situation has been imperfectly understood? Much time and energy could be spent on improvements, but if there has been a misapprehension at the start, the research enterprise (and the outcome of attempts to redress the balance regarding social justice) is flawed.

In English Language Teaching (ELT), AR frequently loses this overtly political edge. Wallace, for example, leaves out the revolutionary dimension when he describes AR as '… the systematic collection and analysis of data relating to the improvement of some aspect of professional practice' (1998: 1). He, like Nunan (1989, 1993), focuses on a more pragmatic interpretation, and concludes that AR offers opportunities for practitioners to:

> improve their own teaching and perhaps also to raise the level of performance generally in their working situation (Wallace 1998: 254)

More recently, a major authority on AR in the field of ELT, Burns (2005, 2010, 2015), has returned to the transformative element of AR. Drawing on the work of others (eg Cohen and Manion 1994), she distinguishes three main approaches (the technical, the practical, the critical) and highlights the inherent tension between the linked concepts of *research* and *action*. Here, the agenda of action for change has solidified as the main plank of AR, and Burns acknowledges that the driving force is to promote change, whether in the social/political arena (eg educational policies), or improvement in pedagogy, or even more locally in individual classrooms. She positions AR as a research paradigm, explaining that AR promotes a moral and ethical approach to research in ELT, one which is 'explicitly interventionist and subjective' (Burns 2005: 60). And she argues persuasively that it:

> … contributes to teachers' professional development in at least three ways: knowledge construction becomes both personal and collective; new teaching and learning practices are scaffolded and supported by others;

professional confidence in one's own efficacy as a teacher is enhanced by those colleagues. (Burns 2015: 15)

Stances range, then, from the highly politicised end of the spectrum, focusing on social justice and change (Atweh et al. 1998; Carr and Kemmis 1986; Kemmis and McTaggart 2003), to the more pragmatic, improvement-oriented work in English language teaching (Burns 1999, 2010, 2015; Nunan 1989, 1993; Wallace 1998). Burns has helpfully summarised the various definitions of AR, noting the importance of context as AR 'identifies and investigates problems within a specific situation' (1999: 30). Above all, she suggests that the political dimension of AR has wider implications. Although local and small-scale, with individual teachers investigating problems in their classrooms and trying to solve them, it is argued that AR can also lead to institution or curriculum reforms or calls for change in the education system.

> **Concept 4.1: Key Themes Common to Definitions of Action Research**
> Emphasis on education as a social/political process
> Emphasis on empowerment of teachers through participation in research
> Emphasis on a problem-to-solution approach
> Emphasis on action for social/political, local/global, theoretical/practical change
> Involvement of academic 'advisors' to help teachers doing research

Broadly speaking, as Concept Box 4.1 indicates, AR involves teachers, often working with academics, investigating problems they have identified, with an *explicitly change-oriented agenda*. That is to say, with the aim of *working towards solving a problem*, whether locally (in the classroom) or more widely (in the field of education or society in general). AR takes

> … an explicitly interventionist and subjective approach […]. This element of change and improvement represents a key distinction from other forms of research. (Burns 2005: 60)

But as a result of this emphasis on 'change and improvement', AR is often in danger of becoming focused on a product rather than a process. A note of caution is needed. And although Carr (2004) has rightly challenged the prevailing agenda of seeing education as a form of instrumental and institutionalised technology entirely focused on externally imposed targets (see Quote Box 4.5), he tends to be rather a lone voice.

> **Quote 4.5: Carr on the Negative Effect of Technologisation on Education**
>
> Technologisation, institutionalisation and bureaucratisation [...] effectively ensure that education is now construed as a species of *poeisis* [...] guided by *techne* [technical knowledge or expertise], and hence as an instrumental capacity directed towards the achievement of externally imposed outcomes and goals
>
> (2004: 68)

Carr's rejection of this popular form of technicism resonates with Breen's (2006) castigation of state-imposed targets and the continuing acceptance of an externally imposed focus on 'improvement' or 'efficiency', which undermine the position and potency of teachers' contributions. As we shall see in Chapter 5, this is an important thread in the EP argument, and one that should not be ignored.

So what about another, very powerful, form of practitioner research?

Working for Improvement (ii): Reflective Practice

AR has developed alongside another practitioner research movement: Reflective Practice. Strong mutual influences (see Adler 1991; Griffiths and Tann 1992; Osterman and Kottkamp 2004) lead to a blurring of the boundaries between them. For example, Liston and Zeichner (1990) and Wallace (1998) make an explicit link between the two movements, while Atweh et al. (1998) describe the spiral of self-reflective research in which participant-researchers plan-act-observe-reflect-plan using elements from both AR and RP, and Farrell (2007) positions AR as a possible outcome of RP. Nevertheless, there are aspects of RP which are distinct from AR, and which therefore merit careful consideration.

> **Quote 4.6: Schön on Reflective Practice: Identifying What Needs to Be Changed**
>
> In real-world practice, problems do not present themselves to the practitioner as givens. They must be constructed from the materials of problematic situations which are puzzling, troubling, and uncertain. [...] When we set the problem, we select what we will treat as the 'things' of the situation, we set the boundaries of our attention to it, and we impose upon it a coherence which allows us to say what is wrong and in what directions the situation needs to be changed.
>
> (1983/1991: 40)

In the early 1980s, Schön (1983) put forward the ideas of RP, where practitioners (architects and psychoanalysts as well as teachers) are encouraged to reflect on their own practices with a view to making sense of '... the situations of uncertainty or uniqueness which he [sic] may allow himself to experience' (Schön 1983: 61). In the oft-cited 'reflection-in-action and reflection-on-action', Schön suggested playful experiments which help to 'get a feel for things' (ibid.: 141) from within the working situation, and argued that a practitioner 'understands the situation *by trying to change it*' (ibid.: 151, emphasis added).

This has proved a popular approach. From the late 1980s, RP has pervaded the fields of education and healthcare (amongst others), proliferating in a multitude of ways. Perhaps as a result of the name, which focuses on reflection, RP is often seen as inward-looking (though it need not be). It has become a central part of initial and ongoing teacher education, often being used as a form of continuing professional development. Adler, for example, frames RP as 'an ongoing conversation' (1991: 148), which impacts in different ways on 'teaching practice, on learning, and on relationships with all those involved in the schooling process' (ibid.). More recently, Farrell (2007) takes a stronger stance, as outlined in Quote Box 4.7, but once again, although laudably the focus is on teachers doing the bulk of the work and taking responsibility for their actions and their development in collegial ways, learners, their potential agency and contributions, are left in the background.

> **Quote 4.7: Farrell on a Bottom-Up Approach**
>
> Reflective language teaching [...] is a bottom-up approach to teacher professional development that is based on the belief that experienced and novice language teachers can improve their understanding of their own teaching by consciously and systematically reflecting on their teaching experiences. It starts with the internal rather than the external and the real centre of the process is teaching itself, and it uses the teacher's actual teaching experiences as a basis for reflection.
>
> (2007: 9)

Based on Schön's (1983, 1987) ground-breaking work, RP considers actions and events in the classroom from two perspectives: reflection-in-action and reflection-on-action. These have been helpfully defined further in Edge's (2011) work where he argues that RP helps teachers to 'discover more about the ways in which knowledge, experience and thought interact in decision-making and action' (Edge 2011: 16). RP is often (wrongly) criticised for being too introspective, but there is a clear requirement for reflective practitioners to work towards improvement too. This might be encapsulated by Farrell's notion of 'reflection for action'. The emphasis in RP, then, remains on contemplation and problem-solving, with the aim of improving *teaching* practices.

> **Quote 4.8: Edge on Two Types of Reflection**
>
> [reflection-in-action] ... situations where the expected flow of a class is interrupted for some reason and the teacher has to rethink, improvise, re-prioritize, or reorient the direction of the lesson.
>
> [reflection-on-action] ... the more contemplative type of reflection that takes place beyond the immediate pressures of the teaching moment, when one can think back over what happened and consider what has been learned from it and how this might be used in planning the future.
>
> (2011: 16)

Like AR, the starting point is usually for the teacher to begin with a 'problematic situation' (Schön 1983: 63) and consider how to develop or improve it using the double vision of reflection-in-action and reflection-on-action. Schön argues that practitioners can use reflection in this way to 'surface and criticise the tacit understandings that have grown up around the repetitive experiences of a specialised practice' (1983: 61). Valli, too, has argued for problem-focused RP:

> teachers must be prepared to solve complex educational problems, make wise decisions, reflect in and on action, and collaborate with colleagues (Valli 1992: xiv)

and Wallace cites the potential for RP to create a 'cadre of teachers who have the skills, ability and motivation to develop their practice' (1991: 166). In the USA, Liston and Zeichner (1990) go even further, by arguing for a socially aware, politically active form of RP, which links directly with AR as a way of implementing change. In other words, as we see in Concept Box 4.2, RP is often concerned with problems and problem-solving, and is transformative in intent.

Concept 4.2: Key Themes Common to Definitions of Reflective Practice

In essence, RP involves:

- Practitioners identifying a *problematic situation* in their working practices
- Pausing to *reflect on their work*
  - as they are teaching, looking into their own teaching practices
  - after they have taught, looking back on their teaching
- Aiming to use the results of their reflections to *change* or *improve* the situation in their classrooms

---

Although Liston and Zeichner (1990) attempted to highlight the active nature of RP, suggesting that teachers and teacher educators need to work together, this seems not to have been taken up more widely. For example, Griffiths & Tann argue that '[t]he reflective practitioner reflects on his or her *own* practice' (1992: 71), while Wallace suggests that:

It is (or should be) normal for professionals to reflect on their professional performance, particularly when it goes especially well or especially badly (1991: 13)

More recently, a critical approach to RP has emerged. Akbari, for example, argues that RP needs to focus on improvement and "more efficient teacher performance" (Akbari 2007: 204). Sadly, Akbari is not alone in failing to notice that this discourse of 'improvement' may in fact be a cipher for the very technicism that Allwright (2003) and Carr (2004), amongst others, have challenged.

Nevertheless, at the turn of the twenty-first century, there was clear enthusiasm for different forms of practitioner research. Yet despite the many calls from across the field of education for practitioner research to be encouraged (Clandinin and Connelly 1995; Clandinin and Rosiek 2007; Zeichner and Noffke 2001) and for practitioners to be engaged in investigations of their own complex and dynamic classrooms (van Lier 1996, 2009), the take-up has apparently been scant, with Borg concluding that it is 'a minority activity in our field' (2010: 391). More than fifteen years after Zeichner and Noffke's call for investigations into 'the conditions that facilitate and obstruct the ability of educators to conduct research on their own practice' (2001: 324), why is practitioner research still seen as an activity practised only by the few?

So Why Don't Practitioners Engage in Research?

Although much was being written *about* teachers researching, and opportunities were being offered for teachers to *do* research, it seemed that teachers themselves were not engaging in research as much as had been hoped. Borg (2009, 2010, 2013) asserts that teachers rarely engage in researching their classrooms without the impetus of some form of study, and indeed, a closer look at websites, journals, and conferences reveals that they are usually populated by academics and/or novice researchers writing up the results of their Masters-level or PhD-level studies. It seems rare for practising teachers to write up classroom research publicly without the impetus of studying for some sort of formal qualification. But if we consider the working conditions of many practitioners, this may be understandable, in Concept Box 4.3 indicates.

> **Concept 4.3: What Hinders Practitioner Research?**
>
> – Lack of *time*
> – Lack of *resources* (financial, physical, mental)
> – Lack of *expertise* in traditional academic research practices
> – Lack of *relevance* of the research agenda to the participants
> – Lack of *relevance* of the findings of research to the participants
> – Lack of *respect* for the work of practitioners
>
> Are there other 'lacks' that should be added to this list?

One reason might be that more pressing demands intervene. When teachers are asked (Borg 2007, 2013; Burton 1998; Kirkwood and Christie 2006; McDonough and McDonough 1990) what hinders them from engaging in research, they regularly cite lack of time, relevance, or resources. But there may be more to it.

Lack of Time and Resources

Turning to the first and second of these 'lacks', a brief vignette illustrates the problem for teachers wishing, or as is more often the case, being *required* to engage in research.

> **Vignette 4.1: Teachers Required to Do Research**
>
> Claire is a teacher of English. She works full-time, and has a demanding workload of preparing and teaching her classes, doing the required administration, marking, and preparing her students for the International English Language Testing System (IELTS) examination. Often she spends her evenings or weekends marking student work, or preparing lessons and materi-

4 Perspectives on the 'Family' of Practitioner Research

> als. She attends teacher development workshops occasionally, but often she is teaching, or she's too tired to go, or she wants to spend a little time with her family. Recently, however, her employer has changed the terms of her contract to include 'scholarship/research' as a duty she needs to perform as well.
> 'What can I do?' she wails; 'I'm already exhausted by the demands of teaching, marking, admin! How can I add research activity to my very full workload?'

Claire's story indicates the many conflicting demands faced by practitioners contemplating research. As Burns rightly points out:

> Teachers don't get paid or given time off to do research as academics do; they have full teaching loads which means that any time spent on research needs to be added onto a busy teaching schedule. (Burns 2010: 6)

The lack of time and resources should not be underestimated. Many forms of practitioner research are seen (by teachers as well as academics) as imposing a heavy commitment. Observation schedules such as Interaction Analysis (Flanders 1970), Foreign Language Interaction, or FLint (Moskowitz 1968, cited in Allwright and Bailey 1991) originally designed for teacher education and/or evaluation purposes may end by increasing the burden on overworked teachers to intolerable levels. If the requirement to 'disseminate' findings (via journal articles, book chapters, or conference presentations) is added to this, practitioners understandably reject the imposition. At a time of austerity, financial resources are scarce, and many (overworked) teachers struggle to find the money, the time, or indeed the headspace to engage in research.

Lack of Expertise

A criticism frequently levelled at teachers doing research is that they are not proficient in the techniques of research itself. Again, this often stems from very traditional notions of what methodologies might be used, and rigid ideas of how knowledge might be gathered or generated as Borg (2009) has discussed. His evidence shows that teachers themselves may have very strong ideas about what constitutes research. Borg argues that for many teachers 'barriers also exist which are attitudinal, conceptual, and procedural in nature' (2009: 29). Powerful images of large-scale surveys, statistical analyses, and extensive written outcomes abound, and these barriers are difficult to overcome. In sum, a lack of knowledge of the varied methodological and technical resources available to teachers may be a significant factor in preventing practitioners from engaging in research. This is exacerbated when we consider how teachers are often positioned in the field (see Johnson and Golombek 2002, in Quote Box 4.9).

> **Quote 4.9: Johnson and Golombek on the Positioning of Teachers**
> Teachers have been marginalized in that they are told what they should know and how they should use that knowledge. Even though many teachers personally reject this model, most of them continue to work and learn under its powerful hold in teacher education programs and the schools where they teach.
>
> (2002: 1)

This is of crucial importance for education more generally, as practitioners are routinely marginalised. Their views, their experiences, and their knowledge count for little, when weighed against the powerful pronouncements of (government-funded) academic research, which then influences policy-makers, institutions, and teacher education. Learners, and learner-teachers (ie teachers-in-training), are in an even worse position, as their voices are overpowered by received (but critically unquestioned) wisdom. But if, as advocated by Johnson and Golombek, we interrogate the status quo, we find that all is not well. Questions are raised not only about who does the research and who has the right to judge it, but also about who the research is for, and how/whether it helps the learning.

Borg (2013) has tried to suggest conditions that might facilitate teacher engagement in research, such as:

- Allocate time for research on teachers' timetables
- Create an awareness of the value of research to teachers
- Include research in teachers' job descriptions

4 Perspectives on the 'Family' of Practitioner Research   71

- Provide teachers with access to research journals
- Provide training/workshops on how to do research (see Borg 2013: 221 for the full list)

Yet this is only a first step (however welcome). Realistically, in current conditions, a second or third step is unlikely to be achievable in anything more concrete than the usual lip-service we see offered by institutions. And some well-meaning intentions to support can all too easily become burdens. Borg rightly identifies the 'definitional uncertainties' (2013: 230) about research as one major reason why teachers hesitate before engaging in such practice. As he points out, there are misunderstandings on both sides: professional academics and practitioners. In calling for stronger research cultures in institutions, and in arguing for certain facilitative conditions, however, the benign face of such institutional shifts can gloss over some of the hazards. For example, 'including research [or scholarship] in teachers' job descriptions' (ibid.: 221) can lead to intolerable pressure on already busy practitioners as we saw in Claire's story (Vignette 4.1) above.

But at the very least, this form of practitioner research, as Borg argues, affords 'undeniable transformative potential to enrich' (2013: 230) the lives and work of all involved in language education. Done well, with appropriate support, it is, therefore, one might playfully argue, a step towards the EP principles for practitioner research.

So, as Zeichner and Noffke (2001) have argued, we need to investigate the conditions which either facilitate or obstruct the ability of practitioners to research their classrooms. As pressures on teachers and learners increase, so too do pressures on researchers. 'Research' (sometimes also called 'Scholarship' – the distinction between the two has not yet been clearly identified) has been written into the contractual obligations for many teachers, as well as researchers, and is often used in criteria for promotions. Increasing numbers of teachers are undertaking Masters or even doctoral work involving classroom research in their own classrooms, and even undergraduates are encouraged to begin researching their own classroom language learning (or teaching) experiences. The notion of a self-motivated practitioner, researching ('scholarshipping'?) their own practice, for their own purposes, is not impossible, but with increasing workloads it is increasingly rare.

Lack of Relevance of Research Agenda/Findings

It is also worth noting that teachers may be dismissive of the efforts of academics. As McDonough and McDonough maintain:

> teachers do not always perceive the findings of such research as relevant to their classrooms and their own teaching practices (1990: 103)

Following this up, Burton (1998) suggests that ELT practitioners who are interested in issues to do with learning and teaching have often found research publications so esoteric and distanced from their 'real world' that they rejected the findings or simply ignored the results as irrelevant. When investigating this question in the late 1990s, Burton eloquently captured the conundrum, which remains relevant today.

> **Quote 4.10: Burton on the Problem with Orthodox Research**
> … orthodox research does not provide what teachers want to know; teachers seek understanding and illumination rather than explanation and definition.
> (1998: 425)

This question of 'lack of relevance' to the participants is crucial. If both the research agenda and the research findings of many projects are perceived as external and irrelevant to those most closely concerned with teaching, then why would practitioners bother?

Edge (2011) notes that the two sides (practising teachers and academics) have often taken up hostile positions. One reason for this may be, as Breen explains, that there are 'vested interests' (2006: 220) at stake, with academics keen to protect their (beleaguered) territory. At the same time, academic research is often seen by practitioners as too esoteric or too remote to be of practical use (see Quote Box 4.11).

4 Perspectives on the 'Family' of Practitioner Research

> **Quote 4.11: Borg on Attitudes Towards Research Engagement**
>
> Constrained by definitional uncertainties about what research and teacher research entail, attitudes towards research engagement are polarised by an uninformed dichotomy between 'theory' and 'practice' in which research for teachers is conceptualised as either irrelevant academic activity or informal reflection on practice.
>
> (2013: 230)

Such attitudes may also indicate a lack of respect on both sides for the achievements and potential of all concerned.

Lack of Respect

Questions are frequently raised (eg Brown 2005, cited in Borg 2010) about the reliability, validity, and quality of the research produced by practitioners, and, in general, more traditional assumptions of what research is, and what it looks like, are pervasive throughout the field. And not only in the field of education, but in social sciences more generally. For example, Gergen (2013) describes how, even quite recently in the field of psychology, battles have raged over the acceptance (or otherwise) of qualitative research at the 'table' of the American Psychological Association:

> In spite of the fact that the grounding work of many of psychology's major theorists – Freud, Ebbinghaus, Piaget, Lorenz, and Vygotsky, amongst others – was primarily qualitative in nature, such inquiry was not accepted or even considered, by virtually any of the major journals of the field. So strong was the grip of 1930s philosophy of science, and the derived quest for truth through experiments and statistics, that qualitative inquiry was essentially an embarrassment to the discipline. (Gergen 2013: 38)

Such attitudes are pervasive throughout academe, and education is no exception. We see similar (subjective? emotive?) comments and reactions from those who are positioning themselves as 'scientific'. But, as the scare quotes indicate, this is in itself a flawed reading of what it means to be 'scientific'. As Borg points out, the comments are based on a narrow, even outmoded, way of thinking about research:

> The common criticism of teacher research that it is of poor quality, methodologically-speaking, is also often underpinned by conventional scientific notions of research (e.g. large-scale, replicable, quantitative). (Borg 2010: 405)

In a similar vein, Burns (1999) acknowledges that AR is frequently criticised for its 'inability to test hypotheses or establish cause & effect relationships, for its resistance to the basic techniques and procedures of research and for its lack of generalizability' (Burns 1999: 27). But, she adds, this is a mistaken attempt to measure AR (and, indeed, other forms of practitioner research) against criteria that are 'inimical to its central principles of action and reflection within practical social situations' (ibid.: 27–28). The reality is that many practitioners (and many researchers) see little point in testing hypotheses when the parameters are too broad, and there are too many uncontrolled/uncontrollable variables (as in classroom language learning), for any meaningful conclusion to be drawn.

On the other hand, '… much of the AR conducted by teachers stays unpublished or is disseminated, often verbally, only to a localised audience' (Burns 2005: 63). Perhaps one reason for this is that putting their work into the public domain leaves the practitioners vulnerable to the criticisms of professional academics, some of whom appear not to recognise the 'research' or give it equal value with their own endeavours, as Vignette 4.2 suggests.

Vignette 4.2: A Dean Speaks

Constantly under pressure to produce results and focus on findings, Mick (a university lecturer, teacher, and researcher) does his best to publish as many articles in highly rated journals as possible. He draws on his research in teacher education, and is acutely aware of the rifts between theory and practice. He would like to bridge that gap, and aims to include teachers as much as possible in his research. Such work rarely if ever achieves high-level funding (grants of £100,000 or more), yet it is highly relevant to the participants themselves, and makes significant theoretical contributions to the field.

4 Perspectives on the 'Family' of Practitioner Research

> One day, he goes to a talk given by the Dean of his Faculty in the University. The Dean is himself under pressure to demonstrate results (in the form of high ratings in the nationally run 'Research Excellence Framework'), and seeks to encourage staff to engage in recognised research activity, with large grants of money from funders. At the same time, he wishes to draw their attention to the threats that poor performance in the ratings system will bring. Since he can only recognise traditional forms of 'scientific' research, he fails to acknowledge the benefits of practitioner research, which is often poorly funded or not funded at all, but takes place at the will of the people involved. In the course of his speech, he thunders; 'Research that does not draw down large sums of money from grants or government funding is just a posh hobby.'
>
> Mick leaves the room demoralised: Is his hard work, which seemed to meet a very real need in education, just a 'posh hobby'?

Such profound changes may be difficult to consider in the current political and economic climate. In order for them to come about, academics as well as teachers and learners would have to undertake a deep examination of their own identities, as well as their belief systems, and practices. If practitioners enter the realm traditionally held by professional academics, then questions about ownership, relevance, and rigour become more personal. This might explain some of the vehemence with which some professional academics attempt to denigrate, downgrade, or reject practitioner research.

Positioning teachers as the disempowered '*recipients* of information on academic research' (McDonough and McDonough 1990: 103) has meant that research into language teaching is distanced from the nominal end-users. Worse, positioning teachers and learners as the subjects of study has objectified them, rather than allowing a degree of respect for their insights. So all the optimistic work of the 1970s and 1980s appears to have been crushed by the social/political/economic forces at work at the beginning of the twenty-first century.

Whatever the reason, '… the record is bleak. The kind of research and theory produced tends to be held in little theoretical regard by disciplinary scholars and held to be of little practical value by practitioners' (Clandinin and Connelly 1995: 6). As a result, 'a great deal of potentially extremely relevant knowledge fails to be constructed and a great deal of motivation fails to be engendered' (Edge 2011: 16).

Problematising Practitioner Research (ii): The Discourse of 'Improvement'

In much practitioner research there is an emphasis on improving the existing situation, an explicit desire to solve a problem. The emphasis on 'improvement', which permeates the world of education, has unfortunately become an unquestioned assumption in many situations, frequently leading to a reliance on problem-to-solution approaches. This critique is not intended as a criticism – I am very much in favour of acting for social justice, and would strongly support anyone arguing for respect for practitioners' knowledge. And nobody would want to argue against a genuine desire for improvement. But in unpacking the *discourse of improvement*, it becomes clear that too often this is a veil for a 'deficit discourse' (see Candlin and Crichton 2011), where, to paraphrase Breen (2006), teachers are positioned as deficient before they even start. That is to say, if 'improvement' is needed, then it follows that something is wrong with what went before. In Quote 4.12, Breen unpacks this argument.

> **Quote 4.12: Breen on Two Unproven Assumptions**
>
> The implications for the teaching profession have been palpable in recent years, especially in the 'developed' world. In the context of the wider performativity of nations and communities in a competition for economic survival and dominance, governments have mobilized standards of achievement and competencies in education, the accountability of educators and the new rationalism of 'evidence-based' practices. Such measures have been put in place on the basis of two unproven assumptions: that whatever teachers achieved before is no longer adequate and that systems of bureaucratic surveillance of teachers' work will improve their students' performance.
>
> (2006: 206–7)

Such a discourse can be seen as leading to an eternal cycle of change, with endless iterations of new targets, imposed by others, which continue without room for developing profound understanding. Practitioners are running to stand still, and, as they are constantly told that they need to improve (the sub-text here being 'not good enough'), they may even feel they are running on a treadmill that is set to take them ever faster, but they slip endlessly backwards.

Although the brief overview here implies a list of developments in practitioner research which succeeded and superseded one another, in fact no individual version is ever completely abandoned. Instead a palimpsest exists, with each new movement overlaying but not entirely erasing what went before. Consequently, a teacher, a researcher, or indeed a learner may hold concurrent but conflicting beliefs about the right way to go about researching into language teaching and learning (Schutz 1970, cited in Basturkmen 2012).

The attempt to resolve such cognitive dissonance (Festinger 1957), whether by changing cognitive behaviour or by changing environmental cognitive elements, takes place in a site of struggle, for beliefs around research and pedagogy are ideologically loaded, rooted in conceptions of society, behaviour, and values.

Who decides what is valued in research, and why, and who has the right to decide what is acceptable as research and what is not, has been much debated elsewhere (Breen 2006; Johnson and Golombek 2002; Zeichner and Noffke 2001). Such discussions have profound effects on practitioner beliefs about what research is done, how much can be done, and how it may be carried out.

Zeichner & Noffke's description of the shift from conceiving of teachers as 'merely consumers of educational research' (2001: 299) to 'teachers as producers and mediators of educational knowledge' (ibid.) offers some hope. Yet the hierarchical organisation of education, with academic researchers working in a rarefied, and rigorous, atmosphere, and teachers struggling in the "swamp" (Schön 1991, cited in Edge 2011: 16), is still an issue. Many academics who judge what 'counts' as research still criticise practitioner research for a lack of rigour in the conduct of the research and a lack of concrete (easily measurable?) outcomes. As has been noted elsewhere (Burns 2005; Edge 2011; Zeichner and Noffke 2001), all too often academics dismiss the insights that practising teachers can offer. Such criticisms continue to be levelled, but in the twenty-first century, it is arguable that interpretivist, critical-realist positions, and more generally qualitative methods of research, have become established enough for such attacks to be considered unwarranted.

Practitioner research at its best holds enormous potential for professionals, whether in language education or healthcare or psychology, to carefully and critically consider their own practices with a view to improving. At its worst, however, it can lead to a mechanical, technicist process which focuses efforts on 'improving' something, without actually taking the time to understand the complexities involved. Inevitably, many teachers report 'burnout' as they attempt to reconcile the ever-increasing demands to be researchers as well as educators. Learners are not even asked for their opinions. And although the technicist assumptions that underpin political and academic views of research and pedagogy are questioned, it is not yet possible to say they have been overcome.

But what if teachers (and learners, and teacher educators) are doing the best they can under difficult circumstances? What if rather than struggling for improvement, where the goalposts are constantly moved to just out of reach, a mechanism of control instituted by the powerful over the powerless (see Glynos and Howarth 2007), practitioners took a moment to stop and think? Exploratory Practice, in challenging the 'discourse of improvement', is deeply subversive. It requires us to stop and think, to question the assumptions and the drive for change. It is, then, constantly reflexive and critical, constantly asking 'Why?'.

Summary

Both AR and RP, along with many other forms of practitioner research, offer enormous potential for teachers to engage in classroom research. In offering a critique, I intend no disrespect to colleagues who carefully, thoughtfully, and systematically investigate their own practices with the explicitly stated aim of improvement. Who could argue with improvement after all? Yet it seems that a form of 'cognitive dissonance' is in place in our society, the presence of which 'gives rise to pressures to reduce that dissonance' (Festinger 1957: 263). We are constantly required to 'improve' but nobody stops to ask if the fluid and ever-shifting (externally imposed) targets for improvement are any good. This argument is amply demonstrated by Cochran-Smith and Lytle (2009), as they uncover the vital and conflicting discourses that place practitioner-researchers under constant pressure.

The chapters in this volume, like those of other texts on practitioner research, are suffused with the beliefs of teachers and learners. Their assumptions, conceptions, and presumptions about learning, teaching, and research thread through professional and academic debates, and this gives an insight into the complexities involved when contemplating practitioner research. Adherence to one or other set of beliefs, often held concurrently, sometimes conflicting, brings out the dissonance noted by Cochran-Smith and Lytle (1999) which lies within, around, and between the concepts of research and pedagogy, and this exacerbates further tensions created by attempts to integrate the two.

> **Quote 4.13: Cochran-Smith and Lytle on Dissonance**
> ... teacher research creates dissonance, often calling attention to the constraints of hierarchical arrangements of schools and universities
> (1999: 22)

Practitioner research, then, is problematic for the status quo. It brings out hidden tensions and spotlights ingrained assumptions about education, institutions, and structures. EP, has embraced the dissonance that Cochran-Smith and Lytle (1999) noted more than a decade ago. EP subverts the traditional hierarchical arrangements of research and education, and foregrounds learners as well as teachers in an enterprise of working for understanding. As we shall see in Chapter 5 and beyond, EP reacts against the endless cycle of unquestioned change-improvement-change by shifting the dynamic towards developing understanding(s), and then considering if change is necessary or desirable.

Further Reading

Borg, S. (2013) *Teacher Research in Language Teaching: a critical analysis.* Cambridge: Cambridge University Press. This characteristically comprehensive review considers the 'how' of teacher engagement in research, and begins to look at strategies for promoting such engagement.

Burns, A. (2010) *Doing Action Research in English Language Teaching: A guide for practitioners.* New York: Routledge. This very useful book provides a full and rich account, including teachers as contributors with voices of their own, of AR and the ways it can be conducted in ELT.

Edge, J. (2011) *The Reflexive Teacher Educator in TESOL: Roots and wings.* New York: Routledge. Edge takes a more poetical, lyrical approach to writing, as he discusses RP not only for teacher educators but also for anyone interested in RP in the Teaching of English to Speakers of Other Languages.

Johnson, K.E. & Golombek, P.R. (Eds) (2002) *Teachers' Narrative Inquiry as Professional Development.* Cambridge: Cambridge University Press. In this edited collection of chapters from teachers, we find some fascinating stories of teachers developing for/by themselves. The introduction alone is worth reading for the scintillating argument and a glinting call to arms.

Zeichner & Noffke (2001) Practitioner Research. (pp. 298–330) IN V. Richardson (Ed.), *Handbook of Research on Teaching.* (4th edition), Washington: American Educational Research Association. This seminal article provides a thorough discussion of the complexities of practitioner research in education, and raises a number of key issues that are still relevant today.

5

The Evolution of the Exploratory Practice Framework

Introduction

Exploratory Practice (EP) focuses on *quality of life* and *understanding*, but why is this focus so important? What are the philosophical influences that make EP distinctive and why do they matter? This chapter and the following one will address these questions from two perspectives: to trace the history of the development of the EP principles, showing their philosophical, theoretical, and pedagogical ancestry, and, importantly, to comprehend the importance of profound understanding for EP and for the field. As Allwright maintains:

> For EP, the ethical and epistemological dimensions are the most critical, with the emphasis on understanding rather than problem-solving. (Allwright 2005a: 353)

EP is a theoretical framework which is adaptable and which has the capacity to grow and change in response to new ideas, yet retains a strong core of principles which inform and support EP activities, relationships, and approaches. Positioned between Action Research (AR) and Reflective

Practice (RP) (see Allwright 2001, for further discussion), EP is relatively new in the field. As it has established itself over the past twenty-five years, it has remained flexible and open to further development; thus it could also be represented as an *organic* framework, rather like a living willow fence. This metaphor usefully conveys the idea of the grounded-ness of the structure (the staves of willow are firmly rooted in the ground), while also affording a high degree of flexibility (willow staves can be bent into different shapes) and vivid expansion (new shoots appear, older branches become established), for these staves are alive and growing.

The previous chapters have discussed various forms of practitioner research, but these forms stop short of the inclusiveness that EP offers. EP widens the remit to include *all* those involved in language education: not only teachers, teacher educators, and researchers, but also administrators, educational psychologists, and family members.

Definitions

Having claimed a space for EP in the foregoing chapters, I need now to establish what EP actually *is* (as opposed to what it is not). EP is a process-oriented approach to exploring language learning and teaching, done by, and for, teachers and learners. These practitioners are (i) invited to puzzle about their own experiences of language learning and teaching, and (ii) having identified puzzling issues, (iii) to explore their practice(s) together, in order (iv) to develop their own understanding(s), (v) for mutual development, (vi) by using normal pedagogic practices as investigative tools.

> **Concept 5.1: A Definition of Exploratory Practice**
>
> In 2001, Dick Allwright, Judith Hanks, Inés K. de Miller, Morag Samson, and Zongjie Wu worked together to hammer out an easily accessible definition. This was added to the Exploratory Practice website (2008) and we have used it in a variety of presentations and workshops around the world:

5 The Evolution of the Exploratory Practice Framework

> *Exploratory Practice is an indefinitely sustainable way*
> *for classroom language teachers and learners,*
> *while getting on with their learning and teaching,*
> *to develop their own understandings of life in the language classroom.*
>
> Now lost from the current version of the EP website, the original statement continued:
>
> *It is essentially a way for teachers and learners to work together*
> *to understand aspects of their classroom practice that puzzle them*
> *through the use of normal pedagogic procedures*
> *(standard monitoring, teaching, and learning activities)*
> *as investigative tools.*

The definition in Concept 5.1 has remained remarkably robust as a way of quickly explaining what EP is all about. It encapsulates the distinctive features of EP, and informs the approach on a day-to-day basis. However, we also need to examine the deeper philosophical underpinnings of the definition and the framework. Here I examine the growth of the EP principles over the last quarter-century into a sound, flexible framework for practitioner research.

The Background

In accounts of the inception of EP, Allwright (2003, 2005a) describes an overwhelming sense of language teachers in the early 1990s feeling overwhelmed and 'burnt-out' by the twin pressures of teaching and research. Reacting against this, Allwright and colleagues advocated the idea of practitioners themselves (teachers and learners) taking control of the research agenda. This is underpinned by the principle that in classroom research the *learning* must be central: not 'either/or', but 'both' pedagogy and research taking place in the classroom.

> **Quote 5.1: Allwright on the Beginnings of Exploratory Practice**
>
> I returned [to Brazil] at the beginning of the 1990s to help the project team and the whole Cultura Inglesa in Rio by teaching classroom research skills to

> headquarters and teaching staff. It was at this time that I began to have serious doubts about the wisdom of what I had helped set up in Rio. The classroom-based SLA research project was clearly taking up far too much staff time to be worth pursuing, and it was also requiring staff to learn research skills that were not likely to be helpful in their lives as teachers. So it was heavily parasitic upon their normal working lives, rather than supportive of them, or integrated into them. [...] I soon formed the opinion that what they needed from me was not a new set of doubtfully usable academic research skills, but some recognition of how close they were to burnout...
> (2005a: 354)

Arguing that '...practitioner research is necessarily a first person notion, and a first person plural one at that' (2005a: 357), Allwright rejects what he calls 'parasitical' research projects by third-party researchers, which impinge on teachers and learners, and which, he argues, ultimately lead to burnout. Instead of this type of third-party research, he proposes a focus on development of understanding(s) and thence the 'quality of life' of/by those most closely involved: the learners and teachers themselves. This has been further developed in Allwright and Hanks (2009), Hanks (2015a, b, c), Hanks et al. (2016) and Miller et al. (2015) where examples of learners and teachers conducting their investigations are shown, and still further in Tajino et al. (2016) where EP principles are exemplified in team teaching and team learning.

Where Did It All Begin?

The notion of EP was first articulated as the result of collaborative work between teachers in Rio de Janeiro, Brazil, and Dick Allwright (Allwright 1991a, b, c; Allwright and Bailey 1991; Allwright and Lenzuen 1997), though its roots may be traced even further back, with an early example of EP 'puzzlement' in an article from the early 1980s entitled "*Why don't learners learn what teachers teach?*" (Allwright 1984). I will return to consider the notion of puzzlement and working for understanding in more depth in Chapter 6.

A number of key texts were created as Allwright worked with teachers in Brazil and students in Lancaster to develop EP during the 1990s and beyond. However, some of those texts may now be difficult for the interested reader to access, being either worksheets from workshops or conference talks, or quietly published in journals or book chapters without fanfare. The beginning of this chapter therefore draws extensively on Allwright's pioneering work (both published and unpublished) with the Rio de Janeiro EP group, and PhD students, bringing this together with publications from other figures over the years, to show the development of the principled framework of EP. Concept 5.2 highlights the contributions of *practice* to *theory-building* in this arena.

> **Concept 5.2: Practice-Driven Theory-Building**
>
> It is important to note that the EP principles come from the practice(s) of teachers and learners working to understand their language learning lives. Although Allwright is the main author credited in these pages, he has always been clear that his work was *with* teachers and learners, and *emerged from* their discussions of their practice. Thus, rather than imposing theory onto practice, EP is a form of practice-driven theory-building.

Firmly rooted in the traditions of experience, reflection, empowerment, and social interaction outlined by, for example, Dewey (1963), Freire (1970, 1973) Schön (1983, 1987), and Stenhouse (1975), EP foregrounds the contributions that practitioners can make in the research enterprise: development of knowledge and understanding of human behaviour, particularly in language learning. As such, it is related to AR, RP, Narrative Inquiry, and other forms of practitioner research. It clearly shares many of the democratising, empowering themes of many of these movements. But there are also differences.

> **Quote 5.2: Allwright on the Genesis of Exploratory Practice**
>
> Exploratory Practice (EP) has been developed over the last 15 or so years as an approach to practitioner research that is devoted to understanding the quality of language classroom life. It started in reaction both to academic classroom research and to Action Research, the practitioner research model most in vogue at that time in our field. At first looking for an alternative to current academic classroom research practices on largely ethical grounds, EP developed over time primarily as a set of principles rather than as a set of classroom practices.
>
> (2005a: 353)

Puzzling and Understanding, Rather than Problem-Solving

EP is markedly different from many forms of practitioner research, which have publicly stated aims of 'improvement' and thus easily fall prey to the rhetoric of performativity and efficiency which has so permeated our field. Instead EP asks us to step back from the hectic activity of change; it is an attempt to promote understanding before/instead of problem-solving, and it explicitly aims to develop 'understandings [that] are collective as well as individual' (Allwright 2005a: 360). That is to say, the notion of the Other (Bakhtin 1986) brings the realisation that our understandings are dependent not only upon our selves, but on our interactions with others (teachers, learners, family members), inside and outside our classrooms, in fact with the whole of society. We will return to this discussion in Chapter 6.

It is interesting to note that the vocabulary, in fact the *discourse*, of EP has drifted into other areas (eg AR), and has almost unconsciously been absorbed over the last decade. Thus we find use of the word 'puzzle' (Burns 2010; Nunan 2012) and incorporation of the notions of collaboration and sustainability (Burns 2015), and even an attempt at hybridisation, as in 'Exploratory Action Research' (R. Smith 2015; Wyatt and Marquez 2016). This is entirely understandable (to extend the metaphor of sibling relationships from Chapter 2, brothers and sisters may frequently influence one another), and if such debts are acknowledged and referenced, there is no need for competition or territorialism.

However, there is also a profound difference, for while AR sees 'problems' and 'puzzles' as more or less interchangeable terms (Nunan 2012), both of which demand solutions, EP focuses on 'being puzzled' or 'puzzling about', both of which invite explorations of 'how human beings exist in the world' (van Manen 1990: 4). Wu (2006) has explained it as a form of Tao or Dao: of the way towards harmonisation via being, understanding, and naming.

5 The Evolution of the Exploratory Practice Framework

> **Quote 5.3: Wu on Understanding**
>
> In the epistemological domain, teacher knowledge is seen as the unity of knowing and doing where a deep unspoken understanding is flowing in the spiritual encounter of pedagogical engagements. Such an understanding merely stands out from the things themselves before they are named by language in the process of investigating the lived world of the teacher.
>
> (2006: 347)

Wu (2004, 2005, 2006) successfully merges the philosophical arguments of EP with personal stories from teachers and learners, thus making complex thoughts accessible through the more mundane realities of narratives grounded in people's lives. The perspectives of two teachers/teacher educators who were involved in his work on the RICH project (RICH stands for Research-based study, Integrative curriculum, Community learning, and Humanistic outcomes) are presented in Chapter 10. The importance of taking time for our understanding(s) to develop in/out of our own experience(s) has frequently been overlooked, but here in EP it is deeply significant. To my knowledge, EP is the only approach that takes the notion of prioritising understanding over solutions so very seriously. In doing so it asks us to stop and think before taking action; it asks us to understand first.

Breen (2006) has commented on these distinctive aspects of EP, highlighting the orientation towards *process* rather than product. He points approvingly to EP's resistance to the ubiquitous demand for performance.

> **Quote 5.4: Breen on EP, Resisting Performativity**
>
> ... Exploratory Practice may be seen to go beyond earlier forms of reflective practice and action research in being process-oriented, integrated within everyday ways of working rather than something added to it and driven by the local concerns of both teachers and learners. It is distinctive in explicitly resisting performativity and a preoccupation with effectiveness by replacing these with a focus upon teachers' quality of life or professional wellbeing through the cooperative understanding of everyday puzzles in practice.
>
> (2006: 216)

EP reminds us that it is important to retain the sense of 'dwelling in the present that the notion of Being concerns' (Gieve and Miller 2006b: 29). It cautions us not to be led astray by the common instrumental attitudes of much research, and returns us to the notion of *Dasein* as proposed by Heidegger (1962), or 'being-in-the-world' (Dreyfus 1991). This focus on the moment, on the experience, and the experiential, is crucial for practitioners who wish to understand the practice of learning and teaching.

But where did it all start? Taking a more historical approach might help to unpack the principles of the EP framework.

The Evolution of the Exploratory Practice Framework

In order to understand why EP positions itself as a *related but separate* form of practitioner research, it is necessary to review the roots. There are three major stages in the development of the EP framework. In the first period (approximately 1991–1997) the 'defining characteristics' of Exploratory Teaching (the term Exploratory Practice began to be used only in 1993) proposed criteria for integrating research and pedagogy. The second period (roughly 1997–2003) saw a new emphasis on 'working for understanding', while the third period (2003 to date) included 'Quality of Life' as a driving force for EP. There is some overlap, and the framework is still (rightly) subject to ongoing changes, but a brief history of EP and the evolution of the principles that underpin it shows that a number of themes remain constant.

Stage One: Relevance, Collegiality, and Theory-from-Practice

In early texts (Allwright 1991a, b, c), the core principles of EP were still being worked out. Allwright was reporting on a series of workshops with teachers at the Cultura Inglesa in Rio de Janeiro, Brazil, in which the first

5 The Evolution of the Exploratory Practice Framework

ideas of EP were collaboratively developed. These ideas coalesced into publications (Allwright 1993; Allwright and Bailey 1991). Alongside many others, Allwright had noticed the 'rift' between academic researchers and practitioners. In response, and inspired by working with teachers in Rio de Janeiro, Brazil, in 1990, he proposed 'Exploratory Teaching' (Allwright and Bailey 1991) as a way forward. Shortly afterwards the notion of integrating research and pedagogy was clarified, and a number of criteria were identified (see Quote Box 5.5 and Concept Box 5.3 below) which discussed seven aims and outlined possible problems to be expected when attempting to integrate research and pedagogy.

> **Quote 5.5: Allwright on Healing the Rift**
> Teaching is often seen as an isolating sort of job, and we could therefore surely aim to use the integration of research and pedagogy to bring teachers together more, to bring teachers closer to learners. Even more pertinently [...] we could (I am sure 'should') try to use the integration of research and pedagogy to try to heal the highly damaging rift that has frequently been noted between teachers and researchers.
> (1993: 129)

In this chapter, Allwright also put forward seven steps for this new form of practitioner research, but these steps were later abandoned as being too prescriptive, too much of a 'recipe' which might be followed unthinkingly (see Allwright 2005a, for a comprehensive narrative). Likewise, the initial term 'Exploratory Teaching' (Allwright and Bailey 1991) was quickly superseded when interested early EP-ers such as Ralph Bannell, Bebel A. Cunha, and Inés K. de Miller (sometimes also known as Inés Miller) argued for a more inclusive approach, which welcomed administrators, family members, and, above all, *learners*, to join in. In discussion (see Part Four of this volume for Dick Allwright's and Inés Miller's memories of this), it is reported that Bannell suggested that the term 'practice' would be more in tune with pedagogic practice, not just 'teaching', and this was swiftly acknowledged.

Allwright's main points were to emphasise the *relevance* of the research to the practitioners themselves. This clearly has links with the various 'lacks' identified in the previous chapter (see Burton 1998; McDonough and McDonough 1990) and to find ways to avoid 'burnout' of teacher-researchers who were already close to exhaustion due to the pressures of balancing one or more teaching jobs, marking, lesson preparation, admin, and examinations.

Reflection, continuity (ie sustainable work), and theory-building were central to the budding framework at this point. Encouraging practitioners to work together ("collegiality") was also a central issue, as was the notion of using the research to help learners and teachers develop. Concept Box 5.3 summarises the main aims, as well as some of the possible problems, that Allwright foresaw for practitioner research at the time.

Concept 5.3: Integrating Research and Pedagogy

The seven major aims
1. Relevance
2. Reflection
3. Continuity
4. Collegiality
5. Learner development
6. Teacher development
7. Theory-building

The major problems to be expected
1. Time commitment
2. The skills-learning burden
3. Threats to self-esteem

(summarised from Allwright, 1993: 128–130)

Allwright was also keenly aware of the difficulties facing anyone wanting to do research and pedagogy rolled into one – he lists some of the issues that we discussed in Chapter 4 (lack of time, lack of expertise, or skills) and adds another: threats to self-esteem, particularly if starting by announcing a problem with practice (see Chapter 6 for further discussion).

The essence of these early aims remains constant throughout the development and extension of the EP framework, and they can be traced right up to the most recent iterations. But the principles continued to evolve, and understanding began to emerge as a key theme. Other, related issues, such as collegiality, relevance, reflection, and teacher/learner development, were reassessed and extended at the turn of the century.

Stage Two: Developing Understandings

The second stage of development re-framed the aims outlined above as principles, and shifted the emphasis to place 'working for understanding' first. A major shift in the late 1990s re-framed the aims as a set of *principles* (Allwright 1997a, b, 1998a, b) for practitioner research. Themes touched on earlier, such as collegiality, relevance, reflection, and teacher/learner development, were also reassessed and extended at this time. Working with Miller, Allwright focused on the issue of sustainability of using EP to help, not hinder, learning.

> **Quote 5.6: Allwright and Miller on Sustainable Ways of Developing Understandings from Practice**
>
> Exploratory Practice is being developed precisely to offer a sustainable way of developing our understandings within our practice, with the absolute minimum of intrusion, and the maximum possible of practical benefit.
> (1998: 1)

From 1998 to 2001, a series of workshops, events (in the UK and in Brazil) which explained the 'defining characteristics' of EP, took place. Through fruitful discussions from/with practitioners, it became clear that because reflection informs action, and since meaningful action needs to be based on work for understanding, EP sits 'right in the middle between reflection for understanding [RP] and action for change [AR]' (Allwright 2001: 105). But why was understanding given such prominence? Doesn't all research promote working for understanding?

One of the key points that EP highlights is that much research in the twentieth and twenty-first centuries is in a tearing hurry to improve before taking the time to understand. The twin drives for efficiency and effectiveness seem to have overridden the need to comprehend. This very quickly leads to the demoralisation of practitioners: to burnout as Allwright and Miller explain.

> **Quote 5.7: Allwright and Miller on Burnout and the Beginning Teacher**
> Focusing on measured performance is highly stressful, then, not just because it increases the workload, but also because it compromises the teachers' intellectual and pedagogic freedom. It is seen as *anti*-educational, we suggest, because it rests on a technicist view of teaching, rather than the more 'human' one teachers might prefer to prioritise.
>
> (2013: 102)

Thus the principle of practitioners working to *understand* now came to the fore. Avoiding 'burnout' was still a major theme, with a new notion proposed: that of using already familiar classroom techniques to explore puzzles without increasing the burden on participants (Allwright and Lenzuen 1997; Allwright and Miller 1998). The aim of EP is to make life more liveable for teachers and learners by 'adopting an investigative stance which they can enjoy and sustain' (Miller 1997: 3). This was perhaps most succinctly expressed in a handout expressing the defining characteristics of EP in a workshop given by Dick Allwright in Rio de Janeiro, Brazil:

Defining Characteristics of Exploratory Practice
Exploratory Practice involves

A. Practitioners working to understand:
   (a) what *they* want to understand, following their *own* agendas;
   (b) not necessarily *in order to* bring about change;
   (c) not primarily *by* changing;
   (d) but *by using* normal pedagogic practices as investigative tools, so that working for understanding is *part of* the teaching and learning, not extra to it;
   (e) in a way that does not lead to 'burn-out', but that is *indefinitely sustainable;*

B. in order to contribute to:
   (f) *teaching and learning* themselves
   (g) *professional development*, both individual and collective.

5 The Evolution of the Exploratory Practice Framework

Note: the term 'practitioners' is intended to cover learners as well as teachers.
(From a workshop handout first developed by Allwright 1997a)

It is clear from this, and a number of other publications from the period (Allwright and Lenzuen 1997; Allwright and Miller 1998), that 'working for understanding' has taken precedence, and this sets up a direct contrast with the notion of 'working for change' associated with many other models of researching practice. Although understanding might seem an obvious aim for research, it is worth placing in the context of ever-changing targets in the education sector, which emphasise 'efficiency' and 'performance'. EP's re-appropriation of research as a search for understanding, rather than a way of solving (practical? mechanical?) problems for instrumental purposes, is a challenge to a political situation where change, any change, is advocated to exhaustion.

Another defining characteristic of EP from this moment is that it advocates using 'normal pedagogic practices as investigative tools' (Allwright 1997a) rather than complex research instruments. In other words, teachers and learners are encouraged to do *what they would normally have been doing* in the classroom, not trying to add the complexities of research training to an already complex life.

Again, van Manen (1990) is helpful here. Discussing a methodological structure for what he calls 'hermeneutic phenomenological research', he begins by suggesting the following activities:

1. turn to a phenomenon which seriously interests us and commits us to the world; [in EP this might be characterized as 'puzzling']
2. investigate experience as we live it rather than as we conceptualize it;
3. reflect on the essential themes which characterize the phenomenon (summarised from van Manen 1990: 30)

He adds also that the research must maintain 'a strong and oriented pedagogic relation to the phenomenon' (ibid.: 31). This speaks to the need highlighted in EP principles to try to reduce the burden on teachers, and contain the institutional demands for more time from them. There are links here to the Aristotelian notion of *phronesis* as described in Chapter 4 (see also Carr 1987, 2004; Flyvbjerg 2001). That is to say, 'the most advanced form of understanding is achieved when researchers place themselves within the context being studied' (Flyvbjerg 2001: 83) – and in fact EP takes this a step further, by conceiving of the context being studied as the natural habitat of the researchers (ie teachers, learners, teacher educators, etc.).

Thus, in responding to the tensions outlined at the end of the previous chapter (see Cochran-Smith and Lytle 1999), EP overturns hierarchical assumptions associated with research in education. It offers opportunities to step back from the hectic pace of change (which is all too often 'change for change's sake'), and instead develop profound understandings of the 'lived experiences' (van Manen 1990) of those involved in the language education enterprise. In a chapter titled 'Three major processes of teacher development and the appropriate design criteria for developing and using them' (Allwright 2001) such questions are examined in depth. Allwright argues that change has become an imperative in our world, and that there is an unquestioned assumption that all changes will be 'improvements' on whatever previously existed. In challenging these assumptions he presents a picture of AR, EP, and RP as three models for language teacher education and development which, if considered together (rather than separately), offer the possibility of productive relationships for the maximum benefit of all (Allwright 2001). Allwright's representation of these relationships has recently been updated for a one-day seminar held at the Centre for Language Education Research, School of Education, University of Leeds (6 May, 2015) (see Fig. 5.1).

Contributions from Lancaster-based PhD and MA studies were also important in the development of the EP framework at this stage. Pinto da Silva (2001) examined teacher intentions and interpretations in language classrooms in Portugal. She took up Argyris and Schön's (1974) concepts of espoused theory, and attempted to make sense of the 'intricate, dynamic, an often contradictory relationship between observed teaching practice and expressed espoused theories' (Pinto da Silva 2001: 301). She concluded that EP would be an appropriate way to allow teachers and learners to explore their beliefs about pedagogy. Meanwhile, my own early work (Hanks 1998, 1999) investigated the differences between 'problem' and 'puzzle', concluding that there are significant 'moments of

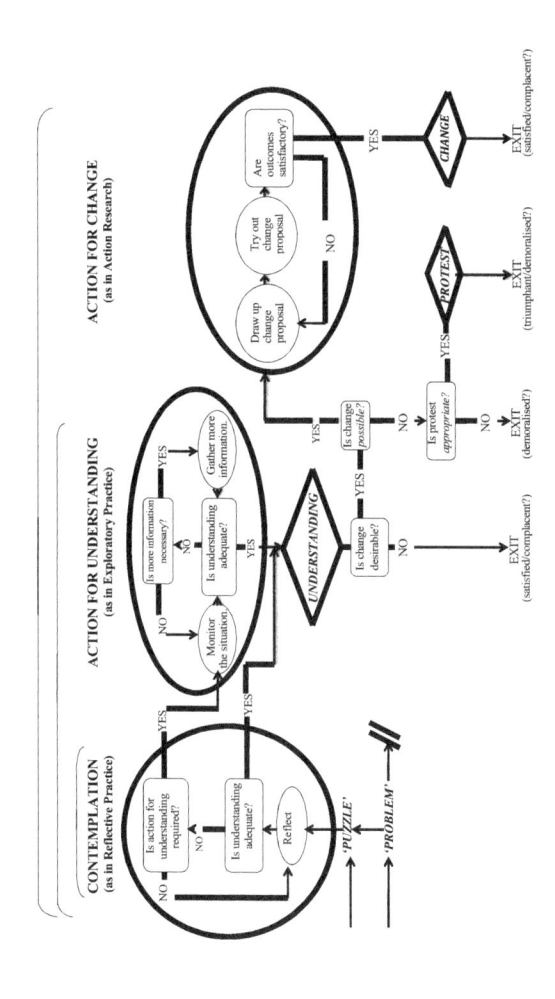

Fig. 5.1 Three processes of practitioner development (by permission of the author: D. Allwright 2015) (Adapted from Allwright, D. (2001): Three Major Processes of Teacher Development and the Appropriate Design Criteria for Developing and Using Them. In B. Johnson & S Irujo (eds): Research and Practice in Language Teacher Education: Voices from the Field. CARLA, University of Minnesota, p. 133)

transition' as practitioner-researchers move from an initial expression of a 'problem' to a stance of 'puzzled inquiry'. In other developments through doctoral work, Perpignan (2001) used EP as a way of investigating learner perceptions of written feedback on their work in an Israeli university, and concluded that enhanced quality of life resulted from sharing the work together. Concurrently, Miller (2001) adopted the EP framework as a way of understanding her own practices as a teacher-consultant working with beginner-teachers in Brazil, examining prosodic features of interviews with her student-teachers, and emphasised the co-construction of teacher-consultancy. Later (eg in Gieve and Miller 2006b), she connected this with Bakhtin's (1986) notion of the relationship between self and Other(s), relating Bakhtinian theory to language learning and teaching. At roughly the same time, in his doctoral thesis, Wu (2002) brought together Western and Chinese philosophy, and argued for the notion of *Dasein* (Heidegger 1962) and Tao as a way of incorporating learning and understanding, and as 'nourishing life for teachers' (Wu 2002: 373) in the language classroom. The effect of these explorations was further growth of the EP principles for practitioner research – to extend the metaphor from the beginning of this chapter: the willow structure was getting stronger staves, and developing deep roots, while also sending out new, green shoots.

Stage Three: The Importance of 'Quality of Life'

As the ethical and epistemological aspects of EP (see Allwright 2005a) began to coalesce, and, thanks also to essential work by Miller (2001, 2003) and Wu (2002, 2006) amongst others working with Allwright (eg Frahm 1998; Graves 2003; Gunn 2001), a new principle emerged for the EP framework: working for 'quality of life' in the classroom.

> **Quote 5.8: Wu on Life, Being, and Understanding**
> Teachers' *life* is conceived here as *being* led by the natural curiosity of knowing towards authenticity. Teachers' *understanding* emerges from their authentic life
>
> (2004: 309 original emphases)

5 The Evolution of the Exploratory Practice Framework

The new set of EP principles (as shown in Concept Box 5.4 below) can be seen to overlay the previous ones, without obliterating them, in a palimpsest of historical developments. For example, a revised order for the principles of EP was established in 2003, with the publication of a special issue of the journal *Language Teaching Research*. This special issue was dedicated to EP work from around the world, and addressed key themes relevant to the EP framework such as collegiality, puzzlement and working for understanding, and sustainability.

> **Concept 5.4: Exploratory Practice as a Set of General Principles**
> Principle 1: put 'quality of life' first
> Principle 2: work primarily to understand language classroom life
> Principle 3: involve everybody
> Principle 4: work to bring people together
> Principle 5: work also for mutual development
> Principle 6: integrate the work for understanding into classroom practice
> Practical corollary to Principle 6: let the need to integrate guide the conduct of the work for understanding
> Principle 7: make the work a continuous enterprise
> Practical corollary to Principle 7: avoid time-limited funding
> (summarised from Allwright 2003: 128–130)

Although the main principles are clearly recognisable from earlier iterations, two 'practical corollaries' now appear, the first of which encompasses the injunction to 'integrate research and pedagogy' of a decade earlier, the second of which expresses a new worry: that of avoiding time-limited funding. The latter comes from a pre-occupation with the 'projectisation' of research. In trying to ensure sustainability, and also in avoiding the colonisation of research by the funders, this is a practical suggestion. If the enterprise is to be truly continuous, it is argued, it needs to be independent of funding; if truly empowering, then it needs to be separate from the politically motivated agendas of many funders.

In his introduction to the Special Issue of the journal *Language Teaching Research* featuring articles on EP, Allwright (2003) also unpacks the notion of *collegiality*, noting that it is 'multiply problematic, but crucial to the enterprise' (p. 135). Gunn (2003), working with students in Thailand to investigate second language communicative competence with/through EP, exemplified this:

through researching what puzzles me about my classroom in my own way, using pedagogical activities that I am comfortable with, and involving my students right from the beginning, I have a better understanding of why things happen in my classroom in the way they do. (Gunn 2003: 255)

In the same volume the question of group work is more extensively investigated as Assia Slimani-Rolls highlighted some of the paradoxes of group work in classrooms. Slimani-Rolls (2003) argued that 'only the teachers themselves, and their learners, [...] can be expected to ponder on such issues because they underlie the core of their daily activities' (2003: 237). Slimani-Rolls elaborates this theme in 2009, noting again the potential for conflicting agendas and warning against casual assumptions.

> **Quote 5.9: Slimani-Rolls on Group Work**
>
> The understanding about this group work that the teachers and the learners reached at the end of this exploratory process brought to the surface a constellation of overlapping cognitive, affective and social variables which highlighted the complexities of the groups' dynamic, the participant's motives, their perceptions and conflicting agenda. The outcomes of these collegial efforts made it obviously clear that it was not a change in the pedagogical procedure that was required but a change in the general understanding that the teachers' unilateral assumption of putting students in groups should automatically enable them to work cohesively
>
> (2009: 62)

Slimani-Rolls has continued her work in the context of teaching French (and other languages) in the UK for business purposes, and working with experienced teachers for Continuous Professional Development. She examines the complexities of classroom work and classroom dialogue, with the aim of helping teachers to understand their own puzzles in more depth (see Slimani-Rolls and Kiely 2014), while Miller (2009, 2010, 2012) has written about her work with initial teacher education in Brazil using EP as a framework for developing their understandings of the mysteries of teaching. Most excitingly of all, she exemplifies EP collegial principles by frequently writing, publishing, and presenting together with other practitioners. This is often, but not always, novice teachers, or teachers, or learners, from Brazil (see Barreto et al. 2015; Miller and Barreto 2015; Miller et al. 2015) or the UK (see Hanks et al. 2016).

> **Quote 5.10: Allwright on Collegiality**
>
> Since life in the language classroom is necessarily social, then the conduct of any practitioner researcher carried out there will also be a social matter. So, for example, learners will be involved not as objects of research but as fellow participants, and therefore as co-researchers.
>
> (2003: 129)

In promoting a collaborative atmosphere in which participant-researchers work together to develop mutual understandings, EP is clearly attempting to combat the 'theory-practice gap' noted by Allwright (1993), Freeman (1996), and others. My own work has scrutinised the concept of collegiality further; I have discussed the related notions of collegiality and inclusivity (Hanks 2009, 2013a) from the perspectives of learners and teachers working together to investigate their puzzles in classes of English for Academic Purposes (EAP) in the UK. At that time (2006) little or no EP work was being done in EAP in the UK, so this was a new development. As part of my explorations I focused on how collegiality and inclusivity could be operationalised in EAP classrooms, and concluded that a central concern was the need for trust (Hanks 2013a, b). Teachers and learners working together can access powerful insights into classroom language learning life. The most exciting example of this can be seen in the annual Teachers and Learners Conferences held in Rio de Janeiro, Brazil. Here, teachers and learners (as well as novice teachers, teacher educators, etc.) report how they share puzzles, explore together, and develop insights with others in the language teaching/learning arena. But we need to *trust* that learners and teachers both can and will do this. This notion of trust is crucial for EP, and we will therefore discuss it in more detail in Part 3.

From 2004 to 2009 Dick Allwright and I collaborated to further express, explain, and exemplify the principles of EP. We argued that research should focus on deep lived understandings because they 'reflect our acceptance of all the complexity we live with and through every day' (Allwright and Hanks 2009: 148) and we proposed EP as 'a form of research that encourages people to try to articulate their developing understandings' (ibid.: 149). Important in our view was the notion that learners should not be left out of research activity any more than teachers. We conceived of learners as intelligent, capable individuals who are, as we put it, 'key developing practitioners'.

> **Quote 5.11: Allwright and Hanks on Five Propositions About Learners**
>
> Learners are unique individuals and social beings who are capable of taking learning seriously, of taking independent decisions, and of developing as practitioners of learning.
>
> (2009: 15)

The drive to involve learners shows EP addressing the issues of (ir-)relevance of research to the participants raised by Burton (1998), McDonough and McDonough (1990, 1997), and many others since (as discussed in Chapter 4). The argument went that if teachers and learners set the research agenda by asking puzzled questions about their own experiences, and if the learning (of language) is prioritised, then the work must, by definition, be relevant to the practitioners. The EP principles were now framed as follows:

> **Principles for Fully Inclusive Practitioner Research**
>
> *The 'what' issues*
> 1. Focus on *quality of life* as the fundamental issue.
> 2. Work to *understand* it, before thinking about solving problems.
>
> *The 'who' issues*
> 3. Involve *everybody* as practitioners developing their own understandings.
> 4. Work to bring people *together* in a common enterprise.
> 5. Work cooperatively for *mutual* development.
>
> *The 'how' issues*
> 6. Make it a *continuous* enterprise.
> 7. *Minimise the burden* by integrating the work for understanding into normal pedagogic practice.
>
> (Allwright and Hanks 2009: 260)

5 The Evolution of the Exploratory Practice Framework

In a subtly radical move, EP positions learners as co-researchers alongside teachers investigating language learning and teaching, in other words as active researchers, rather than as objects or subjects of study. This has links to the seminal work of Freire (1970, 1973), as well as to the learner autonomy movement (see Dam and Gabrielson 1988; Holec 1988; Trim 1976, as discussed in Chapter 4 of Allwright and Hanks 2009), and, of course, to processes of ideological becoming as we see other (Other) people within and outwith classrooms engaged in dialogic interactions with their worlds, Bakhtin (1986).

In EP we seek to break down the barriers between work and life (after all, we spend a lot of our lives at work) and depict classroom language learning and teaching as a life-work performance which points towards the principle of 'quality of life'. Some thought is required when considering the new emphasis on 'quality of life'. It is a phrase that is all too often used, perhaps glibly, in the areas of advertising, healthcare, marketing, and social policy, to cover a multitude of meanings, including a general sense of well-being. However, it is clear that in EP, the phrase carries a specific meaning. It challenges the 'work/life balance', suggesting, in place of a dichotomy, that life and work in the language classroom should be seen as one:

> … our thinking reveals a 'life' orientation *as well as* a 'work' orientation. We are trying to highlight the strong integration we see between 'life' and 'work' – 'work' being a part of 'life' and 'life' being a part of 'work' […] And we are doing so because we are observing that the 'work' part has been hitherto predominant, while the 'life' part has been forgotten or suppressed. (Gieve and Miller 2006b: 20)

Quality of life does *not* mean that all things are good and/or easy; rather it may include working very hard, but on something that is interesting, rewarding, and relevant to those working on it. Thus it conveys a sense of *texture* both within and outside of the classroom. In other words, 'quality of life' relates particularly to learning and teaching in a classroom, and EP positions it as an intellectual and social enterprise, seeking to unite life and work, as Gieve and Miller explain.

> **Quote 5.12: Gieve and Miller on Quality of Classroom Life**
> We believe that [Quality of Classroom Life] *is* what teachers and learners understand, and/or try to understand about their joint experience in classrooms, and these understandings are of greater intrinsic importance to them than how productive or efficient classroom outcomes are by external standards.
>
> (2006b: 23)

As mentioned earlier, Gieve and Miller analyse the notion of 'quality of life' in language classrooms and link it to Bakhtinian theory. They note the connections that Bakhtin (1986) makes between emotion, memory, and meaning, as well as individuals interacting with one another. This dialogic approach is reflected also in the concern found in EP for learners as 'social beings' and 'individuals who learn in idiosyncratic ways' (see Allwright and Hanks 2009), and, we might add, teachers, teacher educators, administrators, psychologists, family, and friends. Thus, the stage is set for a 'discursive analysis of what a classroom feels like to live in: how care, affect and relationship grow alongside work on knowledge-construction' (Gieve and Miller 2006b: 32).

A practitioner researcher wishing to develop his or her understanding of classroom language learning would need to consider this principle above all in EP. It links all the other principles together. For example, the recognition that language learning in the classroom is a social event, in which the people involved (learners and teachers) are interacting on many different levels, is crucial. In acknowledging the arguments of others (Clandinin 2007; Tudor 2001; van Lier 2009) that learners and teachers bring multiple identities to the classroom and interact in infinitely complex ways, EP offers opportunities to address the complexity of human relations and learning (see also Tarone and Swierzbin 2009, for further discussion of the contributions of EP to/for the field of Second Language Acquisition research).

Interestingly, as noted in Chapter 1, the notion of 'quality of life' also now appears as a criterion for 'Impact' (with a capital 'I') in the literature around the Research Excellence Framework (an attempt to measure the quality of research) in the UK. Similarly, key EP principles such as collaboration, working across boundaries to include non-academics as well as academics in research, and sustainability of research have appeared in definitions of 'Impact'.

Bringing the Story Up-to-Date

There is now evidence that EP has been tried out in a number of different local contexts. For example, in teacher education, the relationship between relevance and motivation has been investigated (Rose 2007), while Gunn reports on a teacher educator's puzzle about MA TESOL students' resistance to reflection (Gunn 2010). In Japan, Akira Tajino takes a systemic approach to EP (Tajino 2009) and has extended his interest to combine EP with team teaching, reconfiguring it as team learning (Tajino and Smith 2016). Meanwhile, in a rare moment in the practitioner research literature, Craig Smith (2009) discusses student involvement in decision-making in an EAP course in Japan, using EP principles, with positive results. Following on from this, Alison Stewart, in Stewart et al. (2014), has discussed her work in EAP with Japanese learners, to critically analyse the EP principles, particularly the notion of 'Quality of Life'.

Involving language learners as active participants in the investigative process, Zhang (2004) has described using group work as a way of developing mutual understanding and harmony in English language classes in China. Working in the UK, Slimani-Rolls has taken a slightly different view as she teases out the 'paradoxical world' of the classroom (2009: 236) which poses problems for teachers and learners of business French in the UK. She argues that although teachers and learners know how they should behave in class, they often act in ways that diverge from such knowledge (Slimani-Rolls 2009). In Australia, learners in an EAP/MA TESOL context use EP to compare their own experiences with the literature on language learning (see Rowland 2011). Rowland's EAP learners are in fact also teachers on a pre-sessional course preparing for further study in the area of TESOL in Australia, and thus they are also teachers-in-training. This brings an interesting confluence of identities: language learners, learners of teaching, and teachers (whether experienced or not) all rolled into one.

In the UK, EAP has proved fertile ground for the ideas of EP, as my own work has shown (Hanks 2013a, b, 2015a, b). In addition, recent MA dissertations report enthusiasm for EP. For example, Dar (2008) describes involving her students in investigating her puzzle as part of their classroom work in a TESOL setting (see also Dar 2012, 2015). And Dawson (2012) used Narrative Inquiry techniques to report on how she involved students in reflections on her own puzzle (see also Dawson 2016). Salvi (2012), on the other hand, compares EP and Learner Autonomy, involving her EAP students in puzzling over their own practices in their classrooms (see also Salvi 2014, 2015). We will return to these narratives in Parts 2 and 3.

In a more philosophical vein, Wu (2002, 2004, 2005, 2006) has reported on his investigations using EP as part of curriculum change in China. As mentioned earlier, he has discussed the notion of teacher learning as 'nourishment', concluding that language is often inadequate for the purposes of expressing understanding. He was also deeply influential in helping to develop the philosophical ideas underpinning the next stage of development in the EP framework: considering quality of life in language classrooms.

Moreover, EP is also being successfully implemented in state schools in Brazil (Allwright and Hanks 2009; Kuschnir and Machado 2003; Lyra et al. 2003), and at Masters or doctoral level in tertiary institutions in Brazil (Miller 2003, 2009, 2010, 2012; Miller and Barreto 2015), Taiwan (Chu 2007), and Turkey (Bartu 2003; Dikilitaş 2014; Özdeniz 1996). It has been adopted in different areas in the USA, in the field of Second Language Acquisition (Tarone 2006; Tarone and Swierzbin 2009) and teacher research (K.A. Johnson 2002) and in continuing professional development for language teachers teaching French, Italian, Spanish, etc., in the UK (Slimani-Rolls and Kiely 2014).

EP, then, appears to offer an exciting alternative to previous notions of research, one which draws on Freirean notions of learner empowerment, critical pedagogy, and problematising rather than problem-solving. It is less explicitly political than Freire's (1970, 1973) work, and more process-oriented than the work of Carr and Kemmis (1986), but shares many of the values and theoretical underpinnings of these movements. EP, then, takes its place alongside AR and RP, as well as Narrative Inquiry and many other forms of Teacher or Classroom Research, as a way of inquiring into language learning and teaching. However, as with all forms of practitioner research, there are potential criticisms.

Problematising Exploratory Practice: A Critical Look

I will not repeat here the criticisms levelled at practitioner research more generally (see Borg 2010, 2013; Burns 2005 for extended discussions of these), though of course the points could equally apply to EP. Such criticisms are ideologically rooted, and stem from a particular, subjective, way of seeing research and scholarship. They are therefore quite limited. Instead, I focus on questions specific to EP.

The EP principles may be criticised as overly idealistic and failing to take into account the very real constraints of busy practitioners with tight deadlines and goal-oriented courses. For example, Allwright and Hanks (2009) promote the idea that 'working primarily to *understand* the "quality of life", as it is experienced by language learners and teachers, is more important than, and logically prior to, seeking in any way to improve it' (Allwright and Hanks 2009: 149), but what does this really mean? Can working for understanding really take precedence over seeking to improve things?

Furthermore, what does it mean to 'involve everybody' (Allwright 2003: 129), and why does this need to be specified? Why say 'work to bring people together' (ibid.)? Even allowing for the fact of the much-discussed rift between academics and practitioners, is it really necessary to include this as a principle for research? And what does 'mutual development' mean? How does it work out in practice? What if someone doesn't want to be involved in mutually developing? Whose development takes precedence? Is it possible to say that there is equal development of both/all parties? Supposing they disagree (on priorities, topics) or simply fall out socially? More practical questions arise too. How would EP relate to the curriculum of a real-live course? How does this notion 'fit' into a pre-existing syllabus? What are the 'lived experiences' of practitioners if/when they try out EP in their own classrooms?

In Parts Two and Three we will focus on these questions. But before we look at the practical challenges of implementing the EP framework, and discuss what we can learn from (EP) practice, we need to take a closer look at the notions of 'understanding and puzzlement'. Why is this so important in EP?

Recommended Readings

Language Teaching Research: Special Issue 7(2) (2003). This special issue contains seminal articles by key figures in the EP world, as mentioned in this chapter, and is essential reading for anyone interested in the practice and theory of EP.

Allwright, D. (2005a) Developing principles for practitioner research: the case of Exploratory Practice. *The Modern Language Journal. 89(3)* pp. 353–366. Provides the beginnings of a history and rationale for EP as an ethical and epistemological way of doing research.

Gieve, S. & Miller, I. K. (2006b) *Understanding the Language Classroom.* Basingstoke: Palgrave Macmillan. This thought-provoking volume provides chapters from a range of authors on issues such as *What do we mean by 'Quality of Classroom Life'?* (Gieve & Miller, 2006b) and *Collegial development in ELT* (Breen, 2006). It is a must-read for anyone interested in practitioner research in language education, especially with an EP flavour.

Wu, Z. (2004) Being, understanding and naming: Teachers' life and work in harmony. *International Journal of Educational Research* 41 pp. 307–323. Bringing philosophy, curriculum change, and activity theory together in superlative fashion, Wu explicates his view of how Heidegger relates to Chinese philosophy, through narratives of teachers engaged in teacher learning in EP. His meaning becomes clear through poetical narratives of teachers working through their own puzzles.

6

Puzzles, Puzzling, and Puzzlement

Introduction

Resting on the assumption that puzzling about an issue is more conducive to developing understanding than trying to solve a problem, Exploratory Practice (EP) recommends commencing with 'puzzlement', and encourages the practitioners themselves to investigate, rather than relying on external researchers, as a way of developing understandings. In 2009, we merely touched on these issues:

> A key term for us in getting started is 'puzzling' – reflecting on situations and asking 'why' questions about them, rather than rushing into looking for 'solutions'. (Allwright and Hanks 2009: 176)

It is now time to enquire more deeply into the twin notions of understanding and puzzlement. What do they really mean? And why are they so important in EP?

Why Does Exploratory Practice Promote 'Working for Understanding'?

Wenger's (1998) elegant phrasing about understanding, though not about EP itself, provides a partial answer to this question.

> **Quote 6.1: Wenger on Understanding**
> Words like 'understanding' require some caution because they can easily reflect an implicit assumption that there is some universal standard of the knowable [...]. In practice, understanding is always straddling the known and the unknown in a subtle dance of the self.
>
> (1998: 41)

This 'subtle dance of the self' (Wenger 1998: 41) conveys the fluid, dynamic tensions of working for understanding. And since working for understanding (rather than problem-solving) is central to EP, the sweet tensions it produces can be both enjoyable and productive, as a teacher, 'Bella' (not her real name), demonstrates in Vignette 6.1.

> **Vignette 6.1: Bella's Story: Why Do They Find English Spelling Difficult?**
> Bella has been teaching English for Academic Purposes (EAP) for many years. She has a class preparing learners for their future academic studies; these learners come mainly from two geographic areas: Japan and Saudi Arabia. Even though both groups have a different orthographic system, and therefore should struggle equally with writing in English, Bella notices that the Saudi students have great difficulty with English spelling, while the Japanese find this the least of their difficulties in writing.
> At first, her instinct is to investigate 'how': How to improve her students' spelling in English? But she takes a step back and thinks for a while. Encouraged by the EP framework, she asks instead 'why': Why do my Saudi students struggle with spelling? She reads books and articles, but, she says: 'I've read some stuff, but it's all about "how" – how to improve spelling – but it's not about "why they find it difficult", which is what I want to know'.
> Consequently, she shares her puzzled question with the students in her class, and they discuss together; she talks to other teachers (colleagues in the EAP field and at her son's primary school). As she shares her question

> with her students in class discussions, they too become interested (it is, after all, their struggle too… and since the Listening part of the International English Language Testing System test penalises spelling mistakes, the importance of spelling is becoming more obvious to them). As Bella goes about her daily practice, other teachers also become interested – she finds that two of her colleagues have also been working in this area. Working together, teacher(s) and students investigate the issues to do with learning/teaching spelling in English, and develop their own 'shared understandings'. This leads her to the realisation that actually English spelling is much more complex than at first she had thought; she listens to her students' views and experiences, and she draws a number of preliminary conclusions.
>
> After 10 weeks of working collegially on her puzzle, Bella reflects on her EP work:
>
> *'It's helping me to answer the question why they find it difficult. There's lots of different reasons why, I think. Yeah, I feel like I understand more about the problems that they have and the things that I need to think about as a teacher.'*
>
> (For the extended story of 'Bella' and her students, see Hanks 2015b)

A question like 'Why can't my students spell?' initially invites technicist solutions such as including a more explicit focus on spelling in lessons, marking student written work with this in mind, or incorporating weekly spelling games, spelling bees, other competitive spelling games, and even spelling tests. But if that first impulse to rush for solutions is resisted, in its place a reflexive focus on trying to understand… but really trying to *understand* why are my students struggling with English spelling and why am I (the teacher) struggling to teach it, a very different picture emerges. We will return to Bella's story at various points in this book, as her narrative illustrates the many ways in which puzzles and puzzlement change and develop over a longer period of several years.

In place of the powerful drive towards solutions (the 'discourse of improvement' alluded to earlier), EP advocates developing understanding as an end in itself. For example, in an unpublished transcript of a talk given in Brazil in 1997, Allwright firmly rejected the starting point of 'find a problem' so often found in Action Research (AR) at the time: '… if by chance you do hit upon a good solution to a problem, it does not necessarily help you *understand* why it was a good solution' (1997a: 9). Gadamer's comments on understanding are helpful here:

> ... understanding is always more than merely re-creating someone else's meaning. Questioning opens up possibilities of meaning, and thus what is meaningful passes into one's own thinking on the subject. (1975/2013: 383)

In puzzling about practice we are engaging in playful questioning of the theoretical and the practical; we open up those 'possibilities of meaning' and begin to explore. Reminiscing about his childhood activities, Manguel (2015) describes this process as 'the thrill of the quest'.

> **Quote 6.2: Manguel on the Thrill of the Quest**
> I discovered that questioning could be something else, akin to the thrill of the quest, the promise of something that shaped itself in the making, a progression of explorations that grew in a mutual exchange between two people and did not require a conclusion. It is impossible to stress the importance of having the freedom of such inquiries. To a child they are as essential to the mind as movement is to the physical body.
> (2015: 31–2)

Manguel is talking about *childhood* play and puzzling, but this is equally essential for an adult. From the field of psychotherapy, Winnicott's notion of 'play' (or 'playfulness') extends the boundaries to enable creativity in/through experience:

> ... playing is an experience, always a creative experience, and it is an experience in the space-time continuum, a basic form of living. (Winnicott 1971: 59)

This idea has been taken (much) further by, for example, Peter Stratton and Helga Hanks, who instruct practitioners (in their case, therapists engaged in personal professional development) to: 'have the most fun (wacky, uncritical, playful, ribald, energetic, irreverent, novel) discussion you can manage' (Stratton and Hanks 2016: 14) as a 'way in' to accessing creative thought. In other words, play, playfulness, puzzlement, and puzzling are essential aspects of what it is to be human, and a crucial part of the learning (and researching) process.

If playfulness and puzzlement are part of our humanity, though, they are also a powerful resource for human resistance to the mechanisation of our lives. Such mechanisation often stems from institutions, ministries, government, and 'the field'. In a word, authority. As Gadamer points out:

> Authority, however, is responsible for one's not using one's own reason at all. (1975/2013: 289)

Often we are so distracted (chasing after those ever-moving targets, for example), and so much in awe of authority, that we forget to use our own reason; we assume that 'they' know best. Gadamer adds a call to battle:

> The false prepossession in favor of what is old, in favor of authorities, is what has to be fought (ibid.)

To this I would add the very real and pressing need to fight the authority of what is 'new'. In other words, the prevailing assumption that 'new-is-good' and that in the world of English Language Teaching at least, the latest thing is automatically the best thing, superseding whatever went before – this, too, carries a strange authority, and this, too, has to be fought. But, even if we accept this need to thoughtfully challenge authority, the question remains: How can we ensure that we are working towards a productive notion of deep understanding?

Arguably, the best place to start is by considering our own practice as language teachers, language learners, teacher educators, and educational psychologists. This is presented in van Manen (1990) as an intimate relationship between theory and practice: a form of practice-driven theory-building.

> **Quote 6.3: van Manen on the Relationship Between Practice-Theory-Understanding**
>
> In contrast to the more positivistic and behavioral empirical sciences, human science does not see theory as something that stands *before* practice in order to "inform" it. Rather theory enlightens practice. Practice (or life) always comes first and theory comes later as a result of reflection.
>
> (1990: 15)

There is, then, an invitation to readers here: to follow their own puzzles as and when they occur. Threaded throughout this text are a number of learner and teacher puzzles, which may prompt further thought, a kind of 'meta-puzzling'.

Why Does EP Promote Puzzlement? What Is It, and Why Is It Seen as Somehow Different?

Puzzlement is a way of developing profound understandings – of our practice, of our world, of each other – not superficial solutions. It rejects the politically motivated 'discourse of improvement' (in which powerful forces keep practitioners constantly struggling to achieve fast-moving, ever-shifting targets) and focuses instead on thoughtful interrogation of practice. In Concept 6.1 (see Wyatt et al., 2016), I explore the notion of puzzling and its relationship to puzzles and problems, in more depth.

> **Concept 6.1: Aren't Puzzles and Problems Just the Same Thing?**
>
> Having encountered both EP and AR for the first time, I noticed the emphasis on starting with a 'puzzle' in the former, and a 'problem' in the latter; I wondered: What IS the difference between a problem and a puzzle?
>
> To begin with, I noted that '... "puzzles" like "problems" generally aim for a solution (eg a jigsaw puzzle, or a word puzzle)' (Hanks 1998: 5–6).
>
> So at first glance they do look very similar. But I wanted to understand more. Following investigations with teachers/colleagues/friends, I found that the difference lies in the form and purpose: '... perhaps "puzzle" was the wrong word, at least in count-noun form, as it would then fall into the same problem-setting, problem-solving paradigm as found in AR. As a verb on the other hand (or an adjective), the sense of questioning, or a desire to investigate and explore seems to be conveyed more accurately (eg "what puzzles me is why…?")' (ibid.)
>
> I found that the *attitude* of the puzzler is crucial in differentiating between a problem and a puzzle. My investigations then, and more recently a brief survey (2012) using Sketch Engine, showed that a 'problem' seemed to be inherently negative, collocating with negative things, and with a powerful pull towards a solution. But a 'puzzle' *also* tends towards solution-seeking. Who can forget the satisfaction of solving a crossword puzzle, for example?

> However, in its verb form, *'puzzling'* seems to be more open-ended, offering more avenues to explore. So the real difference emerges when the count-noun form of 'puzzle' shifts into 'being puzzled' or 'puzzling about'... Or, very productively, it develops into the question:
> What puzzles you about your language teaching/learning experiences?

This is central to the EP approach, and links directly to the principle of 'working for understanding' *before* trying to find solutions. The attitude of open-minded, reflective, and reflexive curiosity about our own practice is crucial. That is not to say that EP has sole rights to such things – they can surely be found in all sorts of practitioner research, and have their roots in much older thinking (for example, Freire, Gadamer, Heidegger, van Manen) as discussed previously. But it is nevertheless important to note that this notion of curiosity, of *puzzled enquiry*, is a defining characteristic of EP.

> **Quote 6.4: Hanks on Puzzled Enquiry**
> ... starting with a problem almost inevitably means a negative view of the existing situation, which can result in feelings of frustration, guilt and at times even engender a need for secrecy (if a teacher's job depends on projecting competence in all areas, for example, s/he is unlikely to admit to problems, and for good reason). In contrast, [...] EP's emphasis on a starting point of puzzled inquiry is, in my opinion, a more productive opening, as it offers more room for, indeed requires, work towards greater understanding(s).
>
> (2009: 36)

In framing the work as puzzled enquiry, EP allows for investigation of positive aspects of classroom life too. Questions such as 'Why am I happy with my teaching?' have appeared alongside questions about the anguish of teaching and learning. I found this in my own work, when one of my students asked:

> Why do I feel like learning more every time I attend English class?
> (Learner puzzle in Allwright and Hanks 2009: 277)

No inducements of any kind were offered to the students – they had all written their puzzled questions down on Post-it notes, I couldn't see what they were writing, and I didn't offer any sort of a reward or payment – I was just genuinely curious to know what puzzled my learners. And, in turn, this person seemed genuinely curious to know why English lessons were so attractive.

Crucially, then, the notion of *being puzzled* or engaging in *puzzle-driven practice* affords the possibility of positive questions, not just negative.

> **Quote 6.5: K.A. Johnson on Positive Puzzling**
>
> The notion of puzzling is far less threatening; a *puzzle* is, by its very nature, less clear-cut and more open-ended, and puzzles are more suited for discussion of successes as well as failures.
>
> (2002: 61)

K.A. Johnson (2002) opened up her puzzle about the sequence of activities in any given lesson to her students to discuss, and without 'solving a problem' (there was no problem to be solved, but rather a sense of questioning the habits of years), she found that her students enjoyed being asked, were involved in practising the language, and developed a sense of ownership of what decisions were being made in their classes. She describes the personal and professional satisfaction she gained from this work. Intriguingly, though, in this relatively early stage of EP engagement (at the turn of this century), she talks about 'solving' her puzzle – which suggests that even those who are sympathetic to EP are susceptible to the powerful pull of looking for solutions.

A helpful example of more extended puzzling comes from Ursula Erik, working in tertiary education, who came across EP for the first time when she attended my EP Plenary at a conference in Estonia. She was inspired to think about her puzzle, and the next day wrote me the e-mail that forms Vignette 6.2 (published with her permission).

> **Vignette 6.2: A Teacher in Estonia Writes About What Puzzles Her**
>
> The feedback that puzzled me (and still does, or I wouldn't be sending it to you :D).
>
> The question [to my students] was: what were your expectations to the course?
>
> *I thought this course will be about normal English lessons, I mean grammar, listening etc, but this course which we had, it was much much better. And not boring like normal English lessons.*
>
> It was by an exchange student from a group of 3 (=from the same country), and they all clearly thought their English is better than it really was. The rest of the (international) group were fairly fluent mostly, but lacked confidence (to speak). The exchange students had plenty of confidence, but 'lack of language', so to say.
>
> The things I'm puzzled about:
>
> 1. What's this *'normal English lessons'* that are boring?
> 2. Why are the *'normal'* lessons boring?
> 3. Actually we *did* do grammar and listening etc. – why didn't she notice we did it and didn't mention it was 'boring'? Was it because it was always 'grammar for...' (coping with tricky questions after your presentation, expressing your opinion etc.) or 'listening for...' (getting used to various accents, getting the main point of a lecture, taking notes on a topic etc.)
> 4. There really seems to be a cultural (or traditional?) aspect to language teaching/learning – what are the best practices all over the world? Is it more about that, or about how much it is influenced by the mother tongue of the learner?
>
> So, just a few things that puzzle a teacher of English (for Specific Purposes).
>
> Ursula Erik, Estonia, 2015

What is interesting about Ursula's questioning process is that it emerges from her practice. Although she/we might still struggle with the desire to 'solve' the puzzle, it is this non-defensive, questioning process that helps to open up avenues for exploration.

In inviting learners to participate in the research work alongside teachers, EP takes the notion of empowerment one step further. Learners are encouraged not only to investigate questions that have puzzled their teachers, but also to formulate questions and investigate issues that they themselves are interested in. This move is strongly influenced by Stevick's 'humanistic' approaches (Stevick 1976, 1980, 1990) and Freire's (1970, 1973) ideas regarding pedagogy and liberation. Crucially, EP adopts the Freirean notion of:

> ... an education of 'I wonder' instead of merely 'I do' (Freire 1973: 36)

Such an approach is markedly different from trying to find the solution(s) to discipline problems in the classroom, and offers the opportunity at least to develop greater understanding of the different perspectives of participants in the classroom.

> **Quote 6.6: Miller on the Discourse of Puzzlement**
> ... the special contribution of Exploratory Practice lies in creating pedagogical time and space for the *discourse of puzzlement* to be understood *as* syllabus, and, thus, develop in the lives of teachers and students.
> (2009: 90)

EP, then, represents an explicit attempt to move away from the 'problem-to-solution' paradigm presented in many forms of practitioner research, and recommends instead an attitude of 'puzzlement' (Allwright and Miller 1998; Hanks 1998, 1999), as discussed previously. Using the words 'puzzling' and 'puzzlement' is presented in the EP framework as offering more opportunities for investigation from/in practice – above all, practitioners are encouraged to prioritise understanding and 'quality of classroom life'. This discussion, then, informs my use of the words, so even when I use the word 'puzzle' (as a noun), I acknowledge the understanding outlined here.

> **Quote 6.7: The Rio EP Group on Sharing Puzzles**
>
> When students see their teacher's questions and puzzles, they see a humanised professional. When students can understand a teacher better, they see a chance to open up *their* inner selves as well. As teachers and students gain possibilities for constructing mutual understandings about the classroom environment, practitioners – students *and* teachers – show growth in their intellectual and critical perspectives.
> (The Rio de Janeiro EP Group, Chapter 14 in Allwright and Hanks 2009: 226)

This process of puzzling, investigating, developing understandings, and then, from those (partial, incomplete) understandings, developing yet more puzzled questions is thus central to EP, then. But the interested practitioner could ask: Where does it come from? Where can we find/how can we access puzzlement?

Where Do Puzzles Come From?

The issue of puzzlement itself has been investigated in some detail elsewhere. For example, in the special issue of *Language Teaching Research* (2003), articles considered the question of where puzzles originate (Kuschnir and Machado 2003), and what teachers puzzle about (Lyra et al. 2003). In my own work, I have discussed puzzlement in the area of teacher education (Hanks 1999) and in the context of teaching EAP (Hanks 2013a, b, 2015a, b). And Miller (2009) has proposed the idea of 'puzzle-driven language teacher development' in teacher education (see also Miller et al. 2015). In future, Bebel A. Cunha and other Rio EP group members intend to publish their work on the many puzzles collected from teachers and learners since 2003 (Cunha et al. Forthcoming).

An example might be to consider the often-raised question of 'Why do my students speak their mother tongue in the L2 classroom?' – solutions to the *problem* are many and varied (ranging from rewarding 'good' behaviour with points or praise, to punishing 'bad' behaviour with extra work or even fines). But all too often such solutions fail to lead to an understanding of *why* the students feel the need to speak their mother tongue. An EP approach might be to open the question up for discussion with the students (in either language), perhaps even considering times when L1 might be useful, as well as talking about why L2 is expected, and what the benefits of that might be (Hanks 1999, 2009; Miller 2009; Miller et al. 2015).

Kuschnir and Machado (2003) playfully adapt Vygotsky's notion of the 'zone of proximal development' (1986) and propose a 'puzzlement zone' for EP, where, they argue, questions that drive the investigative work are generated. They conclude that both researchers and practitioners are in continual motion in this zone, and that it has potential as a means of professional development.

> **Quote 6.8: Kuschnir and Machado on 'Puzzlement Zones'**
> … these zones should be seen as constructs of mental and personal interactions, where processes of linking, mediation and scaffolding are developed in order to better contribute to understandings in classroom settings.
> (2003: 177)

In the same issue, Lyra et al. (2003) describe how they investigated the puzzles brought to their EP group over a number of years by teachers working in (state, private, private language) schools in and around Rio de Janeiro. They collated and analysed 88 puzzles, and considered what happened to the teachers who originated the puzzles over a period of months. Most of the puzzles were categorised into issues to do with motivation (teachers' own or students'), anxiety, teaching, discipline, institutional lack of interest, and EP itself (2003: 150). Examples of questions they had collected over a number of years were:

- Why are students so much afraid of making mistakes?
- Why do teachers face so many problems?
- Why do students have so many difficulties to learn?
- Why am I happy with my teaching?
- Why is homework important?
- Why do some students never seem to be motivated?

- Why are the boys in 702 (class) so violent?
- Why does 'anguish' keep us in EP?
- Why do the government do what they do with the educational system?
- Why do we have only 2 classes a week?
  (selected from Lyra et al. 2003, Appendix B: 158–161)

So What Differentiates These Questions from the Kind of 'Problems' (or 'Puzzles') Found in Other Forms of Teacher Research?

One key difference between 'problems' and 'puzzling' is the emphasis on starting with a 'why' question, rather than a 'how' or 'how to'. As we have seen, EP argues that if the (very strong) temptation to 'solve a problem' is resisted, then options for deeper explorations are made available. Likewise, the inclusion of the learners as equal partners with their teachers in the explorations offers an opportunity to develop mutual understanding for all who are in this particular classroom community.

If we take the question 'Why are the boys in 702 (class) so violent?' as an example, we see that in EP it might be opened up to discussion with those very boys. Drawing the learners into shared puzzlement might help to unpick the initial 'why' question, and further, deeper, questions may arise: Are these boys really violent? How is violence in the classroom defined? Do the learners have a different perception of what they are doing and why they are doing it? This might lead to further questions for discussion in the classroom: What causes violence? How is it expressed and why do people feel the need to express it, and what effects does it have on others? What is an acceptable way of behaving in the classroom (and society more generally) and what is not? What happens to the students who stand out against it? Are they coerced, persuaded, or, perhaps, joining in because they are afraid to be different?

In engaging in such work, the teacher and the learners may discover ways of interacting that are more productive: the learners may realise that a degree of consideration for others is required, or, perhaps more importantly, they may gain an understanding of what triggers their violence. They haven't solved the problem of the violence – that was not the purpose; since the violence may well be an expression of the frustrations, and alienation, not to mention despair, these boys experience in their lives, it may not be a solvable problem. But, as a result of the EP work, the teacher may discover that what s/he perceives as 'violence' is in fact merely the exuberant expression of teenage emotions; or s/he might understand the awfulness of the boys' lives (proximity to crime, desperate poverty, despair over the future) and acknowledge their right to anger; or the boys might understand that the teacher is not responsible for these things, and is in fact suffering under the yoke of his/her own oppression. Thus the goal of 'developing understandings' may be both a greater comprehension of the phenomenon itself and an acknowledgement of different perceptions of those in the room.

At any one time, a practitioner may have many different puzzles in mind at once. Through sharing our puzzled questions, and investigating collegially, we gain in developing our understandings. But these developing understandings then raise further questions about our practice, so just as human understanding is always developing, always incomplete, but always redolent with the promise of deeper understandings, so too do we discover an inner motivation to learn more, to understand more profoundly what is happening in our learning and teaching. Figure 6.1 gives an indication of how puzzled enquiry might emerge from the 'messiness' of practice (Fig 6.1).

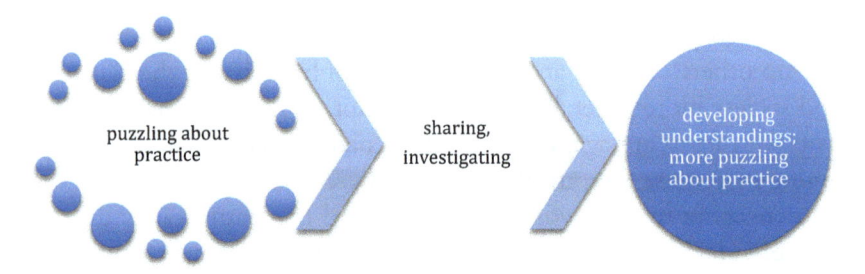

Fig 6.1 Puzzling about practice

In EP we might begin with an invitation to the participants: 'What puzzles you about your language learning/teaching experiences?'. This sounds unproblematic, but a concern to be faced by anyone wishing to try EP was expressed by my colleague Jane (see Vignette 13.1 in Chapter 13) as she planned her first EP lesson some years ago: 'What if they don't come up with anything?'. This is a reasonable fear: Why should we expect learners to have puzzles? What if they do not have puzzles that they feel able to share with the class? If the lesson has been built around the assumption that there will be puzzles to be discussed, and if the puzzles are then not forthcoming, what happens then?

Despite such worries, I have not yet come across any evidence of people without puzzles – quite the reverse. Many practitioners (both teachers and learners) reported a flood of different puzzles, and most participants were able to choose from at least two. In trusting the learners, or 'key developing practitioners' (Allwright and Hanks 2009), as well as the teachers, to have opinions, questions, and experiences, EP opens up opportunities for discussion, collaboration, and mutually beneficial learning. EP strongly encourages collegial ways of working, and this implies sharing of puzzles. But the first step is both exhilarating and scary. The vignettes in the next section give a sense of what it feels like to start puzzling in EP.

What Do Learners Puzzle About?

An under-reported phenomenon in practitioner research is the learner perspective – what puzzles learners? In published work elsewhere (eg Allwright and Hanks 2009), I have listed puzzles elicited from learners in previous years on in-sessional courses teaching EAP at my university. Examples of puzzled questions from my own practice include:

- Why don't I speak English after nine years' study?
- Why I need so long time before I learn and use a new verb or word?
- Why do I always make mistakes of the tense?
- Why do I have such problems to write an essay?
- Why one days can I speak/understand better than other days?
- Why do I feel like learning more every time I attend English class? (selected from Allwright and Hanks 2009: 179)

The process of eliciting and then exploring these questions is potent indeed (see Furman & Ahola for a discussion of 'the power of questions to seed ideas' (1992: 16)) and can lead to very fertile ground for developing shared understandings. The puzzles cited in the following vignettes come from a doctoral study lasting over six years, and involving more than a hundred learners from a range of different countries, as well as teachers from the UK and New Zealand. On being asked, 'What puzzles you about your language learning/teaching experiences?' many participants found they were bursting with puzzled questions, all at different stages of development.

> **Vignette 6.3: Meow and Cheer: What Puzzles Learners?**
>
> There was a degree of commonality in the themes expressed by many of the learners on my EAP course. For example, they puzzled about their difficulties in remembering and actively using vocabulary; their (in-)ability to speak fluently (even after many years of study); their difficulties in listening and their difficulties understanding variations in pronunciation. Not all the learners focused on language issues, however. Some students expressed interest in psychological aspects of language learning, such as retaining concentration over long periods, or issues to do with motivation.
>
> One learner, 'Meow' (from Thailand), reported having a wealth of puzzles. It was as if asking the question and giving her space to think about it had opened the floodgates for her:
>
> > **Meow:** *I think it's very helpful for me if I can understand er what puzzle I have. And I- I just find 'Oh' I find 'Oh I have a lot of puzzle that I never thought about it before'*
>
> The words on the page fail to convey the excitement conveyed in Meow's voice: her exclamation of 'Oh' was high-pitched and she seemed delighted by the number of puzzles. She had written down five or six puzzles but, encouraged by her teacher, had settled on just one: *'Why can't I speak English well, after studying for a long time?'*. As she was talking about it, her group-mate 'Cheer' (from Japan) who rarely interrupted or initiated speech, broke in saying *'It's exactly same as me!'*

What Do Teachers Puzzle About?

Like many learners, teachers often begin by expressing their frustrations, their annoyances, and their irritations. For example, in both John's and Bella's initial answers to the question 'What puzzles you about language teaching?' we can clearly detect a great deal of emotion. The repetitions, the emphases, and the intensity conveys a deep sense of dissatisfaction.

> **Vignette 6.4: John's Puzzle**
>
> **Judith:** What puzzles you about language teaching?
> **John:** *[speaking slowly with much emphasis]*... my puzzle is: why – **why** do some students come on a course not prepared or willing to learn? ... not ready to... Why do they even **bother**?... so are there sociological factors... like pushy parents? ... um what are the factors that cause a student to come and yet not to work? Not be motivated... what *is* that?

John took the decision to share his puzzle with the students in his class, and found a form of resolution through discussing it with them. The fact that they considered his question seriously, and discussed their opinions with him, confirming some of his suspicions but also suggesting alternative perspectives, reduced the levels of irritation, and opened up avenues for exploration. It was this 'moment of transition' (Hanks 1998) which allowed John to turn what was initially a *problem* (frustration about students' lack of motivation) into an area that he could explore.

Interestingly, if we return to Bella (whose story was first presented in Vignette 6.1), we see that her initial puzzle was presented in surprisingly similar language, with a similar vehemence, even though the two of them had not been in contact (and indeed, Bella was engaging in EP a whole year after John).

> **Vignette 6.5: Bella's Puzzle**
>
> **Judith:** What puzzles you about language teaching?
> **Bella:** I think it's, yeah, what we were talking about yesterday... How much do I have... Do I have any impact on them at all really?

> Because we're here in the UK the students that make most progress, it seems to be more to do with their own motivation and ability than anything I do in the classroom. And then the Learner Autonomy – why are we bothering? *Are* we teaching them to be independent? *Should* we be teaching them to be independent? Are we teaching them to be independent because it's cultural and therefore actually as long as they get by without being independent, does it matter as they get to what they need to get to anyway? And umm, I dunno... coming down to language learning: Why – *Why* can't Middle Eastern students spell?
>
> **Judith:** mmm
>
> **Bella:** It's my main problem at the moment – I cannot... and... How do you teach? I don't know how to teach them spelling... Actually it drives me mad.
>
> **Judith:** Odd isn't it? Why?
>
> **Bella:** *Why* can't they?

The discerning reader will note that although these puzzles use 'why' as a starting point (usually cited in the EP literature as a way of generating puzzlement), they are framed negatively, focusing on what the participant 'can't' or 'doesn't' do, or what the students find 'difficult' to do. Initially, there appears to be an implicit assumption of wanting to improve the situation or solve the problem, as in other forms of practitioner research such as AR and Reflective Practice. This is something that the EP literature has tended to argue against, positing instead the need to understand in depth before 'improvements' are initiated (Allwright and Hanks 2009; Allwright 2009; Gieve and Miller 2006b; Miller 2009). However, as I write, I wonder if a 'sense of irritation' with a particular situation is a necessary impetus for the practitioner to want to investigate. This sense of irritation shifts over time, with some participants taken by surprise as they become so fascinated with an apparently simple puzzle. On more than one occasion (see Bella's story in Vignette 6.1 above, for example), teachers and learners have reported being so deeply engaged in the explorations that their EP work expanded into other classes. We will return to this point in Part Two.

The shift in underlying attitudes is very similar to the 'moments of transition' that I had identified in Hanks (1998). Here, I propose two conceptual definitions that helped me navigate these tricky waters, and which, while partial and incomplete, may prompt readers to puzzle over the issues themselves.

> **Concept 6.2: Initial Definitions of Problems and Puzzles**
>
> *Problem:* Connotative language is used to express negative emotion, for example irritation, fear, distrust, or frustration. An expression of the ISness of things, showing evidence of unwillingness to investigate further because questions are closed down or blocked with easy explanations (eg 'Well, just give the learners lots of spellings to learn week-by-week, test them regularly, and they will learn' or 'I can tell your learners how to activate their vocabulary! Just do x, y, z.').
>
> *Puzzle(ment):* Often combined with an expression of surprise or interest. An articulation of the positive uncertainty of things, implying a willingness to investigate further, and to develop deeper understandings of the issue at hand. These understandings may be partial or incomplete, and they may raise further questions, but this is seen as a good thing, something to be celebrated as part of the uncertainty and complexity of life.

In sum, if there is a distinction between problems and puzzlement, then a shift can be made, from viewing an event as needing a solution ('quick-fix' or thoughtful and careful), to viewing it as a puzzling phenomenon which requires further thought, further investigation. Through investigating collaboratively, and developing shared understandings, it is even possible that what was initially perceived as a problem turns out not to be problematic any longer. This is not to say the problem has been solved, but rather that reflexive enquiry, released from the problem-to-solution paradigm, opens up a world of further questions. Not adding to the burdens of practitioners, but, by acknowledging complexity, making life more liveable.

Problematising Puzzling

These stories chart the move from irritation or frustration to a more curious attitude. A challenge for EP, then, is that work is often needed in order to shift from the default position of problem-setting (and thence problem-solving) to an attitude of puzzlement, being puzzled, and thence towards developing deeper understandings. The importance of curiosity cannot be ignored.

A Note of Caution

Despite the imaginative possibilities of meaning and questioning, this should be accompanied by a word of warning. Perhaps we cannot fully realise those possibilities; maybe we should be kind to ourselves, and allow the possibility of incomplete understandings. Dick Allwright has talked of 'understandings too deep for words' (see Allwright 2009; Allwright and Hanks 2009), which calls to mind the argument outlined by Dreyfus:

> Heidegger questions both the possibility and the desirability of making our everyday understandings totally explicit. (Dreyfus 1991: 4)

This is not to say that we should not *try* to understand, merely to note that all human understanding is inevitably partial, incomplete, and leaves us wanting more. Because these everyday understandings enable us to make sense of our world, they are always assumed, and making them fully explicit may be problematic. It is, in fact, a problem, but a lovely problem. It is this drive to understand more that is central to the principle of 'working for understanding', the issue of puzzlement, in EP.

> **Quote 6.9: Allwright and Hanks on Attempting to Articulate Our Understandings**
>
> ... in spite of the potential impossibility of our ever fully expressing our deepest understandings, *attempting* to articulate them can, ironically, be extremely valuable in practice as part of the process of trying to deepen them. Discussions where people push each other to think every more deeply about their developing understandings, without expecting them to be able to articulate them fully and finally, can be a very satisfying and productive collegial process. We need therefore a form of research that encourages people to try to articulate their developing understandings even if they are ultimately 'too deep for words'.
>
> (2009: 149)

The Risks of Sharing Puzzled Thoughts

EP has on occasion been accused of a lack of criticality. But then, we have to ask, what definition of 'criticality' is being used by these critics, and what is their purpose? As Feyerabend talks about criticism as 'the Holy Word' (1975/2010: 149), he identifies the petty jealousies between different disciplines, and different individuals within them. Could this be an explanation for the refusal of some in the field to accept the 'critical-reflexive perspective' (Miller & Barreto, 2015: 58) of EP? Whatever the reason, the joy with which practitioners have reported their experiences is regarded in some quarters with suspicion. It may be that critics have failed to see that in reports of EP, like many other forms of practitioner research, the practitioner-researchers' enthusiasm has hidden a deeper critical edge which is in fact ever-present. In trying to establish an innovative form of research, the positive outcomes may have overshadowed the pre-existing criticality of asking 'why'. This, I believe, is a mistaken reading of the nature of EP – after all, what can be more critical than asking 'why' of the status quo? Surely attempting to *understand* by working with others exemplifies critical thinking?

Thus far, for example, I have shown a generally positive picture (though I have also aimed to honestly draw attention to caveats and flaws). But no picture can be dissociated from the wider social and political context. At this point I want to move towards 'meta-puzzling', to scrutinise the notion of sharing puzzlement with others in the classroom. What if the puzzle is so personal, or so potentially disruptive, that working with others is not appropriate?

Ahmad's story in Vignette 6.6 below gives an indication of the infinite complexity of intercultural issues that learners and teachers have to negotiate as a matter of course in their daily lives (for more on Ahmad's story, see Hanks 2013b, 2015a).

> **Vignette 6.6: Ahmad's Story**
>
> 'Ahmad' (a young man studying EAP in preparation for his undergraduate degree at a British university) started with a question that was deeply personal:

> *Why don't I like [...] to learn another language [English] from my mother tongue?*
>
> but he stated firmly that he did not want to investigate his puzzle. Instead he joined another group investigating a puzzle about preferred learning situations. This puzzled me. Why didn't he want to investigate such an intriguing question? However, I felt it was important to respect his decision, and although we spoke about it privately, we did not pursue it in class.
>
> Over time, it became clear that Ahmad's question implies questions of power and politics, linked perhaps to the 'linguistic imperialism' of English (Canagarajah and Ben Said 2011; Pennycook 1998; Phillipson 1992). What did it mean to be a young man from an Arabic culture who has to learn English in the political and economic climate of 2010? Ahmad mentioned in the interviews that some of his compatriots refused to speak English in the classroom, reverting instead to Arabic whenever they could. He, however, made an effort to distance himself from them, and claimed to speak English at all times in class, despite his apparent distaste for learning the language.
>
> Ahmad showed great maturity and wisdom in deciding what he wanted to investigate publicly, and what he wanted to reflect upon privately. During our conversations we both gained in deepening our understandings: of his question, of the world, and of the importance of social relations in the classroom. To have opened his question up for investigation and public discussion could have led to difficulties, with students expressing political opinions that could either cause problems for them in their home country or cause social disruption in the class, if strong disagreements were encountered.
>
> Was his decision to join another group (with a less explosive puzzle) a way for him to keep the peace? A pragmatic approach which allowed him to continue his class work without disturbing the social/political waters of the classroom?

Raising questions and giving space to develop understandings might appear to be offering, or even promising, solutions. Practitioners often use the words 'problem' and 'puzzle' interchangeably, and many of the investigations in this book were initially framed as finding solutions to problems. But it soon becomes clear that the *process* of investigating, and the discoveries they make, often taking advice from other learners or teachers, based on their experiences of language learning and teaching, is an essential part of EP. Sharing puzzles (or problems), working together to investigate them, sharing what they find out, and above all *owning* the process, from start to finish, is what makes the EP work worthwhile. A challenge for anyone interested in implementing EP, though, is to successfully convey the difference between problem-posing and puzzling, and to give enough time for a problem to transmute into puzzlement.

Summary

In asking practitioners to step away from the rush to find 'solutions' (the scare quotes indicate unease with the drive for solutions), EP creates space for practitioners to stop and think. In an endlessly pressured world of deadlines, targets, and assessments this is rare, but in doing so we rediscover how necessary understanding is for our humanity. It is not a random word – there is a serious, almost magisterial, weight to seeking profound understanding, which adds depth and texture to the quality of our lives. If we look beneath the surface, we can see that it (whatever *it* is that we are puzzling about) isn't as easy as it first appears; in fact working for understanding requires really hard work… but this is work that is deeply satisfying when it is relevant to our lives.

Recommended Reading

Hanks, J. (2009) 'Inclusivity and collegiality in Exploratory Practice' IN T. Yoshida, H. Imai, Y. Nakata, A. Tajino, O. Takeuchi, & K. Tamai (Eds) *Researching Language Teaching and Learning: An integration of practice and theory.* Bern: Peter Lang. (pp. 33–55). Here the authors begin to unpack the notions of 'inclusivity' (ie including learners as well as teachers in the research enterprise) and 'collegiality' (ie practitioners working together with the aim of developing mutual understandings.

Kuschnir, A. & Machado, B. (2003) Puzzling, and puzzling about puzzle development. *Language Teaching Research* 7/2. (pp. 163–180) In this robust investigation of the question 'where do puzzles come from?' Kuchnir & Machado play with the Vygotskyan notion of the Zone of Proximal Development and propose as an addition the idea of a 'Zone of Puzzle Development'.

Lyra, I., Fish Braga, S., & Braga, W. (2003) What puzzles teachers in Rio de Janeiro, and what keeps them going? *Language Teaching Research* 7/2. (pp. 143–162) In this comprehensive study, 88 puzzles from teachers in Rio de Janeiro are analysed and discussed. They remind us that we should not rely on first impressions, and that if we take the time to think about it, we can gain insights and draw strength from one another as practitioners. Interestingly for our purposes, they provide in the appendix a full list of puzzled questions from the teachers.

Miller, I. K. (2009) 'Puzzle-driven' Language teacher development: the contribution of Exploratory Practice. IN T. Yoshida, H. Imai, Y. Nakata, A. Tajino, O. Takeuchi, & K. Tamai (Eds) *Researching Language Teaching and Learning: An integration of practice and theory.* Bern: Peter Lang. (pp. 77–90). Miller presents here the notion of using the EP principle as the syllabus for initial teacher education. She proposes a positive 'discourse of puzzlement' which enables relations of power and trust to be examined by/for practitioners.

Part II

Developing Understandings from Practice

7

Introduction to Part 2

Introduction

In Part One, I looked at notions of 'Research' and 'Practitioner Research'. I noted some of the issues with practitioner research that have been raised: practitioners (whether teachers or learners) lead busy lives, and there are common complaints that there is no time (or money) to enable them to engage in research. I then turned to Exploratory Practice (EP) as a 'younger sibling' in the practitioner research 'family' which aims to address these issues. I examined the development of the EP principled framework, considering each of the principles in turn. However, just stating the framework can leave the concept of EP somewhat opaque.

Part Two elucidates the principles and the framework, through the experiences of practitioners rooted in a variety of situations and countries. As Gieve and Miller (2006b) have argued, the views of classroom 'insiders' are central to our attempts to deeply, seriously understand what happens in the practice of language education.

> **Quote 7.1: Gieve and Miller on the Agency Potential of Classroom Insiders**
>
> By integrating teachers, learners and pedagogic practice within a collegially developed investigative attitude, Exploratory Practice strengthens the agency potential of classroom insiders as those necessarily pivotal in any search for serious understanding of what goes on in classrooms.
>
> (2006b: 21)

I start by looking at how practitioners have been developing their understandings from/through their situated practice. The ideas of Iedema et al. (2013), though they are situated in a different field (healthcare), are equally valid in the complex world of teachers and learners in language education. I want here (and throughout) to establish the notion not only of *research-as-practice* (see Iedema et al. 2013, for extensive discussion of this notion in healthcare) but also of (Exploratory) *practice-as-research*. Just as Iedema et al. depict nurses, doctors, and surgeons as frontline actors in healthcare, so too are teachers and learners at the cutting edge of cultural and intercultural issues in the classroom. These go far beyond mere national characteristics or national boundaries (see Holliday et al. 2010, on intercultural communication, or Holliday 2013, on the 'grammar of culture'), but rather are fluid cultures, co-created by the actors in the classroom, and constantly in motion (see, for example, Bauman 2005, on 'liquid modernity').

> **Quote 7.2: Iedema et al. on the Potential of Existing Practice**
>
> We have been interested in the richness of existing practice and the already-present acumen than is embedded in and evident from *in situ* [situated] practice. That is, our focus has been on how front-line actors negotiate the complexity of in situ practice, on the often tacit resources they harness to do so, and on their capacity for confronting workplace complexity and for designing work processes in more considered ways.
>
> (2013: 172)

Before going further, however, it is worth noting the influence of, and our resistance to, the 'discourse of change', or 'discourse of improvement', which so dominates our field.

Resisting the Discourse of Improvement

With an emphasis on action and attempts to emulate more traditional versions of research instruments, and associated narrow notions of rigour, replicability, and validity, many forms of practitioner research fall into a trap. As noted in Chapter 5, the 'discourse of improvement' means that *change* (endemic, but in the end superficial, because there's always another change just around the corner) is the driver, not action for understanding. The image created in my mind (see Fig. 7.1) is of the practitioner-researcher being pulled in opposing directions: on the one hand is the reflective, introspective, analytical pull of *research*, on the other is the outward-facing, dynamic tug of *action*, and action for change, at that (Fig. 7.1).

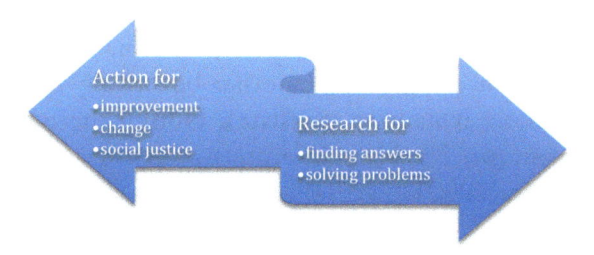

Fig. 7.1 Pulled in opposing directions

Our experiences as teachers, teacher educators, and learners exemplify the problematic nature of current obsessions with change and improvement. We have only just got used to one set of changes when a new set sweeps the field. So as practitioners we never get the chance to really deeply investigate the last lot of changes (which may or may not have value for our practice) before the next lot overturn the old. The new is triumphantly unveiled, and practitioners sigh as they consign the previous changes to the dustbin of history, and gird themselves to take on the 'latest thing'. Practitioners may be forgiven, then, for viewing the newest set of changes with a jaundiced eye.

EP explicitly seeks to turn the two arrow-heads around (see Fig. 7.2), bringing the explorations into/from the practice itself. So rather than something new, EP suggests using what we already do as an investigative tool.

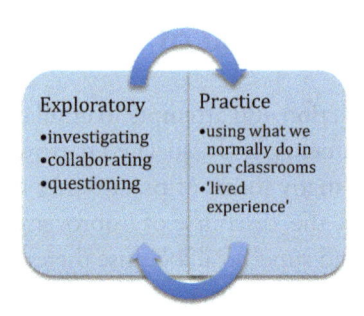

Exploratory
- investigating
- collaborating
- questioning

Practice
- using what we normally do in our classrooms
- 'lived experience'

Fig. 7.2 Bringing explorations into/from practice itself

Using what we would be doing anyway in our teaching/learning as a way of doing research is a very simple concept, and yet quite difficult to explain to those who have not experienced it for themselves. It is, as mentioned in Chapter 3, intimately related to the Aristotelian notion of *phronesis* (another beautifully simple concept that is difficult to explain or translate). Noting the untranslatableness of the concept, Flyvbjerg interprets *phronesis* as 'a sense of the ethically practical' (2001: 57) and adds that it involves '[d]eliberation about values with reference to praxis' (ibid.). Importantly, Flyvbjerg argues that 'the concreted, the practical, and the ethical have been neglected by modern science' (2001:59). Flyvbjerg draws a direct line from Aristotelian *phronesis* to Bourdieu's (1991) notion of '*habitus*' and calls for the development of 'case knowledge' (examples rooted in praxis) with explicit consideration of power. These ideas inform and colour the approach in Part 2: as we look at examples of EP rooted in different situations, we keep a watchful eye on the power relations that govern our world.

However, it is important to note that in the rush towards change, *phronetic* action can too easily become *frenetic* action. We often need to stop and think before we 'improve' or otherwise change our practices, because we need to thoroughly understand the 'good praxis' that may already be in place as well as the weaker areas that need to be addressed. As we shall see, EP resists the pull of 'improvement', of 'technicism' of 'solutions' so roundly criticised by Allwright (2001, 2005a), Breen

(2006), and Carr (2004). Instead, the idea is to develop understandings which are locally relevant and deeply rooted in our contexts. EP promotes a principled and ethical approach to practitioner research (see Quote Box 7.3 below) while retaining its own distinctive features of fully including learners as co-researchers exploring issues to do with classroom language learning and teaching. Examples of this duality can be found, for example, in Hanks (2015b), which looks at the teachers' perspectives, and Hanks (2015a), which foregrounds the learners' perspectives, on EP.

> **Quote 7.3: Allwright on an Ethical Approach to Practitioner Research**
>
> For EP, the ethical and epistemological dimensions are the most critical, with the emphasis on *understanding* rather than *problem-solving*. I find the common emphases on practical problem-solving and making measurable improvements in student achievement not only unhelpfully short-sighted but also potentially counterproductive. I argue instead for a return to the traditional research aim of understanding, and for focusing our work for understanding on *quality of life* (rather than *quality of output*) as the ultimate value. This focus also prompts us to address the ethical issue of the researcher-researched relationship, and to insist that learners, as well as teachers, should be seen as classroom practitioners developing their own understandings of language classroom life.
>
> (2005a: 353)

EP suggests a more measured approach: to step back from change, to resist the discourse of 'improvement', and instead to assess what is genuinely appropriate to the local situation (see Quote Box 7.3 above). That doesn't mean not (ever) changing; it just means putting understanding first, comprehending – and only if our comprehension indicates that recalibration is needed should we attempt adjustments. Without such a stance, change and improvement become merely the tools of oppression: practitioners are run ragged as they chase after chimerical change, impossible-to-achieve improvement.

> **Quote 7.4: Allwright on Resisting Imposed Changes**
>
> Change proposals may well be based on expert understandings of the general educational situation, but, if they are to be successfully implemented, particular local understandings are required, not just general ones. [...] Such local understandings may therefore:
>
> - Inform intelligent resistance to any imposition of the proposed changes.
> - Inform intelligent local modifications to them.
> - Set up the optimal conditions for their successful implementation. [...]
>
> Prioritising understanding itself constitutes a fundamental change of perspective on change, complexifying it considerably, but it should not predispose anyone against change. It should only dispose people against changes that are locally inappropriate.
>
> (Allwright 2002, cited in Allwright and Hanks 2009: 283)

Inviting Practitioners to Dare to Question

As a relative newcomer to the field of practitioner research, EP can be seen to be responding to issues raised in previous years (as outlined in Part 1), namely, the relevance of the research (to whom? for whom? by whom?); the hierarchical relationships between teachers, learners, teacher educators, academics (who decides to do the research? who carries it out?), and empowerment (who sets the research agenda? who reports the findings? to whom? for whom?). But does this theoretical EP framework hold in the complex and sometimes contradictory world of the classroom?

The experiences of the people in this book, and many others, indicates that it does. And that the theoretical, philosophical aspects of the principles afford multiple opportunities for EP to be adapted and adopted in a wide range of language teaching/learning situations. So, for example, when venturing into a new (for me) part of the world, building an EP Network with teachers, learners and teacher educators in Turkey, I asked EP colleagues in the UK and Brazil to send messages to those new to EP. We have already seen the message from Jess (in Chapter 1); now we turn to a communication from Brazil.

Vignette 7.1 is an e-mail (published with her permission) from Carolina Apolinário, an educational psychologist working with children, teachers, and family members in a state secondary school in Rio de Janeiro designed to be shared with people interested in EP. Her commentary on EP conveys the essential features that we will investigate further in the following chapters: daring to ask questions about the unknown; listening to one another (with all our different roles and identities, professional and personal) with respect; positioning all of us as both learners and teachers, each with something to learn, each with something to teach, in our social world.

> **Vignette 7.1: A Message to Practitioners Wondering About EP**
>
> In my opinion, Exploratory Practice is a means of developing a researcher attitude towards life and towards our professional practice. EP considers teachers and learners as responsible for learning in partnership with one another, respecting their idiosyncrasies, backgrounds and opinions.
>
> EP invites practitioners to dare asking questions they probably don't have answers to yet. It reminds us we how much we can learn from one another if we are brave enough to face unpredictability and surprise. We will never be able to foresee all possible answers to a puzzle elicited. At the same time, we should be humble to listen to each answer with no judgement, fostering more understandings and reflections.
>
> The contemporary scenario we live in suffered positive and negative impact of globalisation and the widespread use of technology. One of the pitfalls of this change is that people became used to fast stimuli and consumerism. We feel demanded to be highly productive, highly competent and the happiest as possible. Time became our most valuable treasure. It's not hard to conclude that this kind of behaviour drives us away from attentive listening, empathy and genuine care. As a result, we have become more narcissistic throughout the decades (Baumann 2007; La Taille 2009).
>
> It's not unlikely for teachers to come across more and more children and teenagers presenting symptoms like attention or social interaction difficulties in schools. Environmental and cultural aspects as play a big role on those symptoms.
>
> What enchants me the most about EP is that it still values listening, and deep understandings about the relationships we have in and out of school. EP may be a great tool for teachers to develop social competences, such as resilience and empathy in students.
>
> As for my psychologist role, I believe the Exploratory Practice philosophical/ethical propositions have been helping me reflect in a more caring and critical way in partnership with students, teachers, parents and outside agencies.
> Carolina
> Carolina Apolinário
> Educational Psychologist and EP practitioner, Rio de Janeiro, 2015

We will return to Carolina in Part Two, as she gives us a deeper understanding of her involvement in the complexities of classrooms, people, and practice from a psychological point of view.

So How Might this Work in Practice?

Part Two presents a number of stories and case studies which illustrate and illuminate the ways in which practitioners enact EP in situ. Crucially, in addition to the vignettes and quotes, there are contributions from people around the world, some who have worked with EP extensively, others who have come to it relatively recently. The writers are clearly acknowledged here as authors and contributors in their own right (eg by using bio-boxes to introduce each Case Study). Their work provides useful exemplars of a range of approaches, techniques, and procedures, employed in different contexts from around the world. We consider teaching/learning English in secondary schools, working with teenagers and young adults at tertiary level, teacher education, and continuing professional development. Some narratives cover a long period of time (eg up to three years), while others show EP in action over as short a period as three lessons. These examples are provided as ways of provoking inspiration for others, but *not* a step-by-step guide for 'how to do EP'. They offer the potential for 'what can be' and 'what might I do myself' through the many and varied situations they describe.

Mapping Part Two

So the emphasis in Part Two is on praxis and reflexivity. The focus is on using EP as a lens for developing our profound understandings of *in situ* practice, and for developing yet more puzzled questions, thus playing with Kuschnir & Machado's notion of the 'puzzlement zone' (2003: 172 ff). In particular I will draw upon the work of the EP Group in Rio (see Allwright and Hanks 2009; Kuschnir and Machado 2003; Lyra et al. 2003; Miller et al. 2008), as well as discussing recent developments of EP in an English for Academic Purposes (EAP) context (Gunn 2010;

Hanks 2015a, b; Rowland 2011; Smith 2009; Stewart et al. 2014) and in language teacher education (e.g. Bartu 2003; Dikilitaş 2014, 2015a, b; Miller 2009, Miller et al. 2015; Slimani-Rolls and Kiely 2014; Tajino and Smith 2016; Zheng 2012.

Part Two focuses on the understandings the field can gain from practice: What have practitioners been doing in/through/by EP? And what can we (teachers, learners, teacher educators, educational psychologists, etc.) begin to understand from our practice? The next chapters examine a number of ways to answer the question 'But… what do you actually *do* in EP?' This is the crux of the book. We discuss the importance of working to understand: How have others done this? What might you do? For example, Chapter 8 considers EP in English Language Teaching more generally, while Chapter 9 focuses on EP being tried in EAP, and Chapter 10 looks at EP in Language Teacher Education and Continuing Professional Development. I use these lenses to critically examine the principles of EP described thus far. Threaded throughout the book are questions about quality of life; working for understanding; working to bring people together; working for mutual development; working in sustainable ways; and integrating research and pedagogy.

8

Integrating Research and Pedagogy

Introduction

This chapter, along with Chapters 9 and 10, examines a number of ways in which practitioners have experienced Exploratory Practice (EP) in different contexts, with different groups of practitioners. In the following pages, we see EP inviting practitioners to use their research activities as a way of getting their work done as advocated by Allwright and Hanks (2009). We follow up the vignettes begun in Part One: What happened when teachers and learners like Bella, Cheer, John, Meow, and others tried out EP in their own classrooms?

In addition, we consider a number of case studies from around the world. Each case study stems from a person engaged in teaching, learning, and researching, in and through EP. I contacted various people from around the world, explained that I was writing this book, and asked them to consider the following questions from the point of view of potential readers of this book:

- Why did you become interested in EP?
- How did you use EP in your context?
- What puzzled you/your learners?

© The Author(s) 2017
J. Hanks, *Exploratory Practice in Language Teaching*,
DOI 10.1057/978-1-137-45344-0_8

- What did you actually do?
- How did you combine research and pedagogy?
- What did you find out?
- Was there any follow-up?
- What is EP about for you?
- Is there anything else you would like to tell readers?

The case studies presented in this chapter, and, indeed throughout the rest of the book, were provided by teachers, learners, teacher educators, researchers, and educational psychologists working in different types of institutions and in different parts of the world. As an ethical stance, I have clearly identified them, with a brief biography (supplied by the writer, as s/he gave permission for their text to be used). Rather than positioning them as anonymous (and therefore disempowered) subjects, or even objects, of study, I have invited them to take their rightful places as authors of their own texts, and of their own destinies.

Of course, each individual interpreted these questions in his or her own way, and each person had a very different story to tell. The combination of all of them shows the sheer variety of interpretations possible, in the different contexts (state schools, private language schools, universities, colleges), different countries, and different personalities involved. Through the case studies, and the vignettes (which are drawn from real individuals I have worked with at various points over the past fifteen years), readers can make use of the ideas, thoughts, doubts, and puzzles that arise. You might want to compare what these people did with your own experiences, and you might begin by asking, 'What puzzles you about the stories you read here?'. This process of puzzling, and indeed, meta-puzzling (ie *puzzling about the puzzles*), is one (of many) productive way(s) of doing-being EP.

Puzzling Over Bringing Research and Pedagogy Together

Practitioner-researchers are continually pulled in different directions. On the one hand, they wish to investigate their learning and teaching lives; on the other, they need to ensure that their learning and teaching is prioritised. EP offers a way through this dilemma, by bringing research and pedagogy together, as Wright (2005) suggests.

> **Quote 8.1: Wright on Different Types of Professional Knowledge**
>
> Exploratory Practice holds promise for a more healthy relationship between different types of professional knowledge than the traditional 'theory-practice' dichotomy that so dominates professional discourse.
>
> (2005: 429)

But (as mentioned at the end of Chapter 5) how does EP attempt to bring pedagogy and research together? What might it look like, and what possibilities does this raise for pedagogy, for practice, and for research? In short, how have others enacted EP, and what can we learn from our/their practice?

As discussed in Part One, this concept of researching 'lived experience' (van Manen 1990) is deeply personal and cannot be simply replicated (see Concept 8.1).

> **Concept 8.1: The Relevance of Your Own 'Lived Experience'**
>
> If you have questions to ask about language, language learning/teaching, about pedagogy or research, a good place to start is by examining your own 'lived experience'. Working with your colleagues (learners, teachers, teacher educators, psychologists, administrators, etc.) in order to develop your own understandings might bring joyful epiphanies or sad wisdom or a mixture of the two.
>
> However, by definition, 'lived experience' can't be copied from someone else (though another person's experience might add depth and meaning to your own experiences). The key thing is *being there* – living in the moment, and by a process of serious, thoughtful, questioning, to begin to find glimmers of understanding.

If we return for a moment to the vignettes presented in Chapter 6, it is clear that what puzzled the teachers and learners about their language learning/teaching experiences was not 'how to improve', but rather 'why'. As we saw in Vignette 6.4, John wanted to know *Why do some students come to class unready to learn?* But he was worried about the extra work that a traditional research project would entail. This is an entirely reasonable concern. The course he was working on (a very intensive, high-stakes pre-sessional course, teaching English for Academic Purposes (EAP) to students preparing for their academic degrees) was time-consuming and demanding. To add research to his already considerable workload would be to make the burden almost intolerably heavy. So what could he do? We return to his story in Vignette 8.1 below.

> **Vignette 8.1: Teachers Engaging with Research: John's Story (Continued from 6.4)**
>
> John, an experienced language teacher, and a researcher in his own right, is excited by the thought of exploring his own classroom practices. He is puzzled by the fact that over the years he has met many students who spend a lot of time and money on language courses preparing them for study in a British university, but who seem unprepared to learn. He would like to develop his understanding of this issue, asking, *'Why do some students come on a course not prepared or willing to learn? Why do they even* **bother***?'*
>
> However, when invited to explore his question, he hesitates, saying, *'I'd be really interested, but I think it would turn into a hugely time-consuming thing'*.
>
> Although he is fascinated by the topic, and it is one that has bothered him for some time, he concludes that he would really rather not take it on. Worriedly, he asks, *'What have I got to produce?'* He has always understood 'research' to consist of collecting and analysing data, then writing up the results in a five-to-ten-thousand-word essay or article. This he finds very off-putting: he already has a heavy workload of teaching, marking, and administration, and adding traditional concepts of research to this burden would simply be too much.
>
> Could Exploratory Practice offer a way through the dilemma?
>
> On discovering that EP offers a 'low-key' way of investigating, which includes learners and learning, John brightens up: *'Oh I could do that. I'm quite happy to do that. I thought I was in for writing up a project'*. Later he explains, *'I didn't want to commit myself to a five thousand word essay'*. However, he still hesitates, saying after a fortnight of apparent inactivity, *'I haven't done anything about it. [...] I think I already know the answer to my question'*.
>
> Integrating research and pedagogy in this case means opening up the question for discussion in class, and with other teachers. As soon as this idea occurs, John brightens again: *'Maybe that would be a way to go about it. Discuss it with the students I've got and then maybe discuss it in a staff meeting briefly. That's a good idea. I might do that. Instead of coming up with a questionnaire, I'll just do that'*.

> Two months later, he has thoroughly enjoyed finding out about his students' puzzles (which focused on activating passive vocabulary), and he has also enhanced his own understanding of the situation: '*I did some verbal discussion with my class about that [...] and **they** felt that it was because of a whole lot of reasons: the student not wanting to come; being pushed by his parents [...] having to come because it was a status symbol [...], those type of factors. They didn't feel that those kinds of students came with good intentions and then changed their minds, they thought they came with... um disaffection*'.
>
> John shared his puzzle with the students in his class, and they shared theirs with him. In discussions, they gave him insights into the demands of parents, sponsors, and the learners themselves (he had suspected these already, but could only express his frustration at them). As he realised that the students in his classes shared his puzzlement, that they were serious about their learning, but they were also struggling with factors beyond their control, John's annoyance melted away.
>
> He did not (could not) solve the problem, but he could (and did) gain a profound understanding of his learners: their struggles, their perspectives.
>
> How could you incorporate EP into your practice? Would you take the same route as John? Or would you do something different?

John's story in Vignette 8.1 gives a flavour of what it means to implement EP. The process of moving from eliciting puzzles through investigations rooted in praxis to dissemination of locally relevant findings was absorbing and satisfying. But is this enough to illuminate 'researchable pedagogy' in EP? The next section will examine the question in more detail.

Exploratory Practice as Researchable Pedagogy

A question that is frequently asked is 'But what do you actually *do* in Exploratory Practice?' Since we have explicitly rejected the 'steps' (presented once in Allwright (1993), but abandoned shortly thereafter), it is difficult for those new to the framework to imagine what to do or how to proceed. But if interested practitioners begin to examine their own practices as learners and teachers, if they *start* with 'what you normally do' (whether that is information-gap activities, or dictation, or paragraph writing, or pair-work activities asking about likes and dislikes, or…), then the clouds begin to clear away. This lightening of the skies is clarified further if we look beyond learning and teaching towards research itself as a form of social practice. We see then the richness of practice that Iedema et al. (2013) have indicated, and the agency potential alluded to by Gieve & Miller (2006b).

By inviting the teachers and learners to puzzle about their language classes, opportunities for mutual development are enhanced. Rather than imposing extraneous research activities which would have taken time *away* from the business of the classes (teaching and learning), typical Potentially Exploitable Pedagogic Activities (known as PEPAs) are used as a means to investigate. Thus, several ends are achieved: (i) crucially, students are able to practise key language skills, (ii) teachers begin to understand the complexities of the challenges facing the learners in their classes, (iii) learners begin to realise that they need not always rely on their teachers for the answers – their experiences, their discoveries hold as much validity as those of their teachers, and (iv) both teachers and learners can experience enhanced interest, motivation, and enjoyment of their classes. This 'researchable pedagogy' is summarised as follows:

Learners and teachers
- set their own research agendas (puzzles)
- worked together to explore their agendas
- worked with (other) teachers to collect/generate data, analysed the data, and so on
- prepared presentations of their findings
- gave poster presentations to other learners and teachers
- practised key language skills (and academic skills) while conducting their research

However, the above example should *not* be taken as a series of 'steps' to be slavishly followed. This is merely an example taken from my own experience of trying out EP in my own (EAP) context, with my own colleagues. To try to apply it thoughtlessly to other situations would be to miss the point entirely. Instead, you might think about what *your* normal pedagogic practices are, and consider how you might use them appropriately as investigative tools in your context.

More detailed examples given in this and the following chapters demonstrate the wealth and variety of ways in which the EP principles can be interpreted. Of paramount importance is that the work is driven by the practice of those who are most closely affected. In other words, the research-practice emerges from and is intimately intertwined with the teaching/learning-practice.

So What Do You Actually *Do*?

Some of the most exciting work, and often the most *avant garde* thinking, has come out of the EP Rio de Janeiro group discussions and activities. Inspirational teachers, teacher educators, and learners, such as Walewska Braga, Inés Miller, Bebel A. Cunha, Mariana de Souza, and Felipe Guedes, are strongly featured in another book about EP (Allwright and Hanks 2009), with a whole section (Chapter 14) devoted to the EP Rio Group's own narrative, as well as stories and messages from Brazilian learners of English. In addition, in a chapter for an IATEFL Research SIG publication, (Miller et al. 2015), an extended example of EP in action is given. Moreover, Inés K. de Miller is currently in the process of preparing an edited book on EP experiences from the Rio de Janeiro EP group. Therefore, while recommending these publications to readers, we focus here on the experiences of practitioners from other parts of the world, with just two (very valuable) narratives from the EP group in Rio de Janeiro.

We begin with Caroline de Andrade, an English teacher in a secondary school in Rio de Janeiro. She used her normal pedagogic practice (PEPAs) as a way of exploring a question that deeply puzzled her.

Case Study 8.1: 'Why Are Some Students Not Interested in Learning English?': A Story of Developing Mutual Understandings

Caroline de Andrade works in a tough area of Rio, and the lives of some of her students may be particularly hard. Motivation to learn English is understandably low for these pupils, and some said they hated English. Like many teachers, Caroline is constantly busy, always rushing to meet targets and deal with student disaffection. Her struggles may be familiar to many secondary school language teachers around the world. But what she did about it was intriguing.

Caroline de Andrade

My name is Caroline Rodrigues de Andrade and I'm a novice teacher at a primary state school in a poor community of Rio de Janeiro. I was hired to teach kids from the first to the fifth year due to a project for the 2016 Olympic Games in the city. In 2013, I started attending Exploratory Practice group meetings while I was taking the specialisation course in English at PUC-Rio.

Exploratory Practice and Group 1403's Likes and Dislikes

I'm an English teacher at Escola Municipal República Dominicana, situated in a poor community called Serrinha, in Rio de Janeiro. In 2013, there was a specific group that called my attention – the fourth graders from 1403. They used to say that they hated me and that they hated English too. It was the strongest resistance that I had ever seen and the first group that even expressed their hatred for me, making me feel really uncomfortable with that. That's why I started asking myself what I was doing wrong and thinking I was unqualified to be there. My mind started contemplating some puzzles; then, it became necessary to do something beyond thinking.

While working with this group and the EP principles and ideas, a lot of questions sprang to my mind. Why are some students not interested in learning English? What do the students think about English? Is it fun? Do they like the material – the book, the topics, the songs? Do they see any connections with their reality? Do they really hate English? Do they really hate me? All of this claims for understanding – Why does this happen? How can we improve the quality of life in our classes? Let's understand and maybe change this uncomfortable situation!

In order to understand the behaviour of 1403 students towards me and their lack of interest in the English classes, I proposed a PEPA (Potentially Exploitable Pedagogical Activity) to the learners. This PEPA consisted of investigating their likes and dislikes not only concerning life in the classroom, but also concerning life outside it. This activity wasn't part of the syllabus, but they had seen this topic in the end of the previous year – so I decided to revise the vocabulary. It was divided into three steps: firstly, I wrote on the board 'I LIKE...' and students had to tell the class what their favourite things were: going to school, riding my bike, playing soccer, playing videogames, playing hide and seek, surfing on the internet, and playing with animals.

After that, I asked them to write it on a piece of paper or to draw. The same thing was done with their dislikes. They mentioned: school, studying, violence, *"bate bate"* (a popular toy amongst them which produces an irritating noise), my group teacher, indiscipline, and animal cruelty.

About life in the English classroom they said they liked when we played games, the book, the activities, the school, when they had to draw things, and that they also liked me! With reference to their dislikes they mentioned the fights, the mess made by the boys, when I called their attention, when I shouted at them, and when I used the microphone.

Their answers to this activity were really surprising: I had totally different assumptions about the possible answers. First of all, I used to think that the 1403 group didn't like the book. I always thought they considered it extremely difficult, because some students used to refuse to open it during my class and just threw it on the floor. After the PEPA, I realised that they thought the characters in the book were really interesting and fun. I also thought they didn't like me, as one of them had already told me and I had felt horrible about it.

The things they didn't like were totally the opposite of my ideas. I thought that they were used to all the fighting, the mess, and that they were ok with my microphone. Every time I entered the classroom, I observed paper, books, and things on the floor. Besides, there was always someone fighting verbally or physically. They had never mentioned that they didn't like the noisy environment.

We talked about students' answers and I asked them to draw them on a pieces of paper. Some students didn't want to draw so I helped them to write. When we finished drawing and writing, we decided to make a poster with the likes and dislikes and we put it on the classroom wall.

Some students had never seemed interested in what we were doing and it was extremely frustrating. During our PEPA I could notice that students were really surprised when I mentioned that I wanted to listen to their opinions about their lives and our classes. However, some students took a long time to understand my interest and refused to take part in the PEPA because they said it wasn't about our English book.

These same students used to throw their books on the ground and tear the pages and because of these actions I had the belief that the English book didn't appeal to them. I was terribly wrong! They said they liked it and the activities proposed. After their statement I asked, Why do you refuse to do the book activities? Why don't you take care of the material appropriately? One boy said, 'It's our way, teacher'.

> Understanding is sometimes responsible for changes and my decision was to take action for understanding rather than for change. My first step was to contemplate the situation I was living so I could understand it better. Some changes occurred while working for understanding but the most important change occurred in my own behaviour.
>
> Finally, I understood that learning also depends on the learners. One of the great achievements was the understanding that being part of the decision-making process motivates students. You can have the best materials and resources, but if you don't let your students have a voice in the classroom, you will never get them motivated.
>
> The group finally had a voice in the English class and they started to show some motivation. From September to the end of the year, students had the opportunity to vote for the most interesting topics on the book for us to work. They kept on misbehaving at the school, but observing the small changes, I started to feel more motivated too and the fifty minutes per week didn't seem like a burden anymore.

Caroline's story was not triggered by any form of academic study – she was not carrying out work for an MA dissertation or a PhD. She was simply puzzled by the difficult behaviour she encountered in her classes. As she began her investigations she was continuing to work in a situation that many teachers will recognise. Her EP work focused on action for understanding rather than action for change. As she listened to her students, she noticed how surprised they were that she wanted to listen to them. And as she began to understand their points of view, their troubles, their likes and dislikes, she realised they did *not* hate her (or the course book). In fact they rather liked her (and the book), but they were subject to forces beyond their control. Caroline describes the resulting sense of release from the emotional burden that she had been carrying. The transformation was in her (and their) understanding (and thinking); it was a transformation in *affect* rather than a transformation in circumstances or techniques.

Caroline's narrative links very closely with a story sent from the other side of the world. We begin to see how classrooms are linguistically and culturally complex, and why simple 'solutions' are inadequate; instead, deeper understandings (of the different perspectives, not only of language, language teaching, and learning, but also of culture) are required.

Case Study 8.2: 'Why Are My Learners Not Taking Responsibility for Their Learning?': A Story of Gaining Deeper Understandings

Working in very different circumstances, Yasmin Dar experienced a similar sense of puzzlement about her learners' motivation. The teaching of English to Speakers of Other Languages (ESOL) to adults, mainly refugees or asylum-seekers, has a beleaguered status in the UK, where cuts to funding and a lack of support positions ESOL as the 'poor relation' in language teaching. Students of ESOL face daily struggles in their new country of residence, grappling with financial problems, or registering with a doctor, and everything in-between. ESOL classes represent access to the language which will help them to negotiate these difficulties as they try to take their place in society. We might expect the learners to be highly motivated in such a situation, but their behaviour did not seem to bear this out. Yasmin takes up the tale as she writes about her first experience of EP, investigating with her learners.

> **Yasmin Dar**
>
> Yasmin Dar teaches English for Academic Purposes (EAP) at the English Language Teaching Unit (ELTU), University of Leicester, UK. She has presented and published her Exploratory Practice and EAP classroom case studies at IATEFL, BALEAP, and International Teachers' Research conferences. Yasmin is interested in integrating language teaching and learning with ethical classroom research.

> **My Context**
>
> I carried out my research in 2008 with six adult learners (aged 25–50) who enrolled onto an ESOL course in the academic year 2007/08. The students were from India, Iran, Somalia, and Egypt. They had decided to settle in the UK due to the economic and political problems in their own countries. The ESOL course lasted one academic year and the students were expected to attend two classes a week which were two hours per session. It was a pre-intermediate level ESOL course held in a community centre in Leicester. The learners in my classroom had expressed the following motives for enrolling on the course: to find employment in the UK, and to communicate (speaking,

listening, reading, writing) confidently with professionals face to face and on the telephone (e.g. their young children's teachers, their local doctor, or General Practitioner). By spring, the learners and I had become comfortable with each other, and during that time I was puzzled by the following question: *Why are my learners not taking responsibility for their learning?*

Why I was interested in Exploratory Practice

I wasn't sure if there was a framework that would suit my priorities of doing classroom research that was meaningful for me and my learners, as well as meeting the criteria for my MA dissertation. I knew that I didn't want to use an action research framework where I had to think of a problem and then carry out a cyclical action research project to find a solution. So, after making my classroom research priorities clear to my MA supervisor Simon Gieve, he introduced me to the Exploratory Practice framework (Allwright 2003, 2005a).

How I used the Exploratory Practice framework in my classroom

I used normal classroom activities to collect data about how much English my students used at home to practise for their speaking exam. Below are the questions that I had prepared for the classroom pair-work activity. The learners were instructed to answer the questions individually before turning to their pair-work partner to carry out a 'questions and answers' role play and to record their partner's answers.

Pair-work activity: Practising English for your speaking exam
The questions were as follows:

1. Is it important for you to pass your speaking exam? Yes/No
2. How do you feel about your speaking exam? Ok/Not ok
3. Does your teacher tell you to practise at home for your speaking exam? Yes/No
4. Do you practise speaking English at home?
5. Do you think practising in the classroom is enough to pass your exam? Yes/No

While they were engaged in this activity, I was able to monitor the class for common language errors which would be dealt with in an error-correction slot towards the end of the session.

Mismatch of expectations

After monitoring the responses in the pair-work activity above, I was surprised to hear my students tell each other that they did not practise English at home. I was able to exploit this common theme from their pair-work activity by asking the follow-up discussion question 'Why do you like to learn English in class and dislike learning English at home?' This question was based on the class topic 'Likes and Dislikes'. This particular example clearly demonstrates how I could easily combine collecting data for my research without reducing the normal teaching and learning activities in my classroom.

Here are two of the students' responses to question 4:

Shlen: 'My husband, he does not like English for me to speak at home. He is strict as well with my daughter. He says speak English at school and at work but not inside home.'

Adir: 'My children laugh at me if I try to speak with them in English. They say: "Mum you can't speak good English" and keep laughing at me every-time, so that is why I don't talk in English at home.'

Their responses gave me a valuable insight into what was happening in their lives outside the classroom and how their life at home had an impact on their progress in the classroom. After hearing the students' group discussion, I changed my attitude from feeling slightly impatient at times when they keep making the same errors to feeling empathy with their individual situations.

Thus, I had reached a deeper understanding about this particular group of students. The principles of Exploratory Practice provided me with a framework to reach an understanding that I may not have reached, for example, by simply asking my students direct questions at the beginning of a class.

Follow-up

I decided not to take this issue any further in this class; my students were not looking for a solution related to their problems at home and I didn't want to place an extra burden on them. Instead, I adjusted my expectations because my students needed me to understand their daily life outside the classroom. I felt humbled and satisfied with reaching a better understanding and the principles of EP allowed me to stop at this point. However, my own involvement in EP did not stop there.

I think it is refreshing and empowering that EP does not promote or prioritise a 'problem' and 'solution' focus to classroom research. Instead, it advises practitioners to consider classroom research as an 'ongoing' project, and I was able to explore the general issue of learner autonomy when I started teaching in an English language unit in a university context. I noticed that in my pre-sessional General English class of international students, only a few would complete their homework. Thus, I was curious to find out about their reasons by carrying out another Exploratory Practice case study to explore the re-occurring theme that had originally emerged from teaching ESOL learners.

Yasmin shows how a very simple, and crucially, a *pedagogic,* activity, which was designed to help learners practise their speaking skills for an upcoming examination, was adopted to give air-time to learners' opinions. Instead of trying to solve a problem (student commitment to homework), Yasmin gained immeasurably as she began to comprehend the complexity of the daily struggles her students faced. As she says, it was her own attitude that changed as a result of this new comprehension. And it led her to further questioning in other areas of her work-life. She developed her interest in learner autonomy in other situations as well as ESOL. For example, she has gone on to explore other puzzles in her EAP classes, and publish accounts of her explorations (Dar 2012, 2015). As she says, 'Exploratory Practice appeals to me because my personal priority is to use a research framework that allows me the opportunity to explore "why"' (Dar 2012: 9).

We now fly from Brazil and the UK to another part of the world: Japan. Darren Elliott, like Yasmin and Caroline, was focusing on *understanding* what was going on in his classroom.

Case Study 8.3: 'Why Do the Students Seem Reluctant to Take Responsibility for Themselves?': A Story of Stepping Back for Understanding

Working in a very different context – teaching undergraduate students at a university in Japan – Darren Elliott had a question about his learners. Like Caroline and Yasmin above, Darren also examines the notion of learner autonomy.

He investigates the possibilities afforded once the teacher steps back from the role of 'motivator-knower-chivvier'. Darren provides an account of his 'experiment' with a group of teenagers learning English at undergraduate level. There wasn't a serious *problem*: his students seem comfortably well-off. They were not saying they 'hated' English, and they were making reasonable, if not spectacular, progress. So this is not a story of a struggle to survive, but rather an attitude of 'inquiry as stance' (Cochran-Smith and Lytle 2009). His second puzzle may seem very familiar for language teachers in all sorts of contexts, though. In puzzling deeply, and not leaping to conclusions or accepting initial perceptions, Darren was pushing the envelope, challenging complacency, as he researched his context.

Darren Elliott

Sugiyama Jogakuen University, Nagoya, Japan

Darren Elliott (MA ELT, DELTA) has taught at universities in the UK and Japan and currently teaches at Sugiyama Jogakuen University in Nagoya, Japan. He is also a freelance teacher trainer. He has published and presented on learner autonomy, teacher development, and reflective practice, particularly guided by internet technologies. His current research interests are the connection between metaphors for learning and propensity for learner autonomy, and language learners' exploration of online digital video genres.

A Class with No Teacher

The Puzzle

At the heart of Exploratory Practice is 'the puzzle'. Here was mine. A class of intelligent young students, many of whom had lived overseas and spoke English rather well. Smart, engaging, likeable, and with good class chemistry, but perhaps a little too relaxed. The class met twice a week and worked on a combination of textbook activity and freer project work. It wasn't that they were performing poorly – they were doing everything I asked of them – I just felt that they could do more.

At the time I saw this as a problem, but my attempts to address the situation as a teacher addressing a problem were ineffective. I'd tried the carrot, and I'd tried the stick, but the students were happy to continue doing enough to get by without really pushing themselves to the limit.

Re-framing the problem as a set of puzzles generated two key questions:

1. *Why do the students seem reluctant to take responsibility for themselves?*
2. *Why do students slip into Japanese so easily when they are capable of staying in English for the length of the lesson?*

I didn't feel that asking these questions directly would elicit useful answers. Perhaps the students didn't really know themselves. I decided to take a different approach by removing one important element from the class to see what would happen.

I started the class at the usual time by projecting this message on the screen at the front of the room:

Today, you are going to take responsibility for your own learning. I am not in charge of today's class. We will work on pages 38–44 of the textbook. The CD and the CD player are at the back of the room if you want to use them. Please make your own groups, and decide which parts of the book you want to study. And how you want to study them.
Of course, you will use English to do this.
Thank You.

At first, everyone looked a little surprised, but it didn't take long before the students formed groups of four... and within ten minutes, everybody was talking in English comfortably.

At 9:32 the first group moved to the back of the class and used the CD player to check their answers in the pronunciation section. It seemed that each group was working through the book exercises in order, and also following the instructions in the book directly. Why was that?

By 9:40 there was a really nice buzz.

By 9:55, most students were on to the discussion section, and some started listening to the CD (a radio interview from NPR) to take notes and prepare for a case study activity. This was one of the biggest challenges for me – one group had difficulty finding the right track on the CD, but rather than doing it for them, I let them do it themselves. It's hard to let go as a teacher!

By 10:30, students were talking actively about the topic, although I tried not to walk around as much as usual, to remove myself as a presence from the class.

At 10:35, I projected this message onto the screen:

How did you feel at the start of the class?
Did you speak more or less English than usual today? Why?
Did your group have a particular style?
How did you choose what and how to do, and when to move to the next part?
Would you like to study this way more often?
What were the best and worst things about today's class? Why?
Do you need a teacher?

To finish the class, I showed this message. I didn't say anything at all – not a single word – all class.

Please leave your homework and your attendance card on my desk.

Please do page 46, exercise II (vocabulary) before Friday's class. Visit the class blog, too. I will write more about today's lesson and I would like to read your comments.
In Friday's class, I will probably talk to you again.

The Reflection
Exploratory Practice 'is best done as a social enterprise' (Allwright and Hanks 2009, p. 182). In this case I didn't make my intentions clear to the students, nor did I negotiate the puzzles or the method of research. This made cooperation with the students in the reflection stage essential; to some degree, I had compromised the students' trust by imposing this research upon them, and that needed to be addressed. I wrote a letter of explanation to the students on our class blog, and invited comments. We discussed the class together the following week. There were a number of very interesting outcomes that emerged from the students' feedback.

1. *A particular result may not mean what you think it means*

At the time of this experiment, I was a fairly active blogger. I posted about the lesson and received a number of comments from other teachers. The general consensus, from a professional perspective, was that the end result (constant discussion in L1) sprang from the joy of freedom, the taking up of responsibility and other positive emotions. But actually, according to the students, they were terrified:

"We actually thought that you were angry at us and abandoned us because we use too much Japanese in class."

"I took it for granted that you were angry and you didn't want to give our class."

Despite the cause being the negative emotion of fear, the result was very positive.

"To do task without your help was difficult for me. However, I were able to hear much English. And I could speak more in English than usual!"

"...if we have no teachers, we must think how we should study. However, this situation is very important to us too I think. Actually we try to look for the answer more harder than usual. I spoke in English more. Moreover I heared (sic) more opinions of them than usual. Though we had much difficulties, it was very interesting to me."

When teaching teenagers we do sometimes need to wield a big stick. However, I don't want this to be the dominant motivating force in my classroom, which leads us onto our next point.

2. *Although mystery can be effective, we must ultimately provide transparency*

When the students realised what I was trying to do, they were very happy. This was a vital step – revealing the mystery.

> "*But I read your comment, you tried to see our class from all kinds of directions.*"
>
> "*After reading this article, I noticed you care about us more than I expected. So I'm happy that you are our teacher!*"
>
> "*We were so puzzled! Me, K., M. and M. were discussing about 'what's happening!' through out the whole class. K. and I were even talking about it the rest of the day!*"

So had I left the class cold, with no feedback or no discussion of what had happened, the positives of confusion might have caused longer-term damage to the rapport we have been building. I kept the next class very light, and the students kept up their good habits from the previous class.

3. *Perceived teacher beliefs do not always reflect actual classroom practice*

If you had asked me before this class if I believed in learner autonomy and a hands-off teaching approach, I would have given you an emphatic yes. But what I was actually doing in the class belied this. It was only by removing myself completely from the lesson that I could see how students had been relying on me to prompt them, feed them, and cajole them into using the language. Looking back at my class notes from the time, it seemed to have an effect on my teaching practice. I stepped back, and noted that my students surprised me by speaking fluently in English for longer than I had expected.

Had I been unwittingly restricting learner autonomy by doing too much, by jumping in too soon, by shutting down an activity simply because I was ready to go on to the next one?

This experiment wasn't conceived as Exploratory Practice, just an attempt by a working teacher to break a cycle and shake things up. The fact that it was initiated by the teacher-researcher without consultation with the students is also slightly counter to the spirit of EP. But the main beneficiaries of what we discovered, together, were those who had invested in the research. Teacher and students collaborated to answer the teacher's puzzle, and our class became better.

NB: *This text is adapted from two blog posts written by the author at the time. They can be accessed at:*
http://www.livesofteachers.com/2010/05/25/a-class-with-no-teacher/
http://www.livesofteachers.com/2010/06/04/a-class-with-no-teacher-part-two-feedback-and-reflection/

This case study took place over just three sessions (the lesson that Darren describes, followed by a blog post, student comments, and the next 'light' lesson) – it would be fascinating to find out what happened over a longer period. And indeed, in Chapter 9 we shall see EP taking place over a much longer timespan.

Darren raises an interesting question about the EP principles. If EP advocates using 'normal pedagogic tools' to investigate what puzzles us, what happens when we try out something not-normal (eg teacher refusing to talk for the entire lesson)? Arguably this means it is not EP, and yet in Darren's story there are so many elements of the EP principles in evidence: taking action for understanding, working collaboratively (later on, if not at first), working for mutual development. So are we to say that Darren did not engage in EP? That seems unnecessarily restrictive.

Like many others in EP, Darren had rejected the ubiquitous 'problem-to-solution' approach, in an attempt to take action for understanding. His dramatic experiment shook up the class, and although the students reported themselves startled at first, once they had the opportunity to read Darren's explanation on their blog, they began to develop their own understandings about their language class. This dialogic exchange, which established the teacher and learners as real people in a classroom, who experience puzzled questions and can communicate with each other, with agency, in a variety of ways, is rich in possibilities, and very much within the scope of EP.

Case Study 8.4: 'Why Do My Students Want Lectures While I Want Discussion?' – A Story of Collegiality

Thus far, we have looked at case studies situated in the field of *English* language teaching (ELT). But is EP limited to just ELT? Cori Crane's story from the USA shows us that it is just as applicable in the field of teaching German as a foreign language.

Cori Crane provides two narratives from her work in the USA. The first story she sent shows teachers of German working together with colleagues and learners to share what puzzles them about their practice (the second story appears in Chapter 10). Cori was particularly interested in the contrast between her learner-centred approach to teaching and the demands of her learners, who wanted a more lecture-based format (see also Crane 2015). Sharing her puzzlement with colleagues led to a sense of warmth and a realisation that she was not alone; sharing her question with her students gave her an insight into their concerns and desires.

Cori Crane, Ph.D.

University of Texas at Austin

Cori Crane is an assistant professor in the Department of Germanic Studies at the University of Texas at Austin, where she teaches German, applied linguistics, and foreign language pedagogy and coordinates the lower-division undergraduate German programme. She received her PhD in German from Georgetown University. Before coming to UT-Austin in 2012, she served as the German Language Programme Director at the University of Illinois at Urbana-Champaign. Her scholarly interests relate to understanding and improving learning and teaching in the classroom and include foreign language writing and systemic functional linguistics, postsecondary curriculum and programme development, language teacher education (particularly the training of graduate student instructors), and reflective teaching and learning.

Experiences Working with Exploratory Practice in Language Programmes

I first discovered Exploratory Practice (EP) in 2006 when I was searching for something that could help explain how collaboration and collegiality work to strengthen understanding and innovation in foreign language curricula. As a language programme coordinator responsible for lower-division German courses at a large state university in the USA, I regularly saw how changes in our curriculum, such as developing new course units or introducing new materials, evolved through informal discussions with teachers about student learning, mid-semester student surveys, and professional development experiences.

This work would not have been possible without the teachers being able to identify, reflect on, and voice their thoughts on our programme's specific needs. What we were doing was meaningful and important to us as instructors, though the conversations did not fit into traditional definitions of action research. After all, we were not collecting data for rigorous analysis and we were not responding to any one discernable 'problem' that needed attention. As I began reading more about EP (with Dick Allwright's (2005a) *Modern Language Journal* article as my introduction), I was delighted to find a framework that resonated with the knowledge construction process I felt was happening in our programme, one that prioritised *quality of life* as a central concern for teacher reflection and, importantly, involved learners in this process of understanding.

Working towards Understanding across Multiple Language Programmes

It took a few years following my initial reading into EP before I started to actually practise the guidelines in my own teaching. In spring 2010, I worked with three language programme directors representing Japanese, Korean, and Swahili to develop a reflective teaching group that could support more advanced graduate student instructors who were no longer taking pedagogy coursework but desired continued professional development. Over two months, our small group of seven teachers (three graduate student-teachers ended up joining us) met for two-hour periods once every two weeks to talk about our puzzles.

Our first meeting focused on developing familiarity with two key readings (Allwright 2003, 2005a) with the goal of exploring EP's main tenets and brainstorming ways to go about developing our own specific puzzles. Each group member came to subsequent meetings with short written accounts of what we were exploring and where our puzzling was taking us.

Looking back, it is difficult to put into words how meaningful this group was to me in my professional development at the time. While we were initially conceptualised as a support structure for graduate student-teachers, it became clear to us coordinators how much *we* were benefiting as teachers through participation in this EP group. Our puzzles, all localised within classrooms or language programmes, reflected our own specific work contexts – from teaching small classes to dealing with unmotivated students to wanting to expand our curricula.

My own puzzle in this group stemmed from a graduate course on second language writing that I was teaching at the time and which, in its first run-through, simultaneously excited and terrified me. Though this course was not about teaching language, I felt EP's guidelines were broad and flexible enough for me to consider their application in this seminar. As I began puzzling about my course, a central concern emerged for me: finding the right balance between my second language pedagogy training in learner-centred approaches, which relied heavily on learner participation and open discussion, and a growing sense that my students wanted more input and lecture from me in seminar.

Trying to deal with this conundrum, I posed the following question for myself: 'How can I foster independent learning while giving students enough background to support their own developing knowledge about

> the subject matter?' In researching my puzzle, I talked informally with two colleagues about their experiences over the years in teaching graduate seminars. One colleague confided that she had been struggling with this very same question for over ten years of graduate teaching. How comforting it was to hear that more seasoned faculty members were having similar concerns!
>
> A second colleague revealed that he had changed his approach from an almost exclusively open-discussion format to increasingly more structured seminars over the years – a story that initially surprised and challenged my own thinking about teaching, yet made me consider for the first time how a teaching philosophy on graduate education could evolve.
>
> In addition to these conversations, I looked to my students' final reflective journal assignments for guidance on my puzzle. Drawing on an end-of-semester writing exercise from one of my own favourite seminars as a graduate student, I had asked students in the course to write up a synthesis of the major themes and insights that came up over the semester for them.
>
> This was not an assignment that I had asked them to do *because* of EP, as the essay was on the syllabus well before our reflective teaching support group began meeting that spring. But now with the EP framework, I began to re-imagine the assignment as a tool for understanding the students' perspectives on my puzzle. In particular, their written reflections and our final class conversation illuminated for me what the class had taken away from the seminar and how they were processing the material and in-class discussions. In the end, looking to my students' work through the EP lens allowed me to see how central student understanding was to my question about how much support to give graduate students in learning and engaging with the content material.
>
> But more than my own puzzle exploration, working with six other teachers who cared so much about their teaching gave me renewed energy in the classroom. Towards the end of our two-month group, I noticed how aligned many of our discussions were, despite our very different puzzle topics. Our conversations were full of new ideas and book suggestions, empathetic sentiments, and much laughter as we gave ourselves space and permission to be honest about our fears and hopes as teachers, listening to each other and giving each other constructive feedback along the way. I always came away from our sessions feeling that something quite magical had happened as each conversation seemed to come back to exploring important, core values that we shared as teachers.

In this case study, Cori highlights the importance of collegiality (colleagues sharing experiences and supporting one another) as well as the need to understand learners' wants, needs, and desires. She did not change anything – she used what she normally used (in this case a written assignment), but using the EP framework as a lens for her analysis. In uncovering her students' beliefs, and learning about what they valued, she developed a keen awareness of their needs. In sharing puzzlement, and explorations with other teachers, Cori describes a 'magical' sense. We see here the importance of compassion and empathy in language teaching/learning. The positive emotional atmosphere clearly contributed to the boost in energy she describes. Is this the 'Quality of Life' principle in action?

Summary

The experiences conveyed in these narratives echo the experience of the teachers in Wu (2002, 2004, 2006) who, he tells us, had to find new ways of being in the classroom, new identities, and new interpretations of their 'life-world' as a consequence of the innovation of EP in their curriculum. The teachers in Pinto da Silva's (2001) study also struggled with conflicting identities, belief structures, and the contrast this made with their daily practice in the classroom. Beginning EP, indeed perhaps any form of practitioner research, demands a re-conceptualisation of the world of classroom language learning, and the roles, functions, and relationships of teachers and learners within. EP promotes a focus on quality of life and developing understandings in the language classroom (Allwright 2008, 2015).

From the stories in this chapter, we can see that Quality of Life comes from understanding the situation better, from asking questions that are relevant, and from sharing lived experiences. Understanding comes from daring to question, and from being courageous enough to ask the students themselves for their opinions. In doing so, the learning was still prioritised, but an added benefit was an understanding of the human condition in education. Practitioners gained glimmers of understanding in potentially demoralising situations. In their very different contexts, they shared an attitude of puzzled enquiry, and the effects of *affect* on their daily lives are quite startling.

Recommended Readings

Dar, Y. (2012) Exploratory Practice: Investigating my own classroom pedagogy. *ELT Research, 26,* pp. 8–10. An inspiring account of how 'normal pedagogic practices' can be utilised in an ESOL classroom. This article has also been used as a springboard for discussion in the IATEFL ReSIG discussion group, inspiring vigorous and sometimes heated debate from practitioners (researchers, teachers, learners) around the world.

Hanks, J. (2015a) 'Education is not just teaching': Learner thoughts on Exploratory Practice. *ELT Journal* 69(2) 'Editor's Choice April 2015' pp. 117–128. This article discusses EP as experienced by a group of learners in a British university. It conveys their thoughts as they encountered EP for the first time in EAP and asks what can we learn from them. Through their posters, writing, and interviews, the learners highlight EP's potential for mutual development, and the mutual respect that results from working together to develop understandings.

Miller, I.K., Côrtes, T.C.R., Oliveira, A.F.A., & Braga, W.G. (2015). Exploratory practice in initial teacher education: Working collaboratively for understandings. In D. Bullock & R. Smith (Eds.), *Teachers research!* pp. 65–71. Canterbury: IATEFL. This chapter is of particular interest, not least because it is a joint production, very much in keeping with EP principles of collegiality. It also provides a thought-provoking analysis of the posters that were produced as part of the explorations.

9

Collegial Working

Introduction

This chapter focuses particularly on collegiality, with a particular emphasis on Exploratory Practice (EP), and language education more generally, as a social practice. The stories presented here show the making visible (Iedema et al. 2013) of our everyday understandings, of working together to gain understandings from our practice as language teachers, language learners, and learners as teachers. As the Rio de Janeiro group indicate, one of the major issues we face in classrooms is the need to be seen as humanised professionals. But in order to do this, we need to be willing to make ourselves vulnerable. And this requires trust. So how can we generate such trust in our classrooms?

> **Quote 9.1: The Rio de Janeiro EP Group on Seeing a Humanised Professional**
> When students see their teacher's questions and puzzles, they see a humanised professional. When students can understand a teacher better, they see a chance to open up *their* inner selves as well. As teachers and students gain

> possibilities for constructing mutual understandings about the classroom environment, practitioners – students *and* teachers – show growth in their intellectual and critical perspectives.
> (The Rio de Janeiro EP Group, in Allwright and Hanks 2009: 226)

One place where trust is urgently needed, but sometimes in short supply, is in the field of teaching/learning English for Academic Purposes (EAP). This chapter therefore considers a number of case studies and vignettes situated in EAP. They present an invitation: not only to consider the stories that they tell, but also to begin your own process of puzzling. What questions do these stories raise for you?

Is Exploratory Practice Transplantable to/in Other Contexts?

Having worked in the EP arena for some time, and having also co-authored a book on the subject with Dick Allwright, I knew that EP could take place in all sorts of situations. So, back in 2006, it seemed odd to me that EP was *not* happening in my own context of teaching EAP in the UK. I was puzzled: Why wasn't EP taking off in EAP in the UK? Vignette 9.1 tells my story of exploring this puzzle.

> **Vignette 9.1: A Teacher Attempts EP in EAP: Judith's Story**
>
> In the early 2000s, despite interest internationally, no one seemed to be doing EP in an EAP context in the UK. This puzzled me. I wondered: *'Why don't we do EP in EAP here?'*... And then *'What happens if we try EP in my context?'*
>
> I had worked in EAP since 1999, and had noticed that it is often seen as goal-oriented, intense, and rather dry. The focus is on preparing students for their academic careers in universities, with a heavy emphasis on academic writing, listening to lectures and taking notes, group work, and oral presentations. I wondered, *'How would the principles of EP (which promote understanding over problem-solving, and which might be seen as antithetical to the very intense atmosphere of a pre-sessional course) stand up in this 'hot-house' atmosphere?'.*

> To begin with, I was worried that the goal-oriented nature of EAP would run counter to the principles of EP, or at least present some sizeable challenges. To my surprise, though, the teachers were overwhelmingly enthusiastic about EP, particularly after several weeks of working with their students to investigate what puzzled them. What seemed most salient was the sense that the work they were doing was *relevant* to the needs of their students, that it did not take valuable time away from their studies. Rather, they said; EP enhanced the work that they were already doing by including students in the questioning, puzzling, researching process. And the students themselves seemed delighted to have been asked to take part.
>
> We utilised our normal EAP practices (for example, skills development such as students listening to lectures and taking notes, or students designing and administering questionnaires and interview schedules, and delivering oral presentations) as tools to investigate whatever it was that puzzled us. As we did so, two things became apparent: (i) individuals discovered they were not alone in their puzzled arena; (ii) we developed a heightened respect for colleagues (whether learners or teachers) and what we could learn from one another.
>
> This process of 'doing-being' EP led to an enhanced quality of life in our classrooms, common rooms, and teachers' rooms. Far from the frustrations and daily grind of our usual EAP work, we experienced a lightening of spirit and a drive to explore our puzzlement together that was rare indeed.
>
> All the support that was needed was the space and permission to try out EP for ourselves. Could this work for others?

Vignette 9.1 suggests that if we are willing and able to create a classroom based on trust, where learners are taken seriously, as are teachers, where the work is relevant to the participants, and where we can be curious, we all stand to gain. This stance resonates with Candlin and Crichton's position.

> **Quote 9.2: Candlin and Crichton on Mutual Trust**
>
> ... language learning and teaching, like language use, is always a social, cultural and personal act. It is governed by varying degrees of mutual Trust where teachers and learners can feel freer to make communicative choices driven by their own individual investments of understanding, energy, motivation and commitment.
>
> (2013a: 80)

A common theme that emerges when puzzles are elicited and shared is the sense of isolation that practitioners feel. Some puzzles are deeply personal to the participants, and they believe, at least to begin with, that they are alone in suffering these doubts. Many participants appear to believe their questions are unique to themselves, and of no interest to others. Others may be unsure of the consequences of making such questions public: Would they be exposed to ridicule if they admitted to an imperfect understanding? This is reminiscent of the worries expressed by the learners in Cherchalli's doctoral study: 'Sometimes I feel like asking the teacher a question, but just realising that perhaps the rest of the class understand, I hesitate' (Cherchalli 1988, cited in Allwright and Hanks 2009, p275). But when they share them with others, they find that someone else has been worrying about just the same issue, or pondering the same theme. Vignette 9.2 illustrates this point, as we follow John's story.

Vignette 9.2: John's Story *(Continued from Vignettes 6.4 and 8.1)*
John was quietly confident as he started EP with his students, even though he, like them, had never heard of it before. His focus remained on the pedagogic value of EP, as he described the excitement they, and he, experienced in starting off: *'Everybody seemed engaged. A real buzz'.*

John invited the learners to investigate what puzzled them about language learning. As he conducted a pyramid discussion (moving from pairs to small groups to large groups) sharing their puzzled questions, he encountered a surprise: *'They all, independently, wanted to investigate the same theme: "Why do we struggle to use new vocabulary, even when we know the words?"'.*

John then invited his students to investigate their puzzles, and they leapt at the chance. In class, they used the same EAP teaching techniques as normal, and followed the syllabus of the course: students did a mini-project, just as usual; they attended 'Language Development' classes as usual. But the focus of these classes had shifted from looking at, say, grammar or vocabulary points, to investigating the learners' puzzles.

As part of a standard project activity, the learners collected data (via interviews, questionnaires, and library and internet searches) and analysed their data in preparation for their poster presentations with and to the whole cohort. John takes up the tale: *'they've been analysing and collecting the data. And they're really enjoying it. To the extent where when I asked them to close everything down and sit in their seats, they didn't come! They were so involved, I don't think they registered that I'd asked them [to stop]'.*

> Far from feeling annoyed at being ignored, he ended the session by telling them, *'We'll finish now but if you want to stay in the classroom and continue, you can, just lock up when you've finished'*.
> At the end of the 10 weeks, John reflected on the EP work he had been doing with his students. He was enthusiastic in his endorsement of the approach: *'It is entirely relevant to what they're going to be doing. [...] As teachers, we are constantly looking for authentic materials, and EP gives the students their own authentic materials'*.

Once they begin to talk with students and colleagues, teachers and learners report a surprised realisation that others, too, have been puzzling about the same issue. However, it is only through sharing their puzzles with others that they find the question is common to more than one person. The relief at discovering that many others were not only interested in their puzzles and take them seriously, but are also grappling with similar questions is palpable. A student from the same course as John commented on EP:

Gina: *That is the first time I tried to understand my difficulties in studying English. And I found that not only me, but a lot of interviewees and classmates want to know the answers. They ask me 'How about the others' answers?' [...] Because that's our puzzlement!*

Gina's contribution at this point raises an important question: What about the learners?

What Do Learners Think About It?

In 2009, Dick Allwright and I argued strongly for the inclusion of learners as 'key developing practitioners' (Allwright and Hanks 2009) who not only have meaningful experiences, but can actually help with developing the understandings of everyone. Many of the stories in this book include not only teachers but also learners, and all those other roles and identities that we perform at different times. Any individual is flexible enough to incorporate different identities (eg a teacher may at times be learning, a learner may teach the teacher, and so on). Thus the EP classroom is a microcosm which accommodates multiple perspectives, many identities, and even extends beyond the classroom to include those invisible 'ghosts' who exert their influence, and can sometimes, in turn, be influenced. This multifaceted, multi-levelled experience is captured by Rowland (2011).

> **Quote 9.3: Rowland on the Importance of Including Learners in Research**
>
> ... my learners related their own learning experiences to literature research findings in a number of insightful ways [...]. Our research together certainly revealed a number of valuable themes concerning my learners' perspectives on learning English. From their spirited defence of their personal knowledge about language learning, to their highlighting of 'life before work' as an important principle of learning, my students certainly provided me with some understanding of what was really important to them. In a way they took me into their individual learning lives with their comments and opinions, and I found that although we, teachers, and researchers, might feel that we are closely connected to these lives every day by virtue of our occupational proximity to learners and learning, it is often the case that, in trying merely to provide broad language learning strategies to our very individual and life-sensitive learners, we are in fact drifting further and further away from them.
>
> (2011: 265)

Several students on a 10-week pre-sessional course learning EAP were particularly helpful in drawing attention to the potential EP holds for developing understandings by working together. We met Meow (a Thai student) and Cheer (a Japanese student) in Chapter 6; both students were in the UK preparing for a Masters degree in healthcare. Now we return to their story.

> **Vignette 9.3: Struggling with Speaking: Meow and Cheer's Story**
> *(Continued from Vignette 6.3)*
>
> Meow and Cheer asked, *Why can't I speak English, even after many years of study?* Their delight in discovering another person who shared this perplexity was palpable, and they worked together to find out more about it. However, as they continued their investigations it became clear that the reasons for their difficulties were quite different.

> Meow highlighted the language side, explaining that in the past she had never investigated her own language learning processes: '... *we just think "oh we have the weak point" but we never want to, er never wanted to investigate them'*. From her investigations (involving interviews and questionnaires with other learners and teachers) Meow realised that she had never engaged her own thinking when speaking English, and as a result began paying attention to her own grammar and pronunciation as she spoke: *'Oh yeah, it help my puzzle. I tried to speak more and speaking with [undecipherable] and now I speak and I thinking when I speak "Oh did I do some grammar mistake when I speaking?" Because act-... normally, I speak without thinking of grammar, so now I ... [am] thinking about grammar before I speak'*.
>
> Interestingly, despite working closely with Meow in the same group, Cheer came to a very different understanding. She identified her own personality (quite quiet, withdrawn, shy, private) as a key factor: *'... personality, my personal problem, and environment also'*.
>
> Meow and Cheer offer two perspectives on the same story. Cheer was disappointed at what she perceived as a failure to improve significantly (even though I could hear a marked increase in clarity and fluency of speech in the recordings of the interviews). She blamed her personality and returned to the desire for an 'answer' to her problems with speaking several times. Meow on the other hand was uniformly positive: she attributed her difficulties to a lack of attention to monitoring for grammatical or phonological accuracy when speaking, and in later interviews can clearly be heard self-correcting. This did not 'solve the problem', but she gained insights into what she needed to do to develop as an independent and responsible learner.
>
> Do you think learners in your classes would respond in similar/different ways?
> What about asking them?

It is worth stating again that these examples are not presented as templates to be copied, or as generalisable texts. The questions they ask and the understandings they convey are locally situated, with relevance to the people involved. Thus, it would do no good for the teacher to simply 'tell' Cheer to buck up and find excuses to talk more, or to 'tell' Meow to monitor her spoken output for accuracy. They needed to explore independently and find this out for themselves. At the same time, they needed to develop trust in their own strategies for coping.

Lynne (a student from China), working in a different group on the same course, was also intrigued by difficulties with speaking. Like Meow and Cheer, she was from a different linguistic and cultural background, but had chosen to study in the UK, and was having to adjust to British academic culture. Although she had been learning English for some time, and, like the other students, had achieved a certain score on International English Language Testing System (IELTS) which allowed her to enter the country, and the course, she was shocked at how difficult it was to understand/make herself understood in this new situation.

> **Vignette 9.4: Finding Out for Ourselves: Lynne's Story**
>
> Lynne had cited speaking, specifically issues with vocabulary and pronunciation, as something that bothered her. She framed her puzzle as *'Why I have accent and how should I improve pronunciation?'*. She had identified pronunciation and accent as factors impeding her communication with others and wanted to investigate: *'when I have first class when I ask some questions to the, the teacher, they don't understand what I said, so I think maybe I have an accent, yeah'*. First she thought of asking her teachers for help with pronunciation, but she later broadened her investigations to gather information from course-mates too.
>
> As she did so, she began to notice a number of different ways of pronouncing English: *'And maybe different countries' people have different pronunciation and I could hear other countries' pronunciation mistakes and I could ask them a lot of questions about pronunciation and they gave me answers. I think it is very useful'*.
>
> Through her investigations, Lynne noted that she and her classmates had not only engaged with the language but also with the learning process: *'If just in class the teacher said something and we just accept some answer, I think it's easy to forget it…*
>
> *I think every student take part in this process and we found the answer by ourselves'*.

The cultural and intercultural issues that Cheer, Lynne, and Meow were dealing with are significant. As they cast and re-cast themselves in ways that had been set up for them (ie as students aspiring to be accepted into the community of practice of British academia), we need also to be aware of how students' questions and answers can be sources of puzzlement for us all. Such a process takes Wingate's (2015) call for an inclusive, and critical, model of academic literacy even further by including students alongside lecturers, teachers, and literacy experts, as people able to critique and engage in/with the process of 'ideological becoming' (Bakhtin 1986).

Another student on the same course, also encountering EP for the first time, was Gina (from Taiwan). As we saw earlier, she was surprised to find that others were also struggling with studying English – had she assumed that everyone else was fine, and she was the only one?

> **Vignette 9.5: The Spirit of Exploratory Practice: Gina's Story**
>
> Like many others, Gina began by framing her question as a problem, and began looking for solutions: *'Why can't I remember and use new vocabulary?'*. Over time, though, she began to think about different ways to approach her language learning: *'Sometimes I ask the teachers and the students and they give me some feedback. I gather the question and solutions and I try to do that. So EP gives me a useful method'*.
>
> Gina, like many others, noted her surprise at finding out she was not alone in struggling with her puzzle: *'I am surprised because originally I supposed that's my personal problem, but after that I found out "Oh everyone has that problem". So that's a good way to finding out your puzzle and solutions, but that's just the beginning I think, yeah, just a beginning'*.
>
> Reassured by the discovery that her puzzle was shared with many others, Gina described how *'we opened the door and meet each other. Some interviews is not in the class because the time is not enough. So we have a date and visited in our flats, in our accommodations and sit down – that's a good environment'*. In addition to the classroom activities, she said the students were interested enough in their puzzles to want to spend their free time discussing in the evenings and at weekends: *'the classmates can give me more deep information. They can give me more examples of their puzzlement'*.
>
> Gina demonstrated a thoughtful, critical approach. She was eager to develop understandings and language learning skills alike. Above all, she progressed from thinking that something is unique and personal to realising that others face similar issues and may have helpful advice to offer: *'I think this spirit of EP means you need to discuss with others your personal problems. Don't just hide it in your mind. [...] But most important – most important thing is to discuss with others'*.

At this point, we need to consider further the intercultural issues of inviting learners to engage in researching their language practices alongside their teachers. The learners in these pages clearly enjoyed puzzling, and, crucially, because they had set the puzzles themselves (rather than investigating something designed by someone else), the questions and the developing understandings were *relevant*. Nevertheless, we need also to play with the possibility that the ways in which they responded to EP might themselves have been linguistically and culturally located (see Wedell and Malderez 2013, for a discussion of the importance of context). These were, after all, learners on the cusp of starting academic degree programmes in the UK. The whole purpose of being on the pre-sessional course was to accommodate themselves, perhaps even inculcate themselves, with/to British academic cultural mores. A puzzle for us, then, could be to ask whether this person or that was judging themselves against a standard that is not their own.

Puzzles, then, should not be taken at face value. We need also to recognise the broader social, political, cultural context in which the puzzling takes place. And in puzzling about the puzzles, we can move to a productive stance of 'meta-puzzling': linking the questions that people ask to their intersecting linguistic and cultural backgrounds and aspirations, and to searching for deeper understandings, not accepting first impressions. This resonates with Holliday's (2013) discussion of Geertz's (1973) notion of 'thick description'.

> **Quote 9.4: Holliday on the Search for Profound Interconnections**
>
> This discipline searches for profound interconnections through what has been called thick description. This can be defined as interconnecting different facets of a social phenomenon to arrive at a deeper complexity of meanings. Thick description is arrived at by being open to what is going on in the wider vicinity of the events one is directly involved in. It is related to putting aside easy answers and making the familiar strange in that one must not be complacent about what the answers and solutions may be, and always be prepared to look further and wider. This also requires a preparedness to understand what is going on and what may be connected to what, even in a culturally unfamiliar setting.
>
> (2013: 35)

How Does All this Relate to the Exploratory Practice Principles?

In Part One, we saw the emergence of the EP principled framework for practitioner research. We have argued that EP is an indefinitely sustainable way for classroom language teachers and learners, while getting on with their learning and teaching, to develop their own understandings of life in the language classroom. It is essentially a way for teachers and learners to work together to understand aspects of their classroom practice that puzzle them, through the use of normal pedagogic procedures (standard monitoring, teaching, and learning activities) as investigative tools. So how might all this work out in EAP practice?

In the following case studies, we hear from Susan Dawson, Ana Salvi, and Alison Stewart, all of whom (like myself and Yasmin Dar) have been working with EP in EAP. In her work, Susan Dawson eloquently conveys the humanising effect that the Rio EP Group highlighted at the beginning of this chapter: as the learners began to see the teacher as a humanised professional, the teacher also rediscovered her (very human) learners.

Case Study 9.1: 'Why Do I Ask My Students to Reflect on Their Learning?': A Story of Mutual Development.

Working in a language school in the north of England, Susan Dawson describes how she first came across EP, and then was emboldened to try it out for herself. She incorporated this work for understanding into her practice with two groups: a general English class and an EAP class.

> **Susan Dawson**
>
> I have been involved in the world of TEFL/TESOL since 1985 and have worked in a variety of contexts in Spain and the UK, from teaching CLIL in a Spanish state primary school on the Ministerio de Educación y Cultura/British Council bilingual project and running professional development courses for Spanish language teachers, to teaching asylum-seekers and refugees in London. Most recently I have been teaching EFL/EAP to international students in a Further Education Institution in the north of England. I am interested in practitioner research and love teaching low-level learners.

I have been teaching English in one way or another since I left university and went to Spain to do part-time voluntary work with an international student organisation. I taught English to support myself, and apart from the odd foray into other areas (a rather grim year in an office job in Wales, for example), have never done anything else. However, a few years ago I began to get very bored with what I was doing. I felt stale and was just going through the motions, which had a negative effect on both myself as teacher and subsequently the students. I seriously considered changing careers, but then decided to give teaching a last chance and enrolled on a two-year, part-time MA TESOL course. I loved it from day one, finding the intellectual challenge from both the course content and my course colleagues extremely stimulating, and I began to enjoy my teaching again.

Once into the second year, I needed to think about the dissertation. I decided on some sort of Action Research (AR) project as I wanted it to be directly relevant to the EAP classes I was teaching at the time. Learner reflection was a major theme of these classes and this became my focus. To help, I attended a BALEAP Research Training Event Series (ResTES) in Sheffield in November 2011, mysteriously entitled 'Issues in EAP classroom research: Action Research vs. Exploratory Practice'.

At this point I had never heard of Exploratory Practice and went with the aim of getting feedback on my projected research question: 'How can I help my learners to reflect on their learning?'. The feedback I got was helpful, but disconcerting at the same time: the question itself was considered a normative one assuming that reflection is both a good thing and will happen if learners are given the opportunity to reflect; it implied my learners were not reflecting. Suggestions included turning my question into an exploratory puzzle, a question framed with 'why': 'Why do you think I ask you to reflect on your learning?'. This, they suggested, would enable me to discuss the topic with my students and understand their thinking on the subject.

This last idea is very much based on the principles of EP, but at the time it seemed very alien and so I dismissed it. However, later in the day, Ana Salvi spoke of the EP work she had done amongst EAP learners on a pre-sessional course, particularly with regard to learner autonomy. Something here resonated deeply with me, and consequently I decided to discover as much about EP as I could.

Over the next few months, I used the EP principles to work with different classes: a General English (GE) class and an EAP class. In both cases the primary focus was on the learners: the puzzles they had about their language learning and the understandings that they reached. However, my approach with each class was slightly different because of the different aims and goals of the syllabus. I built on what I had learnt from my reading (particularly Allwright and Hanks 2009) and from Ana's presentation, adapting them to my own classes. The GE class did a mingling activity looking at different aspects of their language learning, and the puzzles which arose from that. In contrast, I gave the EAP students a live lecture about language learning and how EP might benefit them, which served as a stimulus for their puzzles. After that, both groups followed a similar trajectory in terms of deciding which puzzle to explore, coming up with ideas for exploration, collating their findings, and presenting those findings to others. The GE class did most of their work in the class wiki, which also opened the process of their explorations up to feedback and comments from both classmates and myself. The EAP students did final presentations (using Prezi or PowerPoint) to disseminate their findings.

So what did I learn? The enthusiasm and engagement of both classes in this work was exciting to see, and their appreciation of being allowed to pursue this sort of work in class was palpable. According to the end-of-course feedback, the overriding benefit for the EAP learners was the realisation that they were not alone in their language learning struggles: other learners also worried about not remembering vocabulary, making mistakes when they were speaking, not being able to write a perfect English paragraph, or come up with good ideas for an IELTS essay. Working together on their puzzles not only gave them a huge confidence boost but also helped them work out strategies for coping with these issues.

It was not just the learners who benefited. I came to understand so much more about my students: the things they were struggling with; the things they couldn't see a purpose to; the things that they felt unsure about in terms of classroom processes and activities; and areas where they lacked motivation. In fact, the puzzle elicitation part in both classes was the most successful needs analysis I have ever done! I also came to see this sort of work for understanding as being an extension of becoming a reflective learner. It certainly seemed to be more authentic and meaningful than the sort of reflective tasks that formed part of the EAP learning portfolios.

> The whole experience had such an impact on me that I have continued to approach my teaching in this way ever since and could write of many more experiences with very different classes. This is not to say that in every class it is a huge success story. Although I have only ever had one student say that nothing puzzled him, some learners have not been so engaged with the process of seeking understandings. Some only seem interested in solutions, and others have settled for quick, easy answers. This is perhaps the biggest challenge for me as I continue in this work. The pull towards finding solutions is natural and sometimes necessary, while seeking understanding often means being happy to live with ambiguity, which not everyone is. I believe it is extremely worthwhile and rewarding to try and understand, but I do now say to my students that there will be time to work on solutions, if they still want to, AFTER they have done their best to understand. This two-stage process might not be adhering fully to the principles of EP, but it is how it seems to work for both myself and my learners – up until now at least. How that might change in the future is another story for another time …

Susan was using her normal pedagogic practice as a tool to develop her understandings of life in her classrooms. As she did so, she gained a much deeper understanding of what it was that her learners were struggling with (see Dawson 2016, for her development of these themes). In Holliday's terms, she was going wider and further as she put aside easy answers, and instead, tried to really understand what was happening in her learners' lives.

This leads to another question: is EP a form of critical pedagogy and/or liberatory autonomy? In Allwright and Hanks, we considered this (though due to constraints of space, only very briefly), noting the influence of seminal work by Ashworth (1985), Freire (1970, 1973), and Wallerstein (1983). We concluded that if critical language pedagogy could let go of teacher-control (there's no reason to suppose that it wouldn't, once the point had been raised) it was very much in line with EP thinking (or vice versa). To sum up, we argued:

> 'Liberatory autonomy' fits in very well with our Five Propositions. (Allwright and Hanks 2009: 56)

but sadly we also had to note that in the field more generally:

> the 'weak' notion of Communicative Language Teaching, with its largely conventional and asocial view of the learner, still dominates the world's classrooms (ibid.: 57)

Thus, although EP acknowledges its ancestral forebears, these influences seem to have been set as the backdrop to the framework.

So could EP be seen as a form of learner autonomy? Clearly, EP has been influenced by the work of pioneers such as Dam and Gabrielson (1988), Holec (1988) and Trim (1976). And Dick Allwright points to the learner autonomy movement as an early influence in his work (see the interview with Dick in Part Four of this volume). We have commented briefly (and approvingly) on this connection:

> This radical view matches perfectly [our] Propositions 4 and 5 about learners being capable of independent decision-making and development as practitioners of learning. It also assumes that learners will learn by developing their own unique ways of learning, as individuals serious about learning (Propositions 1 and 2) in a mutually supportive environment (Proposition 2). (Allwright and Hanks 2009: 45)

This question of the links between learner autonomy and EP piqued the interest of Ana Inés Salvi.

Case Study 9.2: 'Why Don't We Bring EP and Learner Autonomy Together?': A Story of Integration

Ana Ines Salvi was working with adult learners in the UK. Her experience of incorporating EP into her own EAP classes is instructive, as she explicitly links it to learner autonomy, implicit in the EP framework (in the principles of 'involve everybody, work for mutual development' and the emphasis given to learners' agency potential). Here, she brings the relationship between EP and learner autonomy to the fore and examines it in more depth.

Ana Inés Salvi is currently doing a PhD in Applied Linguistics and has completed an MA in English Language Teaching, both at the University of Warwick. At the same time, she has been teaching academic English at university level in the UK for the last five years and in China for the last three years. She is co-editor of the IATEFL Research SIG newsletter (2012 – present) and has published work related to a pedagogy for autonomy and practitioner research. Previously she did her undergraduate studies in ELT in Argentina, where she taught English at primary and secondary school levels, in language schools, and in pre-sessional university courses, for six years.

The Integration of a Pedagogy for Autonomy into Practitioner Research via Exploratory Practice

I got to know about Exploratory Practice in the summer of 2011 when I went to the IATEFL Learner Autonomy Pre-conference Event in Brighton in the UK and I had the privilege to hear Dick Allwright talk about EP (Allwright 2011) and the work done by his friends in Rio de Janeiro, Brazil. What he narrated resonated so much both with what I was investigating as part of an MA programme at the time, namely Learner Autonomy (Benson 2001), and with my belief that education has an important role to play in fostering authentic being, knowing, and understanding. I therefore decided to explore the feasibility of combining both a Pedagogy for Autonomy (Dam 1995; Dam and Lentz 1998; Kuchah and Smith 2011) and practitioner research via Exploratory Practice in a 5-week English for Academic Purposes Pre-sessional course at a university in the UK as part of both an MA dissertation (Salvi 2012) and the *John Haycraft Classroom Exploration Scholarship* I was awarded by the IATEFL Scholarship Working Party and International House. More specifically I was interested in exploring a) whether these two 'practices' can work together well, and b) my students' perceptions of this innovation. My research plan involved incorporating EP on the one hand and fostering Autonomy on the other based on the literature on each research area. After the experience I used the data collected to find evidence that could illuminate my research questions.

When I started this classroom-based research with 16 international students I was not sure of how to implement Exploratory Practice. I knew that I wanted to foster the EP principles and exploration of the kind of questions that would prompt work for understanding (Allwright and Hanks 2009). What I did was to encourage students to explore why-questions twice during the course: the first time, students decided to explore their questions in small groups and the second time they suggested investigating one question with the whole class together. The questions explored in the first EP session were

Why is it hard to find accommodation around the university?
Why are we sleepy in class?
Why are we here?
Why is it hard to come up with a good idea for our library project?

The question explored in the second EP session was:

Why is the moon festival so important in East Asia?

As part of these explorations students designed questionnaires to find out the views of their classmates and other respondents outside of the classroom, and collected insights from online materials. They discussed their findings in groups and shared them with the rest of the class either via posters or PowerPoint presentations. Speakers were encouraged to include their doubts and partial understandings of the topics they had explored explicitly in their presentations, to foster an understanding of the progressive nature of authentic 'knowing' in them (Wu 2002, 2006). As part of the second EP session students divided themselves into groups and each group explored different aspects of the one puzzle they had chosen. All the students exhibited their work at the same time. Another class group – whose tutor, having been inspired by what we were doing, tried EP with her own students – joined us and showed their work too.

In order to foster autonomy I encouraged students firstly to make decisions regarding content, task, and student-interaction pattern by providing them with options; secondly to work collaboratively in planning, carrying out, and sharing their work; thirdly to reflect on their learning needs and to be proactive in working on them when possible in the class, if not, in their free time (Dam 2009); and fourthly to learn how to find information both in different books and dictionaries scattered on tables in the classroom and on the internet by using the communal classroom PC or their own laptops, smartphones, and tablets. Different groups of students would explore different syllabus topics by using the sources available in class and on the internet; and after working on them in class they would explain them to the rest of the class. These presentations generated illuminating discussions between speakers and listeners, as they tried to gain deeper insights into the topics they were learning.

So far I have discussed what I did on the one hand to foster autonomy and on the other to incorporate EP in an EAP course as part of a classroom-based research project. My interest was in whether these two 'practices' can integrate into each other, and what my students' perceptions were of this innovation. In order to find answers to these questions, I deployed the following research tools: students' daily diaries, their weekly feedback on the experience via e-mail, video-recorded presentations of their EP investigations, end-of-the-course interviews, and their delayed feedback. I analysed

> this data for salient features, and while a first analysis revealed the learners' perceptions of the experience, a second/delayed analysis of the data as a whole sheds light onto how a Pedagogy for Autonomy and EP did integrate with each other. Regarding the former, the results show that the students perceived the experience very positively; as they said, they appreciated working collaboratively, being given the opportunity to decide what aspect of the language each of them needed to work on, and finding answers to their own questions by themselves. Regarding the latter, the study shows that working in the spirit of EP permeated the whole research project, not just the two aforementioned EP sessions. In other words, EP acted as a guiding force when students explored syllabus topics, when they talked to each other. EP fostered Autonomy and added values and principles that made the educative process distinct.

What is important to note here is that Ana Inés used her normal teaching activities as usual, but with a heightened awareness of what she and her students were doing, and why (see Salvi 2014, 2015, for how her thinking and understandings have developed). The *purpose* of her research was to explore and understand the relationship between EP and learner autonomy; the *purpose* of her students' work was to develop their own understandings of questions that were puzzling them. Both parties benefited from the work they were doing.

What is increasingly clear from these stories is the importance of collegiality for EP. Sharing puzzled questions with others, working together to investigate (though individual working is also entirely feasible), and sharing understandings as they develop, articulating thoughts, ideas, and further questions, thus further developing mutual understandings – all this is crucial to the EP enterprise.

Case Study 9.3: 'Why Don't We Use EP in Our 'Zemi' Classes?': A Story of Sustainability

Alison Stewart describes her experiences of incorporating EP into her 'Zemi' class at a Japanese university over a period of three years. She provides a critical account of the highs and lows of her experience over the three years, and raises important questions about the role of assessment and grading. Working over a long period of time, she illustrates the 'slow-burn' effect, with some learners becoming deeply engaged in their Zemi-EP work, even over the long summer vacation with no lessons, and no teacher to encourage them.

Alison Stewart

Gakushuin University, Tokyo, Japan

Alison Stewart teaches in the Department of English Language and Cultures at Gakushuin University in Tokyo. Since completing a PhD in Applied Linguistics on language teacher identity at the Institute of Education, London University in 2005, she has been involved in a number of collaborative and inclusive practitioner research projects in the areas of Learner Autonomy, Critical Pedagogy, and Teacher Identity. She is coordinator of the Learner Development Special Interest Group of the Japan Association of Language Teaching, and has co-edited two anthologies of research within the group, *Realising Autonomy: Practice and Reflection in Language Education Contexts (2012)* and *Collaborative Learning in Learner Development (2014)*.

Developing a Zemi Through Exploratory Practice

I teach in the Department of English Language and Cultures at Gakushuin, a medium-sized, private university located in central Tokyo. Amongst the classes I teach is what is known as the *zemi*, a two-year seminar class for third- and fourth-year students, at the end of which the students write a graduation thesis. Typically in Japan, the zemi is held in special regard, and the bonds that are formed between a professor and her students, and amongst the students, are strong and sometimes endure beyond graduation.

When I was appointed to the position three years ago, I had no prior experience of teaching a zemi, but I knew something about it from my colleagues and from my experience of nearly 20 years teaching in Japanese universities. In addition, I've always been interested in teaching practices based on principles of learner autonomy and critical pedagogy and on the lookout for opportunities to explore them further. For this reason, when I read *The Developing Language Learner* (2009) a few months before starting the zemi for the first time, it seemed that Allwright and Hanks' seven principles of Exploratory Practice could provide a basis on which to conduct and develop the zemi in collaboration with the students themselves.

The first zemi group consisted of 20 students, four of whom were fourth-year students, the rest third-years. The students had chosen my zemi in order to do research on language education and sociolinguistics, and so the main purpose of the class, as I saw it, was to create a 'discourse community' in which we would cover certain topics together, through a mixture of mini-lectures by me and presentations by the students on their research-in-progress, and in which the students would support each other. For this reason, in addition to drawing up a syllabus from a list of topics that the students chose to study as a group, the first meeting included the formation of research circles, groups of three or four, which students were free to conduct as they wanted outside of the class.

At the end of the first semester, I had the students conduct a small-scale interview study on the practices of the research groups. This was a way of killing two birds with one stone: it gave the students hands-on experience of conducting research, including interview techniques, transcription, coding and analysis, and presentation of findings, and it gave all of us a picture of what had been going on with the research groups in the previous 12 weeks. As I had suspected, the findings confirmed that two of the research groups were thriving; the other three never even got off the ground.

As a first attempt at Exploratory Practice, this cannot really be said to be 'inclusive' practitioner research. The research puzzle was really mine, not the students'. Nevertheless, it was with some surprise that I learned, when I raised the subject of the research circles on the first day of the second semester, that all the circles had been active during the long summer vacation, including the previous 'non-starter' groups, which had now all started communicating and sharing materials on Facebook. Fortified by this turn of events, our next venture with EP was an end-of-term poster review of the year. The students worked in pairs to come up with puzzles, which they spent a week discussing and researching before presenting their results in the first half of a 90-minute class. Perhaps not surprisingly, the fourth-year students, who had just submitted their theses, were in a buoyant mood as was reflected in their posters. But the third-year students were more critical and came up with a number of practical suggestions for the following year, including a role for themselves as mentors for the new incoming third-year students.

Since the first year, the puzzles and poster sessions have become a regular feature at the end of each semester as a method of critical review and feedback. Despite the success of the puzzle poster sessions as a means of feedback, however, the class has not been without problems in its development. At the beginning of the second year, in response to a third-year request for more opportunities to write, a Moodle forum was set up so that the students could continue discussion of the weekly topic out of class. But, while two students did use Moodle religiously and extensively every week, few of the other students ever contributed more than a single post. The research circles, too, which the previous year had been relatively successful after a mixed start, fell flat in the second year. Moodle and the research circles were the puzzles identified by three of the student pairs in the end-of-year poster review.

At the beginning of the third year, the class agreed at the outset to give Moodle another try, but, once again, only one or two students ever posted comments. While the class had discussed making the posts compulsory and part of their grade, no one wanted to take this route. Finally, at the beginning of the current semester, the first session returned once more to Moodle and this time the class decided to abandon Moodle altogether and set up a closed group on Facebook instead, which so far is proving a lot more active than Moodle, if only for the number of 'likes' received for each and every post. The research circles have also received a new lease of life, following the last puzzle poster session. Following suggestions of two pairs who came up with similar solutions independently, the research groups were reformed as mixed groups of third- and fourth-year students. Rather than out-of-class sharing, the aim of the research groups is now to support each other in preparing and delivering presentations. Thus, each week, one third-year student, supported by research group members, presents his or her research in progress. Thanks to our EP sessions, it is the students who are seeking and finding new ways to improve their quality of learning rather than me, their teacher.

One thing that I've observed after nearly three years of conducting the zemi along these lines is that similar puzzles come up each year:

Why don't students speak English more?
Why don't students write more?

I've felt at times that these questions mean that the class is not moving forward and I've wondered if I should be more interventionist in implementing methods that I 'know' will solve these issues. For example, I could simply make speaking up in class or writing on Moodle part of their grade. In fact, I have asked the students if they want this and they have declined.

Currently, the third-year students are graded on their production of an annotated bibliography in the first semester and a research report at the end of the second. The fourth-year students are graded on their first draft and receive a grade for their graduation thesis, which is examined by myself and one other member of the department. Although the students have never raised the issue of grading as a puzzle, it is the elephant in the room, the big issue that touches on all questions of power relations and on what constitutes 'quality' in the class.

One final change that has occurred over the past three years is a shifting of focus *outward* from a concern only with the zemi and the individuals who belong to it: I have invited guest speakers and encouraged students to bring in guests of their own (international students and visitors from

> abroad). Many of the students are concurrently studying for a teaching licence, for which they have to undertake a three-week practicum teaching in a school, and time is allotted to them to talk about their experience on their return. As a member of the Learner Development Special Interest Group of the Japan Association for Language Teaching I have invited the students to participate in conferences and in a large, multi-participant project translating essays by junior high school students from Rikuzentakata, a town that was swept away in the tsunami of 2011, and an area where unemployment and housing remain serious problems. This shifting of attention outward to the society in which we live is motivated by my reading of critical education theorists. The works of John Smyth and his colleagues (2011, 2014), in particular, have provided concrete questions that I've used as prompts in the latest puzzle poster sessions.
>
> EP has given the zemi a set of principles for an experiment and experience in democratic living in the classroom, but critical pedagogy reminds us in addition that quality of life is an issue for everybody, everywhere.

Like many of the contributors to this volume, Alison Stewart has developed her ideas elsewhere in print and online (see Irie and Stewart 2012; Stewart 2007; Stewart et al. 2014 for further discussions of learner autonomy, critical pedagogy, and EP).

Summary

In contrast with the 'rift' between academics and practitioners that has so often been cited (for example, Allwright 1993; Burns 1999; Freeman 1996), the EP framework creates an atmosphere of mutual respect. Involving others, inside and outside the institution, is helpful in developing insights into language learning and teaching. 'Problems' are not 'solved' (after all, that's not the purpose of the work), but *comprehension*, both of the issue itself and of the struggles of the self and others, is foregrounded and thus developed.

These stories from EP help us to see that the roles and identities we assume when we enter the classroom are not necessarily fixed. The EP principles of working inclusively, collegially, and for mutual development are empowering. Learners and teachers all stand to gain. But these three principles are not unproblematic. Working in groups involves complex social interactions, as Slimani-Rolls (2003, 2005, 2009) has discussed. There is no guarantee that all those in the group will contribute equal amounts of work or enthusiasm (see Chapter 12 for more discussion of this point). Nevertheless, a clear picture emerges of the potential EP offers for (re-)humanising processes in the classroom. In reminding ourselves of our fallibility, of our human curiosity, we may continue to develop.

Recommended Readings

Gunn, C. (2010) Exploring MA TESOL student 'resistance' to reflection. *Language Teaching Research* 14(2), pp. 208–223. This article works on a number of levels. On the one hand it provides an example of puzzling-in-process as Gunn explores her puzzle with her learners; on the other it demonstrates how EP principles are applicable in other contexts (here, Masters-level teaching in the United Arab Emirates).

Rowland, L. (2011) Lessons about learning: Comparing learner experiences with language research. *Language Teaching Research* 15(2), pp. 254–267. Working in an EAP context in Australia with language teachers preparing for a Masters degree, Rowland uses EP as a vehicle to explore his learners' puzzles. Their questions and their preliminary findings make fascinating reading. Rowland argues that learners need to be acknowledged as experts in language learning.

Stewart, A., with Croker, R. & Hanks, J. (2014). Exploring the principles of Exploratory Practice: Quality of Life or Quality of Learning? IN A. Barfield & A. Minematsu (Eds.), *Learner development working papers: Different cases: Different interests.* Tokyo: JALT LDSIG http://ldworkingpapers.wix.com/ld-working-papers. In this chapter, Stewart et al. discuss the experiences of a group of Japanese university students who use EP as a springboard for their language development. They explore intriguing questions about life, learning, and the quality of both.

10

Continuing Personal and Professional Development

Introduction

In this chapter I consider practitioners (of all kinds) growing, learning, and developing during their language learning/teaching lives. I broaden the scope beyond language teaching itself, to include continuing professional development – and to acknowledge the importance also of continuing personal development – to include others, not only language learners and teachers but also educational psychologists, teacher educators, and teacher trainers. In doing so, it is important to note the frequently overlooked fact that one cannot develop another person, as Slimani-Rolls and Kiely (2014) point out.

> **Quote 10.1: Slimani-Rolls and Kiely on Professional Development**
> Puzzles have been articulated, explanations for some classroom phenomena have been developed, practical ways forward have been identified by the teachers, but these are early stages in professional development. Only they [practitioners] can truly transform their pedagogy.
> (2014: 433)

This calls to mind Freire's comment that:

> In the learning process the only person who really learns is s/he who appropriates what is learned, who apprehends and thereby re-invents that learning; s/he who is able to apply the appropriated learning to concrete existential situations (1973: 101)

Learning as an Ongoing Process

Freire's point is highlighted by language learners too. We saw Lynne and Gina in Chapter 9 explaining that if they are just 'told' by the teacher, they don't remember, while if they investigate for themselves, setting their own questions, and working together to explore them, it becomes meaningful, and memorable. It is for this reason that Dick Allwright and I have called learners 'key developing practitioners' (Allwright and Hanks 2009), because learners are key to the learning process, and because they already have extensive experience of being learners, and the potential for development (just as teachers, or any other professionals, have potential for development). So sharing puzzlement and exploring together is a helpful method of both personal and professional development, but, it is worth remembering that the only person who really learns (whether as a teacher or as a learner or as something else entirely) is the person who 'owns' that learning and takes charge of it for themselves. This process is elucidated in Vignette 10.1, as Chiho (a young woman preparing for undergraduate study in the UK) describes her experience of Exploratory Practice (EP).

> **Vignette 10.1: A 'Key Developing Practitioner' in Action: Chiho's Story**
>
> Chiho is a young Japanese student who has been studying in the UK for 6 months as preparation for her Study Year Abroad. At first a very hesitant speaker, she confided that even in her own language she struggled with a stammer, and with shyness. As time went on, she became much more confident in expressing her opinions, and her hesitations and speech-stumbles could be heard (on recordings) to lessen. Her puzzle, shared with three other students, was, *Why can't we speak like we think we can?*

> Chiho had performed very well in an International English Language Testing System exam, scoring 6.5 (out of 9) in the speaking part of the test, but: *'I-I have IELTS exam and speaking for 6.5 but I don't know why'*. Like many others, Chiho had some thoughts about possible reasons for her difficulties: *'this factor could be... er lack of vocabulary and grammar or, or, and it could be my personal puzzle because even I speaking Japanese I ... [mimes stammer] I, my idea is suddenly disappear and I don't know how to speak... so it's very difficult for me, like this, especially when I'm feeling nervous'*.
>
> Chiho asked me directly if I had any ideas about how to 'solve' her puzzle, so as well as giving her rather anodyne advice about practising more, I also suggested that we work together *'to understand why this thing happens'*.
>
> As she worked with a small group of three other students to investigate their puzzle about the contrast between the language in their heads and their struggles to speak, Chiho discovered a number of interesting issues. She noted what she described as a particularly Japanese trait of being afraid to make mistakes, and compared this with a group of Saudi Arabian students on her course who seemed far more confident when speaking. As part of their EP work, her group conducted a small-scale investigation, interviewing several teachers, and a number of Japanese students. In doing so she noticed, *'to-to interview of course it was part of research but also I can prac-practice English'*.
>
> Very importantly, Chiho continued to think about her puzzle very deeply, and pinpointed a subtlety in the question posed that could easily be overlooked. As she explained, *'the ... "Why we can't speak English" it is simple, but "as we think we can" it is... each of us in our group have difficulties in our brain'*.
>
> Reflecting on the EP experience, Chiho commented, *'I think we can get two things from Exploratory Practice. First thing is a suggestion, and another is, we could think about why we can't [speak fluently]... we could analyse the cause and what affect our puzzlement'*.
>
> She went on, speaking very clearly and emphatically: *'My case, my puzzlement became less. I don't feel any – not any – my **fear** about speaking has a bit reduced'*.
>
> On being asked why, she explained, *'because I could find my friends to help me and we could think, talk about our puzzlement and using some example for [from] our experience'*.

Already a strong person in her own right, Chiho told me she had suffered embarrassment because of her stammer, both in Japanese and in English, and was clearly hoping for help with solving the problem. However, I did not, and do not, want to suggest that EP could 'solve the problem' of the stammer – far from it. I merely wish to note that in her desire to communicate ideas and thoughts that were deeply meaningful for her, Chiho seemed to 'forget' the struggle to express words. Her stammer did not go away (though it did lessen, and when I met her several years later, it was barely noticeable), but more importantly, she had 'owned' it. In giving her space to think about something that was important to her (ie the gap between what was in her head and what came out of her mouth), and in creating time for her to discover that others also struggled to communicate (ie she was not alone in her struggles), Chiho was able to access her 'already-present acumen' (Iedema et al. 2013: 172) and address issues that were truly relevant to her language learning. Over the course of ten weeks, she grew as a 'key developing practitioner', developing not only in her command of the language, but also in confidence and her ability to express mature and complex ideas. Interestingly, Chiho has gone on to further study, going beyond her original goal of a Bachelor of Arts degree in the UK, to take a Masters degree, and to win funded places to study in Italy and Norway.

On first encountering EP, Chiho was particularly interested in the possibilities offered for mutual development, stating in her first interview that she found EP *'very interesting, yes, because of course we can learn a lot of things from the lecture but I think […] we are studying, the teachers are also studying, so interaction is very beneficial to both teachers and students'*.

She liked the idea that learning can also be a two-way process: *'I thought teachers are also learning something from us so it's like I […] try to say to them my question, to the teachers, so maybe they can learn something from me'*. Such a blurring of identity boundaries (teachers-can-learn/learners-can-teach) and playful, purposeful, shifts of agency and power are part of the invisible potency of the EP framework, and represent, therefore, an epistemological challenge to assumptions about research(ers) and pedagogy (learners and teachers, and their roles).

As discussed in Part One, surrounding language teaching and learning are a multiplicity of assumptions, behaviours, and beliefs (Basturkmen 2012; Borg 2009, 2013; Woods 1996; Woods and Cakir 2011). These cognitions are often influenced by teachers' experiences in classrooms, as Breen et al. point out (2001) in Quote Box 10.2 below, both as teachers and, much earlier, as learners themselves.

Quote 10.2: Breen et al. on Teacher Education

Much language teacher education necessarily addresses practice through a focus upon principle. In what ways, however, might the trainer's rationale for a particular practice coincide with the trainee's own principles about teaching derived primarily from their experiences as a learner? Clearly both the dynamic nature of the individual's experiential pedagogy and any evolution in what may be the collective pedagogy of the wider professional community – *and* how these may relate to each other – are significant issues for both teacher education and research on language teaching.

(2001: 498)

This brings us to another question about EP: If the principle of 'involve everybody' is taken seriously, who else can be involved? So far we have talked about learners and teachers, but there are many other people involved in language learning and teaching, some of whom are less visible, but nevertheless contributors to the processes of pedagogy.

Who Else Can Be Involved in Working for Understanding?

One vital group of people is often overlooked: teacher trainers and teacher educators. Most teachers have attended some form of pre-service or in-service training, and/or Continuous Professional Development (CPD) sessions, which transmit and transmute beliefs about teaching and learning held by those in education. For example, assumptions about teacher-fronted input, with learners waiting to be given the information by their teachers, may co-exist (not always comfortably) with beliefs about learner-centred classrooms, with active and autonomous learners who contribute to lessons, learning and teaching. This contrast between practice and 'espoused theories' (see Argyris and Schön 1974) is entirely natural (a part of the human condition perhaps?) but can create internal conflict.

Basturkmen has noted the correspondence between teachers' stated beliefs and practices:

Beliefs in one system, such as beliefs about the use of the target language in the classroom, may, for example, periodically conflict with beliefs in another system, such as beliefs about student factors (2012: 284)

Such 'cognitive dissonance' (see Festinger's ground-breaking work from 1957) is demonstrated by some of the case studies found in these pages. The tension is further underlined when the professional training of language teachers is considered. Much has been written about the 'apprenticeship of observation' (Lortie 1975) of teachers, but it should not be forgotten that the other actors in the room, the learners, have also experienced such an apprenticeship, and bring their own opinions about learning and teaching (see Allwright 1984; Cortazzi and Jin 1996). What matters is not a teacher's ability to master a prescribed strategy but 'their understanding of why (and where and when) they were doing it' (Malderez and Wedell 2007: 12).

In the following case studies, we see Kenan Dikilitaş working with teachers in Turkey, Zhilian Zheng and Meixin Hu with novice teachers in China, and Cori Crane working in initial teacher training in the USA – their stories encapsulate the potential contributions of EP to CPD.

Case Study 10.1: 'What's the Link Between EP and CPD?': A Story of Personal and Professional Development

Kenan Dikilitaş describes his EP work with teachers engaged in Continuing Professional Development (CPD or PD) while working in Izmir, Turkey, and gives an indication of how this gap may be bridged. Although he had not originally set out to do EP in any formal sense, Kenan discovered that some of the teachers had already been operating with the EP framework of principles to good effect. This, in turn, contributed to his own personal development as he describes.

Kenan Dikilitaş

Bahçeşehir University, Istanbul, Turkey
Kenan Dikilitaş has been a teacher for nineteen years and a trainer for the last six years. His teacher training experience primarily includes supporting teachers doing different forms of teacher research for professional development. His primary research interests are language teacher education, educational research, research into language teaching and learning, and linguistics for teaching pedagogy.

Teacher Research Project: Insights into Doing Exploratory Practice

Here I present an exploratory practice (EP) experience with English instructors who work at a prep school programme at Gediz University in Izmir, Turkey. I was working as a teacher trainer in Gediz at this time. Although I did not explicitly give any instruction to the teachers, it turned out that several teachers' teacher research was in the form of EP. I realised that several instructors had 'worked for understanding their students' as suggested by Allwright (2003); Allwright and Hanks (2009).

Here, I aim to share the experiences of those language instructors doing EP in their classrooms, as I was working on a wider teacher research project. The project participants are a mix of experienced and inexperienced teacher-researchers who are intensively teaching in the programme and are required by their institutions to engage in professional development (PD) activities. One way of doing PD is teacher research. The PD programme is designed to help the instructors promote their understanding, knowledge, and teaching practices by researching their own classroom contexts. They began their research in October and completed it in June, when they also presented it at an annual conference held by the same university and everyone submitted a full paper for an edited book.

Interest in EP

Teacher research is an umbrella term (Cochran-Smith and Lytle 1993) that encompasses different forms of research activities for professional development of teachers. Some of the teacher-researchers in the project clearly engaged in action research, while others were obviously engaging in exploratory practice. While action research is based on finding a solution to a problem encountered in the classroom after some kind of intervention, Allwright (2003) suggests taking decisions and finding out solutions first requires deeper understanding of the situation before taking any action in the classroom. It was this perspective that had a considerable impact on how I helped the instructors with their involvement in EP.

What we did

The programme (2014) started with one-to-one or groups sessions where the trainer (me) and the teacher-researchers discussed possible issues or challenges they encountered in the classroom. I helped them understand and locate the reasons for their selection, and elicited the purpose of the study and expected outcomes. Such a discussion led them to figuring out the central principles of the research. This stage was followed by a plan on how to carry out research in the classroom.

I should note that the teachers in the EP studies collected data from their own students to understand their perceptions towards a pedagogical issue, or suggestions for a particular problem, or their preferences for a particular way of teaching and learning. There were also ongoing weekly tutorials offered all year long. In these tutorials, teachers shared their progress, and aired problematic areas of research. As the trainer, I helped them discover ways of investigating the issues they faced, through offering guidance and discussion rather than prescriptions. Based on our discussions, we decided on the following research procedures:

1. Identify focus, purpose, expectations, through 1-2-1 or group discussions.
2. Planning, brainstorming, data collection, and analysis (as a group) over several sessions.
3. Collect data.
4. Meet with external mentor as well as trainer to revisit research issues, clarify what had been done so far, and focus on what needs to be done next.
5. Analysing data (in tutorials and discussions)
6. Collation of data sets (using graphs, tables, charts, figures, etc.).
7. Dissemination, through (i) writing up (drafting and re-drafting for publication) and (ii) presentations at an international teacher research conference.

The teachers collaborated with me over a full academic year to complete the first phases of their work. Their studies were written up and edited over four years, and the full texts can be found in the book *Teacher Researchers in Action* (2015) edited by Dikilitaş, Smith, & Trotman. It was noticeable that eight of 25 of the teacher-researchers had carried out their studies with their students; they aimed to promote understandings of particular issues (eg vocabulary learning/teaching; giving feedback; teaching speaking; peer evaluation; student motivation) from the students' as well as the teachers' points of view.

Findings and discussion

As I informally talked to the teacher-researchers at the end of the programme, I found, as one of the key impacts, long-term engagement in doing research. This, they said, allowed for more reflection. They also reported that this led them to gain deeper insights into the subject of their research. As the trainer, I observed them closely; the discussions amongst themselves and with me provided more opportunities to understand the situation, which also helped them raise more awareness of the scope of their problems. Therefore, once again I realised that teacher-researchers can and should be helped to *understand* rather than immediately trying to come up with solutions. It was clear that these teacher-researchers had developed new understandings of what their students want, and how they want to be instructed. With this knowledge, we have come to better understand the context we work in.

Follow-up
Due to the success and popularity of teacher research more generally in my context, we hope to have more teachers who are willing to participate in EP. In the following year there will be a group of teachers who want to try EP. More workshops will be held to help them develop skills to understand the situations in which they teach.
As a trainer, I have developed several different skills myself through this work, such as learning about mentoring, and supporting educational research for professional development. I also gained insights into the role of such research in professional development in the long run.

Kenan and colleagues were gradually moving away from the notion of trying to solve a problem through some sort of classroom intervention. Instead, they were attempting to promote the idea of action for understanding, of working with and listening to the learners in the classrooms. As Kenan explains, this foregrounds the potential of EP for use in CPD projects and schemes (see Dikilitaş 2015a, b, for further examples of how this has played out in practice). An active practitioner of EP, his various accounts of work with teachers, learners, and teacher educators in Turkey can be seen on the Teacher Research Facebook page: https://www.facebook.com/Teacher-Research-for-Professional-Development-2013-408365679200768/.

Since his initial contact with EP via publications, and a plenary by Dick Allwright, Kenan and I have worked together in a number of areas. In 2015 we worked with a group of teachers, teacher trainers, teacher educators, and curriculum developers in the Izmir region of Turkey, funded by a British Council-Katip-Çelebi, Newton Fund Travel Grant. We encouraged participants to identify and refine their puzzles about their language teaching situations, and over a number of weeks, to begin investigating, while also thinking deeply. Despite being full-time teachers, teacher trainers, and curriculum developers, they themselves expressed the desire to share their work through conference presentations and publications. Our role has simply been to facilitate what they wanted to do, and to provide contacts with the EP and Teacher Research networks worldwide.

Kenan's story in the case study above appears relatively unproblematic – there seem to be no complaints about lack of time, and the teachers seem to have gone through a fairly straightforward process of identifying puzzles, working collegially to investigate, and writing up and presenting. But of course life is usually much messier than this. Many practitioners argue that they don't have time to engage in research (see Borg 2013), and that they need (extensive) support if they are to take it on. We turn, therefore, to Zhilian Zheng and Meixin Hu's account from China. The Chinese educational system is frequently characterised as rigid and inflexible, yet here, these teachers and teacher educators demonstrate that this is a misapprehension. The multi-layered narrative provided by Zhilian Zheng and Meixin Hu gives a flavour of the depth and complexity of EP. They give us a sense of the philosophical underpinnings of the EP principles and note the potential of EP for other areas in education, not just English language teaching, but also initial teacher education.

Case Study 10.2: 'Why Incorporate EP in Teacher Education Programmes?': A Story of Overcoming Burnout

As we consider the links between personal and professional development, using EP as a lens, a number of other issues arise. In many parts of the world, teachers are struggling with heavy workloads; Zhilian Zheng and Meixin Hu use the metaphor of a candle, burning itself out to give light to others, to convey the dark situation for many teachers and teacher educators. Lack of time, lack of energy, and lack of resources are ever-present worries for those working in education. Although the situation is complex, as with many other stories in this book, Zhilian and Meixin indicate that there is still room for hope.

> **Zhilian ZHENG and Meixin HU**
>
> **Zhilian ZHENG** is an Associate Professor in the College of Foreign Languages of Zhejiang Normal University, China. She has been teaching English as a foreign language since 1985 in the college. She specialises in research on exploratory practice in English curriculum. She is one of the main initiators of the RICH programme under the theme 'Research-based learning, Integrated curriculum, Cooperative learning and Humanistic outcomes' developed since 1997 in her college. Since 2002, her research interests have extended to teacher preparation, teacher training, and Exploratory Practice.
>
> **Meixin HU** is an associate professor of linguistics and language education in the College of Foreign Languages, Zhejiang Normal University, Jinhua, Zhejiang, 321004, PR China. Her interests centre on the RICH approach to language education and teacher development, cultural discourse studies, and critical discourse studies, with a common concern of meaning-making dialogue between the East and West.

> **EP in Universities of Zhejiang Province, China**
>
> Exploratory Practice (EP) was first introduced to a group of EFL teachers in Zhejiang Normal University (henceforth ZNU), Zhejiang Province, China in 2002. This group of teachers had been conducting curricular innovation named RICH (acronym of *Research-based learning, Integrated curriculum, Community learning, and Humanistic outcome*) since 1997. Innovation covered course objectives, learning experiences, organising activities, and evaluating methods to *Basic English*, one of the main courses for English majors, who are to be trained as English teachers for middle and secondary schools all over Zhejiang Province. During the learning process, learners and teachers can negotiate with each other about what to learn, how to learn, and how to assess. Self-selected, topic-oriented learning and presenting has become one of the major learning methods employed on the course.
>
> RICH group teachers showed great interest in EP when they were exposed to its key concepts, proposals, and principles since EP seemed more systematic and more deeply rooted in theory and thinking. Quality of ClassRoom Life (henceforth, QoCRL) is prioritised (Gieve and Miller 2006b). Teachers' lives are considered first and foremost and learners are regarded as co-practitioners in the classroom where pedagogy is used as a tool for investigating daily puzzles for gaining understanding.

What a beautiful and encouraging image to envision in the journey of English teaching in China. Understanding QoCRL may give a new life to the effect and efficiency of classroom teaching. The act of understanding may bring about insights which can help address puzzles and console our hearts. Topic-oriented learning in groups, as a social matter, may form collegiality between practitioners by working collaboratively for understanding. Finally, genuine concerns are the meaning of the topics involved rather than the language points (Allwright 2005b). As a result, learners' understanding of the authentic contents may be enhanced, so as to achieve a better quality of teaching and learning. Thus, EP, as practitioner research, provides the same group of teachers in ZNU a new and broader vision.

What do the EP terms like 'QoCRL', 'understanding', 'integrating research with pedagogy', and 'puzzles' mean to us in the local Chinese context?

The strong curiosity surrounding EP leads us to interpret these terms in the local context guided by the limited number of papers available to us (eg Allwright 2003, and Wu's doctoral thesis, 2002).

One case is that of Zhilian Zheng, one of the RICH group teachers, supervised by Wu and influenced by Wu's doctoral research since 2002. She referred to EP principles in her MA dissertation. After investigating her colleague's classroom teaching for one academic year, Zheng (2005) argued that teachers' knowing is embedded within teaching practice and that QoCRL in a Chinese college can be enhanced if the teacher talks narratively in small language, addressing learners' inner voices through interactive activities. In this way the process of understanding may develop 'collegiality' between teachers and learners and amongst teachers. In fact, EP at this initial stage is basically accepted as the framework of principles to guide the RICH team for exploring the project of curricular innovation.

As for college language classroom teaching in China, how can the goal of pure understanding be achieved? In *Basic English*, Aifeng Huang, one of the initiators of the RICH Innovation, posed the question 'Will Christmas replace Spring Festival in China one day in future?' for discussion. At the beginning, the students did not show much interest; however, one student hoped to help the teacher by sharing her opinion, and then another student participated in the discussion to support a certain person from the same town. Gradually, the discussion became more and more heated, and even turned out to be difficult to stop when the class came to an end. This is a typical example of 'talk to understand' in classroom teaching.

It indicates that personal relationships between learners in real life may greatly affect the discussion process. Many students were in high spirits when perceiving the emotional support from friends in class. The result of the discussion turned out to be that Christmas would not replace Spring

10 Continuing Personal and Professional Development 203

Festival in China because it was culturally rooted and valued even though in current China many young people seemed more interested in celebrating some western festivals. This process of discussing served as the tool for investigating the concern of Christmas replacing Spring Festival in the future, and classroom learning can thus be interpreted as a 'social matter', conveying authentic opinions in a safe environment affected by social relationships. During the whole process English was used as 'carrier of knowledge'. Talking to understand real puzzles emerging in daily life is one means of communication for meaning rather than for form in classroom language teaching.

Modern Chinese teachers are frequently compared to 'candles', which means that teachers will sacrifice themselves during the process of cultivating learners, just like a candle that will burn itself out when giving light to others. This bleak image of teachers as burnt-out candles is transformed into a new one of 'teachers as learners'. In classroom teaching, teachers may grow with learners if they communicate with them and create learning opportunities for all. Interaction with learners will bring chances for teachers to develop intellectually and emotionally, which echoes 'mutual development', one of the major principles of EP.

EP may also be interpreted from eastern philosophy as a form of life. Wu (2005) argues that EP in a Chinese context may be interpreted 'as a venture of experiencing authentic being for understanding the quality of classroom life in terms of "what is inherently so"'. Teachers may reach the harmonisation of their professional life as long as they undertake enquiry by following the route from being and understanding to naming. Specifically, in line with EP, Wu interprets 'teaching' as the process of 'revealing being through words embraced by understanding' and 'learning' as the process of 'experiencing what a teacher reveals'.

However, several difficulties emerged when EP found its way into ZNU. First, EP has been partially misunderstood only as a set of teaching principles because it is so closely related w the practice of classroom teaching. Zheng (2009) published a paper in a Chinese tertiary magazine, entitled 'EP as a new means of research for college English teachers', yet it mainly interprets EP as teaching guidance when analysing some relevant cases in it. Secondly, the notion of QoCRL cannot be clearly illustrated with daily teaching examples in the context where instructional efficiency is still greatly emphasised and accepted. Thirdly, the specific means or techniques to understand QoCRL are hardly explored since the teachers here are used to transmitting information by 'improving teaching techniques' in class. Finally, the concept 'key developing practitioners' (Allwright and Hanks 2009) tends to be ignored in real teaching practice so that the information conveyed will be taken more seriously in assessments.

> After doing EP for some years, we have found out that EP is deeply rooted in philosophical thinking, widely planted in daily teaching practice, kindly transformed in qualities of instructional participants, hopefully improved in the environment of schools and colleges. Besides, we believe that EP not only works in language classrooms but also in other subject classrooms. Hopefully, EP will be accepted in middle schools or primary schools for it resonates with the key notions of the *New National English Curriculum* in China.
>
> To sum up, the ideal vision EP hopes to create by 'involve everyone' and 'bring people together' is encouraging and enlightening. 'Understanding' as the ultimate goal of teaching is well grounded in ancient Chinese pedagogical thinking. Emphasising practitioners' growth (both teachers' and learners') and getting insights from understanding our own reality and forming collegiality to improve QoCRL is worth pursuing. Most importantly, all these ideas need to be contextualised in Chinese classrooms and interpreted by the Chinese teachers themselves.

Zhilian and Meixin add: 'Besides ZNU, Wu has helped and guided two other college English teachers in Zhejiang Province in doing EP research in specific courses and published papers in *Language Teaching Research [Journal]*, like Zhang (2004), and Zheng (2012)'.

The vivid metaphor of a teacher as a candle burning itself out to give light to others is redolent with meaning for teachers and teacher educators. Many feel almost burnt-out: they run from one short-term contract to the next, sometimes with good terms and conditions, sometimes not so good. Like many involved in education, they sometimes hold down two jobs (neither of which is well-paid), and often have to take on extra private lessons at weekends or in the evenings in order to pay the bills. Teaching, which was once perhaps been an enjoyable, highly respected, profession, is now infiltrated by ideologies of 'performance-related pay' (but whose performance? Starting at which benchmark? And how were the benchmarks decided upon?) and notions of 'teaching competencies' (but what does it *really* mean to be 'competent'? Who decides what these 'competencies' are? And how are the 'competencies' subject to ideological discourse and the exercise of power?).

This may well resonate for many teachers and teacher educators around the world. Time, always in short supply, is compressed further by the bureaucratic demands of ministries and institutions, and the economic exigencies of poorly paid professionals running from one job to the next. So the EP principle of 'Quality of Life' (or quality of classroom life) is of great importance. Likewise, the principle of integrating research and pedagogy, with teachers and learners as the ones who decide *what* to investigate, *when* and *how* to investigate, is central to the needs of practitioners. As teacher educators, it is worth taking a little time to consider this. *If* the work is relevant to the practitioners, *if* the work considers pedagogy in all its complexity, *if* the work is enjoyable (because relevant to those who are doing it), then life in the classroom has a chance of being more bearable. If we (as teachers and teacher educators) are also learning, we all (teachers and learners and all those engaged in educational practice) stand to gain immeasurably in terms of our Quality of Life.

Case Study 10.3: 'Why Don't We Integrate Theory and Practice in Pedagogy?': A Story of Inclusivity and Relevance

We first met Cori Crane in Chapter 8, where she talked about her work with EP teaching German. Here she provides a glimpse of her work as a teacher educator in the USA (see also Crane 2015; Crane et al. 2013). Drawing on reservoirs of experience, she describes how she developed as an experienced teacher, while also encouraging student-teachers to explore and develop. Cori's story illustrates the EP principles in action: collegial working, inclusivity, using one's own pedagogy to investigate puzzling issues which are entirely relevant to the participants. All of these lead, she says, to an enhanced quality of life for her and for the student-teachers she works with.

Cori Crane, Ph.D.

University of Texas at Austin
　Cori Crane is an assistant professor in the Department of Germanic Studies at the University of Texas at Austin, where she teaches German, applied linguistics, and foreign language pedagogy and coordinates the lower-division undergraduate German programme. She received her PhD in German from Georgetown University. Before coming to UT-Austin in 2012, she served as the German Language Program Director at the University of Illinois at Urbana-Champaign. Her scholarly interests relate to understanding and improving learning and teaching in the classroom and include: foreign language writing and systemic functional linguistics, postsecondary curriculum and programme development, language teacher education (particularly the training of graduate student instructors), and reflective teaching and learning.

EP in Graduate Student Teacher Education

Following the success of the EP group [described in Case Study 8.4], I was inspired to try out the framework in my foreign language teaching methods course for graduate student instructors the following year. During the five years prior when I taught this course, the students wrote for their major project a pedagogy paper in which they were to identify a pedagogical problem (either in their class or in the programme), research the phenomenon, and provide practical pedagogical suggestions for how the problem could be addressed. This project, with a similar problem-solution model to action research, was one I had experienced as a graduate student and, admittedly, I loved it. Yet, once I was in the teacher's seat, I found that few students over the five years really accomplished what I had hoped they would: an integration of theory and practice situated within a clearly defined pedagogical or curricular context. In their papers, some graduate students focused exclusively on the theoretical arguments, forgetting the classroom practice; others lacked a convincing literature review to support the innovative lessons they were creating. Moreover, as I continued to reflect on why the final paper was not working, it became clear to me that this intellectual exercise did not invite the most important players in the classroom experience: the learners! So, as I started to reassess core learning outcomes of the course and consider how I was, or was not, achieving them, I found myself turning to EP, eager to see if the framework could help more novice language teachers in developing meaningful, localised understanding of the learning-teaching process.

10 Continuing Personal and Professional Development 207

> In this EP-inspired portfolio project – the guidelines are spelled out in more detail in Crane (2015) – the graduate students wrote regular journal reflections over the course of the semester on a particular puzzle of their choosing. For the project, they were encouraged to draw on resources around them, e.g., their students, other teachers, peers, published research on their topic, online and campus tools, etc. Using EP with these novice teachers allowed me to see what issues and topics in their classrooms interested them; and they, too, could see which questions were emerging in their fellow classmates' puzzles through repeated check-ins throughout the semester. I also could see which resources the learning teachers gravitated towards and how they were making use of their classrooms to research their questions. The written reflections further gave me, as teacher supervisor to most of these students, a unique and special view into the teachers' classrooms.
>
> Indeed, the graduate students' puzzles – some predictable, others quite unexpected – encouraged me to think much more about my own role as a language teacher educator. In particular, I began to see their puzzles as opportunities to observe and think more deeply about how language teachers develop in their practice. One pattern I began to notice had to do with the difficulty many teachers seemed to have involving their own students in the puzzling process. Some teachers struggled with the idea of using their own classroom activities as resources for gaining insight on their puzzles (the 'PEPAs', as described in Allwright and Hanks 2009), looking instead to other instructors in their programmes for answers. As a result of the EP portfolio project, my own puzzles on teacher development and reflective practice have emerged: *'Why is it so difficult for (newer) teachers to invite their learners into their EP work?'* and *'How can I encourage teachers to include their students more in their own teacher reflective practice?'* I am excited to see where these puzzles lead me.
>
> Reflecting on this meaningful EP work, I see that I have grown tremendously through working with EP as mentor, teacher, and teacher educator. The framework has not only helped me to articulate my philosophy of programme and curriculum development, but has also allowed me to understand better my own vocation as a teacher and teacher educator, which has been deeply meaningful to me professionally and personally.

This account illustrates the importance of sharing, of listening, and of professional development at every level (see also Crane et al. 2013, for more discussion). Cori highlights the gains, not only for learners, and teachers, but also for teacher educators, when they adopt a stance of puzzled enquiry. Tajino and Smith (2016) acknowledge such potential when they argue for a 'team learning' approach, which includes all participants as members of the team.

> **Quote 10.3: Tajino and Smith on Team Learning**
>
> … in place of a 'narrow' definition of a 'team', which considers the teachers as the only team members, a 'broad' view of the concept of team, which includes all of the participants in a lesson, should be adopted. We propose moving beyond conventional forms of team teaching to 'team learning', a more collaborative and inclusive approach to classroom language teaching and learning.
>
> (2016: 12)

As Chick has indicated, there is a rich potential in 'dialogic' discussion, where the teacher educator positions him/herself as open to learning.

> **Quote 10.4: Chick on Exploratory Talk in Teacher-Training Feedback**
>
> Exploratory discussion can thus promote the development of a deeper understanding of the complex nature of language teaching and learning. For instance, attempting to make one's grasp of a concept or issue meaningful to others will often clarify our own understanding.
>
> (2015: 299)

We are interested because we are learning: what is relevant to us (as language teachers, or educators, or learners, or curriculum developers, or …) is potentially relevant to others. But are there people beyond those directly in the classroom who might also benefit from, and contribute to, this sense of quality of life? EP suggests 'including everyone' in practitioner research, but what else could this mean? This puzzling injunction does not mean that all people everywhere must be included at all times. Rather, it flags an intention to ensure that no one is excluded: everyone has a right to be heard, and, if practitioner research is conducted in a (mutually) respectful manner then it is possible that mutual development can go some way towards bridging hitherto chasm-like gaps.

Until now, we have concentrated mainly on stories from teachers, teacher educators, and learners. But they are not the only ones to be involved in classroom learning: family members, administrators, managers, and psychologists may all contribute. Carolina Apolinário, an educational psychologist, highlights the importance of an 'Exploratory Dynamic' inside and outside the classroom.

Case Study 10.4: 'Why Do Teachers and Learners Struggle in the Classroom?': A Story of Quality of Life

Carolina Apolinário

Educational Psychologist and EP practitioner, Rio de Janeiro, Brazil.

I'm a clinical and educational psychologist and I have always been interested in the connection between Psychology, Education, and Language. My first specialisation is in Child and Adolescent Mental Health. I had the opportunity of dealing with challenging cases in a multi-disciplinary team of psychiatrists, social workers, and other psychologists, supporting the patients and their families to overcome their symptoms or deal with existing diagnosis in a healthier way. After that, I got my Masters degree from the State University of Rio de Janeiro in Clinical Psychoanalysis and Research, still focusing on adolescents.

The Intersection Between Exploratory Practice, Language, and Psychology

After having worked for some time in hospital wards and public and private psychology clinics, mainly with children and adolescents, I started studying Educational Psychology and began my work in schools. The role consisted of meeting individual students and families, and offering workshops for teachers regarding the socio-emotional side of the learning/teaching process.

In 2009 I came across Inés K. de Miller and Maria Isabel de Cunha, who were offering a workshop on Exploratory Practice. The identification with the ethical values, the principles, and the concept of practitioner was immediate for me. Exploratory Practice called my attention for its similarities with some psychoanalytical constructs as it considers teachers and learners as responsible for learning and it respects their idiosyncrasies, backgrounds, and roles. EP invites practitioners to dare to ask questions they probably don't have answers to yet. It reminds us of how much we can learn from one another if we are brave enough to face the unpredictability and the surprise of another person's puzzlement.

After this workshop I decided to dwell on my studies of Exploratory Practice and dedicate time to a PhD, at the Language Studies Department. Also, I was very lucky to be advised by Inés Miller, a prominent Brazilian researcher on the theme. In 2012, I was invited to teach topics on Educational Psychology and Applied Linguistics at Veiga de Almeida University (Universidade Veiga de Almeida).

My thesis aims to conduct an interdisciplinary investigation which takes into account three knowledge fields interwoven by language: Educational Psychology (Freud 1914, 1930; La Taille 2009), Exploratory Practice (Allwright 2001; Allwright and Hanks 2009; Gieve and Miller 2006a), and Interactional Sociolinguistics (Goffman 1974; Gumperz 1982; Riessman 2008).

This research took place in a renowned bilingual school in Rio, Brazil, where I have been working as an educational psychologist for some years. The methodology consisted of the analysis of two different moments of intervention. The first moment is the professional meeting with teachers who had referred students for the Educational Psychology sector. In those meetings the teacher not only talked about the students' socio-emotional issues, but also narrated some failed attempts at intervention in class. Throughout the listening process, I found out the hardship (Bastos 2008) was experienced by both students (due to their symptoms) and teachers. I noticed those teachers felt disempowered and anxious in dealing with socio-emotional issues that impaired the child's learning and impacted on the other students in class. In those meetings the teacher and I could weave together new ways of listening to the student's hardships and new strategies to manage their difficulties in school. This exchange between professionals in different knowledge fields has proven to be enriching for both parties.

The second moment is a classroom intervention I called Exploratory Dynamic, which consists of a group dynamic inspired by the propositions of Exploratory Practice. This intervention is conducted in English and is considered part of the PSHE curriculum at the school. It is proposed as a different kind of group dynamic that engages the three types of practitioners (the learner, the teacher, and the psychologist) and is mediated by both teacher and psychologist. The students are encouraged to discuss a puzzling-theme proposed. This theme is selected in the process of the professional meetings (first moment of the process). A Potentially Exploitable Pedagogic Activity (e.g: a story, a fable, a picture, a snippet of a video, etc.) triggers the discussion, arousing the curiosity of students and encouraging the meaning-making through narratives. The main goal is for the students to make free

10 Continuing Personal and Professional Development   211

> associations (Freud 1914) about their own difficulties and strengths in school, listening to each other and re-framing their relationships with their colleagues and with the learning process itself. This dynamic fosters the development of a researcher attitude towards life and towards our professional practice.
>
> The professional meetings were recorded and transcribed and constitute the data of my research. The Exploratory Dynamics were recorded as a field journal and were also included in the analysis. The data analysis is based on the theoretical principles of Exploratory Practice (Allwright 2001, 2003, 2009; Allwright and Hanks 2009; Miller 2010, 2013; Gieve and Miller 2006a; Moraes Bezerra 2007), Narrative analysis, Conversation analysis (Clark and Mishler 2001; Gumperz 2002), and mainly the concept of meaning-making studied by Riessman (2008).
>
> The analysed data indicate the involvement of these practitioners in different phases of the investigative action and promotes the generation of understandings regarding the quality of life lived by the group of students. Regarding the two professionals involved, we could conclude that this joint investigation promotes professional development, as we are both practitioners working together for understandings of life in the school environment.
>
> What enchants me the most about EP is that it still values listening and 'deep understandings' (Allwright 2003) in a contemporary scenario ruled by technology where people are so pressed by time, fast stimuli, and consumerism. Therefore, people have been dedicating less time to attentive care and listening (Bauman 2007 and La Taille 2009). I believe the Exploratory Practice philosophical/methodological view has been helping me grow as an educational psychologist, as well as to reflect in a caring and critical way in partnership with students, teachers, parents, and outside agencies. My thesis will be presented in a few months, but my partnership with the rest of the staff in the school and with students is only getting stronger.

Carolina's story begins to answer the question of what it means to include everyone – when we talk about 'inclusivity', what we mean is that really everyone *can* be involved in this form of practitioner research. And by everyone, we mean not only learners, teachers, or teacher educators, but also family members, school administrators, and, as here, educational psychologists. The principle is to open up opportunities for those who are all too often shut out of research; it is not that they *must*, but rather that they *might*. Consequently, we all have agency in the research process.

The idea that classrooms are sites worthy of research, and, very importantly, that practitioners might be the ones to conduct that research, in ways that help the learning and teaching rather than hindering it (or worse still, attempting to control it), can be a welcome revelation. The stories in this book indicate that not only are teachers, learners, teacher educators, and psychologists willing to investigate, but that in fact they are hungry to contribute to their own development and to that of the field.

Summary

As Allwright (2009) suggests, two major challenges for education are (i) to resist the pull towards performance by prioritising understanding instead and (ii) to at least begin to consider learners as key players in the research enterprise, who have as much to offer as teachers, teacher trainers, and teacher educators. So a question for practice is: how to redress the imbalance between so-called 'learner-centred teaching' (which at least aspires to putting the learner at the centre of classroom activity) and 'teacher-centred research', which, with certain honourable exceptions, has positioned teachers as the centre of practitioner research.

Chapter 10 was about all kinds of practitioners (not only learners and teachers, but also teacher educators and educational psychologists) growing, learning, developing. Here we can see CPD as a truly continuous process of developing both professionally and personally for all concerned in language education. Learners are positioned on a more equal footing with teachers; they too have agency; they have something to contribute, and can even teach their teachers. Teachers, and teacher educators, are positioned as ever-learning, capable of infinite varieties of development; they can enjoy learning from colleagues and from their learners.

The case studies provided by Kenan, Zhilian, Meixin, Cori, and Carolina show how, by questioning roles of teachers and learners, repositioning ourselves as all having the potential to both learn and teach, EP has the capacity (if we choose) to enable Quality of Life, thus replenishing the burnt candles of exhausted professionals. So what of the future? What if a reader wants to try EP? How can s/he make it happen? And where will EP go next? In addressing these questions, Part Three will look at the potential of gaining understanding *for* practice.

Recommended Readings

Allwright, D. & Miller, I.K. (2013) Burnout and the beginning teacher. In D. Soneson & E. Tarone et al. (Eds.) *Expanding our Horizons: Language Teacher Education in the 21st Century.* Minneapolis: University of Minnesota. (pp. 101–115) This chapter focuses on the needs of novice teachers, and considers how EP might be a way of combatting the debilitating phenomenon of burnout in language teachers.

Dikilitaş, K. (2015) Professional development through teacher-research. In K. Dikilitaş, R. Smith, & W. Trotman (Eds.) *Teacher-Researchers in Action.* Faversham: IATEFL (pp. 47–55). This chapter reports on a project undertaken with language teachers in Turkey, and at the same time considers the relationship between Action Research, Reflective Practice, and EP, in the context of personal and professional development.

Slimani-Rolls, A. & Kiely, R. (2014) 'We are the change that we seek': Developing teachers' understanding of their classroom practice. *Innovations in Education and Teaching International* 51/4 (pp. 425–435). This article describes the experience of using EP as a form of CPD for modern foreign language teachers in a British university setting. A helpful article for those seeking to bring EP into the realm of CPD.

Part III

Understandings for Practice

11

Introduction to Part 3

Introduction

Part Three invites you to consider your responses to Exploratory Practice (EP) in your own contexts. How might you, whether you are a learner, or teacher, or teacher educator, or educational psychologist (etc.), begin? What might you actually do to investigate? What can you (we) learn from what others have already done, and what are the pitfalls to watch out for? In the worksheets, vignettes, case studies, and references to published work by others, I hope to demonstrate the range and potential of EP. Once again, though, I should state clearly that these are not steps to be followed; there is no recipe, no 'one right way', but rather a multitude of possible ways, which might inspire readers to engage in their own EP work. Part Three, then, is about developing our understandings for practice, in the sense of 'What might an interested practitioner do (to start off, to continue, to take further) with EP?', adding also 'What questions do we still need to ask of/about EP?'. In sum: 'What can we learn *for* practice?'

Issues of Culture, Identity, and Meta-puzzling

As we have seen, EP plays with ideas of identity and culture, by puzzling, and enquiring into assumptions about who does what, when, where, and to whom. The vignettes and case studies in this book have been drawn from across complex linguistic, cultural, intercultural, contexts, where English is co-present as a language alongside other languages, and situated within intricate webs of institutional and systemic beliefs about language teaching and learning.

Taking a constructively critical approach to EP, I also introduce the notion of meta-puzzlement. Here, I am puzzling, and inviting readers to puzzle, at a 'meta' level, about our own language and culture(s), and the language and culture(s) of others involved in these educational institutions, systems, and processes. In Part Three, I will verbalise my own 'meta-puzzling' thought processes (mine will be shown in italics enclosed in a box on the page, but remain open in the mind) which emerge from the 'puzzlement zone' (Kuschnir and Machado 2003). I encourage readers to begin to start their own puzzling and meta-puzzling processes too.

The Relationship Between Principles and Practices

In this book we have seen how practitioners in a variety of situations have worked with and through the EP principles to explore their own practices in language education. Any framework remains open to further discussion, further development, however, and EP is no exception. Consequently I aim to review the framework, asking, 'What view can we take of the principles in our current, uncomfortable world?'. In doing so, I propose that rather than a *list* of one to seven (or nine) principles, we can see them as deeply interconnected ideas and actions. Quality of life, relevance, the integration of research and practice in the quest for understanding, are at the heart of this network. Pull one thread and they all jingle.

Understanding

Principle 2: Working primarily to *understand* the 'quality of life' [of the classroom], as it is experienced by language learners and teachers, is more important than, and logically prior to, seeking in any way to improve it. (Allwright and Hanks 2009: 149)

EP had started with an attempt to integrate pedagogy and research (Allwright 1993), but in later publications the word 'research' is often eschewed in favour of the term 'working for understanding'. Initially, I had seen these two terms as more or less synonymous, but I now want to distinguish between them.

> *Meta-puzzling: Why is the notion of 'working for understanding' so important in EP?*

In the same way as Richards (2003), who deliberately refers to 'qualitative *inquiry*' and Cochran-Smith and Lytle (2009) who talk of '*inquiry* as stance', the emphasis in EP on 'working for *understanding*' is significant. In part, it is a reaction against the more traditional, sometimes rigid, assumptions about the meaning of the word 'research', which may be off-putting for many practitioners. But as we have seen, it is also much more than that. The Heideggerian notion of *Dasein* – of really deeply trying to access human understanding in/through practice – is potent for our field. As Dreyfus (1991) explains in Quote Box 11.1, this search for understanding is part and parcel of what it is to be human, but it is also something undefined, almost indefinable, invisible, because we do it without thinking, all the time.

> **Quote 11.1: Dreyfus on *Dasein***
>
> Dasein is constantly, in its activities, making sense of itself and everything else. Heidegger, in investigating the question of being, in seeking to understand the understanding of our practices, sees himself as doing thematically what every human being does unawares all the time.
>
> (1991: 29)

This in turn calls to mind Gadamer's comment that:

> Every actualisation in understanding can be regarded as a historical potential of what is understood. It is part of the historical finitude of our being that we are aware that others after us will understand in a different way. (Gadamer 1975/2013: 381)

and Bourdieu's contention:

> But comprehension within established forms would remain empty and formal if it did not often mask a kind of understanding which is both more profound and more obscure, and which is built on the more or less perfect homology of positions and the affinity of the habitus. To understand also means to understand without having to be told, to read between the lines, by re-enacting in the mode of practice (in most cases unconsciously) the linguistic associations and substitutions initially set up the producer (Bourdieu 1991: 158)

Such philosophically, theoretically rooted concepts are central to the EP principles, the EP framework, and to practitioner research more generally. This endlessly imperfect, fragile, always questioning process of seeking understanding is an essential part of the human condition, and the true driver of any decent form of research or pedagogy. But the search for understanding does not take place in isolation.

Collegiality

> *Principle 3:* Everybody needs to be involved in the work for understanding.
> *Principle 4:* The work needs to serve to bring people together.
> *Principle 5:* The work needs to be conducted in a spirit of mutual development. (Allwright and Hanks 2009: 151)

If we accept that the aim of working for understanding is central to the pedagogical/research enterprise, that is a first step. But the questions of *whose* understandings and *whose* work (as raised in Part One) remain. Such questions are particularly relevant to the 'middle' principles of EP, which relate to collegiality and inclusivity. Sharing puzzles with others and engaging in dialogue with others (in a Bakhtinian sense) involves recognising and acknowledging the contributions that others can make to our own understanding(s) and *vice versa*. Many of the participants in my research have reported delight in finding that something they thought pertained only to themselves (with consequent feelings of isolation and inadequacy – see Bauman 2007) was actually relevant to many others. So working together, involving everyone, and working for mutual development afford multiple possibilities for dialogue with others, with the world.

These three principles are not unproblematic, however. Working in groups involves complex social interactions, as Slimani-Rolls (2003, 2005, 2009) has discussed. There is no guarantee that all those in the group will contribute equal amounts of work or enthusiasm, for example. Social relations may break down, too. So it is worth considering more deeply, not taking answers (or questions and puzzles) at face value.

> *Meta-puzzling: Why does collegiality matter? Does collegiality have to include everyone? What if 'everybody' doesn't want to be involved? What if bringing people together actually creates problems for participants?*

In contrast with the 'rift' between academics and practitioners, so clearly indicated by writers such as Allwright (1993), Burns (1999), Edge (2011), and Freeman (1996), the case studies in Part 2 have indicated a sense of mutual respect between the various actors involved in language teaching and learning. Involving others (students, teachers both within and outwith the institution, teacher educators, curriculum developers, and educational psychologists, as well as family members and administrators), is helpful in developing insights into the difficulties that we all (whatever role we are performing) face.

Surface-level 'answers', such as L1/L2 interference or cultural issues, may be raised, but in EP we seek to go beyond that level. For example, in Chapter 10 we met Chiho who pinpointed the pleasure to be gained from *'interaction [which] is beneficial to both teachers and students'.* In Part Three we will meet others who enjoy the collegial aspect of working with others to develop *our* (not 'their') understandings of something that has puzzled *us* (not 'them'). This goes beyond simple enjoyment (even though that might, in some cases, be enough), to encompass activities which are mutually beneficial: what helps a teacher also helps a researcher, and also helps a learner. Such mutual understanding includes empathy, emotional intelligence, and trust in the insights to be gained by accessing the perceptions of others.

Relevance and Sustainability

> *Principle 6:* Working for understanding is necessarily a continuous enterprise.
> *Principle 7:* Integrating the work for understanding fully into existing curricular practices is a way of minimising the burden and maximising sustainability. (Allwright and Hanks 2009: 153–4)

As discussed in Part One, practitioner research may be hampered by four (or more) lacks. Practitioners frequently cite the following reasons for not incorporating research into their practice:

- Lack of time
- Lack of resources
- Lack of relevant research agendas
- Lack of relevant research findings.

The EP framework addresses these 'lacks' by bringing the research into the classroom lived experiences of teachers and learners. The case studies in Part Two frequently end with practitioners raising further questions, or planning further activities. Far from being exhausted by their activities, they seem to have gained in enthusiasm, in motivation. Energised by the realisation that others have also asked similar questions ('I'm not the only one'), and that others also find such questions interesting and relevant ('we can work together on this'), practitioners indicated a sustainable approach to researching their own practices. Because they found it relevant, they enjoyed the work; because they enjoyed the work, and because the puzzles were relevant, they found further avenues of enquiry opening up before them.

> *Meta-puzzling: Why don't teachers engage in research? Why do teachers engage in EP?*

In Part Two, we saw how different people have used their 'normal pedagogic practices' (Allwright 2003) in their contexts. Classroom activities could include writing and administering questionnaires (whether simply asking about likes and dislikes, as Caroline did in Chapter 8, or engaging in more complex project work, as Yasmin and Alison did in Chapters 8 and 9 respectively), interviewing, collecting data and analysing it, and presenting findings via oral presentations or written assignments (as Susan and Ana Inés did in Chapter 9). All of this activity falls within the normal parameters of what a practitioner (of teaching, of learning) might normally do in the course of his/her work. But it is not the kind of high-profile, physically and mentally demanding work that is often associated with research. Quite the opposite: it is deliberately low-key, cognitively satisfying, energising work. As a consequence, a criticism that could be (has been) made is that this activity does not 'count' as research.

> *Meta-puzzling: Why is EP (along with many other forms of practitioner research) frequently positioned as 'not real research'? Why might professional researchers or academics feel threatened by practitioner research generally, and EP in particular?*

Nevertheless, it is clear from the accounts in Part Two that the 'burdensome-ness' of work (whether this is defined as teaching, learning, or research) was relieved. In fact, because of the increase in motivation, in enjoyment, it is arguable that practitioners experience enhanced quality of life as a result of their EP activities. This leads me to consider the last (chronologically speaking) of the EP principles.

Quality of Life

> *Principle 1:* 'Quality of life' for language teachers and learners is the most appropriate central concern for practitioner research in our field. (Allwright and Hanks 2009: 149)

We have argued for 'Quality of Life' to be the central concern for practitioner research, and we have noted its complexity and elusiveness. Some years earlier, Gieve and Miller (2006b) put the notion under the microscope, and in their extended discussion, they highlighted the importance of the humanistic tradition in engaging 'cognitive and affective aspects' (2006b: 29) as well as 'harnessing intuition, creativity, aesthetic sensibilities' (ibid.). As discussed in Chapters 5 and 6, Gieve & Miller make explicit links with Heidegger's notion of 'dwelling in the present' (ibid.) and with Bakhtin's sense of the Other, of practitioners recognising, and interacting with, others in a reciprocal relationship, as contributing to Quality of Life in the language classroom (see Quote Box 11.2). In Part Three, we see how teachers, learners, and all those involved in education stand to gain through becoming aware of the (helpful) existence of others in the search for understanding. The realisation that 'I am not alone', that others also puzzle about the same issue, and that we can work together to delve into our understandings of that issue is significant, and contributes to our sense of quality of life.

> **Quote Box 11.2: Gieve and Miller on Enriched Classroom Awareness**
>
> Through teachers and learners searching together for understandings and articulating them to each other they are developing an enriched 'classroom awareness', by which the nature of the experience of classroom life becomes qualitatively enhanced. [...]
>
> We suggest that there is an empowerment effect in teachers and learners *doing it for themselves* which can both endure and transfer to other parts of their lives.
>
> (2006b: 41)

Prioritising 'Quality of Life' as a principled approach to classroom practice, and to educational research, is intimately connected to all the other principles outlined above. By working with others (Principles 3 and 4), in order to understand (Principle 2), and to do this in collegial, mutually beneficial ways (Principles 5, and 6), which are relevant to the learning and teaching, and sustainable (Principle 7), the agency of learners and teachers is realised.

But working together is a delicate matter, and some may struggle to negotiate the complex social relations involved. Likewise, resisting the lure of technicist problem-solving requires a tolerance of open-ended research which is not equally attractive to all. Empowerment (of whom, by whom, for whom) is a complex undertaking which challenges deeply held convictions.

> *Meta-puzzling: Why is 'Quality of Life' often portrayed as somehow easy, or soft, or gentle? Can quality of life also mean working hard, grappling with the unknown, struggling to find meaning?*

The Importance of Trust

Practitioner research involves different types of professional knowledge (see Wedell and Malderez 2013) and going beyond the generally accepted theory-practice dichotomy. But theory without practice becomes meaningless (see Stevick 1980), while practice without theory risks superficiality (Stevick 1980; see also Candlin and Crichton 2013b). So we need a way of ensuring both. EP offers one possible way to bring them together, merging practice with theory. In related areas, Tudor (2001, 2003) and van Lier (1996, 2009, 2013) have argued for the need to see classrooms as dynamic and complex social systems, which are worthy of further investigation. They, alongside narrative enquirers such as Clandinin and Connelly (1995), Clandinin (2007), Gudmundsdottir (2001), and Johnson and Golombek (2002), suggest it is the participants in such classrooms who are best placed to understand that complexity, and to contribute to understandings developing in the field. In order to enable such contributions, though, the field needs to trust those same participants, and they need to trust themselves.

> **Quote 11.3: Candlin and Crichton on the Discourse of Trust**
> ... trust operates dynamically and reflexively at different scales of social order (the social/institutional and the interactional), and [...] where trust is seen as a discursive practice continually constructed, negotiated, accomplished (as well as potentially jeopardised) among different participants (including researchers), with different interests and purposes, in different settings and critical sites.
> (2013a: 9)

Candlin and Crichton (2013a) suggest that trust can be seen as a discursive practice, which motivates and guides research, and agendas for research, in the field of Applied Linguistics (and, I would add, beyond). Throughout Part Three, then, trust is at once a 'given' and also a discourse open to question. Trust, then is central to a holistic understanding of the EP principles.

The Exploratory Practice Principles as a Network

Hitherto, the principles have been presented in a list format (as shown in the various and developing lists in Part One), but I want now to propose that the EP principles be re-formatted in the form of a network which is embedded in a discourse of trust. The central principle of making Quality of Life the key concern for teachers and learners is fundamentally related to principles of relevance. If/when practitioners conceive of their work (and this includes research alongside teaching and learning) as relevant to their learning/teaching lives, they embrace it.

All the principles act and interact with each other in a complex system. Each is linked with the others by visible or invisible ties, but three principles sit at the centre of an interlocking web: (i) the aim of protecting and/or enhancing Quality of Life inside the language classroom and outside it; (ii) the notion of working for understanding, and (iii) the relevance of the work to the participants themselves. These principles act upon and are in turn affected by any or all of the other principles. This is, then, a deeply interconnected, organic whole, as Fig. 11.1 shows. And this whole is embedded in the linguistic and cultural diversity of classroom language learning and teaching. There can be no understanding of linguistic and cultural diversity without the kind of trust that Candlin and Crichton describe, and there can be no trust without understanding(s) of linguistic and cultural diversity.

Work primarily for understanding rather than problem-solving

Integrate inquiry and pedagogy

Involve everybody

Quality of Life; Understanding; Relevance

Make it a continuous enterprise; avoid burnout

Work co-operatively for mutual development

Work to bring people together

Fig. 11.1 The exploratory practice principles as an interconnected whole

This graphic representation presents a view of EP, and its principles for practitioner research, as an interconnected (and potentially interdisciplinary), organic whole (Hanks 2016). Surrounding the construct and inherent in the discussion is the concept of trust: learners need to trust their teachers to take them seriously, and to know what they are doing, while teachers need to trust the learners to be serious, and to engage seriously with their learning. Arching over all is the need for institutions, and society more broadly, to trust that teachers and learners have important insights into the practice of learning and teaching. The atmosphere that holds the network of EP principles in place is, then, an atmosphere of trust. It is the air that we breathe, the water we drink. So in addition to considering the EP framework, and how it plays with identities and cultures, and in order to enable puzzling and meta-puzzling, we need also to consider issues of trust. Practitioners (whether teachers, learners, teacher trainers, etc.) are endlessly engaged in (co-)constructing, negotiating, and re-negotiating these issues in complex and dynamic ways, and in order to do this they (we) need to trust in our own practices to access our core expertise as practitioners.

Mapping Part Three

I start Part Three by considering the EP framework as it is now, and move on to ask what are the most recent developments, and what might happen next. In previous chapters I have probed the EP principles, and drawn out themes of puzzlement, relevance, collegiality, and ownership. Implicit in the discussion is the issue of tensions between beliefs about research and pedagogy, and attempts to integrate the two. I now broaden the scope to discuss the implications of such themes, setting the discussion in the wider context of practitioner research in education more generally. In keeping with the EP principles, I frame this discussion as a continuing dialogic process with my developing understandings both informed by and informing my puzzlement, and the puzzlement of others. Part Three will examine EP from the perspective of developing understandings *for* practice.

Chapter 12 considers the question of puzzlement from multiple perspectives: What puzzles practitioners working in (language) education? How might we elicit those puzzles, and how can we identify puzzles that are worth further investigation? In other words, how might research begin, how might it continue, and how might it be punctuated with shared understandings, still in development, that lead us to further investigations. Chapter 13 moves on to examine possible ways of conducting investigations with practitioners inside and outside language classrooms. I analyse the notion of 'Potentially Exploitable Pedagogic Activities' (PEPAs) – and suggest some ways of using our normal pedagogic practices as investigative tools. I will also take a critical perspective: What are the more problematic areas of EP? What challenges does EP face, and what challenges does it pose for the field? Throughout this book, I have raised questions around 'What are the important research issues in the field that readers can undertake in a practice-based way?'. Chapter 14 concludes by examining some of the key facilitating factors and key obstacles to the design and accomplishment of research in language classrooms involving practitioners themselves as active and potent agents enquiring into their own practices. It asks, 'What next for Exploratory Practice?' and considers future avenues for fruitful exploration.

In sum, Part Three invites us to problematise (in a Freirean sense) the EP principles, as well as notions of research, scholarship, and pedagogy. As Wenger (1998) rightly pointed out, belonging to a community of practice involves an intricate network of threads, and EP draws our attention to those threads, as we question the overall fabric. Here I invite readers to use EP to open up the potential for understanding pedagogy and understanding research. Looking through the lens of understandings *for* practice, I consider what we still want/need to understand. As we move from the practical (how to start puzzling; what PEPAs have others used) to the theoretical (principles, beliefs, research, scholarship, pedagogy), and back to the practical, I redefine the notion of *research-as-practice* in my own (language learning/teaching) terms, and propose a new development: (exploratory) *practice-as-research*.

12

Puzzles, Puzzling, and Trust

Introduction

This chapter is about understanding *for* practice – if you want to try Exploratory Practice (EP) (and hopefully this book has convinced you that it is worth considering), what do you need to think about? How to access those elusive puzzles that fly around our brains? How to capture life 'as it flies'?

Such work is at once deeply satisfying and yet it also involves risk. As puzzled questions rise to the surface, we begin to question the *status quo*, and in asking why things are as they are, in querying our own assumptions and those of others, we expose vulnerabilities hitherto safely hidden away. It is a risky business. As Candlin and Crichton (2013b) argue, trust, with a capital T, is an essential component as learners and teachers co-construct, and make sense of, their classroom worlds as social spaces subject to emotions as well as systems.

> **Quote 12.1: Candlin and Crichton on Risky Classrooms**
>
> In the messy practices, sites and moments of the classroom, and in the opaque social and institutional worlds beyond, learners as selves, persons, and actors and their associated discourses are co-constructed in interaction with others. We cannot easily talk of *a* learner's contributions since learners are always in themselves plural, and their contributions to learning similarly differentiated and heterogeneous. What needs to be stressed are the social and affective conditions surrounding the making of these contributions. Classrooms, like other learning environments, are challenging, risky and at times intra and interpersonally dangerous places, and thus, as Stevick highlights, the importance of the building of Trust as a counterpoint to such risk and danger.
>
> (2013b: 84)

By extending an invitation to practitioners to puzzle about their learning and teaching practices, this Trust-building can commence. In this chapter I will consider some of the challenges, as well as the opportunities, that practitioners (teachers, learners, etc.) might expect to find when/if they try to conduct EP. First of all, how might someone interested in trying out EP for themselves begin?

What Puzzles You?

EP recommends commencing with 'puzzlement' (distinguishing this from trying to solve a 'problem'), and encourages the practitioners themselves to investigate, rather than relying on external researchers, as a way of developing understandings that are relevant to the people involved. So one way of starting might be to ask, 'What puzzles you about your language learning/teaching experiences?'.

Working with learners, teachers, and teacher educators from around the world, I have found this to be a useful starting point. However, coming to the question 'cold' like this can sometimes be problematic. The question is too wide, or too vague, or too shallow, or too deep, in sum, too daunting, when it is left wide open.

Meta-puzzling: Why do we find it comforting and/or inspirational to look at other people's puzzles first?

So before asking, 'What puzzles you...?' it can be helpful to first scan some questions that have puzzled *other* practitioners. Not to copy, but rather to get a sense of the scope, the variety, and the range of questions other teachers and learners have raised. It is reassuring to see that one's own question is equally valid and valuable. And such questions frequently inspire new curiosities, new enquiries for others. It is helpful to look at a list of these puzzles, but without spending too long on any one list or question (hence the length of the list below, and my use of the word 'scan' above). Here is a selection for you to consider:

- Why do my students always use their bilingual dictionaries, not monolingual ones?
- Why do so many students fail to follow advice about learning *outside* class?
- Why do some students feel their ability is higher than it is, while others remain permanently pessimistic?
- Why do so many board markers disappear from Room 17?
- Why do some students have unrealistic expectations of their ability to do well on IELTS (an international examination)?
- Why do my class bombard me with questions when I'm in the middle of answering questions anyway? Why can't they wait for the end of one answer first?
- Why do my students fall asleep in class?
- Why does a lesson that I took ages to prepare, and that I think will go well, turn out to be pants [= not very good], while others that I think will be boring seem to interest my students?
- Why do students find it difficult to remember or recall vocabulary?
- Why are we bothering with teaching learners to be independent?
- Why do I feel nervous when students ask me questions about grammar?
- Why do some students come on a course not prepared, or willing, to learn?
- Why can't my students learn to spell?

Such puzzled questions are not dissimilar (related, but always individually expressed, with individual nuances and relevances) to those found in Lyra et al. (2003) in Rio de Janeiro. In addition to those listed in Chapter 6 earlier, Rio EP teachers have raised questions such as:

- Why is it so difficult to keep students' interest in the classroom?
- Why aren't we ever happy with our classroom work?
- Why am I supposed to give tests to my students?
- Why would students rather sit, copy and receive the subject matter passively than read newspapers for later discussion?
- Why do I have more and more responsibility and my students less?
- Why can't I motivate students who come from a completely illiterate world? Unfortunately I know the answers but I don't know how to motivate them.
- Why do students lose motivation so quickly? Why don't they find studying important? Why can't I find solutions that really work?
- Why isn't [language – English or other] considered an important subject?
- Why do they make the rules and we make the students citizens?
- Why do we have only 2 classes a week? (selected from Lyra et al. 2003, Appendix B: 158–161)

Having looked at the kinds of questions that puzzle other teachers (or learners, or teacher educators), it is timely to ask people to reflect privately on what it is that puzzles them about their experiences, as in Worksheet 12.1.

> **Worksheet 12.1: What Puzzles YOU About Your Language Teaching/Training/Learning Experiences?**
>
> Please write down the questions that have been puzzling you (either recently or for a long time) about your language teaching/training/learning experiences.
>
> You may have more than one question (write on separate Post-it notes).
>
> It is helpful if the questions begin with 'Why' …

I have found that giving out a Post-it note for practitioners to write on is productive. This may be because a small scrap of paper relieves the pressure to perform, and enables practitioners to focus on something apparently simple. They don't have to write an essay – just a question. And the limited size of the paper encourages a feeling of something achievable in the short time available.

> *Meta-puzzling: Why do some puzzles seem to warrant more attention, or to be more 'serious' than others? What does this tell us about our own internal attitudes/belief systems?*

Some practitioners write more than one puzzled question (even up to 5 or 6) immediately, while others need time to formulate their question(s). It can take a few minutes, or it might take several days. Any question is allowed, even one about board pens (see Vignette 12.1). No one should feel under any pressure: if they don't have an immediate question, that's fine; why should they? It can surely be as much fun working with someone else on their puzzle, and this in turn may inspire further puzzling questions.

> **Vignette 12.1: Puzzling About ...** *Board Pens*??
>
> In 2003, I ran a teacher development workshop with around 20 colleagues teaching English for Academic Purposes (EAP) in the UK. As preparation for the workshop, I asked participants to send me their puzzled questions, which I read in advance of the session. The questions were interesting, sometimes humorous, and usually relevant to the classes they were teaching.
>
> One question, however, caught my eye: *Why do so many board markers disappear from Room 17?* This did not seem to be terribly relevant; maybe it was just a joke? I considered removing it from the pile of questions for discussion. However, I had invited the questions, and I therefore felt honour-bound to consider it seriously. Even if it had been provocative in intent, I was sensitive to 'the power of questions to seed ideas' (Furman and Ahola 1992: 16), and so the question remained.
>
> In the workshop, different groups chose questions to discuss and as there were more questions than groups, they could easily have ignored this one.
>
> However, one group chose to discuss it, and a number of fascinating issues emerged. It turned out that different teachers had been brought up in different traditions/cultures in their previous careers: some had come from schools where you were given a set of pens at the beginning of the year, and only if a pen ran out could you get it refilled, or get a new one.

> You were responsible for your own pens, they 'belonged' to you, and the loss of a pen might mean having to do without. Other teachers came from schools where the pens 'belonged' in the classroom: every classroom had a set of board pens next to the whiteboard, and no one carried them away. Teachers from the former tradition were in the habit of sweeping up all the pens as they left the classroom, while others would expect to find each classroom equipped with pens!
>
> The teacher who had originally written the question explained that he was becoming increasingly annoyed at walking into the classroom and finding no board pens. Through the exchange of experiences and views in the workshop, he began to understand that this was not thoughtlessness on the part of his colleagues, but in fact stemmed from a very reasonable set of assumptions that simply came from a different classroom culture to his own.
>
> In addition, through humorously discussing what seemed to be a silly question, I too found an illuminating insight. What I had originally seen as trivial, and not worth bothering with, was in fact affecting social relations in this group of colleagues. By uncovering the irritation, by sharing experiences, with warmth, with humour, and with curiosity, a renewed atmosphere of mutual respect and understanding developed.
>
> My own position as a teacher educator also shifted: I learned that every puzzle has the potential for developing our understandings. It is this boundless curiosity and joyous learning together that, for me, defines the principle of 'put quality of life first'.

The realisation that all puzzled questions, *and their questioners*, deserve equal attention resonates with the five propositions about learners:

> Learners are both unique individuals and social beings who are capable of taking learning seriously, of taking independent decisions, and of developing as practitioners of learning. (Allwright and Hanks 2009: 15)

In Vignette 12.1, the teachers and I were *all* in the position of learners: we learned from one another, and developed both as practitioners of teaching and as practitioners of learning. So positioning ourselves as teachers as learners was a productive and enjoyable experience. But we had to do this in and through Trust.

So can we trust learners also to have serious, researchable, relevant questions? And if they do have such questions, can we trust that they won't all be the same, limited by experience? So far, the learners I have met have been intrigued by the notion of puzzling, and I, in turn, have been impressed by the depth and imaginative scope of the questions they have raised.

> Meta-puzzling: Why do some people find it difficult to believe that learners can seriously puzzle about learning too?

In my experience, learners, as well as teachers (and everyone else), have all sorts of questions about their language learning activities. But they simply haven't been asked to express these questions before. When they *are* asked, they may well appreciate being given permission to critically question, as we saw in Part Two. The following list, taken from my own database of puzzles from language learners of all ages and nationalities, suggests that this is an untapped resource, well worth investigating more thoroughly:

- Why do I feel anxiety about studying at a British university?
- Why do I struggle to maintain my concentration in lessons and lectures?
- Why do I feel bored while I am studying academic English?
- Why does it always take me so long to use a new word, although I understand?
- Why can't I understand different English (accents/dialects)?
- Why do I never like writing class?
- Why can't I express my feelings exactly in English?
- Why can't I remember the grammar rules while speaking English?
- Why do international students always stick with others of the same nationality?
- Why do I fall asleep in class?
- Why do teachers give so much homework?
- Why am I happy to go to the English lessons?
- Why do I feel like learning more every time I attend English class?

Something that is important to note here is the potential for a puzzled question to include *positive* feelings as well as the more common negative ones. In asking why English lessons make them feel happy, or why they want to learn more, these students are teaching us to look carefully at our attitudes towards teaching and learning. EP is rare in that it not only allows for, but encourages, questions which do not blame the teacher/institution/learner/culture/society, but dig deeper to extract understandings of learning and teaching.

There are, naturally, a number of echoes (as well as personal individual questions) in the lists of puzzles in this book. For example, my attention was first caught by the question about students falling asleep in class when it was raised by a Japanese teacher of English, who was studying in the UK in 2001. Since then, others have asked the same question, or variations on it. Although it seems to have been particularly meaningful for teachers in Japan, and China, where practitioners (both teachers and learners) apparently share a cultural acceptance of a classroom (or an office) as a place to snatch a few minutes of sleep, it nevertheless also resonates with teachers in other parts of the world, who express varying degrees of anger, despair, self-blame, and humour at students' sleepiness. Interestingly, they seem unaware that many *learners* also share this puzzlement. Learners, too, want to know why they struggle to stay awake in a class or a lecture (see Vignette 12.2), even when they are interested in the topic and motivated to learn.

> **Vignette 12.2: 'Why Can't I Concentrate in Class?' Kae's Story**
>
> Kae, a young Japanese student studying in the UK, had noticed how difficult it is to keep focused in classes and lectures: *'I'm thinking about with my classmate: "Why can't I concentrate in class all the time?" [...] Because I can't often concentrate [...] For example during the class I ... my brain goes blank, um, and 'Oh I have to study!'"*. Kae worked with another student (from Taiwan) to explore their question.
>
> The discovery that other people suffered from the same lapses in concentration was a welcome revelation: *'maybe everyone has the same problem as with me'*. Kae and her partner gathered data from other students on the course, and compared their responses. The investigations covered issues such as typical concentration length, the type of lesson and type of activities, and the times of day when sleepiness fell most heavily.
>
> When she presented her poster to the rest of the cohort, a great deal of interest was evidenced by the others. Although she was still describing it as a 'problem' (falling asleep in class is indeed a problem for a virtuous student), she seemed pleased by the realisation that others could be helped by her work: *'I want to share my problem [laughs] to any other people [...] it is interesting to show my problem, show my thinking to others, and they will be excited the problem, yes I'm hap- I'm happy, yeah'*.

Practitioners Getting Started

> Meta-puzzling: Why do teachers often cite lack of time as a reason for not engaging with research or scholarship? Why do we constantly feel exhausted by the demands made on us?

A challenge for teachers is getting the teaching done in the best ways they know how, while the challenge for the learners is getting the learning done in the best ways *they* know how (see Allwright 2006). These perspectives have the same goal, but a degree of negotiation may be required to find the best way(s) to achieve it. So what are the challenges of starting off?

We first saw Bella's initial puzzle and the accompanying irritation (*'Why – **why** – can't Middle Eastern students spell? […] Actually it drives me mad. **Why** can't they?'*) in Chapter 6. In Vignette 12.3 below, her story continues. I have written more extensively about Bella's experience, along with that of another colleague, 'Jenny', in an article for the journal *Language Teaching Research* (Hanks 2015b). Here, though, I want to take a closer look at the 'messiness' of practitioner research, particularly the moments of transition from annoyance, frustration, and half-knowing, or thinking we know, the solutions, to puzzlement, genuinely puzzled enquiry (where the questions are open), and a renewed enjoyment of life in the classroom.

> **Vignette 12.3: Life Cycle of a Puzzle: Bella's Story** *(Continued from 6.1 and 6.5)*
>
> Bella's puzzle *'Why can't Middle Eastern students spell?'* came up during an interview for my own doctoral work. Bella was not scheduled to teach the sessions involving EP and had assumed this would exclude her from the EP work. This created a mixture of relief and frustration: *'I'm not really going to be doing much of it I suppose, so I'm kind of frustrated'*.
>
> After ten years working in the same institution, she described a sense of ennui which was pricked by her interest in EP: *'I think it's nice because my teaching, just everything has gone a bit stale and same-y to a certain extent, and I think things like that [EP] sort of shake you up and make you think a bit'*.

Taking this as a hint, I invited her to investigate her own EP puzzle, saying that there would be nothing to stop her doing it for herself (as opposed to trying it for my study). Despite her professed enthusiasm for EP, Bella hesitated: 'Yeah, I think it's making... making the time, isn't it?'.

This is a common issue for busy practitioners: how to make time to do research on top of an already busy schedule (for both teachers and learners). Trying *not* to add to this burden is one of the principles of EP, so I was interested in her response. Being empowered to investigate or not, as she wished, Bella decided to share her puzzle with her students in class. Their reaction was immediate: *'it's obviously something that has caught their imagination [...] They were all sort of shouting out these, not the answers, but... [...] they've all got their own ideas but [name of student] was saying that it, it's to do with vowels mainly, and I think it is'.*

As the weeks passed, Bella took more active steps to investigate her puzzle, and to explore ways of developing her own and her students' understandings. She sent out a questionnaire (to teachers and students in her workplace) and collected potential reading material. She went to her son's primary school and talked to teachers there about how they taught reading and spelling. As a result of this activity, she found (to her surprise) that there were other colleagues who were also grappling with the same issue: *'I'm talking to other teachers about it as well [...] not just on [my course], I mean, you know, you get very enclosed and [then] you realise that other teachers have thought about the same thing and worried about it, but I think it gives you that kind of push to... about something that's just annoyed you'.*

Yet she still felt anxious about being asked to perform (even though I had no such intentions): *'I keep thinking "Next she's gonna ask me to do a teacher development session on it" and I wouldn't feel comfortable with that because it's just "this is what I think"'.*

Despite all this activity, Bella felt that she wasn't overly burdened:

*'I **haven't** done any extra work, but it has – it has focused my thinking more'.*

By the end of the course, the initial annoyance that Bella had identified with her puzzle had melted away. She explained that the focus on exploring possible reasons *why* her students struggled with spelling had given her a greater understanding of the complexities of the task: *'It makes you realise that actually it isn't as easy as you think it is'.*

She added that her own quality of life had been enhanced by her explorations with students: *'I'm enjoying it as well because I have felt that I've just been regurgitating the same old stuff, for years, and I think it's making me look at things from a different angle'.*

> At this point, Bella concluded:
>
> *'It's helping me to answer the question why they find it difficult. There's lots of different reasons why, I think. Yeah I feel like I understand more about the problems they have and the things I need to think about as a teacher'*
>
> In the months after the initial course (where the puzzle started) had finished, and long after my PhD work was over, Bella worked with another colleague. Together they piloted materials for teaching spelling, and followed this up, entirely of their own volition, with a teacher development workshop for colleagues – noticeably, this was well-attended, in contrast with many of the other TD workshops in the centre.

Bella's initial reaction is not uncommon – she worried about the time it would take, and didn't want to be made the focus of attention by leading workshops or giving formal presentations. Such mistrustfulness resonates with many teachers considering research, and with good reason. Through working collegially, though, Bella moved from a sense of frustration at their struggles (and her own struggles to help them) with the vagaries of English spelling rules, to a shared understanding of the difficulties they faced, and some possible reasons for those struggles. Above all, she gained a sense of *'it's not as easy as you think'* – in other words, a form of empathy for their difficulties, and respect for their attempts to address them.

> *Meta-puzzling: Why did Bella think she would be expected to lead a workshop? Why (later) did she decide to lead a workshop anyway? Why has she stayed interested in EP for more than five years?*

This EP experience has stayed with Bella, and she has taken both her puzzle and her interest in practitioner research much further. Now, more than five years after her first contact with EP, she has incorporated EP into her practice in a variety of ways (as have several of her colleagues). She has given presentations at national conferences, as well as local teacher development workshops, and she has written about her experiences in blogs and articles. EP seems to have become a truly sustainable experience for her.

Refining Puzzled Questions

I suggested beginning with an invitation to participants, 'What puzzles you about your language learning/teaching experiences?', and this is certainly a good starting point. However, as with any research question, the first framing may need some work. Many participants report a flood of questions, and most are able to choose from one or two, but others need time to formulate their nebulous thoughts, and all of us need time to refine our initial questions:

> EP accommodates, even encourages, multi-layered puzzlement, and the refining of messy wonderings 'why' into a short, sharp question 'why can't my students spell?' [...] as an essential part of the process it advocates. The point here being that practitioner researchers may have to go through the fogginess of the broader (unaddressed) issues in order to get to the clarity of the individual question. (Hanks 2015b: 629)

One way to do this is to set aside time to discuss the questions themselves, hopefully finding others who are interested in the same area. The act of sharing questions, looking for common ground, seeking partners who can help, or even colleagues who might form a group helps to set up a collegial atmosphere. Worksheet 12.2 contains a suggestion for how to go about doing this.

Worksheet 12.2: Sharing Our Puzzles

Please use the Post-it notes from last time. If you forgot to bring your Post-it, please write your questions on a new Post-it now. Try to start the question with 'Why...'

Please walk around the room and find out what puzzled the others in the group. Find someone whose puzzle area is similar to yours and sit down together.

Consider:
What happens if you use a 'How...' or 'What...' or 'Why...' question? What difference does this make?
Meta-puzzling: Why do people want a worksheet? Why does it help with getting started? Are there other ways of getting started?

Walking around the room can lead to some interesting revelations. For example, in Northern Cyprus with a group of teachers, two people who would not normally have worked together discovered, to their amazement, that they shared an interest in assessment (specifically, the surprise 'pop quiz' test-type used by the institution). As the conversation evolved, their shared tacit understandings of education systems began to reveal how assessment is often used as a means of controlling student behaviour, and can be loathed by learners and teachers alike. This exemplifies the points made about culture and context by Wedell and Malderez (2013).

> **Quote 12.2: Wedell and Malderez on Invisible Dimensions**
>
> There is also an *invisible* dimension to each of the [...] layers of the Place context. This invisible dimension is a result of the (often unspoken) meanings given to each of the Place layers by the people working in them. For example, what happens in a classroom is determined by beliefs (often unspoken) about what is, and what is not, appropriate behaviour for language teachers and learners. What is considered to be appropriate classroom behaviour is itself a result of deeper and more widespread societal beliefs at the level of nation or world region regarding, for example, the purpose of education.
>
> (2013: 16)

As the invisible dimension is uncovered (through the process of puzzling), we can both examine our beliefs (spoken or unspoken) and activities/behaviours, and begin to question further the societal beliefs that permeate assumptions about education.

A Caveat: How Versus Why

> *Meta-puzzling: Why do EP practitioners insist so much on the 'Why' question?*

Importantly, it can be a revelation to discuss the different responses if a question is framed with 'Why' or with 'How' or 'What'. I would encourage readers to try this out for themselves, and see what different responses they get. As an example, though, we might consider the question of 'How'. The following questions came from some of the experienced teachers and teacher trainers I worked with in Izmir, in response to Worksheet 12.1.

- How can I motivate my students to develop their academic skills further?
- How can I manage such a demanding course and guide my students to 'success' but not to 'failure'?
- How can I meet the needs of the institution and of the students at the same time although there is a discrepancy between them?
- How to improve their ESP skills without burdening them with too much grammar?

After extensive discussion, we realised that all these 'how' questions led us directly towards the kind of 'technicist' solutions that merely scratch the surface of our practice. So, for example, there are countless books and articles and talks and workshops on *how to* motivate students, but there is very little literature on *why* students (and teachers) become demotivated in the first place. We all think we know the answer(s), but actually investigating the question can yield some surprises… and any good researcher needs to come with an open mind, ready to read the data, not impose preconceived ideas.

If we consider another pair of examples: meeting the needs of the institution and the students, and improving ESP skills, seems to uncritically accept an externally imposed set of criteria, without stopping to question *why* the (educational) institution's needs are in conflict with those of the learners, or why ESP is seen as likely to increase the grammar load. Changing these questions into 'why', for example:

- Why are my students motivated?
- And why are they demotivated?

(rather than asking 'How can I motivate them?') sets up a very different set of parameters through which we can engage in our research.

It is, therefore, worth taking the time to work through the initial questions generated, to identify different aspects of what it is that puzzles you, to question assumptions and encourage participants to go beyond just asking someone for 'the answer'. Although many students (and student-teachers) might think it is reasonable to just go and ask the teacher for 'the answer', it is clear from the case studies and vignettes in these pages that practitioners stand to gain enormously from speaking to others, unpacking their questions, and analysing their responses in more depth. In other words, going beyond the 'face value' of the question, and any underlying assumptions, is a productive, and often personally instructive and/or surprising, process.

Moments of Transition

This process of refining puzzles can be seen in the development of questions as practitioners move from the irritation of, for example, *'Why – **why** do some students come on a course not prepared or willing to learn?'* (John), or *'Why – **why** can't they spell?'* (Bella), to a profound interest in learners' motivation(s) for studying (John) or the intricacies of learners' battles to understand and use (and teachers' battles to find ways to clearly convey) English spelling rules. It is these 'Moments of Transition' (Hanks 1998) from initial irritation to a more open and curious stance that are essential for the EP enterprise. They cannot be rushed, and each person (as Bella's story shows) needs his/her own amount of time to transition from a solution-focused approach to genuinely puzzling, questioning, trying to understand.

So how to encourage moments of transition? One way (developed from an idea first suggested by Inés K. de Miller for a workshop in 2001) is to encourage people to write out the story of their puzzle – why did they think of it? What (different events or series of events) triggered the puzzle? What 'critical incident(s)' (Flanagan 1954) began the train of thought? Worksheet 12.3 is helpful here.

> **Worksheet 12.3: Analysing Narratives**
> Please write out your question, along with the story that provoked this question. Just a few lines would be enough (we know you are busy). Maximum 2 paragraphs… minimum, a few bullet points.

> Please work together with a new partner to analyse the stories. Questions that might help:
> (a) Where is the **writer** in this story?
> (b) What are the underlying assumptions in the story?
> (c) Why did the writer make these assumptions?
> (d) What more do we need to know about the situation?
> (e) Who do we need to talk to in order to find out more about this situation?
>
> **Refining our puzzles**
> Now that we have had a chance to discuss together, we may want to change/adapt the initial question(s). We may want to narrow down the scope or we may want to change the focus … please spend some time working with your partner to refine your question(s).
> Think about:
> (a) What do we *not* already understand?
> (b) What do we need to understand?
> (c) Who can help us to understand?
> (d) What do we need to do in order to understand more?

If someone is interested in engaging with EP further, they might want to analyse their own back-stories in more depth, as in Worksheet 12.4. This allows us to question the assumptions underlying the initial puzzle, which can be of crucial importance in developing our understandings. What are the linguistic and cultural lenses through which teachers and learners are prone to make sense of what is going on in their classrooms? How do they interpret their own and others' behaviour(s)? Language classes are linguistically and culturally diverse, and teachers exemplify this just as much as learners do. This diversity both presents a need for, and places pressure upon, Trust.

> **Worksheet 12.4: Linguistic and Cultural Lenses**
> One thing that we have found useful in the past is to conduct a brief analysis of the narratives surrounding our puzzles. How do linguistic and cultural lenses frame our view of the world of the language classroom? Questions we might ask (of our own written or spoken narrative) include:
> (a) Consider the use of *personal pronouns* ('I', 'they', 'we', etc.) – which pronoun is used?
> (b) When is it used? (eg when have you written 'I' or 'you' or 'they' or 'we'?)

> (c) Who are the actors in the text? (eg administrators, students, other colleagues, trainee teachers, trainers, etc. – think about 'self' or 'other')
> (d) Which *verbs* are used?
> (e) Which *adjectives/adverbs* are used?
> (f) What *metaphors* are used?
> (g) What *absences* can we note?
> (h) How is *context* explained?
>   As we analyse our own texts, we might ask ourselves: What is the significance of the choices we make as we write (or speak)?
>
> Look at Hadara Perpignan's second story (pp. 207–8 of Chapter 13 of *The Developing Language Learner*, Allwright and Hanks 2009)
> (a) What was her puzzle? What did she do?
> (b) How is her story similar or different to your situation?
> (c) How can you adapt what she did to your own puzzle?
>   There are other stories (case studies) in the chapter – were there any others that you found interesting? Can you compare/contrast with your own narratives?

But puzzling is not a simple matter, as we shall see.

Puzzling About Puzzlement

Neither teachers nor learners are sitting comfortably in language classrooms in the twenty-first century. Much has been written about the apprenticeship of observation (Lortie 1975) of teachers, but it should not be forgotten that the other actors in the classroom, the learners, have also experienced such an apprenticeship and bring their own opinions about learning and teaching (Allwright 1984; Cortazzi and Jin 1996; Dewey 1963) to the classroom. An example of this can be seen in Vignette 12.4, where Cheer (the Japanese student we met earlier in Vignettes 6.3 and 9.3) explored not only her puzzle about difficulties with speaking, but also a less easily articulated struggle with conceptions of research. Cheer was a deep thinker, who provided a rich mine of information about her reactions to EP. Her story is therefore worth examining in more depth.

Vignette 12.4: Exploring Conceptions of Research

In contrast with the enthusiastic responses of the other participants on her course, Cheer described an ever-deepening sense of puzzlement about her question *('Why can't I speak English well after so many years of study?')*, which was becoming quite uncomfortable for her. The contrast between Cheer's hesitancy in speaking English and the comparatively easy fluency of her course-mates seemed to send her into a spiral of introspection.

In interviews, Cheer also told of a group member's bafflement with puzzlement. In a circular statement he managed to circumvent any possibility of reflective investigation: *'Puzzlement is puzzlement'*. Cheer seemed to endorse her classmate's view as she repeated his phrase several times over the first six weeks.

The disjuncture between her own performance and that of her classmates, the fact that they were not able to understand her when she talked, meant that Cheer became, in her words, *'more deeply'* puzzled. Attracted and repulsed in equal measure by her puzzle, Cheer diligently completed her tasks for the group, and investigated her puzzle alongside her classmates; she even reported taking on work that other group members had abandoned. In addition, she came to interview appointments with me, commenting that this in itself was helping her, by providing extra practice for her speaking.

However, when describing her impressions of the poster presentation, she pointed out that perhaps what she was really looking for was a practical solution to her problems in communication. Although she wanted to understand more, and was grappling with some profound difficulties with communication in a foreign language, she also wanted a straightforward improvement. This contrast between the state of 'being puzzled' and a 'puzzle' (in the noun form) which might be resolved is significant. At first, Cheer seemed uncomfortable with merely 'puzzling' – she appeared to want to redirect the work into a puzzle which offered solutions. In this way she could find a resolution to the difficulties she experienced in speaking – perhaps a more satisfying outcome.

Despite her declared desire to speak English well (and her knowledge that practice would be a good way to do this), Cheer stated that she deliberately chose the shortest, most repetitive, least demanding part of her group's poster presentation: the introduction. As I observed her going about her business on the course, and in the interviews with me, I saw that she tended to keep quiet, waiting to be asked directly rather than volunteering comments.

Nevertheless, in my professional opinion, improvements in her speaking ability over the course of the 10-week programme could be heard: her fluency and range of active vocabulary grew, and these changes are evidenced in the recordings of the interviews. However, Cheer herself appeared not to recognise this, continuing to be dismissive of her progress up until the end of the course. While not rejecting the notion of developing understandings entirely, she repeated several times her desire for practical solutions. She related this preference for solutions to her profession in healthcare, where problem-solving is naturally crucial, and where Action Research (AR) is well-known as a form of practitioner research. I began to assume that she was fundamentally opposed to EP's focus on open-ended, puzzled enquiry.

Perhaps because AR is prevalent in Cheer's field of healthcare studies, she was able to identify the expectations that are often set up in such research projects. Her background may have influenced her apparent preference for a problem-solution approach. However, as time went on, Cheer analysed the fine differences between the two. In a later interview, Cheer contrasted AR with EP, referring again to the desire for solutions: *'understanding is useful for my puzzlement, but I want, mmm I want more useful, like solution'*.

At first, it seemed to me that Cheer had resisted the opportunity to move from what Freire calls 'magic' or 'naïve' consciousness to 'critical consciousness', and therefore she remained, in his terms, "subjugated" by perceptions of reality and causality in a state of helplessness or 'disempowerment' (Freire 1973: 44). Cheer had obediently gone through the motions, completing all the tasks she was required to do, but the bedrock of her question about her lack of fluency had remained unchanged. In fact, as she said in later interviews, she knew the *solution* to her problem (as any teacher would also have advised: 'Practise speaking more often!') but she appeared unable to take action to improve her situation.

This must have been frustrating for her, yet she seemed unwilling to take responsibility for it, seeking instead 'solutions' from an external (authoritative?) source – the teacher. She claimed to understand her puzzle, but at the same time announced that she was unable to find the solution(s) that she craved. This implies a contrast between (i) understanding and (ii) solutions.

However, in the final interview, when I asked her what she would say to other students about EP, to my surprise, she distanced herself from this attitude, saying,

maybe other people like expect some Action Research so through EP they expect their [...] puzzlement solved by EP [...] but a little bit different. But now I can understand

Vignette 12.4 shows how Cheer's understanding **evolved**. As, indeed, did my own. As researchers, as language teachers, as learners, we are all able to develop our understandings, and through the process of deeply questioning, of not accepting things at face value, we delve into the cultural, intercultural, intra-cultural issues of life in the language classroom. For example, Cheer's phrase *'puzzlement is just puzzlement'* initially suggests a resistance to the principles of EP (particularly the notions of working for understanding rather than problem-solving). Reactions like Cheer's seem to present a major challenge for EP. But this is only if that is how we, as outsiders to Cheer's realm, are disposed to understand it. A more interesting reading becomes clear if we keep notions of power and discourse in mind. Bauman (2007) notes that by settling the blame on the individual, 'flexibility' isolates and disempowers:

> The messages addressed from the site of political power to the resourceful and the hapless alike present 'more flexibility' as the sole cure for an already unbearable insecurity – and so paint the prospect of yet more uncertainty, yet more privatisation of troubles, yet more loneliness and impotence, and indeed more uncertainty still. (Bauman 2007: 14)

But there is hope, as Fairclough (1989) argued some years earlier:

> Resistance and change are not only possible but continuously happening. But the effectiveness of resistance and the realisation of change depend on people developing a critical consciousness of domination and its modalities, rather than just experiencing them. (Fairclough 1989: 4)

Consequently, we need to examine our own assumptions more critically.

The circular statement *puzzlement is puzzlement* seemed to block off further questioning by Cheer. Was it enquiring too deeply into very personal feelings? What were the assumptions that guided my own analysis, and indeed behaviour? Cheer's story set off further puzzles for me, as a researcher, as a teacher, and as a learner myself. Attributing her difficulties to personality, or the environment, may have been entirely true, but I was left wondering whether this was actually a convenient belief to hold, which allowed her not to address the real issue. At various points on the course and in the interviews she had said she was disappointed with her (in-)ability to speak, yet she also deliberately chose situations (eg the shortest, simplest part of the presentation) which would, if not *prevent* her from speaking, at least require her to speak *less*.

Classrooms are multi-layered, multi-cultural spaces, however, and picking the easy answer, the obvious solution, will not help in comprehending such complexity. As Wedell and Malderez (2013) warn, we need to avoid the trap of stereotyping individuals, particularly when working in/with/through multi-cultural, multi-lingual contexts.

> **Quote 12.3: Wedell and Malderez on the Danger of Stereotyping Individuals**
>
> ... teachers or researchers must be careful, while seeking to understand typical cultural (however defined) behaviours and preferences, not to fall into the trap of stereotyping individuals. Understanding something of typical cultural behaviours may be of more or less help in understanding something of the way groups or individual learners behave and think, but against this background, personal differences also play a very important role.
>
> (2013: 159)

In blaming her personality and the environment, I felt that Cheer effectively sidestepped taking responsibility for her own learning or development. At the same time, she continued to self-criticise, claiming that her language ability had not improved (even though I could hear more fluency, less hesitation, more confidence and range in her grammar and lexis, when she spoke). Was she setting herself up against an impossible ideal of a proficient language speaker? Kramsch (2009) reminds us of the additional resources available to language learners:

> Speakers who learn, speak, or write more than one language have additional symbolic resources through which they give meaning to things, persons and events. (Kramsch 2009: 124)

As a language learner, operating in a different country (the UK), hoping to gain entry to a highly specialised cultural space (British academic life, specifically, in the discipline of healthcare), Cheer was learning *how* to tell her story. How to understand, and begin to manipulate in acceptable ways, the conventions of research, reporting on research, in academic English, to academics in her field. Kramsch (2009) notes the difficulties faced by students seeking to gain entry to a particular community of practice:

> Part of the socialization into becoming a speaker of culture is learning how to tell one's story in ways that are understandable to others, and for this, one has to abide by the socially accepted conventions of the genre. (Kramsch 2009: 150)

In drawing parallels between the work that Cheer was doing in a few weeks on her pre-sessional course and the research that is carried out in healthcare and medicine, was she also setting herself up against an idealised version of a researcher?

Clearly, the vignettes involving students are about people who are from different linguistic and cultural backgrounds. Backgrounds that are, for want of a better phrase, not English. And yet they are, for the most part, working in a context that is very English, using the English language to communicate in class, and ultimately aspiring to participate in a specifically English-speaking, academic milieu. So their responses to EP might themselves be linguistically and culturally located, as they cast *themselves* in the way that has been set up for them because of what it is that they aspire to. Scarino's (2010) comments on the need for us to learn to communicate our reflections on our own enculturation are helpful here: 'It is this enculturation that constructs a person's linguistic, cultural and social identity; that is, the *intra*-cultural dimension of one's own learning and communication' (Scarino 2010: 168–9).

Cheer showed she had grasped one of the essential, philosophical, differences between AR and EP. Her story offers profound insights into potential challenges for EP, or indeed, any form of practitioner research: the expectations of students (and teachers, and society at large) which feed into the problem-solution mode of thinking. Who teaches? Who learns? Who researches? What 'counts' as research and who decides what counts? Such questions raise cultural, and intercultural, even intra-cultural, issues for language classrooms.

> *Meta-puzzling:* What is the culture of Continuous Professional Development and/or Teacher Development? Why do we still see an international culture of external experts flown in to tell the locals about the 'latest thing'? Why should the locals (or the international expert) accept such positioning? How can the expertise of those who are proficient in the local culture overturn these prevailing assumptions?

In Vignette 12.5, Wayne Trotman, a participant in a series of EP workshops in Izmir, Turkey, writes playfully about his first exposure to EP. He describes his initial scepticism and gradual awakening to the possibilities of EP. His teasing, challenging tone is intentionally humorous but beyond the jokes are some important points for people wondering about EP. His quirky piece raises some key questions for us to consider.

> **Vignette 12.5: Initial Responses to Exploratory Practice: Wayne's Story**
>
> I was recently invited to attend a short course, on which I was reliably informed something called 'exploratory practice' (EP) would be explained to me by a leading light in EP circles. This was with a view to myself and a dozen or so other teacher educators on the west coast of Turkey spreading the good word and helping set up EP projects amongst colleagues also working at university level there.
> Having been involved in teacher research supervision for a few years, I had, I must admit, become rather sceptical, noting how much of this local investigation stuff was on a par with re-inventing the wheel. For example, one colleague recently informed me that, according to her lengthy study, teachers tended to dominate the classroom discourse. Really?! Not for the first time, my jaw fell! Apart from such critical moments, during which I felt life was elsewhere, I'd also not been too enamoured by teacher research when, in a chat with him, Simon Borg politely informed me that unless it took place in one's own classroom, it wasn't teacher research. I shook my head at this recollection and vowed to move on to the much richer possibilities of case study research. Locating, and helping colleagues locate, 'the

complexity, uniqueness and commonality' of a case (Stake 1995) would make it easier for us all to present and publish, or so I thought. One year on, my own seven thousand-word case study on student absenteeism still awaits a publisher. Anyway, armed with what I'd gleaned about action research (AR) from having five years earlier completed my doctoral studies based on Anne Burns' model for AR (2005) to investigate the effects of oral feedback on student essay writing, I thought these sessions on EP would at the very least get me into town to have a natter with colleagues I normally only met at ELT conferences. EP was, after all, merely a lesser known, less regarded sibling of AR, was it not?

Anyway, in session one, the leading light first set out the stall of what EP was, responding well to my questioning as to the where and whom. No, it did not necessarily need to take place in one's own classroom, and it didn't really require language learners as such. The latter was in response to my pointing out that I was a teacher educator, no longer delving into the murky waters of the actual ELT classroom. I was still on board at this stage. Then followed a slot on the ethics of research, an area I'd been pulled up on during my viva, so I was happy to add my sixpenn'orth to that discussion. It was when we got onto the EP principle of dealing with 'puzzles, and not necessarily problems' that my thoughts went back to Burns (1999), which covered the same ground. 'Here we go again', I thought!

Prior to session two we had been asked to write up our own 'puzzle' before listening to and then helping refine each other's puzzle in the session. Frankly, I was no longer on board. Why did we constantly need to refine the damned things? Surely a puzzle is a puzzle is a puzzle, and mine was on how to implement EP in my own institution in the forthcoming academic year. End of story.

I left early with a headache. Session three I missed due to family reasons, but in a late night exchange on social media with a colleague on the course (during which I questioned why we were attending and told her the leading light might have to drag me out of a bar to the next session) she provided me with a moment of epiphany.

'The beauty of EP', she expounded, *'is inherent throughout its framework based on seven principles, key to which are minimising the burden by exploiting normal classroom activities while concurrently practising the target language.'* (I suspected she was reading this from the leading light's session handout, but who cared!; it all began to resonate with me as I fell asleep mulling over the matter. I shuddered as I recalled the intervention phase of my doctoral AR cycle that had had teachers and students missing lunch in order to generate data I required. My colleague continued, *'By implementing in classroom time "potentially exploitable pedagogic activities" (PEPAs) over a period, not only pedagogy and research would be enabled, but collegiality and mutual development on*

> the part of learners and teacher would occur'. This was a far cry from the aforementioned doctoral AR, when learners (who, to my annoyance, my external examiner had pointed out, I had conveniently chosen to ignore when it came to request permission to use their names in the thesis) were simply recorded in conversation with teachers about shortcomings in their essays and then told to clear off back to lessons until the next time. A little bit of EP wisdom back then would have gone a long way to developing collegiality.
>
> My final thoughts on the matter of AR versus EP are as follows: If it seeks to understand a puzzle by minimising the burden to all involved by carrying out the research in classroom time with a carefully refined PEPA and involves all concerned in mutual development, then that's EP. If it seeks to address a problem and provide solutions to improve matters, while at the same time intervening in and possibly interrupting classroom events, then that's probably AR. I can also see, though, how both forms of research can transmogrify into each other.
>
> *Wayne Trotman supervises teacher research at Izmir Katip Çelebi University in Turkey. His special interests are in case study research, action research, and exploratory practice.*

Wayne's story bears a number of resemblances to Cheer's story above. Like Cheer, he seemed to be expressing some resistance to the notion of puzzling. Where Cheer says *'Puzzlement is puzzlement'*, Wayne argues, *'A puzzle is a puzzle is a puzzle. End of story'*. These seem to be defensive moves, ways of blocking further enquiry. And yet, like Cheer, Wayne experienced a moment of epiphany. In his case, it is the realisation that EP is not going to add to the burdens of teachers, but rather, through integrating research and pedagogy, it seeks to *minimise* the burden, and, crucially, to see learners (and teachers, and trainee teachers) as people worth listening to.

The Need for Trust

Zeichner and Noffke (2001) argued that practitioner research is, and should be, justified by the relevance it has to practitioners themselves. The stories in this volume demonstrate that in doing so they (learners, teachers, teacher educators) gained personal satisfaction, as well as, perhaps even as a consequence of, developing their own understandings while engaging in normal classroom practices. Implicit in Zeichner and Noffke's (2001) argument is the need not only for trustworthiness of/in research, but also for trust between all the actors in the field.

> **Quote 12.4: Zeichner and Noffke on the Contextual Nature of Practitioner Research**
>
> Practitioner research is always deeply contextual. Its claims on truth are integrally related to its realisation in practice. For many practitioner researchers, the justification of their labor is as much in the lives of those who practice as it is in in acceptance by those outside the situation.
>
> (2001: 315)

This is still an idea that excites debate, even fifteen years on. It is an even more potent concept when learners are included as active agents, as co-researchers, with a say in what happens in the classroom. Those who hesitate to engage in practitioner research may have excellent reasons for their caution, but underpinning those reasons is, perhaps, a fundamental resistance to the notion of teachers or learners as researchers.

This intimacy with problems is even more challenging for those (teachers, teacher trainers, academics) who consider themselves knowledgeable in the field, and who might prefer classes of compliant learners, who listen to their teacher dispensing knowledge. But as Wenger put it, 'Compliance does not require understanding' (1998: 39). Moving away from the problem-solution paradigm encompasses a wide range of challenges for conventional educational roles and behaviours. In promoting a '*discourse of puzzlement* […] *as* syllabus' (Miller 2009: 90 original emphases), EP suggests a much deeper, and potentially subversive, change. This shift has the potential to enrich our understandings of the hugely complex and diverse worlds we find both within and outside our classrooms.

> **Quote 12.5: Hanks on Trusting Participants to Be Serious**
>
> … in order for learners (and teachers) to be included as researchers in their own right, all the participants need to be able to trust one another to be serious, to make decisions, and to develop as practitioners of learning and teaching.
>
> (2013a: 134)

A key issue which underlies all the examples and suggestions in this book is the question of trust. In Hanks (2013a, see Quote Box 12.5), I called for all participants to trust one another, but, as discussed earlier, this is tricky in an atmosphere of technicist approaches. Trust(ing) is a challenge. It is 'both found in, and a condition of, our experience of the world, one which is at the same time relative, having therefore to accommodate both uncertainty and ambiguity and [...] mistrust' (Candlin and Crichton 2013a: 9). Hence 'working for understanding' requires time and careful thought. It is not always an easy process; indeed it is often complex and fraught with difficulties. But addressing these difficulties can provide a satisfying 'bite' to the notion of Quality of Life.

> *Meta-puzzling: How do issues of linguistic and cultural diversity, as 'lived experiences' of language classrooms, link to issues of Trust? For example, without Trust, can we hope to understand linguistic and cultural diversity? Is there no Trust without understanding of linguistic and cultural diversity? How do these intimately bound concepts form and reform relationships?*

So, for example, many teachers might share Jenny's concerns as she tried out EP with her class as in Vignette 12.6 (for more analysis and discussion of Jenny's experiences, see Hanks 2015b). In challenging her own notions of what a lesson plan should be like (which surely stemmed from her own training as a teacher), she had to be courageous and take risks. But having done so, she experienced a sense of liberation; removed from the constraints of syllabus and expectations, she developed an enhanced respect for what the learners could in fact do.

> **Vignette 12.6: A Question of Trust: Jenny's Story**
>
> Jenny told me she was interested in EP, as she saw links with learner autonomy and creativity. As she planned her first foray into EP, she shared her concerns as well as her excitement: '[I'm] excited, yeah, a little bit, sort of, I wouldn't say nervous, but I'm not really sure where we're going or what this is about... from what I think it's going to be about that's something that goes in line with what I'm naturally interested in, so I'm looking forward to seeing what the students make of it'.

Jenny was concerned about her role in the classroom: *'I wondered what you do in the case when students draw a blank and kind of say "Well, I don't really have any puzzles." How much do you push them, how much do you guide them? [...] I was thinking "Oh, what if they don't come up with anything?"'*.

This fear that the students might treat EP as just another hoop to jump through is entirely reasonable. The fear of emptiness in the lesson, where the teacher is left to fill the gap, is common, perhaps stemming from initial teacher training where teachers are exhorted to not only plan every minute of the lesson, but also to have extra activities 'up the sleeve' for those students who finish a task early. It is rare to find situations where learners are trusted to come up with their own initiatives. Jenny had to trust her learners to take the work seriously, and to come up with ideas of their own.

At the same time, she was worried about too *much* commitment from her learners: *'... there's one very deep thinker in the class and... what if he comes up with "What's the meaning of life?" – you know what I mean, something a bit too deep?'*. Asking deep questions would normally be encouraged, but if the teacher feels obliged to supply the answers, this can be stressful. As she planned her first EP lesson, Jenny thought carefully about such issues: *'If this [forming groups and sharing puzzles in a mingling activity] gets done quite quickly, I don't want to [...] tell them what to do, and that's probably my main question to you is "how much do I guide them?" How much do I say "Right you've got a puzzle, go and find out about it" or should I give them some suggestions?'*.

Giving the learners an opportunity to think of their own questions is clearly a challenge to the teacher's role as 'knower' in that precise outcomes cannot be predicted. In empowering learners, teachers have to be willing to hand over control. Lesson outcomes (always tricky to predict) move out of the teacher's control when power is shared with learners: the teacher has to take on a different role, and lesson objectives require a different formulation, as Jenny highlights: *'it's a learning process for me, I'm in a different role, thinking well – normally I'm going in going "Well I've got a clear idea of my objective" or what I need to be doing, so it's learning to feel comfortable being a bit... reacting really, rather than creating things. But sort of seeing what happens and then working from that. [...] because I was thinking "Oh woah!" [panicky voice] and then I thought "I think that's the whole point" you know "I'm not supposed to know what's going to happen"'*.

In the event, all the students did have puzzled questions (see below) and over four weeks they investigated in groups, giving poster presentations to the rest of the class at the end of the month. Jenny takes up the tale: *'I think those are the best presentations I've seen. [...] I just sensed this real sense of **ownership**. [...] I don't know that they've necessarily done any more preparation for it, but they all knew, they really knew, what they were talking about'*.

Raising learners and teachers to the level of co-researchers, who take the responsibility of setting the research agenda (with their puzzles), means a change in the roles and identities of both teachers and learners, which leaves them unsure of what to do or how to behave. The resulting fear of losing control is natural, and this, together with the need to consider alternative ways of being in the classroom, could cause tension. Yet, as Jenny's story shows, the benefits of letting go, of believing that learners can do it, by themselves, are substantial.

> *Meta-puzzling: Why are we trained to use lesson plans with traditional learning objectives or outcomes? Can we re-frame them using the EP principles? What happens if we try?*

Once again, though, we need to see the classroom in the round. If we look at Jenny's class from the learner's perspective, Vignette 12.7 elucidates the experiences of a Japanese learner, Ted (see Hanks 2013b, 2015a). Ted's puzzle was potentially disruptive – it opened up less comfortable avenues to explore – so Jenny had to decide whether to give it space in the class. As so often, taking an apparently superficial question seriously was a key moment in the development of the EP work.

> **Vignette 12.7: Why Do People Learn Bad Words [= Taboo Words] More Easily? Ted's Story**
> Ted (a Japanese student in his early 20s) began by telling me about his puzzle – participating in student life in the UK, he was going to parties and mixing with many nationalities. He noticed the prominence of taboo words used as a social mechanism:
>
> *Ted: many people teach me bad words and they are having fun with me… I mean having fun when I say something bad in their language*
>
> His teachers, Jenny, and I were a little concerned about this choice of question: Was it just an excuse to say rude words in class and snigger? Could

it be disruptive rather than helpful? But rather than repressing the puzzle or responding as if it were a joke, Jenny encouraged Ted:

Jenny: yeah, Ted really wanted to know 'Why do people learn bad language... before anything else?' and I... the others were going err err err, and I said 'That would be a really good puzzle' [...] because he knows a lot of rude words in a lot of languages! But I was trying to say 'Well,' you know, without giving him an answer, 'you've obviously had that experience and you remember them, so maybe what you learn, you could apply to your language learning', so I- I'd quite like it if he was sort of confident and went on that, but we'll have to see.

Ted had in fact taken the prompt about 'What puzzles you?' extremely seriously. Although his puzzle was potentially an awkward topic, he convinced other students to work with him to truly analyse the question. They conducted a questionnaire, and they interviewed other students in other classes to gather student opinions on why swear words were so prominent in their language learning lives. The work they did generated further questions:

Ted: many people said learning bad words is silly. Ok, but ... why? And why do they think it's a bad thing? I asked [a] guy in my group and he did research about 'Is it really bad thing or not?' And some parts of that research I did, I really didn't know that...

The conclusions that Ted was beginning to draw were quite serious. It is clear that he was not being mischievous or trying to derail the lessons by focusing on taboo words. Instead, he appeared to be making genuine connections and was forming hypotheses around attitudes to swearing. His EP group (of five) focused on the social aspects of learning swear words. After several weeks of investigations, and a poster presentation, Ted commented, 'We focused on what was the attraction of swear words [...] which sources they acquired from and which situations they use [...] and what kind of thing makes them use more'.

The notion of using swear words as a kind of social glue, helping the students to bond with others (British and other nationalities) was an interesting one, and the group was intrigued by ways in which taboo language can break down barriers. In acknowledging Ted's question, Jenny took a risk, and encouraged him to investigate it, rather than guiding him towards more conventional or less challenging questions:

Jenny: I think it [EP] makes them realise what they're capable of and it reminds you... I think it helped me view them in a much more adult kind of way, because I thought 'I really know no more than you about this'. I mean, I have my ideas about why people remember swear words and what-have

> you, but actually the most relevant [thing] is going and doing some research. [...] It's a nice position to say 'Well you tell me the answers.' If you say 'Go and research recycling' I've read so much on it [...] I kind of feel like I know the answers so you're not telling me something new. [...]
>
> So I didn't have to feign interest, and I think that was refreshing for them and for me.
>
> In later interviews, Ted also noted the pleasure he found in identifying his own puzzlement and working with others to investigate it. He also referred to the topic of recycling (a common theme in language teaching and course books), saying, 'like recycling, we know we have to do recycling, and we know we have to reduce [...] rubbish, so I can't find any point to write an essay, but something new I can write about it'.
>
> Several weeks later, Ted reflected on the process of EP, providing profound insights: 'I think it's very useful, but it's hard to find the answer, hard to understand [...] because exploratory practice is for something to understand not like visuable, it's invisuable? [...] Invisible, yeah, so it's hard to answer, like you're doing research many years but you never get a certain answer'. He highlighted the intangible nature of understanding (is it possible to pin down in a few short weeks?), and even after importing his puzzle about swear words into another project in another class, he was still intrigued: 'I found it interesting, to know something, something common, but you don't know any answer. So using swear words, it's common, I know, everyone do it. But I don't know why they do it, so... it's very interesting to review'.

Ted's story further illustrates the need for trust in EP: Jenny had to trust that Ted was serious in his intentions to understand the use of taboo words, and not disrupt the lessons. Ted had to trust his own developmental abilities, and trust in the 'invisible'. The conclusions that Ted was beginning to draw were quite serious. It is clear that he was not being mischievous or trying to derail the lessons by focusing on taboo words. Instead, he and his friends appeared to be making genuine connections between and around the attitudes to swearing held by British and overseas students. Ted's group went on to present a serious analysis of the use of taboo words amongst young people in the UK. They noted the ways in which sharing 'rude words' across languages acted as a form of social glue, enabling humour and bonding through 'safe' linguistic transgressions.

> *Meta-puzzling: Why were both Ted and Jenny motivated by the EP work they were doing?*

I noted earlier Cochran-Smith and Lytle's (1999) point that practitioner research sets up 'dissonance' as it challenges embedded power structures. EP is no exception to this, as it sets up a 'problematic shift in power relations' (Breen 2006: 216), which may cause difficulties for the more traditionally minded. In addition, by 'strengthening the agency potential' (Gieve and Miller 2006b: 21) of the learners and teachers involved, EP provides a means for local understandings to be developed *without neglecting the pedagogy*. So EP sets up epistemological challenges for research culture(s), educational culture(s), and the individuals involved in the (co-)creations, (re-)negotiations, of culture(s) and identity.

Summary

If we engage with EP, and invite learners to puzzle and investigate alongside teachers, if we position teachers as people-who-can-learn, and if we position learners as co-researchers alongside teachers, we all need to begin to trust one another. Learners need to trust the competence and expertise of their teachers as we step away from the course book/lesson plan; at the same time, teachers need to trust that learners can and do puzzle about their learning in serious and productive ways. Thus EP-puzzling is a seriously challenging enterprise.

As Bella noted earlier, the books and articles that we read are often found to be wanting – they often talk about *what* problems there are, and *how* these problems may be solved, but they don't look at *why*. Clearly learners as well as teachers are interested in investigating their classroom language learning experiences, and this can be harnessed as a way of getting the learning done.

Recommended Readings

Candlin, C. & Crichton, J. (2013b) Putting our Trust in the learner. (pp. 79–94) IN J. Arnold & T. Murphey (Eds.) *Meaningful Action: Earl Stevick's influence on language teaching.* Cambridge: Cambridge University Press. A stimulating disquisition on the need to recognise the importance of trust in language education. Candlin & Crichton propose four principles for a new way of seeing research and pedagogy. Although they begin with a problem-base, they soon move on to reflection, acknowledging the agentive capacities of teachers and learners, and call for a multi-perspective form of research, teaching, and curriculum agenda.

Hanks, J. (2015b) Language teachers making sense of Exploratory Practice. *Language Teaching Research* 19/5, pp. 612–633. What are the challenges as well as the opportunities for uniting learning, teaching, and research through EP? This article reports on a critical investigation into the implementation of EP in an EAP context in the UK. How did two language teachers respond to EP when trying it for the first time? From initial puzzlement they developed deeper understandings of their own, and their learners', potential as legitimate investigators of classroom practice.

Wedell, M. & Malderez, A. (2013) *Understanding Language Classroom Contexts: The starting point for change.* London: Bloomsbury. This eloquent disquisition on the visible/invisible aspects of culture in classrooms and social context is a helpful reminder of the need to consider the ways in which language education is construed, and how it might accommodate change in a variety of ways.

13

PEPAs, Culture, and Identity

Introduction

In this chapter I consider the use of Potentially Exploitable Pedagogic Activities (PEPAs) – how can we identify normal pedagogic practices that lend themselves to becoming investigative tools? Essentially, this chapter is about 'making it happen' – how can busy practitioners begin, and continue, to engage in systematic, purposeful, *thoughtful* investigations into practice? And how are their activities deeply embedded in cultural and social beliefs, as well as crossing intercultural boundaries, in and beyond classrooms?

> **Quote 13.1: Hall on Diversity in/of Classrooms**
> What goes on in a classroom is inevitably much more than the logical and tidy application of theories and principle; it is localized, situation-specific, and, therefore, diverse.
>
> (2011: 4)

This, of course, is no simple matter, as Hall (2011) points out. I therefore also consider the challenges that Exploratory Practice (EP) faces and poses. What are the difficult questions to ask of EP? What difficult questions does EP raise for the field? I want to not only convey the many and various successes, but also to examine the EP framework carefully and critically. To purposefully seek out the problematic, as well as the joyful, examples and to think about what we can learn from such experiences.

Byrnes (2013) argues that it is in all our interests to find ways for students to express themselves, in a variety of ways, and to reflect critically upon the prevailing assumptions about language teaching and learning. In doing so, the cultural and intercultural negotiations in/between classroom practitioners emerge.

> **Quote 13.2: Byrnes on Working with a Multiplicity of Expressive Forms**
>
> ... our intellectual and educational interest is to enable students to work with a multiplicity of expressive forms, in the context of different social languages, public life, the professions and institutions, many of which will reflect different ideologies.
>
> (2013: 237)

Byrnes is talking about learners, but the identities of those in the classroom are not fixed. I have argued that teachers can be learners too; we can all be positioned positively as learners. We all have something to learn, as well as something to teach. It is this repositioning of teachers and learners, all of whom also have potential contributions as researchers, that EP has, implicitly or explicitly, promoted. But how might we (whether teachers or learners) co-opt our normal teaching/learning practices to enquire deeply into the complex world of the language classroom?

Identifying 'Potentially Exploitable Pedagogic Activities' (PEPAs)

As we saw in Chapter 12, there are a number of ways of starting off: looking at the puzzles of others (as a way of accessing inspiration); analysing narratives and/or critical incidents from one's own learning/teaching experiences; and questioning, and puzzling further, about one's own assumptions. Having done some, or all, of these, what kind of 'normal pedagogic practices' can be used? What have others done in the same, or similar, situation(s)?

Starting Off: 'Normal Pedagogic Activities'

While some people might prefer puzzles, others may be inspired by looking first at their classroom activities. As an alternative starting point to the puzzles in Chapter 12, we might consider the question 'What do you normally do in your classrooms?' as proposed in Worksheet 13.1.

> **Worksheet 13.1: What Do You Normally Do in Your Classroom?**
> Use the space below to write down some typical classroom activities that you use in language learning/teaching:
> (It might help if you think of what you did in your last two or three lessons.)

By starting from our practice, we become sensitive to issues that we may want to investigate. We can think about using our usual teaching/learning activities as ways of investigating our puzzles, and which, crucially, help the learning/teaching along (rather than impeding it because our attention has gone elsewhere). But many newcomers to EP report high levels of anxiety about this moment of starting in the classroom (see, for example, Jenny, in Vignette 12.4 earlier).

> *Meta-puzzling: Why is it difficult, at least to begin with, to think of one's own pedagogic practices and reconfigure them as investigative tools?*

Some of the stories from Chapters 8, 9, and 10 have given an inkling of how EP uses normal pedagogic activities as investigative tools. But now it is time to analyse these in more detail. What activities could, potentially, be used as a PEPA? In language education there are endless variations of teaching and learning activities, and it is likely that at least some of the following will be employed in any one classroom at any one time. I wonder if your list in Worksheet 13.1 above contained some (or all) of the activities in Table 13.1.

Table 13.1 My normal classroom activities

Information gap activities	Brainstorming of ideas (alone? Together?)
Pair-work	Gap-fills
Group work	Reading and answering questions
Projects	Listening and answering questions
Asking questions (student surveys, interviews, questionnaires, etc.)	Using iPads, mobile phones, internet, etc.
Vocabulary-building exercises	Oral presentations (using PowerPoint or posters or other media)
Writing (sentences, paragraphs, stories)	Writing (essays, reports, assignments)

There is no significance to the order in which the above activities have been presented. They might just as easily be written as a mind-map, thought-shower, or a simple list (please make your own), and they might easily have included the following instead or as well:

- Warmers
- Stories/narratives (spoken or written)
- Input (lecture style or other?)
- Written work (eg assignments? Essays? Other?)
- Dictations
- Note-taking
- Jigsaw readings or jigsaw listenings
- Integrated skills work

The important point here is that these are all *familiar activities*. It is likely that we have all used some of them at different times in our classroom lives, whether as teachers or as learners. They are so familiar, though, that they have become almost invisible in our taken-for-granted world. But if we bring them into focus, it is clear that any one of them can be adapted for use as an investigative tool.

We saw many examples of this in action in Part Two. For example, Caroline de Andrade (Case Study 8.1) utilised a course-book activity about likes and dislikes to investigate her learners' feelings about their English classes (and their teacher), while Yasmin Dar (Case Study 8.2) used a pair-work exercise designed to practise speaking in preparation for an exam to explore her question about learner responsibility. Meow and Cheer (Vignette 9.3) used project work, with questionnaires and interviews, to investigate their difficulties with speaking, while Cori Crane (Case Study 10.3) used a written portfolio project to investigate student-teachers' perceptions of the relationship between theory and practice in language education.

From Activities to PEPAs

However, these examples show that we need to tease out the thread from initial puzzling, through PEPAs, towards developing understandings. So how to work through that middle stage? How to identify a 'potentially exploitable pedagogic activity'? Worksheet 13.2 suggests some useful questions to ask (you are invited to fill in the blanks for yourself).

Worksheet 13.2: From Puzzlement to PEPAs: Initial Thinking-Through Stages
(Adapted from a Worksheet Created by Allwright, Hanks, Miller and Samson, 2000)

1. What do I find puzzling about my learning/teaching situation? Why ……………………………?	1a. What do I need to look into to help me understand my question? (eg underlying assumptions/related issues, etc.) …………………………………… …………………………………… 1b. Reformulated puzzle (if necessary) Why ……………………………………?
2. What familiar classroom practice could I adapt to become a 'potentially exploitable pedagogic activity' (PEPA)? Activity type: …………………… …………………………………… Procedure: ……………………… ……………………………………	2a. What is the pedagogic content of this activity? (What learning/teaching opportunities could be created?) …………………………………… …………………………………… 2b. What is the exploratory potential of this activity? (What could this tell me about my puzzle?) …………………………… ……………………………………

As we refine our puzzles, and use our normal activities as ways of conducting investigations, practitioners progressively narrow the focus. So now the question for an interested practitioner is: How might a PEPA develop?

A 'worked example' may help (see Worksheet 13.3). Here, a teacher in a secondary school had a language class full of students who seemed very dissatisfied with the course book they were using. They tore the pages, refused to do the exercises, and scribbled on the pages. Naturally, she wondered why they hated the book so much.

Worksheet 13.3: Why Do My Students Reject the Course book?

Worked example of a PEPA (Adapted from a worksheet created by Allwright, Hanks, Miller, and Samson, for a workshop in 2000, with thanks to Paula Boyce for suggestions)

1. What do I find puzzling about my learning/teaching situation? *Why do my students reject the course book?*	1a. What do I need to look into to help me understand my question? (eg underlying assumptions/related issues, etc.) *Am I interpreting my students correctly?* *What are their real feelings and attitudes about the course book?* *Do they all feel the same?* *If yes, is it the course book itself or how it is being used in class?* *Do they like some things and not others?* *And so on…*

2. What <u>familiar</u> classroom practice could I adapt to become a 'potentially exploitable pedagogic activity' (PEPA)?
Activity type: Grammar practice page (expressing likes/dislikes)
Procedure: Class Survey
How do you feel about your course book?
  What I really like/dislike is…
  I love/hate …
  I like … very much
  I don't like …. at all
	2a. What is the <u>pedagogic content</u> of this activity? (What learning/teaching opportunities could be created?)
	Practice in manipulating the target exponents accurately and appropriately
	2b. What is the <u>exploratory potential</u> of this activity? (What could this tell me about my puzzle?)
	It could help me understand:
	  How many students actually like/dislike the course book
	  If I was right in thinking they dislike it
	  Detailed information about individual attitudes: What is it that they like and don't like?

The first thing to notice is that the question in Section 1 was not 'How can I use the course book better?' or 'How can I improve my teaching skills?' or 'How can I motivate my students to use the course book?' but rather '*Why do my students reject the course book?*'. This, as discussed in Chapter 12 is an important departure. The second thing to notice is that the puzzling process did not stop at the first question. This teacher was trying to look much more deeply into the situation (in the section marked 1a). She was interrogating the assumptions and beliefs that surrounded the initial puzzle, engaging in critical, discursive, practice. This can be seen as a form of empowerment, though perhaps less dramatic than in Fairclough's vision:

> Empowerment has a substantial 'shock' potential, and it can help people overcome their sense of impotence by showing them that existing orders of discourse are not immutable. The transformation of orders of discourse is a matter of the systematic de–structuring of existing orders and restructuring of new orders (Fairclough 1989: 244)

Meta-puzzling: Why are linguistic and cultural backgrounds so seldom raised as puzzles?

Intriguingly, though, she does not mention the linguistic or cultural backgrounds of herself and her learners as possible explanations for these different attitudes. This intangible, yet pervasive net of filaments exerts an invisible force, for nothing is closer or more familiar to us than our own language and culture. It is precisely where we are most at home, and thus becomes what is most taken-for-granted, and least visible.

Clearly, it is difficult to do this in isolation, so the EP principle of 'working together' may help; by discussing the question with others (other teachers, teacher trainers, and learners) underlying belief systems (which are, at the best of times, slippery) can be brought out into the open. Our own language(s) and culture(s) dispose us to notice, ask, and think in particular ways, though, so it is worth interrupting the flow, taking a moment to interrogate our own dispositions. Such discussions might take varying amounts of time, but this is time well spent for teachers, learners, and all the others engaging in the work for understanding. Insights come from unexpected sources, and what seems ostensibly to be helping one person may, whether directly or indirectly, also turn out to be helping another.

In Section 2 of the worksheet, we can see how a PEPA might develop. The teacher in question looked at the syllabus for the coming weeks, and spotted that in the following week's lesson there was a focus in the course book on the language of expressing likes and dislikes. She looked at an exercise from the book which would normally have focused on questions such as 'Do you like pizza?' and 'What do you like about Italian food?' and re-formed this very familiar exercise into a PEPA, by replacing questions about food, or films, with questions about the course book itself.

> *Meta-puzzling: How would the learners themselves frame their various attitudes to the course book? Could they go beyond the simple 'likes/dislikes' suggested by the exercise in the book?*

Even though the level of linguistic proficiency of the learners was not particularly high, they were competent enough to engage with the PEPA here. They could ask each other about, and clearly express, their likes and dislikes regarding the course book. They could, and did, engage in meaningful discussions about their learning materials as they wrote the questions, walked around the room asking their classmates for their opinions, and recorded their answers. The work did not stop there, of course, because they then worked to collate and analyse the data they had collected, and they shared their findings. Their potential 'symbolic competence' (see Kramsch 2009), then, was immense.

> **Quote 13.3: Kramsch on the Potential of Classrooms for Symbolic Competence**
>
> To view the foreign language classroom as a deficient, less than authentic instructional setting is to ignore its potential as a symbolic multilingual environment, where alternative realities can be explored and reflected

> upon. Language teaching is not just a question of devising the right activities. It has to do with the economy of embodied time – the institutional time of the lesson, the biological, psychological, and emotional time of the participants, the sedimented time of pleasant and unpleasant memories.
>
> (2009: 210)

Section 2 also afforded opportunities for further thinking: box 2a asked how this PEPA would help the *pedagogy* along ('What learning/teaching opportunities?') while 2b asked how it would help the *understanding(s)* develop ('What exploratory potential…?'). Crucially, the final part of box 2b allowed for, even encouraged, a seed of doubt: '*it could help me understand if I was right in thinking they disliked it*'. Such doubt can include helpful self-questioning about the ineffability of the teacher's own linguistic and cultural dispositions. As she worked through her own thought processes, it became clear that she, and her teaching, were another example of linguistic and cultural diversity in the classroom.

This ability, requirement even, to analyse assumptions is central to the processes of EP, and essential for the search for deep understandings. And in her search for profound understandings, the person who supplied the ideas in Worksheet 13.3 reported that through the activity she discovered that her students didn't reject the course book at all. In fact, many of them said they quite liked it. So this raised a new puzzle for her to investigate: '*Why do I dislike the course book?*'.

So a PEPA, despite its mysterious acronym, can be something quite simple, mundane even. Above all, it is a *familiar* classroom activity. It is about taking something so familiar that it is almost invisible, and reconfiguring it to consciously examine the classroom practices that are puzzling to us. It is about using our practices to access the invisible, and to activate our pre-existing acumen (see Iedema et al. 2013) to research our practice. It is about acknowledging the potential that the others in the room (or outside it) offer to help us understand. And it is about the realisation that understanding is not a finite thing: it is fluid, always moving, playing with ideas, and always (potentially) developing.

Avoiding Recipes

From the preceding pages, a reader might be forgiven for thinking 'OK, so I need to first think of a puzzle, then I fill in Worksheets from Chapter 12, then I think of a PEPA by filling in the Worksheets in Chapter 13 … So now I'm doing EP, right?'. However, as I hope the many warnings in these pages have also indicated, this would be a mistaken view of how to 'do' EP.

> *Meta-puzzling: Why do some people look for 'steps' to follow? Why does EP reject steps or recipes or models?*

The aim in EP is not to follow a series of steps, or to adopt a model, and certainly not to provide a template to follow without thinking. Rather, the intention of EP is to ask us to stop, look around, and think. And to think really deeply about our own practice. This is why it is so hard to write about 'doing' EP – because it isn't really about *doing* at all. Rather, it is about '*doing-being*' (as the Rio EP Group elucidated in Allwright and Hanks 2009: 218 ff).

In our society, which is so focused on outcomes, results, speed and solutions, the sense of just being, of living the experience, while remaining alert to it and its implications, has become alien (see Bauman 2007). So in the spirit of 'stop, look around, think', the next section examines some of the challenges that EP faces, while also analysing the broader context in which practitioners live and work, and the challenges that EP poses for that cultural context.

Developing Understanding(s) of Classroom Cultures and Identities

As discussed in Chapter 12, trying out EP with learners as co-researchers alongside teachers for the first time requires trust that (i) teachers and learners actually have any puzzles, (ii) they are willing to share them,

(iii) they are interested enough to spend time investigating them, and (iv) they see the work as relevant, not taking them away from their normal classroom routine unnecessarily. As an earlier EP publication noted, 'Teachers need to trust learners, even if such trust seems hopelessly optimistic. *But trust is a two-way matter*' (Allwright and Hanks 2009: 256, emphases added). This brings to mind Candlin and Crichton's notion of the characteristics of the discourse of trust. All five of the characteristics are in play here, as we look into the ways in which EP can be actualised inside, and outside, classrooms.

> **Quote 13.4: Candlin and Crichton on the Discursive Practices of Trust**
>
> When viewed from the analyst's perspective, then, we may identify five characteristics of the discursive practices of trust:
>
> 1. Trust in the social world being *discursively constructed*
> 2. The discourses of trust being *situated* and *bound by context*
> 3. Trust as a practice being both a *form* and a *condition* of social action
> 4. The meanings of trust being *continuously negotiated in interaction*
> 5. Trust-building (and trust loss) being the basis for the formation of broader *community/institutional/social contexts and meanings*
>
> (2013a: 9)

Such issues may also raise puzzles for *us* (as teachers, as readers, as learners). The stories of people like Meow and Cheer, of Gina and Ted, of Jenny, Bella, and John, and how they have responded to the invitation to try EP, are redolent of meaning, and of meaning-making. As Ahmad (from Vignette 6.6) put it, when reflecting on his experience of EP:

> *I think it's very important because the education is not just teaching, it's teaching from one side and learning from [the] other side.* (Hanks 2015a: 126)

Cultures of Pedagogy

As we (learners, teachers, teacher educators) live and work in our linguistically and culturally diverse classrooms, we need to retain awareness of how practitioners' (learners as well as teachers) responses, their questions, their answers, and their searches for 'one right way' or 'the answer' can be sources of puzzlement for us (teachers, learners, researchers). Adrian Holliday's notion of 'small culture formation' is helpful here, as we begin to realise that every classroom is at one and the same time a site of small culture (where students and teachers engage in constructing rules of interaction, social positioning and social interaction, and mutually acceptable/understandable ways of behaving.

> **Quote 13.5: Holliday on Small Culture Formation**
> **Small culture formation** is the major area where the **underlying universal cultural processes** come into operation. Small cultures are cultural environments which are located in proximity to the people concerned. There are thus small social groupings or activities wherever there is cohesive behaviour, such as families, leisure and work groups, where people form rules for how to behave which will bind them together. Small cultures are the basic cultural entities from which all other cultural realities grow. Wherever we go we automatically either take part in or begin to build small cultures.
> (2013: 3)

Precisely *because* we are working across languages and cultures, though, we need to question the received understandings by which teachers routinely explain themselves and their students, and students explain themselves and their teachers. For, as Holliday continues:

> People do not, however, cross intercultural lines without carrying important cultural identities and structures with them. These cultural resources are the major connection with big national cultural realities; but the relationship with them is never fixed or even easily predictable. (2013: 168)

It is worth remembering Bauman's notions of liquid life and liquid modernity (2005, 2007), when engaging in discussions of this nature.

Bauman argues that in modern life nothing is fixed; life, roles, interactions are constantly in motion and cannot be pinned down, and this has profound effects on our ways of being in the world. In the vignettes that follow, we see individuals struggling to negotiate issues of culture, and of identity, as they begin the questioning process that EP encourages.

In Vignette 13.1, for example, there is a complex interplay between seeking to conform to expectations of what is/should be done in the language classroom, both in terms of pedagogy and in terms of research. I have briefly discussed Jane's story in Hanks (2013a) but it is worth examining in more depth, as it makes explicit some of the cultural assumptions that surround and imbue discussions of pedagogy. Like Jenny in Vignette 12.4, Jane began by expressing her worries (about lesson planning, syllabus design, and how EP 'fits'). Once she began to trust her learners, she entered a similar trajectory of joyful excitement upon finding that not only do learners have interesting questions about pedagogy, but they are keen to investigate and enjoy disseminating their understandings.

> **Vignette 13.1: Worries and Thrills When *Doing-Being* EP: Jane's Story**
>
> Jane had long expressed an interest in EP. She had read a number of articles on the subject, discussed her thoughts with me, and tried out EP for herself on a small scale (a week-long 'project'), with her students in 2006. A short time later, upon finding that we were to be working together on a pre-sessional course, she asked if she could incorporate EP into her teaching that summer.
>
> We met in the week before the students arrived, and, clearly, despite her enthusiasm, Jane had a number of worries: *'I was having breakfast this morning and um...these are the things that are worrying me. First of all: How am I going to ensure the students feel that they are progressing? If they've got their puzzle and I do a bit of grammar and then they start their puzzle... how do they become aware of the language needs they have?'.*
>
> Barely pausing for breath, Jane continued (in a very practical voice): *'How am I going to cope? How are they going to say "I need the 3rd conditional here?" How do they know that? And how am I going to keep them engaged? How much class time am I going to... What am I going to do?'.*
>
> Almost immediately she moved on to think about structuring the syllabus (her responsibility was to teach them 'Language Development' classes for 90 minutes every day of the week for four out of the 10 weeks), and she

> wondered where EP would 'fit': *'Am I going to do ... a bit of grammar and address something for half an hour every day and given them an hour every day? In which case they'll be all over the place doing their stuff and research? How am I going to get them to feel that **that** is actually a lesson?'.*
> The Language Development classes on that particular course were flexible, with no particular syllabus, other than an instruction to teachers to work with the students in their classes to identify which aspects of the language were of most urgent interest to them. The course took students from all over the world, with various linguistic backgrounds, and a range of levels of proficiency. International English Language Testing System (IELTS) 5.5 was given as a general marker, but some students were extremely proficient (up to IELTS 7.0), while others really struggled with the language. At that time, teachers were trusted to listen to their students and respond accordingly. If there were students (eg from Japan or Russia) who needed to work on the articles system in English, this might form the basis of some of the lessons, but if they felt reasonably confident in that area, there would be no sense in spending precious class time on something they felt they did not need, so other foci were agreed (a sort of 'negotiated syllabus'). There was no course book, and although a bank of materials existed, there was no requirement to use all (or any) of the worksheets. This was (deliberately) in marked contrast to the very prescriptive Academic Writing classes that they also had every day.

Such worries point to a clash of cultures (internal and external); in handing over to the learners, there is a contrast with what we, as teachers, are trained to do. It goes against our training of writing lesson plans, lesson aims, and learning objectives and outcomes, all of which seek to impose a sense of control and direction. Even though Jane was well-disposed towards EP (she, after all, had been the instigator), she nevertheless had to grapple with a need for a timetable (etc.), which stemmed perhaps from older habits from her own training, and/or from accepted cultural norms in education: a plan based on linguistic items such as grammar, knowing exactly what will happen when, and so on.

Up to this point in the story, Jane's commentary was all very inward-looking, focusing on the self, and her own learning. However, as soon as she met the students and shared EP notions with them, inviting them to puzzle together, there was a dramatic change in the narrative (see below). In recognising and acknowledging the other (a Bakhtinian Other) actors in the room, the teacher realised she was not alone, not isolated in the decision-making process, that in reality, and most profoundly, she herself and her beliefs about language teaching and learning were examples of the linguistic and cultural diversity to be found in the classroom. For Jane, the innovation was that she could then trust herself to be tentative about her understanding of the learners, to trust the learners to have puzzles of interest to themselves and to her, trust herself, and them, to reflect on teaching and learning, and trust that language learning does not have to be focused only on particular assumptions about language – for example, on expectations about grammar (or lexis or other items).

> **Vignette 13.1: Worries and Thrills When *Doing-Being* EP: Jane's Story (Continued)**
>
> Nine days after our first meeting, Jane had introduced herself to her students, got to know them a little, and begun to establish relationships. Towards the end of the first week of teaching, she had got them to write their puzzles on a piece of paper, and then to share with the rest of the class.
>
> As a result of trusting her learners, and risking her Self, in the classroom, she was filled with excitement. After her first EP class she rushed to describe her students' responses to the invitation to puzzle about their language learning experiences: *'I just want to say that I was thrilled with what they are coming up with. I've got a few that I'm going to read out to you. Everyone's got more than one. And they are really enthusiastic about doing it. So I think it's going to be really exciting'.*
>
> She explained: *'One of them was from India and she was saying how in India, she said "My English isn't very good and I was humiliated so my question is Why is proficiency in English seen as a status symbol?" Others were: "Why can't I remember difficult vocabulary?" "Why can I not express my feelings exactly in English?" "Why do I have anxiety about studying at a British university?" "Why don't I like Academic Writing class?" "Why do international students hang out with each other from the same nationality?" "Why can't I tell if I'm progressing?"'.*
>
> Jane ended our conversation that week by telling me how she had responded, in her turn, to her students: *'I said "I am really excited about your puzzles and I'd love to research them myself". And everyone was going like this [nods]. So tomorrow the plan is that we put all the puzzles up round the walls and then everyone aligns themselves with whichever ones they want to research and then we'll get going'.*

> Jane and her students did indeed 'get going', and using their normal practices of class project work (involving questionnaire surveys, interviews, library and internet work) they investigated their various puzzles over the four-week period. By the end of the third week, Jane (contrary to her initial plan) still hadn't dedicated an entire lesson to EP, but had rather incorporated it into most of her daily practice with the students: *'OK, so I definitely haven't given them a whole lesson on [EP] yet. We've done bits, maybe a bit at the end, and when we finish what we're going to do... [...] the other parts of the lesson took over more, so they've only had about 20 minutes [each time]. But they have done their interviews. And as far as I'm aware, they're doing their research outside the classroom'.*
>
> Jane was learning to trust her students to do the work themselves, and not to feel that she had to control their learning inside (or outside) the classroom. But this was still a risky business: because it wasn't happening in front of her, she could not know if they were doing work outside the classroom or not. This posed a challenge to some of her own beliefs about the ways in which teaching and learning should be conducted.
>
> She went on: *'Tomorrow [Friday] they've got the whole class to finish off [collating and analysing data]. Two of them already came up to me and asked if they could have the poster paper. So for anyone who has finished tomorrow they can mount it'.*
>
> Jane had offered alternative ways for students to present their work (via written essay, PowerPoint presentation, or poster presentation), and they had, as a group, expressed a preference for posters, which they would then present to one another in the class in the fourth week. Following a practice session in their classroom, they (via Jane) invited teachers and students from other classes to join them for the final, public, presentations.
>
> Again, Jane rushed to report on the event: *'They all said they loved it. And I got [to talk to] individuals as well. I said "Brilliant" you know, "Well done" [...] "How did you feel?" And they all said it was lovely. Yeah, they had a really good time'.*
>
> Significantly, she added, *'You ought to hear the buzz that's going on there now. [...] There's two classes of students in there, and three teachers, and they're just "yak yak yak" [...] Oh it's really buzzing'.*

Jane's strong emotional reaction to EP (which is reminiscent also of John's experience in Vignette 9.2) may have partly stemmed from relief at the discovery that her students really had some puzzles. Arguably, the earlier, dominating, culture of Teacher-as-Controller melted away as soon as the learners became real (a kind of psychodrama?) and proved themselves trustworthy to Jane. It was not only relief though. Jane's words and delivery also convey a sense of her excitement at the questions students had, and a genuine interest in their puzzles. If understanding (rather than problem-solving) is positioned as central to this form of practitioner research, it can be enjoyable (as most of the participants in these pages have demonstrated) and productive: a way of enhancing quality of life, by simply enabling the agency, and valuing the contributions, of all the actors.

But what about the learners' perspectives? Did they feel the same way? Or were they just doing as they were told, and obediently producing puzzled questions to order? Vignettes 13.2, 13.3, and 13.4, below, give a flavour of their experiences, in their own words. We start with their reactions at the end of the first week of the course with Jane. Vignette 13.2 presents a snapshot of one of the (many) conversations in the class.

> **Vignette 13.2: Stories of Intercultural Puzzlement: Students from Jane's Class**
>
> At the end of the first week of the course, Jane invited me to come into the class and talk to the students as they worked in groups to share and refine their initial puzzles. One group was puzzled by the status of English, and Tina (a student from India) shared her preliminary thought processes as follows:
>
> *Judith:* [reading] 'Why is proficiency in English seen as a status symbol?' Oh that's really good!
> *Tina:* Especially in India
> *Judith:* Yes, what made you think of the puzzle? [...]
> *Tina:* Because we felt humiliated in our country if we are not very fluent in English. Yeah. And people are very arrogant... feeling very strong, so they see it as a status symbol. In India especially.
> *Judith:* Oh I see. OK... and so how are you going to find out more about this? Because these are very interesting questions.
> *Tina:* Other people. Because we are from different country. So ...

> 1. Are they facing same problem?
> 2. Do they feel the same? Which I feel in my country?
> 3. And er is it true for British people too? [...] Do other people feel humiliated because of their poor English?
>
> Humiliation. Because I was, I felt in India, sometimes I felt, in my college, and other places I worked there. So I wanted to know: do the others feel humiliated because of their poor English?

As Tina's story shows, puzzles can go beyond questions about language itself, to encompass complex cultural issues. Her reference to the continued dominance of English (and a particular type of English at that) highlights issues of ideology and power that lie ever-present, but often unacknowledged, in the language classroom. Such considerations remind us that language learners are whole persons (see Kramsch 2006) who bring partially hidden baggage, of culture, political, and personal history (Holliday 2013), with them as they attempt to transcend national, international, and intercultural boundaries.

> **Quote 13.6: Kramsch on Learners as Whole Persons**
>
> Language learners are not just communicators and problem solvers, but whole persons with hearts, bodies, and minds, with memories, fantasies, loyalties, identities. Symbolic forms are not just items of vocabulary or communication strategies, but embodied experiences, emotional resonances, and moral imaginings.
>
> (2006: 251)

Cultures of Identity

These are questions that go beyond mere nationality, or a monolingual approach to language learning and teaching. In the language classroom of today, students and teachers are constantly navigating immensely complex currents of affect and identity. In beginning the journey to gain access to the desired community of practice (in this case, the British university system), practitioners (of teaching and learning) are transcending national boundaries, and engaging with multiple voices and cultures, as well as co-creating their own 'small cultures' as Vignette 13.3 indicates.

> **Vignette 13.3: Stories of Culture and Identity: Students from Jane's Class**
>
> In the fourth week of the course, Jane again invited me to come into her classroom. This time the students spoke to me as they were practising their oral presentations to accompany their posters of their puzzles. They had spent the last two weeks investigating their puzzles (using the normal pedagogical tools of English for Academic Purposes (EAP) classes: surveys, internet and library searches, interviews) and were ready to summarise what they had found out. One group, consisting of Jamie (Hong Kong Chinese), Oak (Thai), and Kate (Thai), were particularly interested in understanding the difficulties they had in expressing their feelings in a foreign language. As they spoke, other students also listened in with interest, laughing appreciatively at appropriate moments in the conversation.
>
> *Kate: Our group puzzle is 'Why can't I express my feelings exactly in English?'*
> *Jamie: It's our puzzle.*
> *Kate: Yes and we did a survey about our classmates and other classmates. We had questionnaire with 16 men and 19 women, and found most of them have just been in UK less than 6 months but almost all of students have been studying English more than 7 years. And these are the top 10 difficulties why they can't express their feelings in English.*
>
> *[...]*
>
> *Jamie: In our survey most of the people think they are lack of vocabulary and it's difficult to find exactly the word to express their feeling. And second, is sometimes because of their personality they have, they feel shy to speak in English. Yeah. The third problem is they have grammar problem especially in speaking English [...] and fourth problem about the intonation because maybe they are non-native speaker so they don't know how to pronounce the words. Yeah and these [pointing to the poster] are the other top 6 difficulties [laughter].*
> *Oak: Number 6 is '[...] with my culture' because some culture believe, some people think that in their culture they don't want to express their feeling.*

> Another one is 'I only want to express my feeling to close friend or family'. The next one 'I say one thing but think another'
>
> [...]
>
> **Jane:** Thank you. Can any of you express your feelings now about discovering the puzzle or working on the puzzle? Can you express your feelings on that?
> **Jamie:** ... still difficult for us, for me to express the feeling because still lack of vocabulary [laughter].
> **Kate:** And we found that most of us have the same problems.
> **Jane:** So did that make you feel better or worse?
> **Jamie:** Better, because it's a common difficulty for the foreigner...

We see here the emerging dialogue between learners and teachers. The EP principles of 'work together', 'involve everyone', and 'work also for mutual development' can be seen in action. Through such principled activity, the learners realised that they were not alone in struggling to express their feelings: these are difficulties that are *shared*. They are common to any foreigner operating in an unfamiliar situation. And there is a sense of relief at discovering a common struggle – perhaps a realisation that it is not personal inadequacy that is to blame, but rather, that these are difficulties everyone experiences.

The conversation with Jamie, Oak, and Kate was captured as they described their poster following four weeks of puzzling and exploring. Although it is common for posters to be used (common practice in EAP classes, as well as in EP activity), they should not be seen as the end-point.

> *Meta-puzzling:* Why do some people focus on the posters, and see them as the end-product of EP? Why do they need a 'product'? Why do they need an end-point?

Poster presentations are not the product, they are merely a punctuation point in a much longer, more complex, process. They may lead to further questioning around the same topic area, or they may lead to written accounts of the work done so far. With my own students, following their poster presentations, for example, I have asked them to write group assignments explaining what they did, how they investigated, and what they have found out so far. Many of the participants came up with extensions of their puzzles, deeper understandings of the process and themselves, or, indeed, new puzzles, as a result. In some cases, they even tried out puzzling in other classes, or included, even co-opted, other students or teachers to help them in their EP work. As we saw in Chapters 9 and 10, Alison Stewart's 'zemi' class wrote longer assignments as well as making posters, and Cori Crane's students wrote academic assignments (as befitted their contexts in universities).

> *Meta-puzzling: Do you have to work in a group if you are doing Exploratory Practice?*

Most of the examples I have given in this book show people working together in groups to investigate their puzzles. And they have derived great enjoyment from that. But that's not to say that we must all always work in groups. There are alternative ways of being collegial that are just as useful. The vignette that follows shows one individual (Val) who worked alone on her deeply personal puzzle. Ostensibly, then, she was alone. Yet Val gained great confidence from the support of her classmates and teachers as she worked. In the session where she presented her poster, the warmth of the laughter that she seemed to be orchestrating, and the general atmosphere of people working purposefully to investigate and then share puzzles that were of interest to all, made me realise that you don't need to work in a group to investigate. There are many ways of 'doing-being' EP which involve the principles in different, and sometimes surprising, ways.

Vignette 13.4: 'Why Do I Feel Anxiety About Studying at a British University?': Val's Story

When she arrived on my course, Val (an Iranian student) appeared to be a shy, withdrawn young woman. She spoke extremely hesitantly, with long pauses, incomprehensible mumbles, and stumbles. At times it was very difficult to make out what she was saying. Nevertheless, she clearly had a lot she wanted to say, often staying behind after class to convey her thoughts to me.

She began to explain her puzzle, and (as so many do) immediately tried to supply some reasons for it: *'As a general ... [indecipherable] ... anxiety... now er, I er, because I'm studying here in Britain... anxiety. Whether I can do my... can I understand my lecturers in the class... when m y course start... because that time, er, professors just er, expect us to do a lot of works in essays, research. [Speaking clearly and firmly] This is another language. It is not my own language. That's why... I'm worried... the other reason for my anxiety is that: can I do my assessment in my essays, my research correctly if I ... [trails off into silence]'*

Encouraged by her teachers, Val spent the next two weeks investigating her puzzle. She spoke to other students, and realised that they shared her anxiety (though in a less extreme form). She went to her future department and spoke to one of the lecturers there. She touched on the psychological aspects of anxiety (both in language learning and in other areas), and she described a traumatic event in which a low IELTS score had humiliated her (she had even abandoned a previous course because of this).

In the class poster presentations session (after only four weeks), Val spoke publicly in front of the whole class and her teachers. She was still a little hesitant, but expressed herself clearly: *'This poster is... depend on my, my background about IELTS exam which I re-sat it twice and be-became the same [result] and so... that time I... missed my self-confident about English language. But at the moment I, er, I feel much better'.*

Despite the pressures of performance in front of the class, she spoke fluently, clearly and loudly, and even used humour. There was much supportive laughter during the whole poster presentation session, and in her presentation Val even seemed to be orchestrating the laughter by joking and smiling: *'For me was very strong... my anxiety was very strong. [Pauses and smiles, followed by group laughter.] Not now'.*

She described what she had found out: *'But totally they [her interviewees] mention the causes of anxiety for them is changing environment and, er, teaching method, er because it is different to their national culture and difficulty to understand, for example accent problems, and, er, about vocabulary [...] But I think that in that research, is my reference [pointing to her poster] some researchers believe that anxiety at the beginning of the semester is high but during the term and second semester it is reduced'.*

> It was noticeable that Val's language skills had improved: there was a marked increase in fluency, range of vocabulary, and structures, and she expressed her ideas clearly. The hesitations apparent in her first interview had more or less disappeared. Her confidence had improved and this in itself may have enabled her to access language and skills already present, but blocked by her high levels of anxiety.
>
> Moreover, she was beginning to engage with important research processes during her EP experience: everything from visiting the library and reading widely, to collecting data and analysing it, and presenting her initial findings in a public forum. She was able to critically analyse the causes of anxiety (her own and others'), relating this to literature on student anxiety more broadly. The process of investigating her puzzle was crucial for her Quality of Life. As she realised that others also suffered, she realised she was not alone, and gained sustenance from the support of others. In addressing her puzzled question, she was able to manage her anxiety and focus on her studies.

Three years later, I met Val again. Not only had she successfully completed her Masters degree, she had also gone on to gain a PhD in the UK. Her struggles with anxiety were a dim and distant memory for this confident and successful young woman.

I do not want to suggest that EP 'solved' the problem of anxiety, nor to imply that EP 'improved' Val's language skills. That would be a very simplistic interpretation, with a naïve belief in causality. Rather, I want to suggest that as Val went about uncovering her anxiety, which had become quite debilitating for her, she discovered that others also suffered (though perhaps not to the same extent) from nerves, fear of the unknown, fear of losing face. This shift from an internal world towards recognising Others, in itself, was reassuring. As she continued to investigate, she developed a sense of her own agency; *she* decided who to interview, *she* interpreted her data, *she* decided what to present to her classmates. It was at this point that she began to grow in confidence, and, I believe, was able to access language that was *already there*. This was, and will always be, a tall order, as Byrnes points out:

> … communication and its success are potentially even more fragile because ownership is not simply given and cannot simply be claimed. Recognising

> the fragility but also the surfeit of meaning making potential that inheres in the situation, communicative partners must develop a sophisticated, multilayered awareness of the innumerable transculturally and translinguistically derived meaning potentials that a particular context affords in order to position themselves and others responsibly and constructively within them. That is a tall order when communication takes place among members of the same social and linguistic group. It is a particularly tall order for the foreign language classroom to prepare students to operate in such contexts. (Byrnes 2013: 232)

Despite the magnitude of the task, though, it is achievable. Particularly if teachers and learners become aware of the need for collegiality, of the need to support one another as they negotiate these complex meaning potentials. These vignettes indicate that there are many ways of being collegial, many ways of being empowered. No one can tell you how to do it; no one can tell you what to do. Only you.

The vignettes also show that learners had to trust that (i) their puzzles would be taken seriously, (ii) sharing their puzzles could be done safely, without negative social impacts, (iii) the time spent investigating would be well spent, and (iv) their language learning/teaching would be helped and not hindered by the work. Identifying PEPAs or learning/researching opportunities was central to the latter. The notion of trust, then, is applicable not only to learners, but also to language teachers and teacher trainers.

Summary

In EP the rules of the game have changed, and this can be unsettling, not only for those who prefer more traditional approaches in the classroom but also for those who are open to innovations. It requires teachers to have faith in the learners' ability to take learning seriously, make independent decisions about their learning, and develop as practitioners of learning, as proposed in Allwright and Hanks (2009: 5–6). It also requires learners to trust in their teachers' ability to take them seriously, and allow them independence and room to develop. In sharing ownership of research, and enabling learners and teachers to contribute to discussions in the field, the resulting surge of energy and enthusiasm not only encourages teaching and learning to take place, but also creates space for small-scale, local, and situated research.

In the vignettes we can see some of the issues emerging from trying to marry different expectations, understandings of how things should be done. In the classroom these expectations are between teachers and learners (as well as teacher trainers, curriculum developers, managers, institutions, and the like). In the research project these expectations are between professional, experienced researchers from different disciplinary backgrounds. In both situations, belief systems clash, cultural norms and expectations need to be negotiated, boundaries transgressed, and new ways of being found which are at once respectful of yet challenging to established ways of doing.

The teachers, teacher trainers/educators, psychologists, researchers and learners in these pages are enquiring into their own practices, in their own contexts and with the aim of extending their understandings of educational processes and human behaviour. Their work is purposeful, systematic, and critical, and is made public via their presentations and written work, whether at a conference (large or small), on a Facebook page (as in the, very active, Exploratory Practice, IATEFL ReSIG, and Teachers Research Facebook pages), or through journal articles. In the pages of this book, as well as the work of many others, there is in fact a wealth of evidence of teachers and learners engaging in practitioner research. So, in fact, practitioners *are* engaging in research in a variety of interesting, exciting, and above all, *relevant*, ways.

In this chapter I have discussed such tensions, moving the discussion from beliefs about research, pedagogy, and integration of the two, on to consider issues of ownership, curiosity, and trust. Exploratory Practice is not named thus by accident: the clue is in the name – exploring our own practices in language teaching and learning.

Recommended Readings

Candlin, C.N. & Crichton, J. (2013a). From ontology to methodology: exploring the discursive landscape of trust. In C.N. Candlin & J. Crichton (Eds.) *Discourses of Trust* (pp. 1–18). Basingstoke: Palgrave

Macmillan. This book explores the issue of trust in professional life (not just in education but in all areas of society), and raises key questions about how trust (and mis-trust) pervades attitudes to practice.

Hanks, J., Miller, I.K., Salvi, A.I. (Eds.) with Xavier Ewald, C., Mendes Lima Moura, S., Apolinário, C., Slimani-Rolls, A., Bond, B., Poole, J., Allwright, D., Dar, Y. (2016). "Why Exploratory Practice?" A collaborative report, *ELT Research*, IATEFL Research SIG Newsletter, 31. This account of a one-day seminar held at the University of Leeds, on 6 May 2015, provides snapshots of EP work from Rio de Janeiro, Leeds, and London, and covers EP in Continuing Professional Development , English for Academic Purposes (EAP), English as a Foreign Language, and Educational Psychology, with particular emphasis on PEPAs.

Holliday, A. (2013). *Understanding Intercultural Communication: Negotiating a grammar of culture.* Abingdon: Routledge. Holliday's work on culture and intercultural communication is keenly relevant to themes in EP. This book is just one of his publications in the area. Of particular interest is the notion of moving across boundaries.

Kramsch, C. (2009). *The Multilingual Subject.* Oxford: Oxford University Press. Considering learners' experiences of language learning/teaching culture, Kramsch proposes the notion of 'symbolic competence', and suggests that learners have multidimensional, multi-lingual experiences that contribute positively to classroom language learning.

14

Conclusions

Introduction

In writing this book, I have sought to engage with Zeichner & Noffke's call for investigations of the 'the conditions that facilitate and obstruct the ability of educators to conduct research on their own practice (2001: 324). The challenges of practitioner research are many and varied, and Exploratory Practice (EP) is not exempt. We grapple with beliefs about practice and pedagogy, about methodology, and about research. Questions about what 'counts' as research, who does it, who reports on it, and who benefits from it are a necessary ethical as well as practical part of any research, and they are thrown into sharp relief by the work reported on here.

On taking an EP approach teachers and learners become deeply involved in explorations of their lived experiences in the classroom. Throughout the book I have addressed questions about what puzzles practitioners, and the knotty question of the difference between 'puzzlement' and 'problem'. Central to these issues is a critical analysis of what 'understanding' means, and what it means to practitioners situated in linguistically and culturally complex educational settings. By inviting you to consider puzzling, working to develop understanding(s), both individually and with others, and exploring ways of integrating research and pedagogy, the case studies and vignettes exemplify the spirit of EP. In sum, this book is an extended invitation to readers to join exactly the kind of dialogue that EP is all about.

From Research-as-Practice to Practice-as-Research

I began by using Allwright's (2003) more inclusive definition of 'practitioner' to include the notion of learners, as well as teachers, teacher trainers, and others, as researchers. I have examined this proposition and found that not only are practitioners capable of engaging in actively working to develop their understandings of questions or puzzles they have themselves set out, but that the field can gain immeasurably from such work. In foregrounding the perspectives of learners, in re-conceptualising researchers and teachers and teacher educators as people who continue to learn, while practising as language education professionals, we stand to gain a unique insight into the cognitive dissonances (Festinger 1957) surrounding the practice of research and pedagogy in what are (and always were) linguistically and culturally diverse contexts.

In Part One, I surveyed the existing literature on practitioner research, ending with a particular emphasis on EP, the notion of understanding, and its relationship with *Dasein* (Heidegger 1962). As I did so, I raised a number of questions about the practicalities of investigating practitioner research. I also noted the often entrenched ontological and epistemological perspectives regarding research. Research has cultural capital (Bourdieu 1991) which is politically and contextually situated. Some will never be convinced of the value of practitioner research, simply because it does not fit their conception of what research is. Others, however, not only accept it, they enthusiastically promote it, *because* it is an expression of their own deeply held beliefs about what constitutes research. As I surveyed the historical background to, and the philosophical and theoretical underpinnings of, the principles of EP, I argued that EP has a strong individual identity, which distinguishes it as a distinctive member of the practitioner research 'family'. Part One of this volume, then, placed EP firmly in the tradition of practitioner research and critically examined the EP framework.

> *Meta-puzzling: Why has understanding become so important? Why should teaching/learning languages take understanding so seriously?*

Part Two looked at potential understanding(s) *from* practice. I asked, 'What have we learned from the practice(s) of Exploratory Practice?', examining this question from a variety of viewpoints and contexts. These contexts were not only international (ranging over Brazil, China, Japan, Turkey, the USA, and the UK), but also inter-institutional, considering examples of EP in state secondary schools, colleges, and universities, as well as private language teaching institutions, and included EP as enacted in continuing personal and professional development, in General English, English for Academic Purposes (EAP), and Modern Foreign Languages.

> *Meta-puzzling: It is interesting to note that English as a Foreign Language seems generally to be categorised separately from Modern Foreign Languages. Why? Is it not modern? Not foreign? Not a language?*

The case studies and vignettes both illustrated and interrogated the EP principled framework. In charting the participant responses and analysing their contributions alongside them, I traced the lived experiences of practitioners engaging with EP within their own practice. The learners and teachers did more than respond positively to the notion of combining research and pedagogy: they were alternately thrilled, excited, fascinated. They brought renewed creativity, energy, and enthusiasm to their classes. Since they were investigating their own questions, and since they were concurrently practising the skills they needed, in the language of their choice, the work was, in one person's words, '*entirely* relevant to them'.

> Meta-puzzling: How do we need to understand Exploratory Practice now? It is, by definition, evolving, in response to and against understandings of the nexus of practice-participation-research perspectives. So what are we to make of it in the current climate?

In Part Three I argued that EP is not a panacea for all our ills. Far from it. But the same is true of any other form of practice or, indeed, of the outcomes of any research: at best they can only develop our understandings in small, incremental steps. In bending to societal demands to seek 'quick fixes' we (practitioners of research, of teaching, of learning) are pushed into superficial solutions which meet neither the demands of rigorous research nor the urgent needs of pedagogy and practice. So the EP principle of stepping back, resisting the pull towards 'solving' problems, and instead investigating deeply, questioning, critiquing, is worth examining in more depth. How does it relate to pedagogy? How does it relate to research? And how can both research and pedagogy benefit from such integration?

It is clear that trust, and indeed, what Candlin and Crichton call 'trust-in-action', is central to such questions. The stories of practitioners – learners, teachers, teacher trainers, educational psychologists – were narratives of trust. EP invokes the understanding of others, and in doing so it both requires and encourages trust.

> **Quote 14.1: Candlin and Crichton on 'Trust-in-Action'**
>
> The analysis of *trust-in-action* does not end with its effects; it is always dynamic and reflexive, a form of *praxis* that mutually implicates the concepts of the Conceptual Framework [of Trust] in the lives of individuals across micro and macro scales of social order – including the interpretations, actions and agendas of researchers.
>
> (2013a: 15)

According to Wright, 'learners are more aware about their learning and are more deeply concerned about learning than is often portrayed' (2006: 84), and it is evident that both teachers and learners (and others) have profound, serious concerns about teaching and learning. In the stories of the learners and teachers (etc.) in Part Three, we saw a range of puzzled questions, which probe deeply into the complexities of language classrooms. EP, through Potentially Exploitable Pedagogic Activities, takes this a step further; going beyond the notion of research-as-practice, I propose practice-as-research.

Language, Culture, and Identity in Exploratory Practice

Questions about identity, language, culture, and power (who does what, to whom, where, and when) arise when we engage in EP. Learners are included as researchers alongside teachers (Allwright 2003), but we have also seen that teachers may be learners. Identity is fluid: teachers become learners, learners become teachers, and both learners and teachers become researchers. This is well expressed in Tajino and Smith's notion of 'team learning' where teachers and learners jointly construe their learning and teaching:

> … the practice of team learning can be a sustainable way to promote improvements in language learning through the growth of better understandings by teachers and students of classroom teaching and learning processes. When teachers and students share the construction of their learning environment in a harmonious team-learning partnership, the full collaborative potential of team teaching may be realised. (Tajino and Smith 2016: 23)

Meta-puzzling: What makes Exploratory Practice special?

If, as I have argued, puzzlement is to do with understanding how classrooms are, the 'being' of classrooms, of how students and teachers (etc.) *are* in the world, then one of the things that makes EP special is the combination of epistemological, methodological, and ethical understandings of pedagogy. It is the notion of understanding, and therefore puzzlement, as a way of bringing together pedagogic research and perspectives, of participation and empowerment of those who are usually disempowered and unable to participate in the 'big decisions' about education.

All these questions and questioning processes bring the wider remit of language, culture, education, and research into play. As Kramsch (2009) argues, it is a highly complex scene.

> **Quote 14.2: Kramsch on Subject Positions in Multi-lingual, Multi-cultural Situations**
>
> The negotiation and power struggle that surround subject positions in published work as well as in private written or spoken communication are not special to the multilingual subject. Every language variety, dialect or sociolect carries with it memories of personal experiences attached to each of its variations, and for every author, positioning oneself within a discipline, a field, or across readerships, is a challenge. But multilingual and multicultural situations increase exponentially the semiotic resources available – as well as the risks of miscommunication.
>
> (2009: 21)

This brings us back to the notion of *Dasein*, Heidegger's term for human 'being', a kind of being that is characterised by being an issue (a puzzlement) for itself. As he argued:

> Dasein is an entity which does not just occur among other entities. Rather it is ontically distinguished by the fact that in its very Being, that Being is an *issue* for it. [...] *Understanding of Being is itself a definite characteristic of Dasein's being.* (Heidegger 1962: 32)

And this, as Dreyfus (1991) explains, is an integral part of what it is to be human: to try to understand understanding is to engage unconsciously or consciously in/with/through our humanity.

But the tension of the unknown can be uncomfortable. There is a drive to solve problems, find answers, resolve the unknown by turning it into a quantifiable known. A naïve response to the puzzles raised by the practitioners in this book would be to argue that the teacher should simply *tell* the students how to improve their speaking (or vocabulary, or concentration, or whatever else was puzzling them). This is a powerful temptation for teachers, teacher educators, and academics, perhaps too powerful for them to resist – after years in the field, the 'answers' often appear obvious, and it seems heartless to refuse to provide them. But on careful reflection it is clear that 'telling' the answers is not satisfactory. Solutions might range from seeking out more opportunities to practise with others (whether native speakers or not) to focusing on improving pronunciation or accuracy or fluency, or developing vocabulary. Developing understandings, on the other hand, begin to capture the complexity of speaking in a foreign language: the social, personal, political, and cultural issues that need attention. So EP presents epistemological challenges to the cultural norms and expectations of education *and* research. In gaining understanding of the different perspectives of all those in the classroom, and in treating puzzled questions with respect, greater trust between the participants is engendered.

> *Meta-puzzling: Why is the 'problem-to-solution' paradigm so attractive? Why is Exploratory Practice so keen to promote understanding instead?*

Problematising Problem-Solving

Solutions are seductive, and problem-solving is clearly deeply attractive. Staying within the problem-to-solution paradigm means that problems can be identified relatively easily (there is a societal pull towards such a technicist approach), and 'fixes' are sought ever more avidly. So a question like '**How** can I improve my vocabulary learning?' (or speaking skills, or writing ability) begs for technical, practical solutions, which are clear, thorough, and based on evidence of previous successes, as researched by distant experts. This sounds ideal, and for many (teachers, learners, and researchers) it is enough. But as Wright points out, such an approach

> … tends to be problem-focused, setting up a professional discourse of problem-solving. This has the danger of limiting the practitioner to the status of 'trouble-shooter' (Wright 2005: 429)

Despite EP's emphasis on understanding, many of the questions in the stories in this book were initially framed in such a way as to promote a problem-to-solution approach. Even when the questions began with '*Why…*' (a way of trying to encourage an attitude of developing understandings rather than problem-solving) some participants returned to the problem-to-solution paradigm. It requires some effort to refocus on trying to understand rather than leaping to problem-solving. EP suggests a much deeper, and potentially subversive, change in thinking about research, teaching, learning, and language. Enabling teachers to see themselves as learners, and learners to see themselves as teachers, and encouraging all to propose and investigate their own questions in an approach of puzzled enquiry, means a move from acquiescence to active (and at times challenging) practitioners. In Freirean terms, this is 'problematising' rather than technical problem-solving, to put his earlier quote in its context:

> We needed, then, an education which would lead men [*sic*] to take a new stance towards their problems – that of intimacy with those problems, one oriented toward research instead of repeating irrelevant principle. An education of 'I wonder,' instead of merely 'I do'. (Freire 1973: 36)

Questions, particularly questions that ask 'why', are concomitant for understanding. In EP, the difference is that we are no longer driven by methods, no longer entrapped in a machine, no longer focused on change and change for change's sake. By focusing on questions rather than solutions, we (re-)discover how necessary understanding is for humanity. But how can we get understanding that is shared and communicated? How to set up our practice to make understanding visible?

This raises the Aristotelian notion of *phronesis*. This form of 'practical wisdom' (Flyvbjerg 2001: 57) has a strong ethical and pragmatic orientation which 'focuses on what is variable, on that which cannot be encapsulated by universal rules' (ibid.). Practitioner research more generally, and EP specifically, may therefore be conceived as a form of *phronesis*: ethical, practical, and concerned with values in *praxis*. Although Flyvbjerg goes on to say that *phronesis* is oriented towards action, I would frame this as 'action for understanding' more than anything else.

Talking about safety research in healthcare contexts, Iedema et al. maintain:

> Safety research does not just require the enquirer to participate (as researcher) in practice, but also requires the practitioner to participate (as practitioner) in the enquiry. (2013: 65)

They go on to challenge the prevailing discourse of 'objective' knowledge, also referring to *phronesis*:

> Of course, important knowledge may be acquired and negotiated 'objectively', as I can read a treatment guideline, a care pathway or a medication administration protocol. But knowing-*that* exists at one or removes from *in situ* practice. Knowing-*how* – phronesis – needs to complement knowing-that. Knowing how involves doing, but doing without understanding actors' reasonings, trade-offs, workarounds and shortcuts does not engender phronesis. [...] Could it be that in the marginalisation of phronesis, and attendant inattention to what we do and say in the here and now, are behind organisations 'drift into failure'? (ibid.: 184)

From this discussion, further puzzling, and 'meta-puzzling' (puzzling about puzzlement, about puzzles and puzzlers, and about systems, cultures and beliefs), is engendered. As Holliday (2013) points out, we are all travelling with/through/around society; we bring our baggage with us, but we are not fixed: we cross boundaries (even the very subtle ones) that others in society might seek to establish as barriers.

Quote 14.3: Holliday on Crossing Boundaries

...**personal trajectories** comprise the individual's personal travel through society, bringing histories from their ancestors and origins. Through these trajectories, they are able to step out from and dialogue with the **particular social and political structures** that surround them and even cross into new and foreign domains. This domain thus crosses the subtle boundary with **underlying universal cultural processes**.

(2013: 3)

Holliday continues:

[I make it a theme]… that individuals are not only very capable of crossing intercultural lines, but that they can do this creatively and innovatively given the potential. Holliday 2013: 168

What these individuals in multi-lingual, multi-cultural classrooms need, though, is the space to engage in dialogue, as Chick maintains.

> **Quote 14.4: Chick on Dialogic Spaces**
> Despite the challenges inherent in creating dialogic spaces on courses that require formal assessment, viewing the feedback discussion as reflective conversation, can nevertheless assist in alerting learner teachers to the importance of socio-cultural factors, to an appreciation of what learners bring to a classroom, and to the fact that the path to language teaching expertise is a lifelong endeavour.
> (2015: 306)

Too often, practitioners (of teaching, of learning, of research itself) have accepted very traditional descriptions of what research is. Typically, as Borg (2013) has depicted, it is seen as consisting of large-scale surveys or projects involving intensive and time-consuming observation schemes, with high-profile outcomes such as giving conference presentations or writing articles for academic journals. This creates a problem for practitioner research, with practitioners peering anxiously into the depths, and wondering, 'How on earth am I going to manage to do this on top of my normal workload?'.

Many practitioners are hampered by the net of beliefs that surround research; their work is often downgraded by themselves as 'it's just what I think', and by others as 'it doesn't really count'. In other words, it is given little value. So what 'counts' as research in an educational context? What are the beliefs about research itself as a social practice, and can we unpack them?

Looking Ahead: What Next for Exploratory Practice?

Calls for alternative ways of doing research in education proliferate (eg Allwright 2009; Burns 2010; Borg 2013; Freeman 2006), and it is clear that there are options available for practitioners wishing to essay practitioner research. But if the practitioners have taken over the role of judging what research is relevant, and doing the research themselves, then where is the space for the academics? Are the criticisms noted above masking the protection of 'vested interests' as Breen (2006: 220) has argued? Practitioner research, and EP in particular, has the potential to be subversive, challenging the right of academics to adjudicate knowledge from afar, and may even be perceived as a threat. So trust is needed not only inside the classroom, between teachers and learners, and between and through the languages and cultures that they bring, but also more broadly in the field. Although EP was initially conceived within an educational context, its principles may have a broader appeal, and wider applications.

Exploratory Practice as a Form of Research

Interestingly, there have been recent developments in seeing EP not only as a form of pedagogy, but also as a form of research. In my own doctoral studies, I was attempting to bring together my own 'lived experiences' not only as a teacher but also as a researcher. But recently this has been extended even further.

Case Study 14.1: 'What Happens When Exploratory Practice Moves Beyond the Classroom?': A Story of Explorations in Research

What happens when those principles are taken away from their original 'home' of the language classroom and used in a different context? Richard

Fay and Susan Dawson explore just such an undertaking in Case Study 14.1.

> **Richard Fay**
> *University of Manchester, Manchester, UK*
> I'm a Lecturer in Education (TESOL and Intercultural Communication) at the University of Manchester with a long-standing interest in practitioner-oriented, collaborative research, and in researcher thinking and development. Exploratory Practice has been on my radar for some time but the extension of it for a researcher learning context (i.e. for the AHRC-funded project outlined in this case study) represents my first real foray with it.
>
> **Susan Dawson**
> *University of Manchester, Manchester, UK*
> I'm a final year PhD student at the University of Manchester. My doctoral research uses Exploratory Practice as both methodology and pedagogy, with a particular focus on the different types of knowledge that are generated through inclusive practitioner research. As part of my studentship, I get to do lots of interesting things, such as being affiliated to the AHRC project in this case study.

> **What Happens When EP Moves Beyond the Classroom?**
>
> *The Research Project Context*
> The possibility of extending EP – from its concern with understanding the life of the language classroom to a concern for understanding the life (or work and workings) of a complex research project – occurred to us in the early stages of a particular project: *Researching Multilingually at the Borders of Language, the Body, Law and the State* (AH/L006936/1 – www.researching-multilingually-at-borders.com) or 'RM@Borders' for short. This project is large in scale, lengthy in duration (2014–17), and complex in character, being multi-sited, multi-disciplinary, multi-modal, and multi-lingual (this explains why we call it a 'multi-multi' project). It has five case studies, each with different sites of operation, different disciplinary anchors and practices, different sets of researchers spread across different institutions, and different research questions. It also has two 'hubs' which interact with the case studies as well as with each other – the Creative Arts and Translating Cultures (CATC) and the Researching Multilingually and Translating Cultures (RMTC) Hubs. We are part of the RMTC Hub, and we suggested EP as a way of enabling it to fulfil its remit within the larger project.
>
> *A Role for EP?*
> Through our shared work outside the RM@Borders project (ie for Susan's PhD), we were already in the habit of discussing EP and its applications, and

doing so from a position of comfort, that is, EP was something we not only felt we knew something about, but also felt that its underlying principles were ones we largely shared. EP was thus readily available to us as a resource which might be extended (and adapted) for the RM@Borders project. EP was not, however, familiar (to any large extent) to other members of the team.

The RMTC Hub is an Education/Critical Applied Linguistics unit within the overall project. It is charged with advising and supporting the five case studies and the CATC (creative arts) Hub with regard to Researching Multilingually (RM-ly) practice, but it also seeks to learn with and from these other project units about RM-ly practice. Thus, the project proposal states that '... *the members of the RMTC "hub" will lead the development of integrated conceptual and methodological approaches, tools, and methods for researching translation processes and practices at borders where bodies are often at risk, in pain and/or in transition*'and'... *together with the CATC "hub" they will work with all researchers in the team, both in the field and remotely, at strategic stages and milestones throughout the project, to collate, consolidate and improve research practices in multilingual contexts*'.

However, the initial (and unhelpfully enduring) project discourse of 'shadowing' and 'researching the researchers' was at odds with this remit, and raised many ethical concerns. Consequently, we were achieving only partial success in developing a shared understanding (across the project) of this bilateral relationship between the RMTC Hub team and the case study researchers and CATC Hub colleagues. This partial understanding of the remit was the source of an operationalisation stumble but it also provided an opportunity for proposing the extension and adaptation of EP for Exploratory RM-ly Practice. We argued that, if EP '*is an indefinitely sustainable way for classroom language teachers and learners, while getting on with their learning and teaching, to develop their own understandings of life in the language classroom*' (Allwright 2005a: 361), then for our RM@Borders project, 'Exploratory RM-ly can provide a sustainable way for all RM-ly project researchers (including those in the CATC Hub and in the 5 case studies), while getting on with their project activities, to develop their own understandings of life in the RM-ly field of activity'.

Exploratory RM-ly Practice – initial steps

Initially, our team (RMTC Hub) developed our own curiosities (sometimes also called 'puzzles') and identified the 'data' being naturalistically generated which might help us explore these curiosities. Then we invited everyone in the project (ie case study researchers and hub members) to develop their curiosities, puzzles, or research questions (there were differing preferences regarding terminology). Susan's notes (in italics below) provide an initial critical analysis of these questions:

Sustainability – *some of these 'puzzles' are huge; research questions in their own right. How will they develop understandings of them through their 'normal' research activities?*
Relevance – *some of them seem more concerned with the intricacies of their individual projects and mostly unrelated (in my limited understanding) to the whole process of researching multilingually, which is your main aim, no? Does this matter?*
Technical problem-solving or understanding? – *which comes first? In EP it's the understanding, but a lot of these questions seem primarily technical ones. EP is exploring* **practice**, *whereas some of these puzzles seem more about exploring theoretical and technical issues. So does your EP base need extending/broadening?*
Quality of life – *the CATC Hub pick up on the idea of well-being which I think is related to QoL issues. They ask (last puzzle) if this could be a link between all case studies. Interesting.*
Researcher/Project development – *it seems to me that this whole process has enabled all to articulate concerns at an individual and group level that might not have surfaced in any other way, or at least might not have made it onto paper. Many of the puzzles seem related to ways of working together across different case studies and Hubs which is positive for the whole concept of* **mutual development and collegiality.**

For Richard, the key questions (prompted by his reflections on our EP activity to date) were 'Will our extended use of EP enable us – collaboratively, sustainably, and with consideration of quality of life issues including ethics – to develop insights into the Researching RM-ly practice strand of the overall project and, thereby, make a contribution to the objectives of the project more generally?'

Taking Stock
A year or so after EP was introduced as a way of negotiating an implementational obstacle, talk of puzzles or curiosities or research questions is largely absent in the project. In that sense, the experiment of extending EP from the language classroom to a research project has not been successful. Initial attempts to understand 'why' include reflections around the nature of interdisciplinary (as opposed to multi-disciplinary) research and the different levels of what might be termed *disciplinary porosity* or *academic hospitality* (vis-à-vis new ideas coming from other disciplines) of each of the project's contributing disciplines. However, it did enable us to get past that initial operational obstacle, and it did provide a new discourse (replacing talk of 'shadowing', etc.) for our shared project endeavours, one which recognised the collaborative and exploratory character of this 'life and work of the research project'.

A substantial body of work critiques practitioner research from a range of perspectives. Common criticisms emanating from professional academics cite the lack of rigorous training, and naïve approaches of novice (practitioner-) researchers which, it is argued, lead to flawed investigations. In addition, there are expectations of large-scale, time-consuming, and rigorous methods, which aim to prove/disprove hypotheses using statistical analyses. The results of these are finally published in (rarefied) academic journals or (expensive) academic books, to be reviewed and read by other academics, and, on occasion, practising teachers. For a teacher (or a learner), this is understandably off-putting. But if, as Dawson and Fay indicate, new conceptions of research itself can be brought into play, then a world of possibilities opens up.

Exploratory Practice as a Form of Scholarship

The overwhelming message from EP is one of enquiry/exploration/research forming a vibrant part of the teaching and learning lives of the participants. But this paints a rosy picture, which, even with some thorns noted, needs filling out. What about teachers and learners researching their own practices? It could be a form of scholarship as defined by van Manen:

> Perhaps the best answer to the question of what is involved in a hermeneutic phenomenological human science research method is 'scholarship!'. A human science researcher is a scholar: a sensitive observer of the subtleties of everyday life, and an avid reader of relevant texts in the human science tradition of the humanities, history, philosophy, anthropology, and in the social sciences as they pertain to his or her domain of interest – in our case the practical and theoretical demands of pedagogy, of living with children. So in a serious sense there is not really a 'method' understood as a set of investigative procedures that one can master relatively quickly. (van Manen 1990: 29)

In Vignette 14.1, Bee Bond reflects on her experiences of EP with colleagues (learners and teachers) in her workplace. These exemplify EP as a form of sustainable scholarship, for both teachers and learners.

> **Vignette 14.1: Thoughts on Exploratory Practice**
>
> For teachers, EP is a way of taking those staff kitchen conversations beyond the experiential 'well it works for me' into a more thought-out and questioning approach to practice. Frequently this stops when the kettle has boiled; sometimes the spark fizzes for a bit longer. Every now and then it develops into a slow burning and sustainable interest in an aspect of teaching and learning that leads to real scholarly outputs and enhanced understanding.
>
> For students, at its base level it is student initiated task-based learning. However, it can also be more than this. For EAP students, entering a research intensive university it is a way in to research cultures. It breaks down hierarchical teacher/student barriers and creates a truly collaborative learning environment where students are required to take the initiative, to question and to think critically, and see this behaviour modelled and mirrored in their teacher.
>
> Bee Bond, Leeds, 2016

The explorations of practitioners leads us to question long-held beliefs about research and pedagogy, with very fruitful results, not only for our own practice as teachers, learners, researchers, and scholars, but also for the field more broadly. In my own work, I link this to the notion (currently very popular in British universities) of 'research-led teaching':

> In an age of 'research led teaching' (as promoted by my own institution), EP's focus on integrating pedagogy and research suggests a rich area for further study. [...] by positioning learners alongside teachers as legitimate investigators of classroom language learning and teaching, EP enhances the potential for understandings in pedagogy and research alike. (Hanks 2015b: 19)

This view is echoed by Bond (2016), who argues that EP is at once scholarly exploration and a form of continuing professional development (CPD).

> **Quote 14.5: Bond on Scholarly Exploration**
>
> Approaching practice through scholarly exploration encourages (re-)engagement but does so as a manageable, continuous enterprise where quality of life is at the forefront, thus meeting the social and academic needs of both students and teachers.
>
> (2016)

If practitioners are entrusted with the responsibilities of investigating their own practices, the resulting contributions are of pedagogic and epistemological value. Because EP explicitly includes learners as well as teachers, and teacher trainers, educational psychologists, curriculum developers, as people who are, and should be, involved in researching language learning and teaching practices, and because EP explicitly encourages the integration of pedagogy and research, it affords creative possibilities for *all* those involved in language education to engage in 'the multiplicity of meaning-making of contemporary societies' (Byrnes 2013: 236). This happens not just in/through texts, but in/through the 'rhythmic alternation between constraining and releasing (structure and process), almost a discursive dance' (van Lier 2013: 249). But they need to trust one another, and they need to trust the 'system' (which so often lets them down), in order to proceed.

Redefining Notions of Pedagogy, Scholarship, and Research

As this discussion shows, there are a number of issues to be negotiated. Beliefs around pedagogy, beliefs around research, tensions around the *integration* of pedagogy and research swirl and coalesce as practitioners bring their own perspectives (conscious and unconscious) to bear. Classrooms are not only nurturing, supportive environments, but also sites of potential misunderstandings. The experiences described in this book are examples of the ongoing struggle between these concurrent and conflicting views, often held by the same person at the same time in the same space. Attempts to reconcile these views are expressions of cognitive dissonance (Festinger 1957), and the complexities of thought this requires can make life uncomfortable.

The notions of 'pedagogy', 'research', and 'practitioner research' are contested territory, and giants in the field of education have grappled with such issues for decades. There are those, for example, who would dispute the characterisation of what has been described here as 'research'. But others would strongly endorse it as precisely the kind of 'deeply contextual' work that Zeichner and Noffke (2001: 315) have advocated. The potential that EP offers is clear: a way of empowering learners, teachers, teacher educators, and all those involved in education to take their rightful place as 'knowers' and 'researchers' of their own language learning and teaching lives. An approach very much in line with that described by Iedema et al.:

> … the approach […] embeds and manifests complexity thinking and complexity talking. It does so by acknowledging that the common practice of maintaining an objective distance and producing research knowledge *in abstracto* needs to be counterbalanced by a new and more dialogic research paradigm. This new paradigm allows – no, *capitalises* –on closeness, on meshing researcher and practitioner interests and practices. (2013: 64)

For an example of this from EP, I return to Jess Poole (who first appeared in Chapter 1). Vignette 14.2 describes how her engagement in this dialogic research paradigm has re-awakened her creativity, and her interest in learning and teaching; in her words it 'is giving me back my mojo'.

Vignette 14.2: Reflections on Exploratory Practice

When I first thought about this question ('What EP have you been doing?') I felt a bit despondent. I'd been feeling stuck for while, and for various reasons like I had lost my mojo. I hadn't been 'doing' any Exploratory Practice. For ages. Well, I'd been to a Poster presentation given by our students – which was inspiring and uplifting. I'd participated in a staff development session with colleagues from Leeds and Leicester – which was motivating and re-affirming. I'd been doing a lot of talking *about* EP, but I hadn't actually been 'doing' any EP, so I was feeling like a bit of a fraud.

I felt stuck for a long time. I wasn't teaching on an EP module in our centre. There was no space in the timetable for EP on the busy summer pre-sessional. How could I do EP?

But, I had creative yearnings. Feeling bored and fed up (perhaps dried up by too much serious EAP?) I started daydreaming as a means of escape. I wondered: 'What makes me tick right now? What gets my juices flowing? What do I love?'

> And then I suppose I started … well wondering, exploring. I had an itch about Graphic novels. I started to wonder whether graphic novels could be used in EAP – I don't really know how, I just have a very strong hunch that they can. So I had a puzzle. I haven't really got very far with that, but it is bubbling away. The beauty of EP means I feel I can dip in and out of it when the time is right (for me and for my students).
>
> Then came the call for papers for the NFEAP (2016) conference on EAP and Creativity. People contacted me: 'Have you seen this?' 'This is right up your street'. Again they met with a grumpy response. 'I haven't been creative for ages! Maybe I'm not creative any more.' But then, I started wondering, 'Well what does it mean to be creative? That's the whole issue! Maybe what we are doing is creative? Could it be more creative? What will the students think if I ask them to be creative? What does creativity mean for them? What can they teach me about creativity?' So again, I was suddenly puzzling and then I just thought 'Well, let's do this in class.' So I have.
>
> I've been exploring with students what it means to do note-taking more creatively. I've been giving them choices about what kind of task they'd like to do in response to a text. I've been asking them what creativity means to them and why or even if we should try to be more creative when we are studying. And then I've been thinking about how I can teach more creatively.
>
> I think what I have realised overall that Exploratory Practice is, for me at least, a philosophy rather than always an activity. I don't always have to *do* EP, but I can *be* explorative. It is an approach, a way in. I find it very affirmative – it somehow gives me both the permission and the means to look at something /work on something deeply interesting to me, but in a very doable way. It is giving me back my mojo.
>
> Jess Poole, Leeds, April 2016

I end by wondering if questioning whether the work that the teachers and learners do 'counts' as research is to ask the wrong question. Those who embrace EP, or other forms of practitioner research such as Action Research, Reflective Practice, and so on, do so because of the immediate relevance of the agenda and findings to the practitioners themselves. EP can incorporate elements of research as part of the explorations, but it does not claim to be 'Research' (with a capital 'R'). This may be seen in the emphasis in EP publications, workshops, and talks on the phrases 'working for understanding' and 'developing understandings', and the deliberate attempts to reduce obfuscation by writing in a more accessible style about the work of practitioners. Such an approach is gaining hold across the field.

Implications and Impact

As I have continued with EP over the years, it has become clear that EP has taken off in a big way. The possibility, for example, of doing EP now seems an entirely viable proposition in all sorts of contexts. The fact that EP has spread across the UK (in the influential field of EAP) and across the world (as CPD or as pedagogy or as pedagogically rooted research) in China, Japan, Turkey, the USA, and, of course, Brazil, indicates a growing impact on/in the fields of applied linguistics and language education.

As I disseminate my own work in conferences and workshops, through social media and publications, as well as simply by living my professional life, I have found that others are adopting EP in their work. Perhaps as a result, more and more practitioners are getting in touch saying they want to try EP. I conclude that the landscape has changed since EP began in the early 1990s. EP is a *living* framework, one which is capable of growing, of developing, and one which has been incorporated into the curricula of many different types of language education. It therefore merits further attention.

So what do we know now that we did not know before? First, that EP can be successfully implemented in a variety of contexts, despite, perhaps even at times because of, the goal-oriented nature of such contexts, but that this is dependent upon a flexible interpretation of the framework, which applies the principles appropriately, rather than imposing a 'model'. Second, that these EP principles are deeply interconnected, with the notions of working for quality of life, of understanding, and of relevance to the participants, at the very centre of the network. Third, that whether EP is positioned as research or as pedagogy is immaterial: it is a growing force in the field, with multiple possibilities for nuanced and multi-layered interpretations. Fourth, that the shift from a paradigm of technicist problem-solving to one of open-ended puzzling offers greater potential for seeing and seeking the solutions to problems, of explorations and investigations of language learning and teaching as well as research itself. Fifth, EP's empowerment of practitioners enables them to find ways of investigating their own experiences, while also promoting the goals of language learning and teaching. And this provides opportunities for co-creation of educational understandings as well as knowledge, with learners teaching their teachers, as much as the other way around.

In sum, the contributions of learners and teachers may lead to greater understanding of the processes of learning, teaching, and researching. Traditional beliefs about research and pedagogy may, in the past, have been holding practitioners back, but if alternative definitions such as the ones afforded by EP can be accepted, even embraced, there is huge potential for practitioners to engage in small-scale, locally and globally relevant, research or scholarship, and this offers significant contributions to the development of pedagogy itself as well as the field more broadly.

Suggestions for Future Research

In keeping with the EP principle of sustainability, I end this book with thoughts of 'what next?'.

The issue of ***affect***, and its contribution to well-being, begs further investigation. For example, although I have provided case studies and vignettes from work in EAP and teacher development, these merely scratch the surface of what might be investigated. The cycles I have described of pre-innovation anxiety, followed by relief, followed by wave upon wave of enthusiasm, seemed common, but would others experience the same, or different, emotions? And how does attending to the quality of life of practitioners contribute to their ***motivation*** (or address ***demotivation and burnout***)? EP can take place over a relatively long time (three years, in Alison Stewart's case, much longer in the case of the EP Rio Group) or a short time (just a few lessons, as in Darren Elliott's or Yasmin Dar's case), or anything in-between. But was the enthusiasm of participants predicated on the novelty of the approach? This links to questions of ***longevity*** and ***motivation***: What happens to practitioners, and their feelings, over a longer period of time (see Brandes and Ginnis 1990)? My own experience (over almost twenty years) is that my interest, and enthusiasm, has remained constant, though my activity has ebbed and flowed, sometimes involving periods of intense work, at others just bubbling away on the back burner. But is this the same for others?

What happens if/when EP is institutionalised? If EP becomes a part of institutional procedures and practices, then the practitioners may lose the very power we have been talking about: it is in danger of becoming a management tool. Is practitioner research, whether EP or another approach, dependent on the interest, activity, and liberty of the participants? What if it is imposed as an integral part of a course (of learning, of CPD, or research methods?): Would individuals be able to object? Would EP, or indeed any form of practitioner research, lose its allure? Where do we draw the line between encouraging practitioners to try something for themselves and forcing them to do something (eg as part of the criteria for promotion) that they don't really want to do?

In the field of *Second Language Acquisition*, there are interesting possibilities offered by EP (as discussed by Tarone and Swierzbin 2009). How might EP contribute to the development of our understandings of SLA? What can learners, as well as teachers and researchers, tell us about the processes, the difficulties, and the triumphs? This book has barely touched upon such issues, but it would surely be a relevant area to explore further.

Similarly, the question of how EP as an educational process relates to *assessment*. Can the work produced by EP practitioners (students or teachers) be assessed? If yes, how? As long as appropriate assessment criteria are used, and in appropriate ways, the answer is likely to be in the affirmative, but this needs to be interrogated. As the assessment of students becomes more and more associated with political gatekeeping, can we retain a sense of the true aims and processes of assessment?

Within EP itself, an area of potentially fruitful research would be to investigate further *the relationships between principles and practice*. My discussion has opened up a range of questions which merit deeper investigation. For example, in empowering learners to investigate their puzzles, are teachers inevitably going to prioritise the learners, leaving their own questions to one side? Or is it possible for learners and teachers to do EP concurrently? And in this case we immediately see rising in front of us the question of how each is to understand and be understood through the diverse linguistic and cultural lenses that define our classrooms. As we have seen, this question is inseparable for questions around trust. These in turn lead us to questions about collegiality: Do we need to work in groups to be collegial? Are there other ways in which collegial working can take place?

The principle of sustainable research is also of interest. Does EP continue for all participants all of the time? What happens if/when someone gets to the end of puzzling about something? Do they just stop?

The beliefs of learners, as well as teachers and researchers (not to mention society as a whole), are omnipresent in any discussion of practitioner research. The **intersections between conflicting beliefs held by practitioners** (of learning, of teaching, of research) are sites of particular interest, revealing as they do not only the palimpsest of beliefs held by any one individual, but also the social, political, and ideological pressures that exist in a world (described so eloquently by Breen 2006) of bureaucratic surveillance, control measures such as checklists and so-called competency frameworks, and all too common mismatch between the rhetoric of education and the mechanisms which we have to survive. We struggle to resolve the cognitive dissonance that this causes, and a better understanding of the forces at work here would go some way to relieve the pressures currently oppressing those who labour in education.

The challenges of implementing practitioner research (whether EP or any of its siblings) are many and varied, and certainly worth investigating in more depth. And the **relationships between research, scholarship, and pedagogy** need teasing out, particularly since no one seems able to provide a clear definition of scholarship. This last is of great importance, as it is now being included in the job descriptions of teachers. Often disappointingly presented as an alternative or watered-down version of 'research', the notion of scholarship is beginning to take on a life of its own, and to generate a whole new discourse. But without a clear definition, a cynical interpretation would be that this is merely another way to move the goalposts to wherever is convenient for those in power. The EP framework could provide a potentially very helpful definition of scholarship, but this needs further investigation.

There are, of course, those who would be most unwilling to accept practitioner research of any kind, and EP in particular, as research. Such arguments have dominated the field for decades, and yet there is, in amongst the disputes, a small patch of common ground. When we consider what research is *for*, it seems uncontroversial to say that (good) research is for developing human understandings of the world (or indeed the universe) of practice(s), and of the relationships that are governed by, and govern, them. So, considering research and pedagogy as central pillars in any educational institution, we need to put critical questions to pedagogy, to research, and to integrated research and pedagogy. Hence there are questions about EP and research that would potentially bear fruit. What are the challenges for practitioners, of teaching, of learning, of research, as well as the potential benefits?

Finally, ***the lure of problems*** is another area worthy of investigation. I have alluded several times to the knottiness of the problem/puzzle issue. It does seem that problems, and technical problem-solving, are deeply attractive, while puzzling, with its open-endedness and aim of developing understandings too deep for words, may not always suit everyone. I have suggested that problem-solving is seductive, and I argue that actively puzzling in the ways suggested by EP *interrupts* that seduction, by asking awkward questions at awkward times. But what does this mean? And why does it matter? My own beliefs (based on years of puzzling over this question) suggest that it matters little in the end – as long as the attitude is one of curious enquiry. Such an attitude takes time to develop (there is always that temptation to leap to solutions), and this, too, would bear further scrutiny.

To sum up, more studies in different institutions, different contexts, and over varying periods of time are needed to see if the potential of EP is a viable, even desirable, form of practitioner research. Each of the areas outlined above requires scrutiny, analysis, and discussion. As EP has begun to impact globally, it requires further examination. Further studies are needed to uncover the deeper relationships between the everyday practices and the principles of all those involved in education and research or scholarship.

Conclusion

Zeichner and Noffke (2001) argued that practitioner research is, and should be, justified by the relevance it has to practitioners themselves. The stories in this volume demonstrate that in doing so they (learners, teachers, teacher educators) gained personal satisfaction, as well as, perhaps even as a consequence of, developing their own understandings while engaging in normal classroom practices.

Teachers and learners (and researchers) are continuously engaged in negotiating conflicting beliefs around pedagogy and research. Attempts to reconcile such beliefs in practice lead to forms of cognitive dissonance as a range of varied, often unexpressed or inexpressible, understandings seem to be at odds with practices. Preconceptions of pedagogy and/or research may, therefore, play a role in preventing the potential offered by practitioner research. If on the other hand, alternative visions, such as EP, with its deeper requirements for interrogating practice and developing understandings, are accessed, then, perhaps, such potential might be reached.

Academics as well as teachers, teacher educators and learners need to respond to Freeman's (2006) call to think differently about professional learning and professional development. It is clear from the EP experience that learners as well as teachers *are* interested, and they *will* inquire deeply into learning and teaching, as long as they are given the space and liberty to do so, and as long as they set the agenda, thus making the work relevant to their needs. As Freire (1973) suggests, the only one to learn is the person who owns the learning, and frames it for themselves. This applies not only to learners, but also to teachers, who are also learning as they continue to teach, in a fruitful cycle of professional development. All too often, practitioner-researchers are pulled in opposite directions: should they give attention and energy to research or to pedagogy? The elegance of Exploratory Practice resides in the opportunity it affords to shift those opposing movements back into a coherent, productively complex and dynamic whole.

Part IV

Resources

15

Exploratory Practice Voices

Introduction

A driving force for this book has been to ensure that it not only establishes the history, and the philosophical and theoretical underpinnings of Exploratory Practice (EP), but also brings the field up-to-date with more recent developments. The book aims to take EP's ethical, practical, theoretical framework, and analyse it thoughtfully, moving from practice to research and theory, back to practice. But as we have seen, there is more than one voice to be heard. Consequently, I now turn to some 'living resources' in the shape of interviews with those who have been doing EP for a while, and who therefore have some useful insights to share. I am enormously grateful to those who contributed, despite heavy workloads, and pressing life/health/well-being concerns. These interviews with some of the central figures in the field, the very researchers that have been talked about in earlier chapters (in alphabetical order: Dick Allwright, Isabel (Bebel) Maria A. de Cunha, Inés Kayon de Miller, Assia Slimani-Rolls, and Akira Tajino), are at once a chance for readers to hear from them directly, and an invitation to readers to join in the conversations.

© The Author(s) 2017
J. Hanks, *Exploratory Practice in Language Teaching*,
DOI 10.1057/978-1-137-45344-0_15

Each interview used six starting points that everyone had the chance to address as they wished:

- How did you first become interested in EP?
- What have been the major influences on your thinking?
- What are the key trends in practitioner research that you'd identify?
- What would you say you have learned so far?
- How do you see the field developing in future?
- What resources would you recommend for someone who wants to begin research in/on/through EP?

Framed as: 'What do you think will be helpful to a reader interested in trying out EP?', the interviews are flexible and open-ended, to allow for discussion of other issues the contributors think germane. Naturally, we all have different points of view, and want to emphasise different aspects or experiences. Some gave all their attention to just one question, while others answered the questions that were most productive for them, and that they thought would be most helpful for others. I hope that this demonstrates the multiplicity of perspectives, and the complexity that EP encourages. The intention, then, is to cordially invite you, the reader, to take your place in this community of practice, to join in the discussions, and to add your puzzles, perspectives, and experiences to the threads weaving in and out of the EP story.

I start with Dick Allwright, who was there at the beginning of the strong form of the Communicative Approach as well as EP. Dick has worked over the years as one of the pivotal figures in applied linguistics to bridge the gap between theory and practice. Despite his modesty, it is logical to start the interviews with him, and find out about what influenced his thinking.

Interview with Dick Allwright

> **Dick Allwright** taught at Essex University, where he pioneered language classroom research, before he moved to Lancaster University in 1978. There, his interest in classroom research shifted towards research as a contribution to teacher and learner development, via the notion of EP. Retired since 2003, he is still actively pursuing his interest in teacher and learner development.

Hello Dick! What made you first become interested in EP?

In a sense there wasn't an EP for me to become interested in, to begin with ... There was other people's classroom practice that I got interested in which later became what we characterised as EP. This developed well beyond what I had originally seen. So what I'd *heard* about (in the very early 1990s) rather than seen was teachers who were already getting their learners to help them, the learners themselves and the teacher, understand what was going on in their classrooms through asking them to address issues in group work that weren't the usual pedagogic stuff of pollution or traffic or whatever, but actually issues that were affecting their lives in their classrooms.

The starting classroom issue I came across, in Rio in 1990, was the old problem of 'How can I stop my learners slipping into their first language instead of keeping on talking English?' Nobody seemed to have found a solution, although they had tried many different alternative teaching techniques. Eventually I came across a teacher who had asked '*why*' instead of 'how'. She had asked herself: 'Why don't my learners manage to stay in English when they're doing group work? They keep slipping into Portuguese.' And then she had asked them to help her understand what was going on. Together they developed an understanding that meant the 'problem' sorted itself out without the teacher having to try any more new techniques.

Having noticed that this was what at least one person was doing, it seemed enough to start looking for signs of it elsewhere, and encouraging it whenever I saw it. That was in Rio in 1990, and it was where I began thinking that, having got disillusioned with the sort of classroom research I was supposed to be teaching Cultura Inglesa teachers in Rio, that here was a viable alternative. I had already been working on it in preparation for the book with Kathi Bailey (Allwright and Bailey 1991), but hadn't actually got much to say at that point so it became an epilogue about how things might be different in the future.

It seemed to me that I was honouring the work of the teachers, and that was what crucially needed to happen. They were in a bit of a crisis—they had an in-house journal 'Research News' that people didn't want to contribute to because they weren't at all sure they were doing research. So when I heard this sort of story of their practice from teachers, I tried to reinforce it as interesting, and not just to me, but also interesting to other people. I tried to encourage them to realise that they were doing something of wider interest. I remember one branch manager who turned to one teacher who'd been telling me her story, and said: 'See! I've been telling you it's interesting what you've been doing. Now will you believe me?'

There was also the massive problem of 'burnout': incipient burnout in the Cultura, and partly fuelled by people like me going and telling people that what they were doing wasn't good enough and they needed something else.

When you say 'people like me' what do you mean?

Academic researchers, experts from the British Council, and so on, flying in, employed by the bosses, however nice the bosses were. I mean, one year it would be new ideas about reading, the next year it might be new ideas about vocabulary. Every year they'd be expected to adopt new textbooks, adopt new practices, without ever having had time to actually get used to the previous year's recommendations. And that was tiring people out, exhausting them, and making them feel life was hardly worth living. In a word: burnout.

And suddenly here was I telling them that what they were doing was actually *better* than what I'd been employed to teach them to do. The joy we got from the early years of Rio work was teachers actually saying: 'Now I know why I started teaching in the first place!' Joy. And that was really crucial to feeling that we were onto something worth having.

When you think about how you got to where you are now, what kind of things had influenced your thinking?

When I went to study applied linguistics at Edinburgh University in 1967, the job of applied linguistics appeared to be to find ways of making language teaching, and therefore learning, more efficient: meaning—take less time to reach a measured level of proficiency.

The influences on that seemed to be:

(a) demand from governments,
(b) demand from teachers,
(c) expectations set up by teacher training,
(d) expectations set up by the available literature, and

(e) the focus of academic research in the 1960s.

All this amounted to *prescription* as the order of the day when I started my career in language teaching and learning.

In the mid-1970s I got involved with TESOL conferences, where prescriptiveness was still thriving, and highly researcher-centred classroom observation, but other viewpoints also got a reasonably good airing. For example, when I first went to TESOL in 1975 in Los Angeles to give a talk about the treatment of error, it got a good response, because apparently I was the first person who seemed to *understand* that teachers had a real problem treating error. Because it was complex, and perhaps not even a good idea (because it was so complex) to expect anybody to be able to do it well, in the terms which people expect it to be. And that encouraged me to think that I was relating to teachers in a way not expected of an academic researcher. And *that* encouraged me to think that there was something there that I should build on; trying to understand the problems teachers face in the classroom was more important than trying to understand the problems theories face being implemented in the classroom.

Can you explain what you see as the difference between those two things?

Going back a bit, to the 1960s, the Pennsylvania Project, for example, tried to teach teachers how to teach for a period of four years such that at the end of the four years you'd be able to say that the method one set of teachers used was better than the methods other sets of teachers used. In the end it failed to show any significant differences, largely because the teachers were sensible and professional enough not to allow themselves to stick to what they'd been told to do. But of course what it meant was the teachers got blamed for the failure of the experiment rather than praised for doing a professional job—of doing their best for whoever's in front of them. And that was an important lesson I think.

It was allied in my own experience in Sweden, also in the 1960s, when, as novice teachers, we were given very highly prescribed materials to teach. They had a script for you to follow—words you could use to do everything with, as well as a plan for every lesson. Once, when I used one of those lesson plans it didn't work very well. I said something to the regional inspector about the plan not being good, and she said: 'Well that's not good enough. It's you teaching them, not the plan. It's up to you to find something that works for you and them. You can't just say "Stockholm has produced a rubbish plan".' That was a crucial lesson in terms of the relationship between the value of having a prescription, which gives you safety of knowing what to do, and the responsibility for *not* doing that if there's a reason for doing something different. Even if you have to invent something that nobody else has invented. You have to do what's right for you and your learners at that particular point in history, in that place, with those particular people. The insight from tutors there was: if what they prescribed didn't work, then you had to work to find something that did work, for you and your learners. You couldn't just blame whoever made the original prescription.

Would you call yours a stance of questioning?

I read Bertrand Russell's *Sceptical Essays* when I was quite young and I took to heart his admonition that people would do well not to believe anything unless they had good reason for doing so. It had a great influence on me, such that I became good at identifying things that were being taken for granted and questioning them.

More practically, when I got to Essex University in 1969, Penguin Books was producing a lovely series of accessible psychology books. That's where I turned to social psychology from individual psychology. I abandoned individual psychology and the experimental method and all that, and I became much more interested in social psychology and management psychology. They were still doing it in the hope of eventually prescribing, but they were at least trying to describe what was going on first, instead of prescribing without having made any attempt to *understand* what was going on in the situations they were prescribing for.

So understanding was already kind of strong in your mind?

Probably not very much at that time… because I think I believed then that description itself would get us a long way. It took me a while to get beyond that and say: 'No. Description isn't going to do the job.' I think much more important was the disillusionment with individual psychology that seemed to me to have very little to say about the classroom. Prescription had been taken for granted and failed. So now prescription was replaced by *description* in the form of observational classroom research. But I also felt disillusionment with the descriptive approach that was putting too much weight on being able to describe and then analyse the description and then come up with a prescription for what would be better, without asking learners or teachers.

You mentioned in your notes for this interview: 'I was inspired by radical work in Hawaii that I knew about from Peter Strevens', and you also mention 'I got interested in Language Learner Autonomy thanks to work in France and Council of Europe project in Scandinavia'. Do you want to pick one of those to talk about?

Learner Autonomy … I had an M.A. student working in France, very interested in Holec's (1980) work. I was also interested in John Trim's (1976) work in Cambridge and got involved myself with a Council of Europe project promoting autonomy across Europe for foreign language teaching. That was extremely interesting. It was the same appeal to me that this was something that was saying: 'Things don't have to be the way they are. There might be an alternative way which is more respectful of people; not trying to prescribe exactly what people do, but helping them develop their own ways of doing.'

Hawaii… I won a scholarship to travel across the states in 1974. Peter Strevens (my Department Head at Essex University) advised me to visit the East-West Centre in Hawaii. Not from the standard language teaching side of things, but because what they were doing was, in a month, getting people up to a level so they could pass the entrance exams for Hawaii University. The *genius* of them was to say: 'You've got 30 seconds' for these apparently simple (in terms of materials) but actually quite complex (in terms of communication) activities. It was magical.

They also had another idea which was central to my mind at the time. It was in the second language acquisition (SLA) literature as well as in their minds as 'peer tutoring'. This was crucial in that one of the basic ideas was that as soon as somebody has learned something, give *them* the job of trying to teach someone who hadn't yet learned it. It doesn't matter how bad they are, however long it's taken them to learn it, just give them the chance to try and teach somebody else. There was a very nice paper I remember, about a little girl who'd been doing rather badly, and was well behind the others, but when she eventually did manage to learn something (to do with reading), they assigned her to someone else to help them, and she absolutely blossomed thereafter. Across the board, not just in that activity.

It was technically, cognitively, the fact that trying to explain your own understanding is helpful for your understanding, but also in terms of self-esteem: if you help someone else to learn, then you're going to feel better about yourself, and your ability to carry on learning. So from there came this connection that the learners interactively can do an awful lot more for each other than a teacher is likely to be able to do, if only you give them the opportunities to do it.

But why encourage learners and teachers to take on a researcher-like role?

When I moved to Lancaster in 1978, Communicative Language Teaching (CLT) was all the rage. But it soon split into a reduced watered-down version, and a much stronger, radical approach that I had been developing (in Essex and Poland), having lost all faith in prediction and control. I became much more interested in how control itself, or the insistence on the teacher's control, could be the hub of the problem. The strong form of CLT, and experience in Learner Autonomy, had taught me that a lot could, productively, be left to chance, and to recognise the richness of learning opportunities that classroom interaction in itself could be trusted to provide.

I lost all faith in academic researchers' ability to produce, even in SLA, productive understandings of classroom language learning and teaching. Teachers, often rightly, viewed researchers as purely parasitic, interested only in their own narrow research questions. By the mid-1980s I was beginning to realise that understanding was key, but *not my understandings* (those of the academic researcher). Instead, I began to trust in the possibility of helping both teachers and learners develop *their own understandings*.

One other important person I'd like to ask you about is Paulo Freire

Yeah. At Lancaster in the 1980s I was trying to get people interested in his ideas; as alternative things that people would read on the M.A. course, as a way of looking at how we might build up a curriculum. I had the notion of the procedural syllabus at the time. That the syllabus would be more interesting if you, instead of focusing on the content, focused on the procedures: 'What procedures do you think it's worth learners undertaking in the classroom in order to develop language?' rather than: 'Do you want this tense before that tense?', or whatever.

The procedural syllabus was a very productive idea for me and I liked very much what Freire was doing— to go into a community and find out what the issues were locally. So the procedural syllabus in terms of content could be based on local issues and then the procedures in terms of pedagogic procedures could be based on whatever that turned out to be, in terms of tasks or any sort of activity that might get people explaining the issues that they wanted to. Whether it was literacy, or access to voting, or access to water.

So would you say that Freire was somebody who influenced your thinking?

Yes… It's difficult to assign any sort of balance, but in practice I was probably more influenced by people I was closer to, like Esther Ramani and Michael Joseph and Prabhu, from India. Prabhu in particular was taking the sort of Socratic approach of saying: 'Well you can't actually teach anybody anything, but you can get them to think better than they've ever thought before'… and that's all you could hope to do. And if they start picking up direct ideas from you, it's probably a bad thing, because they need to develop their own ideas. You can get them to *think* about your ideas. But anything that means *copying* is not going to work out well.

The other thing I got from them was the inevitability of slowness in any sort of development. And that was basically in their Indian experience, not those people, but the previous generation, who had the British Council going across the entire country on *'How to teach…'* or *'New ways of language teaching'*… going to halls and talking to thousands of people one night, then moving on to the next lot, and having the thought that they'd actually now changed the face of language teaching in India.

What Prabhu, Esther, and Michael were saying was: 'Don't even try! It's a total waste of energy. Just influence whoever it is that you are in contact with. In the long run it will be better than it was before.' And it might then eventually get wider, but could be spoiled by that. So again, don't even try to proselytise, unless you really can follow it up and work with people and make sure that they *can* do whatever it is that they've decided they would like to do. That was very powerful.

Something that we haven't really mentioned is Action Research…
I don't know exactly when I first got in touch with Action Research (AR), but it was a natural thing to do in the 1980s. I was sucked into it quite happily as the obvious way of bridging the gap between my academic classroom research and locating what teachers themselves might be able to do in their classrooms.

However, when I went to Rio in 1990 to teach academic classroom research, I did not have in mind teaching AR. I was teaching them the research procedures for an SLA project in the classroom that depended on recording classrooms and analysing what learners did in the classroom. So it was not a classroom research project for pedagogy directly; it was an SLA project in the classroom that depended upon academic research taking place.

AR in those days was basically arguing for the same sort of research experiments but without a control group. But then I had a couple of Danish visitors who gave me lovely anecdotes, and the main one was: 'What are you interested in Action Research for? It's silly. We've done it in Denmark, and it's not going to work.' I cannot remember the substance of their arguments, unfortunately, but it just shook me; saying: 'Here's this lovely idea', and suddenly these two people come from where there's a lot of it happening, and they're saying: 'Don't waste your time'. Basically for them it was already passé. I was prompted by them to worry that perhaps I'd been far too enthusiastic.

We've started by talking about the kind of historical background to EP. So for somebody who has never thought about EP before, what would you say to them?
In the late 1980s I was still focusing on observation as central, but in my book (Allwright 1988) I had begun to question what research based on outsider descriptions alone could offer language teachers and learners in the way of productive understandings. Then, in the book with Kathi Bailey (Allwright and Bailey 1991), I had added an epilogue that questioned all the hitherto taken-for-granted arguments in favour of academic observational classroom research as a model for teacher research. I suggested that what was needed was a new relationship between teachers and researchers, where an academic researcher might act as a consultant

to a teacher/researcher. This seems to be the model adopted in AR circles (e.g. in Australia).

But at TESOL I had experienced at first hand the highly destructive and toxic researcher/teacher split, with neither side trusting the other to be useful for the development of understandings. That made it unlikely that researchers would be willing to act as consultants, or that teachers would welcome their counsel. I had an even more radical idea that was even more unlikely to be acceptable to academic researchers: that teachers should employ teachers on their own (teachers') terms, to explore whatever research questions interested them (the teachers again), not the questions academics wanted to pursue.

It came to a head when I was invited to go to Brazil in 1990 to teach academic classroom research techniques to language teachers at the Cultura Inglesa in Rio de Janeiro. I lost faith in that project when I found I was meeting teachers who had already started asking their learners to help them understand certain aspects of their language teaching and learning. For example, the learners' commonly experienced failure to maintain English as the language of classroom discussions. Thus was born what we originally called 'Exploratory Teaching'. But we soon renamed it 'Exploratory Practice' to avoid the teacher-centred focus of the original term.

What we were calling Exploratory Teaching at that time [early 1990s] was the idea of precisely helping teachers reorient, if they were so inclined (because there's a real difficulty in trying to find a way of suggesting things without appearing to be demanding), was that teachers should in fact start by thinking about anything they didn't understand about what was happening in their classroom.

We did, right from the beginning, try to say: 'We're not asking you to start problem-solving; we'd just like you to think about something you'd like to understand better, something that you are puzzled by. Then think of ways of exploring how you might get a better understanding, using the learners as a source of help, which might at the same time, help *them* understand better.'

We hadn't focused on learners particularly though. That took three or four years, probably. We had a big discussion, and Ralph Bannell said: 'We ought not to call it Exploratory Teaching any more. It's wider than that. Let's call it Exploratory Practice. And that would include the learners, it would include if people want to do it outside language teaching… or outside teaching altogether! Then we've got a name that's not going to put them off.' And that was a good insight, from Ralph.

What cheered me up most was every time I went back to Rio the number of teachers who told me just how much joy they had found in teaching again. It was wonderful to hear.

When you say 'it was working', what do you mean?

Whatever it was that they were doing was helping them, and their learners, *understand* what was happening in the classrooms, and that in turn was helping everyone enjoy more whatever it was they were doing.

It was then, I think, that we started getting quite gung-ho about PEPAs—Potentially Exploitable Pedagogic Activities—as an alternative to standard teaching techniques. So if I ran a workshop with teachers, I would say: 'OK, what do you normally do as a teacher? What is your repertoire of techniques?' And then: 'Of all these things, what do you think might be of any use to you? If you wanted to understand better what was happening?'

And somebody would say: 'A test', and I'd say: 'Well, how would that help? Would that help in understanding? Wouldn't it generate more data, rather than directly help you to understand?' So we'd be gradually working towards finding things that people do already, familiar teaching techniques, that would also be exploitable for the purpose of trying to develop understandings. That meant they wouldn't have to learn to do anything new (such as learn how to use standard research techniques).

It was, I think, very largely *teachers'* puzzles that teachers were seeking help from learners about, not learners' puzzles, at that point. We hadn't got that far, I think. It wasn't until 2003 that Inés Miller phoned me up from Rio and said: 'The annual EP Event is coming up: any ideas about what we should do?' And over the phone we jointly decided: 'Yeah, let's get the **learners** in to present their work for understanding'.

Something that actually probably helped us in the end, because it was so fearsome, was total quality control (TQC)? A management mantra that came in those early years of my association with the Cultura Inglesa in Rio. The management wanted to adopt it, and it had all sorts of horrendous implications for everybody in branches of the Cultura; a sort of box-ticking exercise. Isolation of procedures, not improvement of service—in fact not service at all. So that was a frightening thing; it turned out to have steps just like AR, and it was what we *were* doing in EP. I think we were so shocked at this appalling thing that it made us think: 'For god's sake, we can't let ourselves be associated with **that**'. My Modern Languages Journal article (Allwright 2005a) goes into quite a lot of detail about this whole thing of trying to move away from steps—method if you like… to say 'What really are our underlying principles that make us want to do this?'

So although steps appeared in Allwright (1993), you abandoned them quite quickly.

We didn't start with steps; we started with defining criteria for productive practitioner research and saying: 'It's got to be relevant; it's got to be sustainable,'—we then realised we'd lost sight of that by reducing it to a set of steps as to what to actually do.

So what it meant was that now a group of people in Rio, around Inés Miller and Bebel Cunha, particularly, but from other universities and ex-Cultura teachers too, who in any case would have several other jobs, so people from all over, who discovered they didn't need the steps. What they were talking about was not the steps they were doing but whatever they needed to do to pursue whatever puzzles they were discussing. And the steps were… almost irrelevant. So that made it much easier for us to focus on the developing principles and finding ways of articulating the principles.

And then we wanted to have a sort of appendix to the principles to say: 'While you're doing this, don't let anybody waste any time… And don't let anybody projectise it. And that's all we've got to say. How you do it is up to you. There are steps if you want to look at them, but you know they are not steps that define whether you are doing EP or not.'

I don't think we ever solved that in terms of being that explicit. I mean with AR you could say: 'Well it is defined by those steps' I might be misunderstanding what they intended by them, but I think a lot of people would think if you followed those steps, then you were doing AR. At the beginning, with Carr and Kemmis (1986), for example, there had been a radical, transformative, notion of the whole thing, but I think that by the time we were developing EP, AR, in the language teaching field at least, had become just a set of steps that served to define whether you were doing it or not. It was the emphasis on problem-solving rather than puzzling, that and the technicist emphasis in general, that was to me a very bad thing. Not just another way of doing it that I don't like, but a *bad* way of doing it if what you really want is to help people understand what is going on in their lives.

So if somebody said to you: 'Well what's the difference then? What's the difference between EP and AR? Aren't they just the same thing?'

I am tempted increasingly to say to such people: 'First tell me what you've read.'

Because by-and-large, you discover that they've only read something that was produced relatively early in our thinking. And I don't see, in their objections, any awareness of any of the subtlety of thinking that has come out in what we've published that they could've been aware of if they'd taken us seriously in the first place. So they seem not to have done their homework to find out whether they're right to think that AR and EP are identical.

They may think it's identical at the level of practice… and the steps we *used to* have in the early 1990s would have made it reasonably likely for people to slip into that error. But if you did a side-by-side comparison now, in 2016, you should be able to see the difference.

So what are the actual differences? I mean if somebody said: 'What are the differences?'

I am reluctant to improvise, really. Because I think the major issues get lost.

But I think I would want now to say that if it's true that AR has managed to lose its own roots in radical transformative pedagogy, and has become a method of doing research on a watered-down academic model, then the major difference is that we have rejected that model.

What we have done is instead substitute ethical and epistemological arguments that for us are much more important. And tried to help people and ourselves understand those, so that whatever practice comes out of it reflects those concerns, rather than the technicist ones which still appear to infect the world of AR.

EP makes a big deal out of distinguishing between 'problems' and 'puzzles', and yet David Nunan has been reported as saying that they're just different names for the same thing. Is he wrong?

I'm sure he really *knows* they're not the same thing. They could become the same thing, in terms of their content, but only if you're willing to turn a problem into a puzzle, and to do *that* you have to recognise the difference. For example, finding that your learners constantly slip from English into the first language is certainly going to be seen initially as a clearly practical 'problem'. The first response may be to ask: 'How can I get them to stop it?' But if you turn it into a *'Why'* question the whole situation can look very different, for example: 'Why do my learners find it so difficult to keep talking English?' The underlying classroom issue remains the same, but asking 'why' really shifts the focus from problem-solving to working for understanding, which is at the heart of EP.

Nevertheless, when I was running workshops for teachers, it was difficult for them to perceive the difference, so it's worth acknowledging that there is an issue for people as to what constitutes a 'problem,' and what constitutes a 'puzzle'. Our simple linguistic trick was to say: 'Turn your *how* question into a "why" one', and so ask '*why* do you think it's a problem?'

And that's all you need to do, really. If you are serious about it, you'll see the difference. It's a simple linguistic trick you can play. But you do need to play it, and play it seriously.

We will return to the interview with Dick later, but first we need to hear from two of the key figures that he mentions earlier: Bebel and Inés. We start with Bebel, who has worked with and through EP in Rio de Janeiro for more than 20 years to develop some of the central planks of EP thinking.

Interview with Bebel A. Cunha

> **Maria Isabel (Bebel) A. Cunha** teaches Portuguese and English and has acted as language teaching consultant to private schools. She coordinates the Curso de Especialzação em Língua Inglesa at PUC-Rio, and has been working with the Rio de Janeiro Exploratory Practice Group in the development of practitioner research.

Hello Bebel! What have been the major influences on your thinking?

Being 68 years old, I've been influenced by a large number of people… All the members of my family have always been involved with teaching: all grandparents were teachers of English and Portuguese, my father taught at the medicine school and my mother taught my brother and me, at home, how to read and write with the help of a method she created. In my family, there were also politicians from left and right, inclinations and political discussions belonged in the menu of family Sunday dinners. I believe they represent the strong influence I had in my education, which has always influenced me as a teacher.

One thing has always been of major importance for me: the students' needs and what they thought about learning and studying. This goes back to when I was 10 or 12 and I saw my father helping my brother with his assignments for school. Soon I was doing the same when my younger brother's friends asked me to help them at school.

When I entered the university, I started to teach Portuguese at a community course organised by the students' union for the university personnel. They were janitors, gardeners, elevator men, technicians, and so on. I was not worried with teaching them to pass exams that would prove their literacy but I worried about the needs of the students when looking for a telephone number in a phone directory, the reading of their house rent contracts and drug description leaflets. That was what the students had told me they needed Portuguese for. At that time I had not read anything about the teaching of Portuguese but, as part of the students' union activity, I was taking part in groups to read and discuss Marx, Lukács, and Freire.

In the postgraduate course in educational psychology I read Foucault and Gramsci, two major influences to me. The school where I worked based its pedagogical orientation on Piaget and classes promoted games and activities to challenge the students' involvement with learning. My major influences then were Stevick, Rinvolucri, Penny Ur, and the other authors from Pilgrims.

So, all this was before getting in touch with Dick Allwright's thinking. I'm not sure but maybe the first text I read was: 'Why don't learners learn what teachers teach?' (Allwright 1984). The title was provocative. The reading revealed to me a scholar who expressed ideas I had, but I did not then think my ideas were serious and academic.

After reading everything by Dick Allwright I could find, I also read Rodgers, Dewey, and the educators Rubem Alves and José Pacheco. Another very important influence in the understanding of Dick's thinking was the discussion of his texts with Inés Miller.

Bebel works closely with Inés Kayon de Miller. Together, they have been largely responsible for many of the discussions around central themes, and most cutting-edge thinking, as well as the most avant-garde activities (such as the Learners' and Teachers' annual Exploratory Practice Event in Rio de Janeiro). We therefore turn to interview Inés.

Interview with Inés Kayon de Miller

Inés Kayon de Miller is an associate professor at PUC-Rio, Brazil. She holds a Masters degree in Teaching English as a Second Language from the University of California, Los Angeles (UCLA) and a PhD in Applied Linguistics from Lancaster University UK. She is involved in initial and continuing language teacher education at both undergraduate and postgraduate levels. As mentor of the Rio de Janeiro Exploratory Practice Group, she is involved in developing and disseminating EP—a way of encouraging teachers and learners to engage in practitioner research. She has presented papers at international conferences and published widely. In 2006, she coedited, with Simon Gieve, the book *Understanding the Language Classroom*, published by Palgrave Macmillan.

Hi Inés! How did you first become interested in EP?

I first became interested in the rationale of EP when I was invited to join a course that Dick Allwright was teaching on Teacher Research at the Cultura Inglesa, Rio de Janeiro, Brazil, in 1990. I soon found out that this course was part of a larger institutional Teacher Development scheme, to which I had the privilege of being invited to contribute, despite the fact that I did not work for the institution. What a huge learning opportunity that was! Dick ran the sessions and a small group observed and reflected deeply on what went on in the sessions and planned ahead.... It was all very pleasant, quite enigmatic and highly collaborative.

EP was embryonic at this point, but developed quite quickly among the Rio de Janeiro group and, especially, during Dick's visits, which were very intensive. Locally, Bebel and I worked very closely. We had long conversations on the phone and in my car, as we went to our workshops for public sector teachers. Ralph Bannell and David Shepherd would also come along and contributed with their thinking and feedback on our sessions. Ralph was interested in reflective teaching and David worked with AR. So we got quite a range.

In 1994, I started my Ph.D. degree as Dick's part-time research student and shared what we were doing in Rio, our puzzles and our understandings and challenges with Dick and with other research students in Lancaster University. When in Rio, I always worked in partnership with Bebel, with colleagues from the Cultura Inglesa, and with some of my own peers at the university.

I began to go to TESOL international conferences on my way back from Lancaster. Dick and some of my colleagues became a group. We presented posters together, we ran a pre-convention course at one of the TESOL conferences and we also presented posters together. I believe that all of this, finally, helped me become a professional. In EP terms, I was growing into a practitioner.

But the ideas of EP made even more sense to me when I noticed that I could also make use of them for my own professional development at PUC-Rio, the university where I worked back then and still work nowadays. At the time, I was a contracted teacher, with a UCLA Master's degree in TESOL/Applied Linguistics, but with limited work load and, due to this, not expected to investigate, nor to do research. My only obligation was to teach English to undergraduates, to show good results, and to be positively evaluated by students. But I suddenly realised that there could be so much more...

What have been the major influences on your thinking?

The major influence on my thinking came, I think, from reading and discussing Dick's texts. Another kind of influence came when I realised that I had puzzles or issues that I wished to understand more deeply and that I could think about them together with my students. So, even if the institution did not expect me to research or even to 'reflect' about my classes, I was able to do it. And teaching became a lot more interesting, more fun!

What are the key trends in practitioner research that you would identify?

I think the key trends, aside from EP, and especially in the English language teaching (ELT) world, are AR and Reflective Practice. In other areas in the social sciences, I think teachers engage in academic research, mostly of the qualitative kind. The main problem with AR and with engagement in academic research is that they stop as soon as the research project ends. Only very rarely are these processes integrated into or sustained in daily pedagogic practice, as in EP.

Could you talk about something you have done representing your thinking? (e.g. showing the links and value of your research to practice) Can you give an example of something that exemplifies EP?

My Ph.D. thesis, which was an example of professional reflection integrated with professional practice. It was not my initial objective but, as I was so very involved with EP in other teachers' professional development, again I realised I could do it myself. With Dick's support and supervision, I risked presenting it as a Ph.D. thesis.

In the past two decades, I've been encouraging my supervisees to do the same. To some academics, this does not always count as research, but we are happy to say that EP is helping to contribute to the scene of qualitative academic research carried out in pedagogic contexts in Rio and in Brazil.

What would you say you have learned so far?

That, in pedagogic and professional contexts, working for understanding is key and that this is the most democratising of notions. People who try to understand something of interest to them, in a collaborative way, create a unique bond that intensifies and enhances their quality of life in the context. I have seen people of various ages in different contexts discover that they can enjoy what they are doing, once they find out that they are not 'alone', that they can share their puzzlement with each other and work for deeper understandings.

In Rio, practitioners have found it pleasant and comforting, but not easy to achieve! In some cases, this peacefully subversive attitude has caused them to be accused of not being practical, of not solving problems, of not trying to change things. The value of 'just' understanding has been questioned by some. I have learned that we need to go on expanding our EP philosophy, especially among future teachers.

How do you see the field developing in future?

If you mean 'the field of practitioner research within ELT communities', I see that in Brazil teachers and future teachers are becoming researchers, whether they like it or not. It is expected of them as teachers, now. Also, whenever they engage in M.A./Ph.D. courses they need and wish to do empirical research. It's become part and parcel of initial and/or continuing education programmes. I have been working with EP for the past 10 years in our initial teacher education course at PUC, the university where I work.

Also, my colleagues in the Rio EP group and I have been working with EP in the field of continuing education. We see the effect of our actions during our annual EP Events…. Some manage to bring their learners, others have now been Skyping from their classrooms.

After 14 years of acting as M.A. or Ph.D. supervisor of dissertations or theses that find inspiration in EP, I believe that the EP Group in Rio is beginning to have an influence in the growth of EP as a form of practitioner research which includes teachers and students, coordinators and teachers, educational psychologists and teachers, in short, practitioners of various kinds working together to understand what they find intriguing and useful.

What resources would you recommend for someone who wants to begin research in/on/through EP?

Nowadays resources are easier to find on the Internet or in libraries. But the main thing is to join someone to work with, in order to understand something. Working with somebody else is crucial, in order to have somebody to talk to and to listen to, and to be listened to. Therefore, I guess I'm referring to human resources and ethical values such as respect, trust, and collegiality among others. Unveiling one's own agentivity or autonomy is at the heart of EP.

Another key figure is Assia Slimani-Rolls. Her work in classroom research, first in the area of analysing the complexities involved in group work, and later in the area of modern foreign language (MFL) teacher development in the UK, continues to be influential in the development of EP thinking.

Interview with Assia Slimani-Rolls

Assia Slimani-Rolls is a Reader in applied linguistics and education. She is head of Research and Professional Development in the Institute of Languages and Culture at Regent's University, London. Her research interests include classroom interaction, teacher education, and teacher development. She has, for many years, researched the relationship between language learning and teaching and what learners get out of the classroom. Her interest in traditional academic classroom-centred research has shifted towards teacher and learner development via EP, a form of practitioner research involving teachers and learners working together to foster a better understanding of their learning and teaching environment. Working in the multicultural environment of Regent's University, she has also developed an interest in internationalisation of the curriculum and transnational studies.

Hello Assia! How did you first become interested in EP?

I used to work closely with a group of language teachers of French for whom I acted as Academic Leader. We worked together to organise the content of and procedures for our teaching. However, we hardly ever got similar students' reactions to our preparatory work once rolled out in the classroom. This was particularly true of group work. So I proposed to my colleagues to investigate the students' reactions. We asked the learners the same questions that Safya Cherchalli asked hers many years ago [in her doctoral thesis (1988); see also Allwright and Hanks 2009, pp. 275–277] producing those wonderful sets of inspiring responses, which typically illustrate the students' infinite ways of reacting to classroom events. Our analysis of the students' perceptions of their peers and teachers following a class discussion and a brainstorming session revealed a constellation of social, affective and cognitive variables which, in actual fact, hindered the smooth running of group work.

This was my first encounter with EP, which myself and my colleagues found revealing. What goes on in the students' lives inside and outside the classroom and can impact on the teaching events? EP made us think critically about ourselves and about the demands that we make on our students. Why should the group gel just because we decided to get the students together for a few minutes? What followed is that there was much more flexibility and acceptance of things going the way they go on the part of the teachers. As to the learners who underwent the research process with us, they understood that they also have their share of responsibility to stay on task.

What have been the major influences on your thinking?

My doctoral work (1987), which characterised the learners as idiosyncratic and learning as a social event, has been influential on my professional life. As it happens, both aspects—learner idiosyncracy and the social dimension of learning— are fundamental to EP. Integrating learners brings in the complexity that is representative of the learning phenomenon in instructional settings. Working with teachers and learners has been mostly inspiring. Of course, working with Dick Allwright has helped me to shape my ideas on language learning.

Reflective Practice and AR are widely talked about in the field of ELT. I have been working with EP principles for a number of years with many of my colleagues from the Languages Department but also from the Faculty of Business and Management thus indicating that EP can also work for other taught subjects. I find the principles true to life in the classroom but I also think life in general—inclusivity, collegiality, understanding, and mutual development are basic to getting on with others and helpful in developing a better quality of life in the classroom.

Could you talk about something you have done representing your thinking? (e.g. showing the links and value of your research to practice) Can you give an example of something that exemplifies EP?

Often academic management takes over my life but I find that I am at my best in class when I am involved in understanding better what I am trying to achieve with my students. In those moments, I feel more alert to what is going on around me and more responsive to the students.

There is a difference between managing learning and facilitating learning to advance the students' progress, which I feel I am doing when using

EP. So I wanted to share my knowledge with my colleagues especially in my role of Academic Leader. They find that looking at their teaching from the point of view of EP makes them more discerning and critical about their teaching. Working with colleagues as a collaborative researcher has allowed me to attract teachers not only of languages but also of other disciplines. Perhaps the aspect that is most appealing to them is the possibility to use normal classroom activities to enable them to integrate their search for understanding into their teaching routine. I have to say though that it requires lots of thinking and time for them to use their teaching activities as investigative methods to help them to grasp better what they have set up to understand. Whether they continue with the work afterwards only time can tell.

What would you say you have learned so far?

How important it is to include the learners, and other relevant parties, in the search for developing a better understanding of our teaching practice because we don't operate in isolation. It doesn't come naturally to teachers, at least those I have been working with, to think of including the learners in their investigation. My own experience and those who work with EP know that learner inclusivity opens up a communication channel, which eases tension in the class and improves the relationships between learners and teachers thus creating a better quality of life. Teaching isn't all about techniques. It is also about establishing a relationship with those we work with.

Recently, I worked with a group of academics in Law and Business studies. They wanted to find out why the students didn't engage with their classroom discourse, in other words with their teaching. They resisted the idea of including the learners in their investigation when I suggested it. As I set up myself to be simply a guide in their investigation, I let them get on with it in order to empower them to come up with their own investigative methods. When they completed their analysis, the teachers were surprised to find out that they were so involved in transmitting their expert knowledge and covering the syllabus that they didn't realise that they were not actually acknowledging their students' contributions. At that point, the teachers realised that engagement is a two-way process and that it would have been, indeed, valuable to include the learners in their enquiry. As it is, they felt that their understanding of their practice remained partial.

I note, however, that the lack of learner inclusivity doesn't tend to happen only to inexperienced teacher researchers. It can also happen to teachers working at doctoral level. I recently examined a Ph.D. thesis on exploring teacher knowledge and practices in various tertiary language education contexts. This work was carried out in an intensive research-orientated British university. Given that the main drive of the thesis was to understand why teachers do what they do, one would have thought that if not a full investigation, the inclusion, at least, of a focus group would be useful to provide a view on the learners' perspectives as they were essentially characterised by their teachers as lacking autonomy, initiative, and motivation. But were they? If yes, what might have been the reasons for their behaviour? With hindsight, the author of this thesis wished she had taken a peep into the learners' views to get a fuller picture of the situation.

How do you see the field developing in future?

I believe that teacher research, including EP, will continue to develop and impose itself as a necessary component in teacher training programmes and staff continuous professional development in order for teachers to grow as discerning practitioners capable of contributing to their development, that of their students and to the field in general. I shall use the situation of MFL teaching in the UK to illustrate my response.

In some respects, the situation of teachers of foreign languages is similar to that of teachers of English, except that there is less interest and demand for the learning of MFLs in the UK. Many teachers are hourly paid, especially at university level. There is no mention (at workshops, conferences, and in policy documents) of looking into how foreign languages are taught in the classroom to inspire learners, and why learners should maintain their interest to learn languages to advanced levels. Project leaders have presented on funded and wonderfully sophisticated projects and courses such as transnationalising modern languages, translanguaging, and repositioning languages within other disciplines. However, I believe that without understanding one's classroom practice and managing to recruit and keep students learn foreign languages to advanced levels, such sophisticated sounding courses would not materialise, as there would simply be no students to take them. This is exactly the situation for some languages today in many universities. Of course, one also knows that the situation is complex.

What resources would you recommend for someone who wants to begin research in/on/through EP?

I trust that what is important is to talk to people who engage with EP as I had the privilege to work with many EP practitioners and of course Dick Allwright. It is possible nowadays to bump into EP practitioners in conferences and workshops as the word on EP is spreading. Sharing ideas with EP practitioners and talking and listening to teachers with similar values, goals, and beliefs is one good way of learning about EP.

Another very influential voice in the development of EP thinking, as well as other areas of language education, is Akira Tajino. Now based in Japan, his work spans education, linguistics, and research, and his recent book (Team teaching and Team Learning (2016)) promises another powerful contribution to the philosophical and theoretical underpinnings of language teaching and learning.

Interview with Akira Tajino

> **Akira Tajino,** Ph.D., is a professor of educational linguistics and a founding member of the International Academic Research and Resource Center for Language Education (i-ARRC), as well as the Graduate Course of Foreign Language Acquisition and Education at Kyoto University, Japan. His research interests include English for Academic Purposes, pedagogical grammar, and classroom research. He has served on the Editorial Panel of several journals including *ELT Journal*. He is a recipient of the JACET (Japan Association of College English Teachers) Award for Excellence in Teaching in 2011, and the JACET Award for Excellence in Academic Publication in 2014.

Hello Akira! How did you first become interested in EP?

Traditional classroom research in which the teacher changes the conditions or atmosphere of the classroom by recording data through obtrusive means such as audio recordings, for example, was never very appealing to me because it seemed to disturb the natural environment of teaching and learning. What's more, it is likely that students and teachers may behave in different ways while being recorded or report response biases on surveys. I believed there should be an alternative to traditional classroom research.

So you were disillusioned with these more traditional research methods—how did you then come across EP?

I had been aware of the general idea of EP since my graduate school days at Lancaster, but only fully began to appreciate its importance through my own experience in the language classroom and research. I noticed that when researchers are present in the classroom (e.g. with recording equipment) they may sometimes influence the class in such a way that the lesson does not progress naturally. This is not always the case, but when it happens, it seems that pedagogy and research have been turned on their heads. In these situations, lessons seem to be conducted for the purpose of research, rather than pedagogy. A good balance is important. Through this experience and my own work with 'team learning', I began to understand how to put EP into practice.

What have been the major influences on your thinking?

Dr. Dick Allwright, my Ph.D. supervisor at Lancaster University. Also Dr. Judith Hanks and the other members of the Classroom Language Learning Research Group at Lancaster. They have had a direct influence on me during the opportunities we shared discussing language education and classroom research. In a more indirect way, their research and writing became very relevant to me during my work on team teaching and team learning, through which I became more aware of the importance of mutual understanding in language classrooms.

What are the key trends in practitioner research that you would identify?

It could be said that practitioner research has moved from teacher-centred research, towards a greater focus on student-centred classrooms. Now a more holistic 'classroom-centred' approach, recognising both teachers and students as active members in the classroom, is becoming more prevalent.

Could you talk about something you have done representing your thinking? (e.g. showing the links and value of your research to practice) Can you give an example of something that exemplifies EP?

In my seminars and laboratory meetings, I apply the concept of 'team learning' which shares principles with EP and with team teaching. Whereas EP is a set of guiding principles, 'team learning' could be thought of as a set of value-based collaborative manifestations of the EP principles. For example, behaviours and practices for all members, including teachers as well as students, involved in the learning team.

What would you say you have learned so far?

Involving students in the research process through EP can be a very challenging, yet rewarding experience. It may appear as though EP is difficult to apply, because it consists of a set of principles (rather than concrete directives). However, EP provides an excellent philosophy for both classroom practice and research.

Why do you think this? Are there any areas where it needs to develop?

EP is excellent because it encourages an atmosphere of learning and discovery in the classroom that is inclusive of all members—students and teachers alike. This mutual development may help to promote life-long learning in a new generation of students, while providing consistent motivation for teachers to explore and develop their own practice.

As far as areas needing development, as I mentioned, being principles rather than directives, it may be difficult for novice practitioners to approach. A broader database of demonstrations of EP in practice may provide a beneficial resource for implementing EP.

How do you see the field developing in future?

As there seems to be an increasing focus on practitioner research, I expect EP to become even better known, both as a means for teacher reflection and development, as well as a source of knowledge to further research in pedagogy. Until now, EP has been exclusively concerned with the language classroom, but I expect its influence to expand to other subjects in education.

Finally, a teacher working in Japan has written asking 'How can I get started?'—What would you say to them?

As a starting point, I would recommend Dr. Allwright's plenary speech 'Theorising Down instead of Up', given at KOTESOL 2013, which is available on the KOTESOL website and YouTube. It is an excellent introduction to EP which interested practitioners may follow up with some of the resources listed below. I would also recommend also teacher organisations or associations such as: IATEFL (SIG: Teacher Development, Teacher Training and Education) or TESOL International Association.

They can also start by exploring some of the resources listed to familiarise themselves with EP principles. A research paper written by Professor Yosuke Yanase of Hiroshima University discusses EP in Japanese, available at https://ir.lib.hiroshima-u.ac.jp/files/public/33697/20141016194310252231/CaseleResBull_38_71.pdf.

EP is a process of working towards the development of understanding, and as such practitioners are not expected to be perfect at the start. I believe EP can be most effective when we, teachers and students, enjoy team learning that leads to mutual understanding among all the participants in the classroom.

Having seen countless examples of apparently faceless interviewers asking questions of others, but failing to address these same questions themselves, it seemed in line with the ethos of EP for me to probe my own thinking as well. I therefore spent some time considering the same prompts myself, joining in the conversation too.

Interview with Judith Hanks

How did you first become interested in EP?

I first came across EP when I was doing my master's degree at Lancaster University in 1997–1998. At that time, I had never heard of practitioner research, let alone AR or EP. When someone mentioned AR in one of our seminars and Dick Allwright added EP, my interest was piqued. I wanted to know more, and since AR seemed very problem focused and EP very puzzle focused, I decided to orient my M.A. dissertation (1998) towards finding out what are the differences between problems and puzzles. This has turned into a lifelong interest in puzzlement, curiosity, and EP.

Fortunately, not only was Dick Allwright my supervisor that year, but through the research groups he ran (Teachers Develop-Teachers Research/Classroom Language Learning Research), I also met a number of his Ph.D. students: Inés Kayon de Miller, Bebel A. Cunha, Christina Pinto da Silva, Morag Samson and Zongjie Wu, and later, Assia Slimani-

Rolls, Akira Tajino, amongst others. Interacting with them has enhanced the quality of my life immeasurably.

What have been the major influences on your thinking?

Clearly Dick Allwright has been a major influence, but he's not alone. Before that, the colleagues I met while working at International House and the British Council were influential—Jan Gates, Lesley Golberg, Adrienne Harrison, Roger Hunt, Frank de la Motte, Martin Parrott to name but a few. I was also very impressed by Joan Allwright, Norman Fairclough, Roz Ivanič and Romy Clark in Lancaster, Chris Candlin, Elaine Tarone and Adrian Holliday. More recently colleagues at the University of Leeds such as Bee Bond, Simon Borg, Jane Kay, Jess Poole, James Simpson, and Martin Wedell, and many others, have influenced my thinking in a variety of ways. We have puzzled, discussed, and laughed together.

More than anything else, what has *really* influenced my thinking is the constant contact with learners and teachers and teacher educators around the world. For example, I went to the EP Event in Rio de Janeiro in 2009, and was amazed at the levels of enthusiasm and activity as learners presented their work alongside teachers. That made me wonder if I could do the same back home, which sparked my doctoral thesis.

What are the key trends in practitioner research that you would identify?

I think there's a growing sense of the need to be more inclusive—so it's not just one group of people who do research, and another group who read about it or hear about it. It's becoming a two-way street. The notions of researching multi-lingually, multi-modally, of seeing classrooms as sites of culture and intercultural interfaces, are exciting.

It's also interesting to see how some of the themes from EP are drifting into the wider discourse of practitioner research. We now hear lots of people talking about 'puzzles' as well as 'problems' (though the shades of meaning between these are often missed), the notion of 'understanding' has begun to replace, or at least, to live alongside, 'problem-solving', and there's a much stronger emphasis on collaboration in all areas.

It's hard to see where all this is leading, though. Although there's much more mutual respect amongst practitioner researchers (our points of agreement are, I believe, stronger than our need to differentiate ourselves), there is still an enormously strong lobby which argues *against* practitioner research. I am sometimes astonished to hear grown academics professing views such as: 'But is this [whatever "this" is that doesn't fit their world-view] really research?' or: 'If it hasn't been done by 300 schools, or 1000 teachers, then it doesn't count!' Such comments should make them blush for shame. So one trend that has been there for a long time, but which still needs attention, is the need for us to clearly establish the potential contributions to the field that all kinds of practitioner research offer.

Could you talk about something you have done representing your thinking? (e.g. showing the links and value of your research to practice) Can you give an example of something that exemplifies EP?

I guess the thing that most represents my work is my interest in the difference it makes if you ask practitioners '*What puzzles you about your teaching/learning?*'. So far, I haven't met a person who says 'Well nothing really'. Everyone is puzzled by something. But all too often teachers and learners have absorbed the message that their questions don't matter, that what they do doesn't count. So both the act of asking the question 'What puzzles you…?' and the ongoing activity of listening, but really listening, and giving importance to what the person says and does, exemplifies EP for me. The astonishment and the relief that teachers and learners express when they find out that (a) what they puzzle about is important, (b) the importance is not only for them in their classes, but also for others in other classes around the world, and (c) that what they think and do counts, for both practice and for research, is a constant source of joy.

What would you say you have learned so far?

I'm still learning! But key things I'd say are: (i) to listen carefully to what others are saying, because (ii) what they are saying is significant. Also (iii) that where I say 'others' and 'they', I include myself implicitly, so I need to remember to explicitly say 'I', or better yet, 'we'—that 'first person (plural)' thing. Like many teachers, I often downplay myself and my contribution, and I've had to learn how to allow myself to be present and visible in the discourse too. I've realised that we (all people involved in language education) have to say *matters*. Our experiences and our views are what drive the field forward, and what keep it grounded.

How do you see the field developing in future?

Actually it's quite an exciting moment, because I see more and more people expressing interest in practitioner research. And I see a growing respect for EP itself—the value that it offers for ethically grounded, principled, research, which is directly relevant to the people who are actually working in language classrooms. In this book, I point to the need for the very concept of 'research' to be re-thought—to bring it back to its roots of trying to *understand* rather than merely problem-solve at a superficial level. At the same time, we need to rethink the notion of *pedagogy*—to allow teachers and learners the freedom to explore and develop their own understandings of the world.

What resources would you recommend for someone who wants to begin research in/on/through EP?

I'd definitely recommend meeting and talking with other practitioners. So the first 'resource' is dialogue — whether that is face-to-face (over coffee, in a student or teacher common room, at a conference) or virtual (the EP Facebook page, an EP blog or vlog, or through e-mails). There are a number of videoed talks available on the Internet too—you can just google 'Exploratory Practice' and see what comes up. Reading is good—articles in *ELTJ*, or LTR, or Language Teaching, which focus on EP, and of course, books. All this is to begin a much longer conversation.

We return now to the interview with Dick Allwright, taking up from where we left him talking about 'a simple linguistic trick you can play. But you do need to play it, and play it seriously'. This resonated with my own thinking on play and playfulness, and how important they are, so I asked him to elaborate.

A Final Few Words from Dick Allwright

So EP was born in Rio in the early 1990s. What happened next?

Back in Lancaster, I developed the thinking in publications and in my postgraduate teaching. I was greatly encouraged by colleagues (especially through the sophisticated scepticism of the 'critical pedagogy' movement) and by many of my master's and doctoral students. I was especially encouraged by visits (practically every two years from 1990 onwards) to work with the group of Brazilian teachers who eventually formed the extraordinarily productive Rio de Janeiro Exploratory Practice Group. Of particular importance to my thinking were stories from teachers (at high risk of burnout for a variety of reasons) that spoke of rediscovering pleasure in being a teacher.

One of the things I'm hoping that this book will be able to bring out is this sense of playfulness as well. When you said 'it's a linguistic trick that you can play', some people might think that that's a sort of dismissive thing to say, but I think the opposite. I think that actually playing with ideas is important.

I was very impressed by Bud Mehan (1979) and his notion of ethnomethodology. He showed me a piece of videotape of a class, and with the group of students he had, he was showing them this videotape of an event in the class where a teacher got angry with a student and the student was being rude. Mehan was *not* saying: 'What would you do about it?' as a teacher, but rather: 'What on earth do you think produced that event?' And instead of saying: 'Let's see how closely we can get to the answer' he was asking: 'How many hypotheses can we entertain? About what might have produced *that* learner being rude to *that* teacher on *that* day?'

The class came up with an infinite number of hypotheses: the poor kid hadn't had any food for breakfast, or … anything that you wouldn't, *couldn't possibly* know about, by studying the videotape any longer. And so the question was: 'Well some of those might be preposterous—we may think we can just discard them. But how would we investigate them enough so that we know that we can discard them? What on earth can we do to establish what *might've been* behind it all? Is the teacher particularly provocative in the class?' I mean: 'Why should we think it's the learner's fault for being rude, rather than the teacher's previous behaviour that has led people to lose patience with him?'.

So for me, it was very illuminating in terms of saying we've got to find all possible hypotheses and then see if we can reduce it to a number that are not entirely preposterous, and *then* see if we can think of ways of investigating them.

But actually also illuminating was the notion that there's going to be a lot that you cannot investigate. Things that are beyond investigation. Even if you could… in principle, perhaps the lad's mother was angry with him for leaving dirty socks in the bath or something, but in practice you're not going to find that out, so don't even think of it. Just remember that you really don't know and are not going to know. So you're not going to get a complete explanation; whatever you get is partial at best. That seemed to me very important. I haven't explicitly thought of it in terms of EP before but I think it works very well by saying: 'What we are asking people to do is explore all possible reasons why, but not come to a conclusion that they believe is definitive.'

What would you say you have learned so far?
First off, UNDERSTANDING:
(a) the importance of *working* for it,
(b) the importance of everyone being encouraged to develop *liveable* understandings, not necessarily articulatable ones, and
(c) the possibility of working for understanding being enough, making direct problem-solving intervention redundant.

Secondly, TRUST. Probably the most important thing, and deliberately not prompted by myself, is the trust issue. I'm thinking of the importance of trust and the value of trust, and the importance of it as an outcome of what we were doing. What we discovered was that if teachers shared their puzzles then that helped the learners understand. And the way the learners acted in their trust, helped the teachers to trust them. And that was absolutely magical to a lot of people I think.

It took somebody like Hadara Perpignan to articulate it for her Ph.D. thesis. But it's actually part of the common experience of a lot of people. They might not put it like that—they might just say: 'Life's a bit easier in the classroom'.

So I think trust is the most valuable lesson of all.

The other thing you mentioned earlier was about Quality of Life
What we have been interested in is getting people to understand what's going on in their teaching and learning lives, and understand in particular that solutions are not to be found in technicist thought, but in relationships between people. And what we're interested in is getting practitioner research done in a way that's helpful to the people doing it. So, yes, Quality of Life is crucial.

So I'm perfectly happy to be called a practitioner researcher, are you?

Yeah. That's why, when I was doing the *Journal of Language Teaching Research* subediting job, my section was called 'Practitioner Research'. That label doesn't tell you anything at all about how research should be conducted from a technical point of view. We're more interested in the epistemological and ethical side of it than we are in the technical side of it. And in fact the technical side *follows,* it doesn't lead.

What resources for a debutant can you suggest?

On the 'resources' for EP beginners, I would start with 'other people'. Get involved in the EP network and share your thoughts as widely as possible. Some people have done amazing things in the classroom just after reading one published article, and without any collegial support. But it's likely to be far easier, and much more rewarding, if you can feel part of a collegial group. The Rio EP Group is a great example of what a group can achieve, both in terms of getting EP done in their classrooms, and also, very importantly, in developing the thinking behind the ideas.

The other thing is: read the book (Allwright and Hanks 2009)! You don't have to buy it, just read it. Catch up with the literature; don't let yourself be sucked into reading old texts and thinking you've got everything that it's worth reading.

How do you see the field developing?

I'd put it two ways: What I have some hope of seeing happen, is the spread of *inclusivity* across the practitioner research field. That I think may help. And the second way is wider representation of different educational settings, such as more work in secondary schools and so on.

Any final thoughts?

I'm thinking of the philosophy of science angle. EP is the developing outcome of an epistemological inquiry into what it means to understand, married to an ethical concern for agency—the question of who needs to do the developing of understandings if they are to be of practical value in the lives of actors in situations (rather than just the intellectual understandings of academic researchers who do not know how to communicate them productively to the actors themselves). EP as a classroom practice is a response to the practical question of how actors (e.g. teachers and learners) in social settings like the classroom can in practice (EP), develop their own liveable understandings.

References

Adler, S. (1991). The reflective practitioner and the curriculum of teacher education. *Journal of Education for Language Teaching, 17*(2), 139–150.

Akbari, R. (2007). Reflections on reflection: A critical appraisal of reflective practices in L2 teacher education. *System, 35*, 192–207.

Allwright, D. (1984). Why don't learners learn what teachers teach? The interaction hypothesis. In D. Singleton & D. Little (Eds.), *Language learning in formal and informal contexts* (pp. 3–18). Dublin: IRAAL.

Allwright, D. (1988). *Observation in the language classroom*. Harlow: Longman.

Allwright, D. (1991a). *Exploratory language teaching*. CRILE Working Paper 9, Lancaster University.

Allwright, D. (1991b). *Exploratory teaching, professional development, and the role of a teachers' association*. CRILE Working Paper 7, Lancaster University.

Allwright, D. (1991c). *Understanding classroom language learning*. CRILE Working Paper 8, Lancaster University.

Allwright, D. (1993). Integrating 'research' and 'pedagogy': Appropriate criteria and practical possibilities. In J. Edge & K. Richards (Eds.), *Teachers develop teachers research* (pp. 125–135). Oxford: Heinemann.

Allwright, D. (1997a). *Exploratory Practice: Defining characteristics*. Handout from workshop in Rio de Janeiro, Brazil.

Allwright, D. (1997b). Quality and sustainability in teacher-research. *TESOL Quarterly, 31*(2), 368–370.

Allwright, D. (1997c, May 10). *From academic research to professional development: The story of Exploratory Practice*. Unpublished transcript of talk given at Universidade Federal do Parana (UFPR) in Curitiba, Brazil

Allwright, D. (1998a). *Planning for specific change in a context of endemic change*. Monograph, Lancaster University.

Allwright, D. (1998b). *Playing with words: The puzzling problem of distinguishing between 'problems' and 'puzzles'*. Monograph, Lancaster University.

Allwright, D. (2000). *Some first principles for Exploratory Practice*. Workshop handout, Lancaster University.

Allwright, D. (2001). Three major processes of teacher development and the design criteria for developing and using them. In B. Johnston & S. Irujo (Eds.), *Research and practice in language teacher education: Voices from the field* (pp. 115–133). Minneapolis: University of Minnesota.

Allwright, D. (2003). Exploratory Practice: Rethinking practitioner research in language teaching. *Language Teaching Research, 7*(2), 113–141.

Allwright, D. (2005a). Developing principles for practitioner research: The case of Exploratory Practice. *The Modern Language Journal, 89*(3), 353–366.

Allwright, D. (2005b). From teaching points to learning opportunities and beyond. *TESOL Quarterly, 39*(1), 9–31.

Allwright, D. (2006). Six promising directions in applied linguistics. In S. Gieve & I. K. Miller (Eds.), *Understanding the language classroom* (pp. 11–17). Basingstoke: Palgrave Macmillan.

Allwright, D. (2008). Prioritising the human quality of life in the language classroom: Is it asking too much of beginning teachers? In G. Gil & M. H. Vieira-Abrahão (Eds.), *Educação de Professores de Línguas: os desafios do formador* (pp. 127–144). Campinas: Pontes Editores.

Allwright, D. (2009). Inclusive practitioner research: Why we need it and what Exploratory Practice offers. In T. Yoshida, H. Imai, Y. Nakata, A. Tajino, O. Takeuchi, & K. Tamai (Eds.), *Researching language teaching and learning: An integration of practice and theory* (pp. 15–31). Bern: Peter Lang.

Allwright, D. (2011). *Learners as researchers of their own learning*. Unpublished paper at IATEFL Learner Autonomy SIG Pre-conference Event, Brighton.

Allwright, D. (2015). Putting 'understanding' first in practitioner research. In K. Dikilitas, R. Smith, & W. Trotman (Eds.), *Teacher-researchers in action* (pp. 19–36). Faversham: IATEFL.

Allwright, D., & Bailey, K. (1991). *Focus on the language classroom: An introduction to classroom research for language teachers*. Cambridge: Cambridge University Press.

Allwright, D., & Hanks, J. (2009). *The developing language learner: An introduction to Exploratory Practice*. Basingstoke: Palgrave Macmillan.

References

Allwright, D., & Lenzuen, R. (1997). Exploratory Practice: Work at the Cultura Inglesa, Rio de Janeiro, Brazil. *Language Teaching Research, 1*(1), 73–79.

Allwright, D., & Miller, I. K. (1998). *Exploratory Practice: Our underlying rationale.* Paper presented at the IATEFL annual conference, Manchester.

Allwright, D., & Miller, I. K. (2013). Burnout and the beginning teacher. In D. Soneson & E. Tarone (Eds.), *Expanding our horizons: Language teacher education in the 21st century* (pp. 101–115). Minneapolis: University of Minnesota.

Allwright, D., Dar, Y., Gieve, S., Hanks, J., Salvi, A. I., & Slimani-Rolls, A. (2013). Exploratory Practice: Using class time to help teachers and learners develop as practitioners of teaching and learning. *ELT Research,* IATEFL Research SIG Newsletter 28.

Altrichter, H., Posch, P., & Somekh, B. (1993). *Teachers investigate their work: An introduction to the methods of action research.* Abingdon: Routledge.

Argyris, C., & Schön, D. A. (1974). *Theory in practice: Increasing professional effectiveness.* San Francisco: Jossey-Bass Publishers.

Ashworth, M. (1985). *Beyond methodology: Second language teaching and the community.* Cambridge: Cambridge University Press.

Atweh, B., Kemmis, S., & Weeks, P. (Eds.). (1998). *Action research in practice: Partnerships for social justice in education.* London: Routledge.

Bailey, K. M. (1983). Competitiveness and anxiety in adult second language learning: Looking *at* and *through* the diary studies. In H. W. Seliger & M. H. Long (Eds.), *Classroom oriented research in second language acquisition* (pp. 67–102). Rowley/London: Newbury House.

Bailey, K. M. (2001). Action research, teacher research, and classroom research in language teaching. In M. Celce-Murcia (Ed.), *Teaching English as a Second or foreign language* (3rd ed., pp. 489–498). Boston: Heinle & Heinle.

Bailey, K. M., & Nunan, D. (Eds.). (1996). *Voices from the language classroom.* Cambridge: Cambridge University Press.

Bakhtin, M. M. (1986). *Speech genres and other late essays* (trans: McGee, V. W.). Austin: University of Texas Press.

Bartu, H. (2003). Decisions and decision making in the Istanbul Exploratory Practice experience. *Language Teaching Research, 7*(2), 181–200.

Bastos, L. C. (2008). Diante do sofrimento do outro – narrativas de profissionais de saúde em reuniões de trabalho. *Caleidoscópio, 6*(2), 77–85.

Basturkmen, H. (2012). Review of research into the correspondence between language teachers' stated beliefs and practices. *System, 40,* 282–295.

Bauman, Z. (2005). *Liquid life.* Cambridge: Polity Press.

Bauman, Z. (2007). *Liquid times.* Cambridge: Polity Press.

Benson, P. (2001). *Teaching and researching autonomy in language learning.* Harlow: Pearson Education.

BERA. (2011). *Revised Ethical Guidelines for Educational Research.* Retrieved 5 April, 2012
Bond, B. (2016). The E(A)P of spelling: Using exploratory practice to (re)engage teachers and students. *BALEAP 2016 Conference Proceedings.* Garnet Education.
Borg, S. (2006). *Teacher cognition and language education.* London: Continuum.
Borg, S. (2007). Understanding what teachers think about research. *The Teacher Trainer, 21*(2), 2–4.
Borg, S. (2009). English language teachers' conceptions of research. *Applied Linguistics, 30*(3), 358–388.
Borg, S. (2010). Language teacher research engagement. *Language Teaching, 43*(4), 391–429.
Borg, S. (2013). *Teacher research in language teaching: A critical analysis.* Cambridge: Cambridge University Press.
Bourdieu, P. (1991). *Language and symbolic power* (trans: Raymond, G. & Adamson, M.). Cambridge: Polity Press.
Brandes, D., & Ginnis, P. (1990). *The student-centred school: Ideas for practical visionaries.* Oxford: Basil Blackwell.
Breen, M. P. (2006). Collegial development in ELT: The interface between global processes and local understandings. In S. Gieve & I. K. Miller (Eds.), *Understanding the language classroom* (pp. 200–225). Basingstoke: Palgrave Macmillan.
Breen, M. P., Hird, B., Milton, M., Oliver, R., & Thwaite, A. (2001). Making sense of language teaching: Teachers' principles and classroom practices. *Applied Linguistics, 22*(4), 470–501.
Brown, S. (2005). How can research inform ideas of good practice in teaching? The contributions of some official initiatives in the UK. *Cambridge Journal of Education, 35*(3), 383–406.
Bryman, A. (2007). Barriers to integrating quantitative and qualitative research. *Journal of Mixed Methods Research, 1*(8), 8–22.
Bryman, A. (2009). Mixed methods in organizational research. In D. A. Buchanan & A. Bryman (Eds.), *The Sage handbook of organizational research methods* (pp. 516–531). London: Sage.
Burns, A. (1999). *Collaborative action research for English language teachers.* Cambridge: Cambridge University Press.
Burns, A. (2005). Action research: An evolving paradigm? *Language Teaching, 38*(2), 57–74.
Burns, A. (2010). *Doing action research in English language teaching: A guide for practitioners.* New York: Routledge.

Burns, A. (2015). Reviewing classroom practices through collaborative action research. In K. Dikilitas, R. Smith, & W. Trotman (Eds.), *Teacher-researchers in action* (pp. 9–17). Faversham: IATEFL.

Burton, J. (1998). A cross-case analysis of teacher involvement in TESOL research. *TESOL Quarterly, 32*(3), 419–446.

Byrnes, H. (2013). Renting language in the ownership society: Reflections on language use and language learning in a multilingual world. In J. Arnold & T. Murphey (Eds.), *Meaningful action: Earl Stevick's influence on language teaching* (pp. 222–240). Cambridge: Cambridge University Press.

Canagarajah, S., & Ben Said, S. (2011). Linguistic imperialism. In J. Simpson (Ed.), *The Routledge handbook of applied linguistics* (pp. 388–400). Abingdon: Routledge.

Candlin, C. N., & Crichton, J. (Eds.). (2011). *Discourses of deficit*. Basingstoke: Palgrave Macmillan.

Candlin, C. N., & Crichton, J. (2013a). From ontology to methodology: Exploring the discursive landscape of trust. In C. N. Candlin & J. Crichton (Eds.), *Discourses of trust* (pp. 1–18). Basingstoke: Palgrave Macmillan.

Candlin, C. N., & Crichton, J. (2013b). Putting our trust in the learner. In J. Arnold & T. Murphey (Eds.), *Meaningful action: Earl Stevick's influence on language teaching* (pp. 79–94). Cambridge: Cambridge University Press.

Carr, W. (1987). What is an educational practice? *Journal of Philosophy of Education, 21*(2), 163–175.

Carr, W. (2004). Philosophy and education. *Journal of Philosophy of Education, 38*(1), 55–73.

Carr, W., & Kemmis, S. (1986). *Becoming critical: Education, knowledge and action research*. Lewes: The Falmer Press.

Casement, P. (1985). *On learning from the patient*. London: Tavistock Publications.

Charmaz, K. (2003). Grounded theory: Objectivist and constructivist methods. In N. K. Denzin & Y. S. Lincoln (Eds.), *Strategies of qualitative enquiry* (2nd ed., pp. 249–291). Thousand Oaks: Sage.

Cherchalli, S. (1988). *Learners' reactions to their textbooks (with special reference to the relation between differential perceptions and differential achievement): A case study of Algerian secondary school learners*. Unpublished PhD thesis, Lancaster University.

Chick, M. (2015). The education of language teachers: Instruction or conversation? ELT J, *69*(3), 297–307. First published online April 2, 2015. doi:10.1093/elt/ccv011.

Chu, P. (2007). How students react to the power and responsibility of being decision makers in their own learning. *Language Teaching Research, 11*(2), 225–241.

Clandinin, D. J. (Ed.). (2007). *Handbook of narrative inquiry: Mapping a methodology.* Thousand Oaks: Sage.

Clandinin, D. J., & Connelly, F. M. (1995). *Teachers' professional knowledge landscapes.* New York/London: Teachers College Press.

Clandinin, D. J., & Rosiek, J. (2007). Mapping a landscape of narrative inquiry: Borderland spaces and tensions. In D. J. Clandinin (Ed.), *Handbook of narrative inquiry* (pp. 35–75). Thousand Oaks: Sage.

Clark, R., & Ivanič, R. (1997). *The politics of writing.* London: Routledge.

Clark, J. A., & Mishler, E. G. (2001). Prestando Atenção às histórias dos pacientes: o reenquadre da tarefa clínica. In B. T. Ribeiro, C. C. Lima, & M. T. L. Dantas (Orgs.), *Narativa, Identidade e Clínica.* Rio de Janeiro: CUCA-IPUB/UFRJ.

Cochran-Smith, M., & Lytle, S. L. (Eds.). (1993). *Inside/outside: Teacher research and knowledge.* New York: Teachers College Press.

Cochran-Smith, M., & Lytle, S. L. (1999). The teacher research movement: A decade later. *Educational Researcher, 28*(7), 15–25.

Cochran-Smith, M., & Lytle, S. L. (2009). *Inquiry as stance: Practitioner research for the next generation.* New York: Teachers College Press.

Cohen, L., & Manion, L. (1994). *Research methods in education* (4th ed.). London: Routledge.

Cohen, L., Manion, L., & Morrison, K. (2007). *Research methods in education* (6th ed.). Abingdon: Routledge.

Collini, S. (2012). *What are universities for?* London: Penguin.

Cortazzi, M., & Jin, L. (1996). Cultures of learning: Language classrooms in China. In H. Coleman (Ed.), *Society and the language classroom* (pp. 169–206). Cambridge: Cambridge University Press.

Crane, C. (2015). Exploratory practice in the FL teaching methods course: A case study of three graduate student instructors' experiences. *L2 Journal, 7*(2), 1–23. Accessible on-line: http://repositories.cdlib.org/uccllt/l2/vol7/iss2/art1/

Crane, C., Sadler, M., Ha, J. A., & Ojiambo, P. (2013). Beyond the methods course: Using exploratory practice for graduate student teacher development. In H. W. Allen & H. Maxim (Eds.), *Educating the future foreign language professoriate for the 21st century* (pp. 107–127). Boston: Heinle.

Creswell, J. W. (2003). *Research design: Qualitative, quantitative, and mixed methods approaches* (2nd ed.). Thousand Oaks: Sage.

Cunha, M. I. A., & Members of the Rio de Janeiro Exploratory Practice Group. (Forthcoming). What has been puzzling teachers and students in Rio de

Janeiro. In Grupo da Prática Exploratória do Rio de Janeiro (Orgs.), *A Prática Exploratória no Rio de Janeiro: histórias de um grupo de aprendizes*. Campinas: Pontes Editores.

Dam, L. (1995). *Learner autonomy: From theory to classroom practice*. Dublin: Authentik.

Dam, L. (2009). The use of logbooks – A tool for developing learner autonomy. In R. Pemberton, S. Toogood, & A. Barfield (Eds.), *Maintaining control: Autonomy and language learning*. Hong Kong: Hong Kong University Press.

Dam, L., & Gabrielson, G. (1988). Developing learner autonomy in a school context – A six-year experiment beginning in the learners' first year of English. In H. Holec (Ed.), *Autonomy and self-directed learning: Present fields of application* (pp. 19–30). Strasbourg: Council for Cultural Co-operation, Council of Europe.

Dam, L., & Lentz, J. (1998). 'It's up to yourself if you want to learn.' *Autonomous language learning at intermediate level*. Copenhagen: DLH (video).

Dar, Y. (2008). *An exploration of puzzles in an adult ESOL classroom in Leicester*. Unpublished MA dissertation, University of Leicester.

Dar, Y. (2012). Exploratory practice: Investigating my own classroom pedagogy. *ELT Research, IATEFL Research SIG Newsletter, 26*, 8–10.

Dar, Y. (2015). Exploratory Practice: Investigating my own classroom pedagogy. In D. Bullock, & R. Smith (Eds.), *Teachers research!* (pp. 51–59). Faversham: IATEFL. [online]: http://resig.weebly.com/uploads/2/6/3/6/26368747/teachers_research_.pdf

Dawson, S. (2012). *Exploratory Practice: Its contribution to ongoing professional development*. Unpublished MA dissertation, University of Manchester.

Dawson, S. (2016). Practice to professional development: What practitioners think. *ELT Research, IATEFL Research SIG Newsletter, 31*, 10–13.

Denzin, N. K., & Lincoln, Y. S. (1998). *Collecting and interpreting qualitative materials*. Thousand Oaks: Sage.

Denzin, N. K., & Lincoln, Y. S. (Eds.). (2003). *Collecting and interpreting qualitative materials* (2nd ed.). Thousand Oaks/London: Sage.

Dewey, J. (1938). *Experience and education*. New York: The Macmillan Company.

Dewey, J. (1944). *Democracy and education*. New York: The Free Press (Macmillan).

Dewey, J. (1963). *Experience and education*. New York: Collier Books.

Dikilitaş, K. (Ed.). (2014). *Professional development through teacher research*. Izmir: Gediz University.

Dikilitaş, K. (2015a). Professional development through teacher-research. In K. Dikilitaş, R. Smith, & W. Trotman (Eds.), *Teacher-researchers in action* (pp. 47–55). Faversham: IATEFL.

Dikilitaş, K. (2015b). Teacher research for instructors. In S. Borg (Ed.), *Professional development for English language teachers: Perspectives from higher education in Turkey* (pp. 27–33). Ankara: British Council, Turkey.

Dikilitaş, K., Smith, R., & Trotman, W. (Eds.). (2015). *Teacher-researchers in action*. Faversham: IATEFL.

Dikilitas, K., Wyatt, M., Hanks, J., & Bullock, D. (Eds.). (2016). *Teachers engaging in research*. Faversham: IATEFL.

Dreyfus, H. L. (1991). *Being-in-the-world: A commentary on Heidegger's being and time, division 1*. Cambridge, MA: MIT Press.

Duff, P. A. (2008). *Case study research in applied linguistics*. New York: Laurence Erlbaum Associates.

Edge, J. (2011). *The reflexive teacher educator in TESOL: Roots and wings*. New York: Routledge.

Elliott, J. (1991). *Action research for educational change*. Milton Keynes: Open University Press.

EPCentre Website. (2008). Retrieved 17 September, 2012, from http://www.letras.puc-rio.br/unidades&nucleos/epcentre/links.htm

Fairclough, N. (1989). *Language and power*. Harlow: Longman.

Farrell, T. S. C. (2007). *Reflective language teaching: From research to practice*. London: Continuum.

Festinger, L. (1957). *A theory of cognitive dissonance*. Stanford: Stanford University Press.

Feyerabend, P. (1975/2010). *Against method* (4th ed.). London: Verso.

Flanagan, J. C. (1954). The critical incident technique. *Psychological Bulletin, 51*(4), 327–358.

Flanders, N. A. (1970). *Analysing teacher behavior*. Reading: Addison-Wesley.

Flyvbjerg, B. (2001). *Making social science matter: Why social inquiry fails and how it can succeed again* (trans: Sampson, S.). Cambridge: Cambridge University Press.

Fontana, A., & Frey, J. H. (1998). Interviewing: The art of science. In N. K. Denzin & Y. S. Lincoln (Eds.), *Collecting and interpreting qualitative materials* (pp. 47–78). Thousand Oaks: Sage.

Frahm, G. F. (1998). *Change/innovation in mainstream education in Parana, Brazil*. Unpublished PhD thesis, Lancaster University.

Freeman, D. (1996). Redefining the relationship between research and what teachers know. In K. M. Bailey & D. Nunan (Eds.), *Voices from the language classroom* (pp. 88–115). Cambridge: Cambridge University Press.

Freeman, D. (2006). Teaching and learning in 'the age of reform': The problem of the verb. In S. Gieve & I. K. Miller (Eds.), *Understanding the language classroom* (pp. 239–262). Basingstoke: Palgrave Macmillan.

Freire, P. (1970). *Pedagogy of the oppressed*. New York: Seabury Press.

Freire, P. (1973). *Education for critical consciousness*. New York: Seabury Press.

Freire, P., & Shorr, I. (1987). *A pedagogy for liberation*. Basingstoke: Macmillan.

Freud, S. (1914/2002). *Some reflections on schoolboy psychology*. London: Penguin.

Freud, S. (1930/2002). *Civilization and its discontents*. London: Penguin.

Furman, B., & Ahola, T. (1992). *Pickpockets in a nudist camp: The systemic revolution in psychotherapy*. London: Dulwich Centre Publications.

Gadamer, H.-G. (1975/2013). *Truth and method*. (2nd ed., Trans: Weinsheimer, J. & Marshall, D. G.). London: Bloomsbury Academic.

Garfinkel, H. (1967). *Studies in ethnomethodology*. Cambridge: Polity Press.

Geertz, C. (1973). Thick description: Towards an interpretive theory of culture. In C. Geertz (Ed.), *The interpretation of cultures*. New York: Basic Books.

Gergen, K. J. (2013). The rugged return of qualitative inquiry in American psychology. *Qualitative Methods in Psychology Bulletin, 15*, 38–40.

Gibbons, T., & Sanderson, G. (2002). Contemporary themes in the research enterprise. *International Education Journal, 3*(4), 1–22.

Gieve, S., & Miller, I. K. (Eds.). (2006a). *Understanding the language classroom*. Basingstoke: Palgrave Macmillan.

Gieve, S., & Miller, I. K. (2006b). What do we mean by 'quality of classroom life'? In S. Gieve & I. K. Miller (Eds.), *Understanding the language classroom* (pp. 18–46). Basingstoke: Palgrave Macmillan.

Glaser, B. G. (1992). *Basics of grounded theory analysis: Emergence vs forcing*. Mill Valley: Sociology Press.

Glaser, B. G., & Strauss, A. L. (1967). *The discovery of grounded theory: Strategies for qualitative research*. New York: Aldine de Gruyter.

Glynos, J., & Howarth, D. (2007). *Logistics of critical explanation in social and political theory*. Abingdon: Routledge.

Goffman, E. (1974). *Frame analysis: An essay on the organisation of experience*. Harmondsworth: Penguin.

Gorard, S. (2001). *Quantitative methods in educational research: The role of numbers made easy*. London: Continuum.

Gorard, S., & Taylor, C. (2004). *Combining methods in educational and social research*. Maidenhead: Open University Press.

Graves, K. (2003). *Understanding language classrooms as social practices: Competence, roles and distribution of knowledge in an adult ESL class*. Unpublished PhD thesis, Lancaster University.

Griffiths, M., & Tann, S. (1992). Using reflective practice to link personal and public theories. *Journal of Education for Teaching, 18*(1), 69–84.

Gudmundsdottir, S. (2001). Narrative research on school practice. In V. Richardson (Ed.), *Handbook of research on teaching* (pp. 226–240). Washington, DC: American Educational Researcher.

Gumperz, J. (Ed.). (1982). *Language and social identity*. Cambridge: Cambridge University Press.

Gumperz, J. (2002). Convenções de Contextualização. In B. T. Ribeiro & P. M. Garcez (Eds.), *Sociolinguistica Interacional*. São Paulo: Edições Loyola.

Gunn, C. (2001). *Communicative competence in an enhanced learning context*. Unpublished PhD thesis, University of Bath.

Gunn, C. (2003). Exploring second language communicative competence. *Language Teaching Research, 7*(2), 240–258.

Gunn, C. (2010). Exploring MA TESOL student 'resistance' to reflection. *Language Teaching Research, 14*(2), 208–223.

Hall, G. (2011). *Exploring English language teaching: Language in action*. Abingdon: Routledge.

Hammersley, M., & Atkinson, P. (1983). *Ethnography principles in practice*. London: Tavistock.

Hammersley, M., & Atkinson, P. (2009). *Ethnography: Principles in practice* (3rd ed.). Abingdon: Routledge.

Hanks, J. (1998). *"The thing that puzzled me was…": Implications of teacher perspectives on 'problems' and 'puzzles' for Exploratory Practice*. Unpublished MA dissertation, Lancaster University.

Hanks, J. (1999). Enthusiasm, puzzlement, and Exploratory Practice. *International House Journal of education and development, 7*, 14–16.

Hanks, J. (2009). Inclusivity and collegiality in Exploratory Practice. In T. Yoshida, H. Imai, Y. Nakata, A. Tajino, O. Takeuchi, & K. Tamai (Eds.), *Researching language teaching and learning: An integration of practice and theory* (pp. 33–55). Bern: Peter Lang.

Hanks, J. (2013a). Inclusivity and trust in Exploratory Practice: A case study of principles in practice. In E. Tarone & D. Soneson (Eds.), *Expanding our horizons: Language teacher education in the 21st century*. Minneapolis: CARLA.

Hanks, J. (2013b). *Exploratory Practice in English for academic purposes: Puzzling over principles and practices*. Unpublished PhD thesis, University of Leeds.

Hanks, J. (2015a). 'Education is not just teaching': Learner thoughts on Exploratory Practice. *ELT Journal, 69*(2), 117–128. First published online: December 1, 2014.

Hanks, J. (2015b). Language teachers making sense of Exploratory Practice. *Language Teaching Research, 19*(5), 612–633.

Hanks, J. (2015c). 'Professional language & intercultural studies: What and how to assess and why?' Conference proceedings: *Diversity, plurilingualism and their impact on language testing and assessment* (pp. 30–33). 22–23 November, 2013, Universita' per Stranieri, Siena.

Hanks, J. (2016). What might research AS practice look like? In K. Dikilitas, M. Wyatt, J. Hanks, & D. Bullock (Eds.), *Teachers engaging in research* (pp. 19–29). Faversham: IATEFL.

Hanks, J., Miller, I. K., Salvi, A. I. (Eds.) with Xavier Ewald, C., Mendes Lima Moura, S., Apolinário, C., Slimani-Rolls, A., Bond, B., Poole, J., Allwright, D., Dar, Y. (2016). "Why Exploratory Practice?" A collaborative report, *ELT Research*, IATEFL Research SIG Newsletter, 31.

Hanks, P. (2013). *Lexical analysis: Norms and exploitations.* Cambridge, MA: MIT Press.

Hashemi, M. R., & Babaii, E. (2013). Mixed methods research: Toward new research designs in applied linguistics. *The Modern Language Journal, 97*(4), 828–852.

Heidegger, M. (1962). *Being and time* (trans: Macquarrie, J. & Robinson, E.). Malden: Blackwell Publishing.

Holec, H. (1980). *Autonomy and foreign language learning.* Oxford: Pergamon.

Holec, H. (Ed.). (1988). *Autonomy and self-directed learning: Present fields of application.* Strasbourg: Council for Cultural Co-operation, Council of Europe.

Holliday, A. (2002). *Doing and writing qualitative research.* London: Sage.

Holliday, A. (2013). *Understanding intercultural communication: Negotiating a grammar of culture.* Abingdon: Routledge.

Holliday, A., Hyde, M., & Kullman, J. (2010). *Intercultural communication* (2nd ed.). Abingdon: Routledge.

Homan, R. (1991). *The ethics of social research.* Harlow: Longman.

Iedema, R., Mesman, J., & Carroll, K. (2013). *Visualising health care practice improvement.* London: Radcliffe Publishing.

Irie, K., & Stewart, A. (Eds.). (2012). *Realizing autonomy: Practice and reflection in language.* Basingstoke: Palgrave Macmillan.

Johnson, K. A. (2002). Action for understanding: A study in teacher research with exploratory practice. In K. E. Johnson & P. R. Golombek (Eds.), *Teachers' narrative inquiry as professional development* (pp. 60–71). Cambridge: Cambridge University Press.

Johnson, K. E., & Golombek, P. R. (Eds.). (2002). *Teachers' narrative inquiry as professional development.* Cambridge: Cambridge University Press.

Kemmis, S., & McTaggart, R. (Eds.). (1988). *The action research planner*. Geelong: Deakin University.
Kemmis, S., & McTaggart, R. (2003). Participatory action research. In N. K. Denzin & Y. S. Lincoln (Eds.), *Strategies of qualitative inquiry* (2nd ed., pp. 336–396). Thousand Oaks/London: Sage.
Kiely, R. (2006). Teachers into researchers: Learning to research in TESOL. In S. Borg (Ed.), *Language teacher research in Europe* (pp. 67–80). Alexandria: TESOL.
Kirkwood, M., & Christie, D. (2006). The role of teacher research in continuing professional development. *British Journal of Education Studies, 54*(4), 429–448.
Kramsch, C. (2006). From communicative competence to symbolic competence. *Modern Language Journal, 90*(2), 249–252.
Kramsch, C. (2009). *The multilingual subject*. Oxford: Oxford University Press.
Kuchah, K., & Smith, R. (2011). Pedagogy of autonomy for different circumstances: From practice to principles. *International Journal of Innovation in Language Learning and Teaching*.
Kuchah, K., & Smith, R. (2011). Pedagogy of autonomy for difficult circumstances: From practice to principles. *Innovation in Language Learning and Teaching, 5*(2), 119–140.
Kuhn, T. S. (1996). *The structure of scientific revolutions* (3rd ed.). Chicago: The University of Chicago Press.
Kuschnir, A., & Machado, B. (2003). Puzzling and puzzling about puzzle development. *Language Teaching Research, 7*(2), 163–180.
Kvale, S. (1996). *InterViews: An introduction to qualitative research interviewing*. Thousand Oaks: Sage.
La Taille, Y. (2009). *Formação ética: do tédio ao respeito de si*. Artmed Editora AS.
Lave, J., & Wenger, E. (1991). *Situated learning: Legitmate peripheral participation*. Cambridge: Cambridge University Press.
Lewin, K. (1946). Action research and minority problems. *Journal of Social Issues, 2*, 34–46.
Lieblich, A., Tuval-Mashiach, R., & Zilber, T. (1998). *Narrative research: Reading, analysis, and interpretation*. Thousand Oaks: Sage.
Lincoln, Y. S., & Guba, E. G. (1985). *Naturalistic inquiry*. Thousand Oaks: Sage.
Liston, D. P., & Zeichner, K. M. (1990). Reflective teaching and action research in preservice teacher education. *Journal of Education for Teaching, 16*(3), 235–253.
Lortie, D. C. (1975). *Schoolteacher: A sociological study*. Chicago: University of Chicago Press.

Lyra, I., Fish Braga, S., & Braga, W. (2003). What puzzles teachers in Rio de Janeiro, and what keeps them going? *Language Teaching Research, 7*(2), 143–162.

Malderez, A., & Wedell, M. (2007). *Teaching teachers: Processes and practices.* London: Continuum.

Manguel, A. (2015). *Curiosity.* New Haven: Yale University Press.

McDonough, J., & McDonough, S. (1990). What's the use of research? *ELT Journal, 44*(2), 102–109.

McDonough, J., & McDonough, S. (1997). *Research methods for English language teachers.* London: Arnold.

McNiff, J., & Whitehead, J. (2002). *Action research: Principles and practice.* Abingdon: RoutledgeFalmer.

McNiff, J., Lomax, P., & Whitehead, J. (2003). *You and your action research project* (2nd ed.). London: RoutledgeFalmer.

Mehan, H. (1979). *Learning lessons.* Cambridge, MA: Harvard University Press.

Miles, M. B., & Huberman, A. M. (1994). *Qualitative data analysis: An expanded sourcebook.* Thousand Oaks: Sage.

Miller, I. (1997) *Understanding the Municipio language classroom through exploratory practice.* IATEFL Brazil & BraTESOL Workshop Day, August 1997, Rio, Brazil.

Miller, I. K. (2001). *Researching teacher-consultancy via Exploratory Practice: A reflexive and socio-interactional approach.* Unpublished PhD thesis, Lancaster University.

Miller, I. K. (2003). Researching teacher-consultancy via Exploratory Practice. *Language Teaching Research, 7*(2), 201–220.

Miller, I. K. (2009). 'Puzzle-driven' language teacher development: The contribution of Exploratory Practice. In T. Yoshida, H. Imai, Y. Nakata, A. Tajino, O. Takeuchi, & K. Tamai (Eds.), *Researching language teaching and learning: An integration of practice and theory* (pp. 77–93). Bern: Peter Lang.

Miller, I. K. (2010). Construindo parcerias universidade-escola: Caminhos éticos e questões crítico-reflexivas. In T. Giminez & M. C. G. Góes (Orgs.). *Formação de professores de línguas na América Latina e transformação social* (pp. 109–129). Campinas: Pontes Editores.

Miller, I. K. (2012). A Prática Exploratória na educação de professores de línguas: inserções acadêmicas e teorizações híbridas. In K. Silva, F. G. Daniel, S. M. Kaneko-marques, A. C. B. Salomão (Orgs.), *A formação de professores de línguas: novos olhares* (pp. 317–339). Campinas: Pontes Editores, v. 2.

Miller, I. K. (2013). Formação Inicial e Continuada de Professores de Línguas: da eficiência à reflexão crítica e ética. In L. P. Moita Lopes (Ed.), *Linguística*

Aplicada na Modernidade Recente: Festschrift Para Antonieta Celani (pp. 99–121, 257–266). São Paulo: Parábola Editorial, v. 1.

Miller, I. K., & Barreto, B. C. B. (2015). A formação de professores de línguas nas licenciaturas em Letras da PUC-Rio: horizonte teórico e decisões curriculares. In R. M. de B. Meyer & A. Albuquerque (Eds.), *Português: uma língua internacional* (pp. 77–94). Rio de Janeiro: Editora PUC-Rio.

Miller, I. K., Barreto, B., Braga, W. G., Cunha, M. I. A., Kuschnir, A. N., Moraes Bezerra, I. C. R., & Sette, M. L. (2008). Prática Exploratória: questões e desafios. In G. Gil & M. H. Vieira-Abrahão (Eds.), *Educação de Professores de Línguas: os desafios do formador* (pp. 145–165). Campinas: Pontes Editores.

Miller, I. K., Côrtes, T. C. R., Oliveira, A. F. A., & Braga, W. G. (2015). Exploratory Practice in initial teacher education: Working collaboratively for understandings. In D. Bullock & R. Smith (Eds.), *Teachers research!* (pp. 65–71). Canterbury: IATEFL.

Mishler, E. G. (1986). *Research interviewing: Context and narrative.* Cambridge, MA: Harvard University Press.

Moita Lopes, L. P. (2006). *Por Uma Linguisica Aplicada Indisciplinar*. São Paulo: Parábola Editorial.

Moraes Bezerra, I. C. R. (2007). Com quantos fios se tece uma reflexão? Narrativas e argumentações no tear da interação. Unpublished PhD thesis, PUC-Rio.

Moraes Bezerra, I. C. R., & Miller, I. K. (2015). Exploratory Practice and new literacy studies: Building epistemological connections. *Pensares em Revista* (No. 6, pp. 90–128). São Gonçalo: Rio de Janeiro.

Moskowitz, G. (1968). The effects of training foreign language teachers in interaction analysis. *Foreign Language Annals, 9*(2), 135–157.

Moskowitz, G. (1978). *Caring and sharing in the foreign language class: A sourcebook on humanistic techniques.* Rowley: Newbury House Publishers.

Muir, T. (2015, May). *Spirit photography: Feelings in the EAP classroom.* Paper presented at the 27th Communications Skills Workshop, Tartu.

Nunan, D. (1989). *Understanding language classrooms: A guide for teacher initiated action.* London: Prentice-Hall International.

Nunan, D. (1992). *Research methods in language learning.* Cambridge: Cambridge University Press.

Nunan, D. (1993). Action research in language education. In J. Edge & K. Richards (Eds.), *Teachers develop teachers research* (pp. 39–50). Oxford/ Portsmouth: Heinemann International.

Nunan, D. (2012, June 28). Professional development through action research. Unpublished talk given at University of Warwick. Slides available at http://

www.slideshare.net/teresamac/professional-development-through-action-research-d-nunan

Osterman, K. F., & Kottkamp, R. B. (2004). *Reflective practice for educators: Professional development to improve student learning* (2nd ed.). Thousand Oaks: Corwin Press.

Özdeniz, D. (1996). Introducing innovations into your teaching: Innovation and exploratory teaching. In J. Willis & D. Willis (Eds.), *Challenge and change in language teaching* (pp. 110–125). Oxford: Heinemann.

Pennycook, A. (1998). Borrowing others' words: Text, ownership, memory, and plagiarism. In V. Zamel & R. Spack (Eds.), *Negotiating academic literacies: Teaching and learning across languages and cultures* (pp. 265–292). Mahwah: Lawrence Erlbaum Associates.

Perpignan, H. (2001). *Teacher-written feedback to language learners: Promoting a dialogue for understanding.* Unpublished PhD thesis, Lancaster University.

Perpignan, H. (2003). Exploring the written feedback dialogue: A research, learning and teaching practice. *Language Teaching Research, 7*(2), 159–278.

Phillipson, R. (1992). *Linguistic imperialism.* Oxford: Oxford University Press.

Pinto da Silva, C. M. F. (2001). *Intentions and interpretations in the language classroom: A case study of ELT in a Portuguese polytechnic.* Unpublished PhD thesis, Lancaster University.

Prabhu, N. S. (1987). *Second language pedagogy.* Oxford: Oxford University Press.

Research Councils UK 'Pathways to Impact'. (2015). http://www.rcuk.ac.uk/innovation/impacts/. Accessed 27 Nov 2015.

Riazi, A. M., & Candlin, C. (2014). Mixed-methods research in language teaching and learning: Opportunities, issues and challenges. *Language Teaching, 47*, 135–173.

Richards, K. (2003). *Qualitative inquiry in TESOL.* Basingstoke: Palgrave Macmillan.

Richardson, V. (Ed.). (2001). *Handbook of research on teaching* (4th ed.). Washington, DC: American Educational Research Association.

Riessman, C. K. (2008). *Narrative methods for the human sciences.* Boston: Sage.

Robson, C. (2002). *Real world research* (2nd ed.). Malden/Oxford: Blackwell Publishing.

Rose, J. (2007). Understanding relevance in the language classroom. *Language Teaching Research, 11*(4), 483–502.

Rowland, L. (2011). Lessons about learning: Comparing learner experiences with language research. *Language Teaching Research, 15*(2), 254–267.

Russell, B. (1928). *Sceptical essays*. London: Allen & Unwin.
Salvi, A. I. (2012). *Integrating a pedagogy for autonomy with Exploratory Practice*. Unpublished MA dissertation, University of Warwick.
Salvi, A. I. (2014). Teachers Research! A report from the PCE supported by ReSIG. *ELT Research*, IATEFL Research SIG Newsletter, 30.
Salvi, A. I. (2015). Some issues in practitioner research. In D. Bullock, & R. Smith. (Eds.), *Teachers research!* (pp. 72–76). Faversham: IATEFL. Accessible [online]: http://resig.weebly.com/uploads/2/6/3/6/26368747/teachers_research_.pdf
Scarino, A. (2010). Language and languages and the curriculum. In A. J. Liddicote & A. Scarino (Eds.) *Languages in Australian Education: Problems, prospects and future directions* (pp. 157–177). Newcastle upon Tyne: Cambridge Scholars Publishing.
Schön, D. A. (1983/1991). *The reflective practitioner*. London: Temple Smith.
Schön, D. A. (1987). *Educating the reflective practitioner*. San Francisco: Jossey-Bass.
Schön, D. A. (Ed.). (1991). *The reflective turn: Case studies in and on educational practice*. New York: Teachers College Press, Columbia University.
Schutz, A. (1970). *On phenomenology and social relations*. Chicago: University of Chicago Press.
Senior, R. M. (2006). *The experience of language teaching*. Cambridge: Cambridge University Press.
Simpson, J. (Ed.). (2011). *The Routledge handbook of applied linguistics*. Abingdon: Routledge.
Slimani, A. (1987). *The teaching/learning relationship: Learning opportunities and the problems of uptake – An Algerian case study*. Unpublished PhD thesis, Lancaster University.
Slimani-Rolls, A. (2003). Exploring a world of paradoxes: An investigation of group work. *Language Teaching Research, 7*(2), 221–239.
Slimani-Rolls, A. (2005). Rethinking task-based language learning: What we can learn from the learners. *Language Teaching Research, 9*(2), 195–218.
Slimani-Rolls, A. (2009). Complexity and idiosyncrasy of classroom life. In T. Yoshida, H. Imai, Y. Nakata, A. Tajino, O. Takeuchi, & K. Tamai (Eds.), *Researching language teaching and learning: An integration of practice and theory* (pp. 57–75). Bern: Peter Lang.
Slimani-Rolls, A., & Kiely, R. (2014). 'We are the change we seek: Developing a teachers' understanding of classroom practice. *Innovations in Education and Teaching International, 51*(4), 425–435.
Smith, C. (2009). Developing a new English for academic purposes course: Administrator-teacher-student collaboration. In T. Yoshida, H. Imai, Y. Nakata, A. Tajino, O. Takeuchi, & K. Tamai (Eds.), *Researching language*

teaching and learning: An integration of practice and theory (pp. 95–113). Bern: Peter Lang.

Smith, R. (2015). Exploratory action research as a workplan: Why, what and where from? In K. Dikilitaş, R. Smith, & W. Trotman (Eds.), *Teacher-researchers in action* (pp. 37–45). Faversham: IATEFL.

Smyth, J. (2011). *Critical pedagogy for social justice.* New York: Bloomsbury Academic.

Smyth, J., Down, B., McInerney, P., & Hattam, R. (2014). *Doing critical education research: A conversation with the work of John Smyth.* New York: Peter Lang.

Stake, R. E. (1995). *The art of case study research.* Thousand Oaks: Sage.

Stake, R. E. (2003). Case studies. In N. K. Denzin & Y. S. Lincoln (Eds.), *Strategies of qualitative inquiry* (pp. 134–164). Thousand Oaks: Sage.

Stenhouse, L. (1975). *An introduction to curriculum research and development.* London: Heinemann.

Stevick, E. (1976). *Memory, meaning and method.* Rowley: Newbury House.

Stevick, E. (1980). *Teaching languages: A way and ways.* Rowley: Newbury House.

Stevick, E. (1990). *Humanism in language teaching.* Oxford: Oxford University Press.

Stevick, E. (1996). *Memory, meaning, & method: A view of language teaching* (2nd ed.). Boston: Heinle & Heinle.

Stewart, A. (2007). Teacher development and ad hoc communities. *Learning Learning, 14*(1), 18–27.

Stewart, A., Croker, R., & Hanks, J. (2014). Exploring the principles of Exploratory Practice: Quality of life or quality of learning? In A. Barfield & A. Minematsu (Eds.), *Learner development working papers: Different cases: Different interests.* Tokyo: JALT Learner Development SIG. http://ldworkingpapers.wix.com/ld-working-papers

Stratton, P., & Hanks, H. (2016). Personal and professional development as processes of learning that enable the practitioner to create a self that is equipped for higher levels of professional mastery. In A. Vetere & P. Stratton (Eds.), *Interacting selves: Systemic solutions for personal and professional development in counselling and psychotherapy* (pp. 7–32). New York: Brunner-Routledge.

Strauss, A. L., & Corbin, J. (1990). *Basics of qualitative research: Grounded theory procedures and techniques.* Newbury Park/London: Sage.

Tajino, A. (1999). *Tsukuru Eigo wo Tanoshimu* [*Fun with Creative English*]. Tokyo: Maruzen.

Tajino, A. (2009). Understanding life in the language classroom: A systemic approach. In T. Yoshida, H. Imai, T. Nakata, A. Tajino, O. Takeuchi, &

K. Tamai (Eds.), *Researching language teaching and learning: An integration of practice and theory* (pp. 115–130). Bern: Peter Lang.

Tajino, A. (2011). *Imijun Eisakubun no Susume* [*A meaning-based approach to English compositions*]. Tokyo: Iwanami Shoten.

Tajino, A., & Smith, C. (2005). Exploratory practice and soft systems methodology. *Language Teaching Research, 9*(4), 448–469.

Tajino, A., & Smith, C. (2016). Beyond team teaching: An introduction to team learning in language education. In A. Tajino, T. Stewart, & D. Dalsky (Eds.), *Team teaching and team learning in the language classroom: Collaboration for innovation in ELT* (pp. 11–27). Abingdon: Routledge.

Tajino, A., Stewart, T., & Dalsky, D. (Eds.). (2016). *Team teaching and team learning in the language classroom: Collaboration for innovation in ELT*. Abingdon: Routledge.

Tarone, E. (2006). Language lessons: A complex, local co-production of all participants. In S. Gieve & I. K. Miller (Eds.), *Understanding the language classroom* (pp. 163–174). Basingstoke: Palgrave Macmillan.

Tarone, E., & Swierzbin, B. (2009). *Exploring learner language*. Oxford: Oxford University Press.

Trim, J. L. M. (1976). Some possibilities and limitations of learner autonomy. In E. Harding-Esch (Ed.), *Self-directed learning and autonomy* (pp. 1–11). Cambridge: Cambridge University Department of Linguistics.

Tudor, I. (2001). *The dynamics of the language classroom*. Cambridge: Cambridge University Press.

Tudor, I. (2003). Learning to live with complexity: Towards an ecological perspective on language teaching. *System, 31*, 1–12.

Ur, P. (1996). *A course in language teaching: Practice and theory*. Cambridge: Cambridge University Press.

Valli, L. (Ed.). (1992). *Reflective teacher education: Cases and critiques*. New York: State University of New York.

van Lier, L. (1996). *Interaction in the language curriculum: Awareness, autonomy and authenticity*. Harlow: Longman.

van Lier, L. (2009). Perception in language learning. In T. Yoshida, H. Imai, Y. Nakata, A. Tajino, O. Takeuchi, & K. Tamai (Eds.), *Researching language teaching and learning: An integration of practice and theory* (pp. 275–291). Bern: Peter Lang.

van Lier, L. (2013). Control and initiative: The dynamics of agency in the language classroom. In J. Arnold & T. Murphey (Eds.), *Meaningful action: Earl Stevick's influence on language teaching* (pp. 241–251). Cambridge: Cambridge University Press.

van Maanen, J. (Ed.). (1995). *Representation in ethnography*. Thousand Oaks: Sage.

van Manen, M. (1990). *Researching lived experience: Human science for an action sensitive pedagogy*. New York: State University of New York Press.

Vieira, F. (2003). Addressing constraints on autonomy in school contexts: Lessons from working with teachers. In D. Palfreyman & R. Smith (Eds.), *Learner autonomy across cultures: Language education perspectives*. Basingstoke: Palgrave Macmillan.

Walker, M. (1995). Context, critique, and change: Doing action research in South Africa. *Educational Action Research, 3*(1), 9–27.

Wallace, M. J. (1991). *Training foreign language teachers: A reflective approach*. Cambridge: Cambridge University Press.

Wallace, M. J. (1998). *Action research for language teachers*. New York: Cambridge University Press.

Wallerstein, N. (1983). *Language and culture in conflict: Problem posing in the ESL classroom, a teacher's cross-cultural resource for adult education instruction based on the work of Paulo Freire*. Reading: Addison Wesley.

Watson-Gegeo, K. A. (1988). Ethnography in ESL: Defining the essentials. *TESOL Quarterly, 22*(4), 575–592.

Wedell, M. (2009). *Planning for educational change: Putting people and their contexts first*. London: Continuum.

Wedell, M., & Malderez, A. (2013). *Understanding language classroom contexts: The starting point for change*. London: Bloomsbury Academic.

Wenger, E. (1998). *Communities of practice: Learning, meaning, and identity*. Cambridge: Cambridge University Press.

Wingate, U. (2015). *Academic literacy and student diversity: The case for inclusive practice*. Bristol: Multilingual Matters.

Winnicott, D. W. (1971). *Playing and reality*. Harmondsworth: Penguin.

Woods, D. (1996). *Teacher cognition in language teaching*. Cambridge: Cambridge University Press.

Woods, D., & Cakir, H. (2011). Two dimensions of teacher knowledge: The case of communicative language teaching. *System, 39*, 381–390.

Wright, T. (2005). *Classroom management in language education*. Basingstoke: Palgrave Macmillan.

Wright, T. (2006). Managing classroom life. In S. Gieve & I. K. Miller (Eds.), *Understanding the language classroom* (pp. 64–87). Basingstoke: Palgrave Macmillan.

Wu, Z. (2002). *Teachers' "knowledge" and curriculum change: A critical study of teachers' exploratory discourse in a Chinese university*. Unpublished PhD thesis, Lancaster University.

Wu, Z. (2004). Being, understanding and naming: Teachers' life and work in harmony. *International Journal of Educational Research, 41*, 307–323.

Wu, Z. (2005). *Teachers' knowing in curriculum change.* Beijing: Foreign Language Teaching and Research Press.

Wu, Z. (2006). Understanding practitioner research as a form of life: An Eastern interpretation of Exploratory Practice. *Language Teaching Research, 10*(3), 331–350.

Wyatt, M., & Dikilitaş, K. (2015). English language teachers becoming more efficacious through research engagement at their Turkish University. *Educational Action Research, 1*, 1–21.

Wyatt, M., & Pasamar Márquez, C. (2016). Helping first-year undergraduates engage in language research. *Language Teaching Research, 20*(2), 146–164.

Wyatt, M., Burns, A., & Hanks, J. (2016). Teacher/practitioner research: Reflections on an online discussion. *TESL-EJ, 20*(1), 1–22. http://www.tesl-ej.org/wordpress/issues/volume20/ej77/ej77int/

Yates, L. (2004). *What does good education research look like?* Maidenhead: Oxford University Press.

Yin, R. K. (2003). *Case study research: Design and methods* (3rd ed.). Thousand Oaks: Sage.

Yoshida, T., Imai, H., Nakata, T., Tajino, A., Takeuchi, O., & Tamai, K. (Eds.). (2009). *Researching language teaching and learning: An integration of practice and theory.* Bern: Peter Lang.

Zeichner, K. M., & Noffke, S. E. (2001). Practitioner research. In V. Richardson (Ed.), *Handbook of research on teaching* (4th ed., pp. 298–330). Washington, DC: American Educational Research Association.

Zhang, R. (2004). Using the principles of Exploratory Practice to guide group work in an extensive reading class in China. *Language Teaching Research, 8*(3), 331–345.

Zheng, Z. (2005). *Understanding ways of knowing in the Exploratory Practice of RICH curricular innovation.* Unpublished MA dissertation, Zhejiang Normal University.

Zheng, Z. (2009). Exploratory Practice: College English teachers' new means of research. *Foreign Language World, 130*(1), 30–36.

Zheng, C. (2012). Understanding the learning process of peer feedback activity: An ethnographic study of Exploratory Practice. *Language Teaching Research, 16*(1), 109–126.

Index

A
academic, academically, 3, 5, 10, 12–14, 45, 55, 58, 62, 67–75, 77–9, 85, 86, 89, 99, 103, 105, 108, 138, 140, 146, 148, 152, 153, 168, 174, 176, 182, 188, 198, 202, 221, 233, 235, 237, 244, 252, 254, 256, 278, 279, 283, 285, 290, 293, 296, 300, 301, 304–6, 315, 323, 326, 328, 329, 332, 334, 337, 339–41, 343, 348, 352
action
  for change, 61, 91, 95, 135, 152
  for understanding, 95, 135, 152, 161, 199, 298
action research, 1, 3, 9, 24–6, 28–30, 57, 60–3, 81, 85–7, 95, 109, 154, 162, 178, 197, 206, 249, 254, 255, 309, 328

affect, 36, 98, 102, 149, 152, 165, 193, 202, 203, 224, 227, 232, 236, 283, 311, 321, 339
agency, 3, 17, 65, 134, 148, 161, 181, 194, 211, 212, 225, 262, 281, 287, 352
agency potential, 17, 134, 148, 181, 262
Allwright, D., 1–3, 5, 8, 9, 11, 13, 15, 17, 18, 35, 46, 49–51, 67, 69, 81–6, 88–97, 99–102, 104–7, 109, 113, 116, 117, 121, 124, 126, 136–8, 140, 143, 147, 149, 154, 159, 163, 165, 168, 170, 171, 179–82, 185, 188, 192, 196, 197, 199, 202, 203, 207, 210–12, 219–24, 236, 239, 247, 269, 270, 274, 275, 288, 292, 295, 301, 303, 319–35, 339, 340, 343–7, 349–52

annual EP event, 330, 338
anxiety, anxious, 118, 210, 237, 240, 267, 279, 286, 287, 300, 311
Apolinário, C., 139, 209

B
Bailey, K.M., 11, 28, 46, 51, 69, 84, 89, 321, 328
Bakhtin, M.M., 86, 96, 101, 102, 175, 221, 224, 278
Bauman, Z., 134, 139, 211, 221, 250, 274, 276, 277
being, 'being', 296
being-in-the-world, 18, 25, 59, 88
beliefs, 11, 16, 33, 54, 55, 61, 77, 79, 94, 160, 165, 194–6, 218, 228, 229, 243, 265, 271, 279, 280, 289, 291, 292, 299, 300, 306, 307, 311, 313–15, 343
Bond, B., 305, 306, 347
Borg, S., 46, 48, 54, 58, 67–71, 73, 74, 105, 194, 200, 253, 300, 301, 347
Bourdieu, P., 55, 136, 220, 292
Braga, W., 149
Breen, M.P., 5, 49, 54, 55, 63, 72, 76, 77, 87, 136, 194, 195, 262, 301, 313
Bryman, A., 40
burnout, burn-out, 2, 11, 35, 78, 84, 90–2, 200–5, 207, 311, 322, 350
Burns, A., 1, 28, 59, 61, 62, 69, 74, 77, 86, 105, 188, 221, 254, 301
Byrnes, H., 266, 287, 288, 307

C
Candlin, C.N., vii, 17, 40, 76, 169, 225–7, 231, 232, 257, 275, 289, 294, 347
Carroll, K., 19
Carr, W., 52, 60, 62, 63, 67, 94, 104, 137, 331
challenges, 7, 10, 12, 16, 23, 51, 57, 93, 101, 106, 111, 125, 148, 158, 169, 178, 180, 194, 198, 212, 225, 229, 232, 239, 250, 252, 256–8, 262, 265, 274, 280, 291, 296, 297, 299, 300, 313, 314, 334, 336
change, 4, 5, 26, 30, 43, 49, 58, 60–4, 66, 75, 76, 78, 79, 81, 86, 88, 91–5, 98, 104, 109, 134–9, 150, 152, 162, 165, 180, 187, 246, 249, 250, 256, 259, 278, 298, 338, 343
Chick, M., 208, 300
Chu, P., 12, 104
classroom
 culture(s), 236, 274–88
 identities, 102, 165, 172, 188, 259, 266, 274–88
 language learning, 1, 2, 26, 41, 71, 74, 99, 101, 102, 137, 165, 227, 262, 306, 326, 344, 346
 language teaching, 50, 83, 117, 203, 208, 303
 research, 28–30, 48, 68, 71, 78, 83, 85, 105, 153–5, 178, 320, 321, 328, 329, 339, 343, 344
Cochran-Smith, M., 1, 24, 46, 51, 55, 59, 79, 94, 197, 219, 262
cognitive dissonance, 54, 77, 78, 196, 292, 307, 313, 315
Cohen, L., 34, 37, 38, 61

collegiality, collegial working, 16, 27, 78, 88–91, 97, 99, 161–5, 167–89, 202, 204, 205, 220–2, 228, 254, 255, 288, 304, 312, 338, 340. *See also* principles
Communicative Approach, 320
Communicative Language Teaching (CLT), 181, 326
community of practice, 174, 229, 252, 283, 320
complexity, 29, 47, 48, 50, 99, 102, 125, 127, 134, 156, 176, 200, 205, 224, 225, 251, 254, 297, 308, 320, 340
continuing personal and professional development, 191–213, 293
continuing professional development (CPD), 12, 64, 98, 104, 140, 141, 195–200, 212, 253, 306, 310, 312, 342
control, 5, 37, 38, 44, 46, 54, 78, 83, 147, 152, 180, 212, 243, 258, 259, 278, 280, 313, 326, 328, 330
co-researchers, 8, 26, 49, 51, 99, 101, 137, 256, 259, 262, 274
Crane, C., 13, 161, 162, 196, 205–7, 269, 285
Crichton, J., viii, 17, 76, 169, 225–7, 231, 232, 257, 275, 289, 294
critical
  critical attention, 9
  criticality, 127
  critical pedagogy, 104, 180, 185, 188, 349
  criticism (vs), 54, 69, 74, 76, 77, 105, 127, 223, 301, 305

culture(s), 13, 71, 128, 134, 152, 174, 185, 218, 228, 235, 236, 238, 243, 252, 253, 262, 265–90, 295–7, 299, 301, 302, 306, 339, 347
Cunha, M.I.A., 11, 89, 117, 149, 209, 319, 331, 333–5, 346
curiosity, curious, 6, 7, 17, 18, 96, 113, 114, 125, 155, 169, 189, 202, 210, 236, 245, 289, 314, 346

D

Dalsky, D., 370
Dar, Y., 104, 153, 156, 177, 269
Dasein, 18, 25, 31, 59, 88, 96, 219, 292, 296
Dawson, S., 104, 177, 180, 302, 305
de Andrade, C., 149, 150, 268
demotivation, de-motivation, 311
Denzin, N.K., 33, 34, 38, 48
Dewey, J., 42, 43, 55, 58, 60, 85, 247, 335
dialogic, 45, 51, 101, 102, 161, 208, 228, 300, 308
Dikilitaş, K., 13, 104, 141, 196–9
discourse(s)
  of deficit, 76
  of improvement, 76, 78, 109, 112, 134–8
  of puzzlement, 116, 256
  of trust, 226, 275
dissemination, 8, 9, 44, 69, 74, 147, 179, 198, 277, 310, 335
diverse classrooms, 276
diversity, 34, 39, 227, 246, 257, 265, 273, 279

'doing-being', 8, 144, 169, 274, 277, 279, 285
Dreyfus, H.L., 6, 18, 25, 59, 88, 126, 219, 296

E

Edge, J., 1, 65, 72, 75, 77, 221
education
　language, vii, 8–10, 14, 16, 18, 25, 30, 35, 46, 52, 55, 57, 58, 71, 78, 82, 94, 133, 134, 167, 185, 186, 201, 210, 212, 218, 228, 267, 269, 292, 307, 310, 342–4, 348
　as social process, 3, 42
educational psychology/psychologist, 7, 8, 10, 17, 26, 27, 82, 111, 139, 141, 144, 191, 209–12, 217, 221, 294, 307, 334, 338
Elliott, D., 60, 156, 157, 311
engagement in research
　learner(s), 13, 308
　teacher(s), 8, 44, 70, 308, 337
English
　for Academic Purposes (EAP), 3, 12, 99, 103, 104, 108, 117, 121, 122, 127, 140, 141, 146, 148, 153, 156, 168–70, 172, 177–9, 181, 183, 235, 283, 284, 293, 306, 308–11
　language teaching (ELT), 61, 72, 106, 157, 161, 182, 254, 337, 338, 340, 343
　for Specific Purposes (ESP), 115, 244
Erik, U., 114, 115
ethics. *See also* phronesis
　ethical, practical wisdom, 52–3
ethical research, 15, 35, 41, 47, 61, 85, 137, 153, 291, 303, 319, 349
exploratory practice (EP)
　background, 18, 30, 83, 139, 292, 328
　defining characteristics, 88, 91–6
　definition(s), 3, 14, 27, 30, 82–3, 100, 294, 311
　evolution of, 24, 30, 81–106
　framework, 3, 12–14, 16–18, 24, 27, 30, 43, 47, 57, 81–106, 108, 116, 133, 138, 154–6, 164, 165, 177, 181, 188, 194, 196, 218, 220, 222, 228, 266, 293, 310, 313, 319
　genesis of, 85
　history of, 4, 9, 81, 88
　principles (of), 11, 15, 88, 97, 99, 141, 155, 168, 169, 178, 180, 185, 188, 203, 211, 220, 240, 250, 284, 292
　as research, 310, 313
　as researchable pedagogy, 147–9
　as scholarship, 27, 105, 229, 305–7, 311, 313
　spirit of, 160, 175, 184, 292
　story of, 2, 8, 9, 88, 301–5
exploratory teaching, 88, 89, 329

F

Fairclough, N., 55, 250, 271, 347
family tree of practitioner research, 30
Farrell, T.S.C., 1, 63–5
Fay, R., 302, 305
Festinger, L., 54, 77, 79, 196, 292, 307
Fish Braga, S., 130

Flanagan, J.C., 245
Flyvbjerg, B., 34, 39, 52, 94, 136, 298
framework, EP
  evolution of, 24, 30, 81–106
  stage one, 88–90
  stage three, 96–103
  stage two, 91–6
Freeman, D., 48, 50, 99, 188, 221, 301, 315
Freire, P., 44, 45, 49, 51, 55, 85, 101, 104, 113, 116, 180, 192, 229, 249, 298, 315, 326, 327, 334
frequently asked questions about practitioner research, 25
Freud, S., 73, 210, 211
fully inclusive practitioner research, 12, 13, 18, 100

G

Gadamer, H.-G., 110, 111, 113, 220
Geertz, C., 48, 176
Gieve, S., 2, 9, 17, 88, 96, 101, 102, 124, 133, 134, 148, 154, 201, 210, 211, 224, 262, 335
Golombek, P.R., 39, 46, 50, 54, 58, 59, 70, 77, 225
Gunn, C., 13, 96–8, 103, 140

H

Hall, G., 265
Hanks, J., 1, 2, 8, 9, 11–13, 17, 18, 28, 49, 51, 82, 84, 94, 98–102, 104, 105, 107, 109–11, 113, 116–18, 121, 123, 124, 126, 127, 137, 138, 140, 141, 143, 149, 159, 168, 170, 171, 179–82, 185, 192, 197, 203, 207, 210, 211, 219, 220, 222, 224, 227, 236, 239, 242, 245, 247, 256, 257, 259, 270, 274, 275, 277, 288, 306, 339, 344, 346, 352
Heidegger, M., 6, 18, 25, 31, 59, 88, 96, 113, 126, 219, 224, 292, 296
hierarchy/ies, 45, 60, 79, 94, 138
Holliday, A., 2, 40, 134, 176, 180, 276, 282, 299, 300, 347
Hu, M., 196, 200, 201

I

ideal
  impossible, 251
  learner, 2, 297
  researcher, 252, 297
  teacher, 297
identity/identities, 15, 17, 26, 28–30, 48, 50, 75, 102, 103, 139, 165, 171, 172, 185, 188, 194, 218, 228, 252, 259, 262, 265–90, 292, 295–7
ideological becoming, 101, 175
Iedema, R., 7, 15, 34, 134, 148, 167, 194, 273, 299, 308
impact, 13–14, 28, 34, 64, 102, 103, 123, 139, 155, 180, 197, 198, 210, 288, 310–11, 314, 340
implications, 14, 23, 34, 40, 50, 51, 62, 76, 228, 274, 310–11, 330
inquisitive, inquisitiveness, 4
integration of research and pedagogy, 4, 89. *See also* principles
intercultural communication, 134, 302
involving everyone/everybody, 221. *See also* principles

J

Johnson, K.A., 104, 114
Johnson, K.E., 39, 46, 50, 54, 58, 59, 70, 77, 225

K

Kemmis, S., 60, 62, 104, 331
key developing practitioners, 11, 49, 100, 121, 171, 192–4, 203
Kramsch, C., 2, 251, 252, 272, 282, 296
Kuhn, T.S., 37
Kuschnir, A., 104, 117, 118, 140, 218

L

lack(s)
  of expertise, 68–72, 90
  of relevance, 8, 68, 72–3, 226, 310
  of resources, 68, 200, 222
  of respect, 68, 73–5
  of time, 68–9, 90, 140, 146, 184, 200, 222, 239, 245, 271, 311, 314
Lave, J., 50
learner(s)
  as co-researchers, 101, 137, 262, 274
  as individuals, 181
  puzzles, 170, 330
  as social beings, 100, 102, 236
learner autonomy, 101, 104, 124, 155–7, 160, 178, 181–5, 188, 257, 325, 326
Lenzuen, R., 84, 92, 93
Lincoln, Y.S., 33, 34, 38, 48

linguistic imperialism, 128
lived experience, 'lived experience', 24, 41, 94, 106, 136, 145, 165, 222, 257, 291, 293, 301
Lortie, D.C., 43, 44, 48, 55, 58, 196, 247
lure of problems, 314
Lyra, I., 104, 117–99, 234
Lytle, S.L, 1, 24, 46, 51, 53, 55, 59, 79, 94, 156, 197, 219, 262

M

Machado, B., 104, 117, 118, 140, 218
Malderez, A., 8, 176, 196, 225, 243, 251
Manguel, A., 7, 110
Manion, L., 61
Mesman, J., 19
meta-puzzling, 112, 127, 144, 176, 218, 219, 221, 223, 225, 228, 232, 235, 237, 239, 241–3, 253, 257, 259, 262, 267, 271, 272, 274, 284, 285, 293–5, 297, 299
methodology, methodological, viii, 9, 19, 37–40, 50, 69, 70, 74, 93, 210, 211, 291, 295, 302, 303, 350
Miller, I.K., 2, 9, 11, 12, 17, 35, 82, 84, 88, 89, 91–3, 96, 98, 101, 102, 104, 116–18, 124, 127, 133, 134, 140, 141, 148, 201, 209–11, 224, 245, 256, 262, 270, 319, 330, 331, 335, 346

Index

mixed methods approaches, 40
moments of transition, 124, 239, 245–7
Morrison, K., 358
motivation, motivated, 8, 66, 71, 75, 97, 103, 112, 118, 120, 122–4, 148, 149, 152, 153, 156, 159, 169, 179, 188, 198, 222, 223, 226, 234, 238, 244, 245, 262, 271, 308, 311, 342, 345
multilingual classrooms, 272
mutual development, 17, 82, 97, 100, 105, 141, 148, 161, 177–81, 188, 194, 203, 208, 220, 221, 227, 254, 255, 284, 304, 340, 345. *See also* principles

N

names, naming, 2, 11, 13, 15, 24–5, 28, 29, 39, 42, 64, 87, 108, 150, 152, 201, 240, 255, 289, 329, 330, 333, 347
Narrative Inquiry, 30, 58, 85, 104, 105
Noffke, S.E., 1, 23, 47, 49, 54, 59, 60, 67, 71, 77, 255, 256, 291, 308, 314
normal classroom activities, 154, 254, 268, 341. *See also* principles
normal pedagogic activities/practice, 4, 27, 82, 92, 93, 100, 148, 149, 180, 223, 228, 265, 267–9. *See also* principles
Nunan, D., 1, 61, 62, 86, 333

O

other(s), 9–11, 18, 29, 36, 45, 49, 59–61, 64, 67, 73, 76, 86, 89, 96, 99, 100, 102, 119, 120, 127, 138, 140, 141, 143, 145, 161, 169–71, 174, 175, 179, 180, 184, 188, 191, 193, 194, 197, 200, 203, 204, 206–8, 217, 218, 220–2, 224–6, 228, 229, 231–3, 235–8, 242, 245–7, 252, 260, 261, 266, 267, 270–3, 278, 279, 282, 287–9, 292, 294, 297, 299, 300, 307, 310, 311, 320, 325, 338, 340, 346–8
ownership, 2, 16, 53–5, 75, 114, 228, 258, 287–9

P

pedagogy, pedagogic, 1–4, 9, 10, 17, 27, 28, 35, 49, 55, 61, 77–9, 81–3, 87–90, 92–4, 97, 98, 100, 104, 114, 116, 134, 141, 143–66, 170, 177, 180, 182, 184, 185, 188, 191, 194, 195, 197, 198, 201, 202, 204–6, 210, 219, 220, 223, 227–9, 254, 255, 262, 265–70, 273, 276–83, 289, 291–5, 301, 302, 305–11, 313–15, 321, 327, 328, 330, 332, 334, 337, 343–5, 349
PEPAs (Potentially Exploitable Pedagogic Activities), 148, 149, 207, 228, 229, 254, 265–90, 330
performativity (resisting), 76, 86, 87

Perpignan, H., 96, 247, 351
philosophy, philosophical, 3, 7, 18, 26–9, 31, 40, 42, 73, 76, 81, 83, 87, 104, 138, 139, 164, 200, 203, 204, 207, 211, 220, 252, 292, 305, 309, 319, 338, 343, 345, 352
phronesis, 51–3, 93, 136, 298, 299
plausibility, sense of, 5
play, playful, playfulness, 17, 18, 42, 47, 49, 64, 71, 110, 111, 118, 129, 139, 140, 151, 176, 182, 194, 199, 206, 212, 218, 228, 251, 253, 273, 275, 296, 305, 315, 333, 349, 350
Poole, J., 3, 4, 308, 309, 347
power, 34, 42, 45, 53–5, 60, 122, 128, 136, 187, 194, 204, 235, 250, 258, 262, 282, 295, 296, 312, 313
Prabhu, N.S., 5, 327
practice-as-research, 17, 19, 134, 229, 292–5
practice-driven theory-building, 85, 111
practitioner(s), 3, 5–12, 14, 16–17, 26, 41, 48–9, 67–75, 82, 92, 93, 95, 100, 112, 120, 121, 133–5, 138–40, 143, 165, 171, 192–4, 203, 210, 211, 228, 232–6, 239–41, 276, 292, 300, 306, 307, 311–13, 343
practitioner research
  and agency, 3, 211, 281
  definition(s), 41, 47, 49, 51
  ethical approach to, 137
  as family, 28–30
  inclusivity in, 211, 352
  potential of, 59
  practitioners, who are, 48–9
  problematising, 53–5, 76–8
  purpose of, 51
  subject matter of, 47, 50–1
  underlying assumptions of, 47–8
  what hinders, 68
  working definition of, 41, 51
principles
  as an integrated whole, 277
  avoid/ing burnout, 2, 11, 90
  inclusivity, 205
  integrate/ing work for understanding into normal pedagogic activities/practice, 97, 100, 182
  involve/ing everyone/everybody, 221, 284
  make/ing it a continuous enterprise, 97, 100
  minimise/ing the burden, 100, 255
  principles sustainability, 222, 304, 311
  quality of life, 88, 96, 97, 101
  relationship between principles and practices, 218–25
  relevance, 226, 310
  understanding, 97, 220
  working for mutual development, 141, 161
  working together, 271
problem(s), 5, 6, 27, 28, 31, 34, 40, 44, 46, 52, 54, 55, 60, 62, 64, 66, 68, 72, 76, 81, 86–90, 93–7, 100, 103, 107–9, 112–14, 116–21, 123–5, 128, 129, 135, 137, 147, 153–7, 161, 163, 168, 173, 175, 186,

193, 194, 197–9, 206, 221, 225, 227, 229, 232, 238, 241, 248–50, 253–6, 262, 263, 266, 281–4, 286, 287, 291, 294, 297–300, 304, 310, 314, 321–3, 326, 329, 332, 333, 338, 346, 347, 349, 351
problematising
   Exploratory Practice, 53, 76, 104, 105, 123, 297, 298
   practitioner research, 53–5, 76–8
   problem-solving, 297–300
   puzzling, 125–9
propositions (five), about learners, 18, 100, 236
psychology, 58, 60, 73, 78, 209, 210, 290, 324, 334
puzzlement, 1, 6, 28, 31, 84, 97, 106–29, 140, 147, 153, 162, 165, 169, 171, 174, 175, 192, 193, 210, 218, 228, 232, 238, 239, 242, 247–50, 255, 256, 261, 263, 269, 276, 291, 295, 296, 337, 342
puzzlement zones, 118, 140, 218
puzzles
   positive puzzling, 114
   same as problems?, 86, 112–13
   what happens when Exploratory Practice moves beyond the classroom?, 301–5
   what's the link between EP and CPD?, 196–200
   why are my learners not taking responsibility for their learning?, 153–6
   why are 'normal' lessons boring?, 115

why are some students not interested in learning English?, 149–53
why can't I concentrate in class?, 238
why can't I express my feelings exactly in English?, 237, 283
why can't I remember and use new vocabulary?, 175
why can't I speak English well, after studying for a long time?, 122
why can't I speak English well, even after many years of study?, 248
why can't we speak like we think we can?, 192
why do I ask my students to reflect on their learning?, 177–81
why do I feel anxiety about studying at a British university?, 237, 286
why do my students want lectures while I want discussion?, 161–5
why don't I like to learn another language from my mother tongue?, 128
why don't we bring EP and learner autonomy together?, 181–4
why don't we do EP in EAP here?, 168
why don't we integrate theory and practice in pedagogy?, 205–9
why don't we use EP in our 'Zemi' classes?, 184–8
why do people learn bad words more easily?, 259

puzzles (*cont.*)
  why do so many board markers disappear from Room 17?, 233, 235
  why do some students come unready to learn?, 145
  why do teachers and learners struggle in the classroom?, 209–12
  why do the students seem reluctant to take responsibility for themselves?, 156–61
  why do they find English spelling difficult?, 108
  why do they/I hate the course book?, 273
  why I have accent and how should I improve pronunciation?, 174
  why incorporate EP in teacher education programmes?, 200–5
  why is proficiency in English seen as a status symbol?, 279, 281
puzzling
  importance of, 31
  vs problem-solving, 27, 86–8
  vs solutions

Q

qualitative research, 19, 38–9, 48, 73
quality of life, 13, 14, 41, 81, 84, 87, 96–105, 137, 141, 150, 163, 165, 169, 188, 205, 208–12, 218, 219, 223–7, 236, 240, 257, 281, 287, 304, 306, 310, 311, 337, 340, 341, 351. *See also* principles
quantitative research, 37–9, 47, 48

R

recipes (avoiding), 274
reflection, 3, 52, 53, 64–6, 74, 85, 90, 91, 103, 111, 159, 163, 178, 185, 199, 297, 337, 345
reflective practice, 1, 3, 9, 25, 26, 29, 60, 63–7, 124, 157, 207, 309, 337
reflexive, reflexivity, 12, 17, 78, 109, 113, 125, 127, 294
relationship(s) between principles and practice, 312
relationship(s) between research, scholarship and pedagogy, 313
relevance
  as EP principle, 205
  lack of, 8, 68, 72–3
research
  cornerstones of, 48
  'good', 35, 36, 313
  'holy trinity' of, 34
  orthodox, 72
  paradigm(s), 61, 308
  purpose of, 334
  questions for, 47
  subject matter of, 50–1
  working definition of, 35
researchable pedagogy, 147–9
research-as-practice, 17, 292–5
researchers, 11, 15, 17, 33, 36–40, 46, 48, 59, 74, 77, 102, 135, 139, 160, 210, 211, 222, 244, 250, 252, 259, 301, 302, 304, 305, 308, 323, 326, 328, 329, 341, 352
research questions, 182, 291, 302–4, 326, 329

Rio (de Janeiro) Exploratory Practice (EP) Group, 350
risks/risky, 127–9, 225, 231, 232, 257, 280, 296
Rowland, L., 103, 141, 172

S
Salvi, A.I., 104, 177, 178, 181, 182
scholarship/scholarly, 24, 27, 69, 71, 105, 182, 229, 239, 305–9, 311, 313, 314, 325
Schön, D., 64, 66, 77, 85, 195
Second Language Acquisition (SLA), 102, 104, 312
sharing
 control, 147
 decision(s), decision-making, 65, 103, 181, 279
 findings, 8
 ideas, 343
 puzzles, puzzlement, 117, 127, 128, 165, 192, 221, 258
 questions, 242
 understanding(s), 207, 344
Slimani-Rolls, A., 9, 11, 12, 98, 103, 104, 141, 189, 191, 221, 319, 339–43
small culture(s), 276
Smith, C., 1, 12, 24, 46, 53, 59, 79, 86, 94, 103, 141, 156, 182, 197, 198, 207, 262
solutions (and problem-solving), 31, 117, 310
Stenhouse, L., 43, 44, 48, 58, 85
steps (abandoned), 89
Stevick, E., 45, 46, 116, 225, 232, 334

Stewart, A., 12, 103, 141, 177, 184, 185, 188
Stewart, T., 370
sustainable/sustainability/sustained, 7, 14, 17, 28, 83, 86, 90–2, 97, 103, 141, 177, 184–8, 222–3, 225, 241, 295, 303–6, 311, 313, 331. *See also* principles
Swierzbin, B., 13, 102, 104, 312

T
Tajino, A., 11, 12, 84, 103, 141, 207, 208, 295, 319, 343, 347
Tarone, E., 13, 102, 104, 213, 312, 347
teacher(s)
 education, teacher educators, 11, 12, 45, 49, 59, 64, 69, 70, 74, 94, 95, 98, 103, 117, 140, 141, 162, 195, 197, 200, 206, 335, 338, 339
 as learners, 203, 236, 250
 puzzles, 112, 330
 research, 13, 67, 153, 289, 346
 researchers, 10, 13, 17, 44, 48, 90, 160, 197–9, 329, 342
 training, teacher trainers, 191, 195, 199, 200, 212, 228, 244, 256, 271, 288, 289, 292, 294, 307
team learning, 84, 103, 208, 295, 343, 344, 346
team teaching, 84, 103, 208, 295, 343, 344
technicism, 63, 67, 136

technologisation, 63
theory, 9, 13, 17, 38, 50, 55, 73–5, 85, 88–90, 94, 96, 99, 102, 111, 145, 201, 205–9, 225, 269, 319, 320
theory-from-practice, 88–90
Trotman, W., 198, 253, 255
trust, 16, 17, 99, 159, 167–9, 173, 222, 225–8, 231–62, 274, 275, 277, 279, 280, 288, 289, 294, 297, 301, 307, 312, 326, 338, 343, 351
Tudor, I., 1, 50, 59, 102, 225

U

understanding(s). *See also* principles
  articulation of, 125
  collective, 5
  individual, 86
  for practice, 217, 228, 229
  from practice, 16, 17, 91, 141, 293
  sharing (importance of), 207, 344
  too deep for words, 126, 314
  working for, 6, 27, 35, 79, 84, 88, 91–3, 97, 105, 108–13, 126, 129, 141, 152, 195–6, 219, 220, 222, 227, 250, 257, 309, 333, 337, 351

V

van Lier, L., 50, 67, 102, 225, 307
van Manen, M., 6, 19, 24, 41, 86, 93, 94, 111, 113, 145, 305

W

Wallace, M.J., 1, 61–3, 66
Wedell, M., 8, 176, 196, 225, 243, 251, 347
Wenger, E., 50, 108, 229, 256
why, importance of, 1, 7
Winnicott, D. W., 36, 110
Woods, D., 194
working
  for improvement, 60–7
  for mutual development, 141, 161, 221 (*see also* principles)
  together, 8, 17, 99, 109, 128, 161, 167, 172, 179, 184, 192, 211, 221, 225, 271, 277, 285, 304, 338, 339 (*see also* principles)
  for understanding(s), 6, 27, 35, 79, 84, 88, 91–3, 97, 105, 108–13, 126, 129, 141, 152, 195–6, 219, 220, 222, 227, 250, 257, 309, 333, 337, 351 (*see also* principles)
Wright, T., 145, 294, 297
Wu, Z., 11, 12, 25, 82, 86, 87, 96, 104, 165, 183, 202–4, 346

Z

Zeichner, K.M, 1, 23, 47, 49, 54, 59, 60, 63, 66, 67, 71, 77, 255, 308, 314, 256, 291
zemi, 'zemi', 184–8, 285
Zhang, R., 12, 103, 204
Zheng, C., 12, 141, 204
Zheng, Z., 196, 200–3